# THE SURVIVAL HANDBOOK

# THE SURVIVAL HANDBOOK

## ESSENTIAL SKILLS FOR OUTDOOR ADVENTURE

LONDON, NEW YORK, MUNICH, MELBOURNE, DELHI

**Senior Editors** Nicky Munro, Richard Gilbert

**Senior Art Editors** Michael Duffy, Gillian Andrews

**Editors** Bob Bridle, Chris Hawkes,
Philip Morgan, Gill Pitts, Clare Weber

**US Editor** Chuck Wills

**Designers** Sarah-Anne Arnold, Katie Eke,
Brian Flynn, Phil Gamble, Sharon Spencer

**Lead Illustrator** Mike Garland
**Assisting Illustrators** Darren Awuah,
Phil Gamble, Peter Liddiard, Mark Walker

**Production Editor** Tony Phipps
**Production Controller** Norma Weir

**Managing Editor** Stephanie Farrow
**Managing Art Editor** Lee Griffiths

**Art Director** Bryn Walls
**Publisher** Jonathan Metcalf


First American Edition, 2009

Published in the United States by
DK Publishing, 375 Hudson Street
New York, New York 10014

09 10 11 12   10 9 8 7 6 5 4 3 2 1

SD308—April. 09

Published in Great Britain by Dorling Kindersley Limited.

A catalog record for this book is available
from the Library of Congress.

ISBN 978-07566-4279-2

DK books are available at special discounts when purchased in bulk for
sales promotions, premiums, fund-raising, or educational use. For details,
contact: DK Publishing Special Markets, 375 Hudson Street, New York,
New York 10014 or SpecialSales@dk.com.

Printed and bound in Hong Kong by Hung Hing

Discover more at
**www.dk.com**

**IMPORTANT NOTICE**
Some of the techniques desribed in this book should be
used only in dire emergencies, when the survival of
individuals depends upon them. The publisher cannot
be held responsible for any injuries, damage, loss or
prosecutions resulting from the use or misuse of the
information in this book. Do not practice these
techniques on private land without the owner's
permission, and obey all laws relating to the protection
of land, property, plants, and animals.

# CONTENTS

# 2
## ON THE TRAIL

# 3
## CAMP CRAFT

# 4
## TAKING SHELTER

# 5
## WATER AND FOOD

# INTRODUCTION

**HAVING TAUGHT SURVIVAL SKILLS FOR MANY YEARS,** I have learned that four elements must be in place for a survival situation to have the chance of a positive outcome: knowledge, ability, the will to survive, and luck. While knowledge and ability can be learned, the will to survive is hard-wired into our survival mechanism and we may not know we possess it until we're put to the test. For example, people who were fully trained and well-equipped have given up hope in survivable conditions, while others, who were less well-prepared and ill-equipped, have survived against all odds because they refused to give up.

> Always apply the **principle** of the **least** amount of **energy expended** for the **maximum** amount of **gain**

Anyone venturing into the wilderness—whether for an overnight camping trip or a lengthy expedition—should understand the basic principles of survival. Knowing how to survive in a particular situation will allow you to carry out the correct beforehand preparation, choose the right equipment (and learn how to use it), and practice the necessary skills. While you may be able to start a fire using a lighter, for example, what would you do if it stopped working? Equally, anyone can spend a comfortable night inside a one-man bivy shelter, but what would you do if you lost your pack? The knowledge gained through learning the skills of survival will enable you to assess your situation, prioritize your needs, and improvise any items of gear that you don't have with you.

Treat the **wilderness** with **respect**: carry in only what you can **carry out**; leave only **footprints**, take only **pictures**

Survival knowledge and skills must be learned—and practiced—under realistic conditions. Starting a fire with dry materials on a sunny day, for example, will teach you very little. The real survival skill is in understanding why a fire won't start and working out a solution. The more you practice, the more you learn (I am yet to teach a course where I didn't learn something new from one of my students). Finding solutions and overcoming problems continually adds to your knowledge and, in most cases, will help you deal with problems should they occur again.

There are differences between teaching survival courses to civilians and teaching them to military personnel. Civilians have enrolled on (and paid for) a course to increase their knowledge and skills, not because their life may depend on it (although, should they find themselves in a life-threatening situation, it may well do), but because they are interested in survival techniques in their own right. In contrast, the majority of military personnel who undergo survival training may very well need to put it into practice, but they invariably complete the training simply because they are required to do so. While no one in the military forces would underestimate the importance of survival training, it is a fact that, if you want to fly a Harrier, or become a US Marine Mountain Leader, survival training is just one of the many courses you must undertake.

In the military, we categorize the four basic principles of survival as protection, location, water, and food. Protection focuses on your ability to prevent further injury and defend yourself against nature and the elements. Location refers to the importance of helping others to rescue you by letting them know where you are. The principle of water focuses on making sure that, even in the short term, your body has the water it needs to enable you to accomplish the first two principles. Food, while not a priority in the short term, becomes more important the longer your situation lasts. We teach the principles in this order, but their priority can change depending on the environment, the condition of the survivor, and the situation in which the survivor finds him- or herself.

> Understanding your **environment** will allow you to select the **best equipment**, adopt the **best techniques**, and learn the **correct skills**

We also teach advanced survival techniques to selected personnel who may become isolated from their own forces, such as when operating behind enemy lines. The four principles of survival remain the same, but we substitute "location" with "evasion". The military definition of evasion is recognized as: "being able to live off the land while remaining undetected by the enemy". This involves learning how to build a shelter that cannot be seen, how to maintain a fire that doesn't give away your position, and how to let your own forces know where you are but remain undetected by the enemy.

In military training, and with most expeditions, the equipment with which you train will be specific to a particular environment—marines operating in the jungles of Belize will not pack a set of cold-weather clothing, for example; and Sir Ranulph Fiennes won't practice putting up his jungle hammock before venturing into the Arctic! However, the standard practice of being equipped and trained for a specific environment can prove to be a major challenge for some expeditions. During my career as a survival instructor, for example, I have been fortunate enough to have worked on two of Sir Richard Branson's

> The more you understand **how and why** something works, the more prepared you will be to **adapt and improvise** should it be **damaged or lost**

global circumnavigation balloon challenges with Per Lindstrand and the late Steve Fossett. For these expeditions, the responsibility for selecting the survival equipment and training the pilots was a unique, if daunting, task. The balloon would be flying at up to 30,000 ft (9,000 m) and would potentially cross every type of environment: temperate, desert, tropical rain forest, jungle, and open ocean. While it would have taken some very strong winds to blow the balloon into the polar regions, we did fly—after a brief and unplanned excursion into China—across the Himalayas.

We also had to train for the worst-case scenario, which would be a fire in the balloon capsule. A capsule fire would leave the three pilots no option but to bail out, potentially from a great height, breathing from an oxygen cylinder, at night, and anywhere in the world, whether over land or sea. The chances of them landing in the same vicinity as each other under such circumstances would be slim to non-existent, so each pilot would need not only the necessary equipment to address the priorities of survival in each environment, but also the knowledge to be able to use it confidently and alone. We addressed this challenge by providing each pilot with survival packs devised for specific environments, a single-man liferaft (which provides shelter that's just as good in a desert as it is at sea) and realistic training with the equipment contained in each pack. As the balloon moved from one environment to another, the packs were rotated accordingly, and the pilots re-briefed on their survival priorities for each environment.

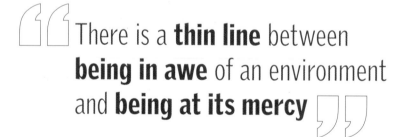

There is a **thin line** between
**being in awe** of an environment
and **being at its mercy**

As you read this book and plan to put the skills and techniques covered here into practice, you will typically be equipping yourself for just one particular type of environment—but it's important that you fully understand that one environment. Make sure you research not only what the environment has to offer you as a traveller—so that you can better appreciate it—but also what it offers you as a survivor: there is sometimes a very thin line between being in awe of the beauty of an environment and being at its mercy. The more you understand both the appeal and dangers of an environment, the better informed you will be to select the right equipment and understand how best to utilize it should the need arise.

Remember, no matter how good your survival equipment, or how extensive your knowledge and skills, never underestimate the power of nature. If things aren't going as planned, never hesitate to stop and re-assess your situation and priorities, and never be afraid to turn back and try again later—the challenge will always be there tomorrow. Finally, always remember that the most effective method of dealing with a survival situation is to avoid getting into it in the first place.

Colin Towell

Twenty years from now you will be **more disappointed** by the things **you didn't do** than by the **ones you did do**

MARK TWAIN

# BEFORE YOU GO

# PREPARE YOURSELF

**Most survival situations** arise in one of two ways: either you are thrust into a situation not of your making and beyond your control, or (as is more often the case) a situation develops because of a sequence of events that could have been avoided had you recognized the danger signs and acted on them at the earliest opportunity. Unfortunately, most survival situations occur as a result of ignorance, arrogance, an overconfident belief in one's own ability, or because the forces of nature have been underestimated.

In the military forces, troops prepare for survival situations by learning the basic principles and techniques and then practicing them until they become second nature. The more you practice a particular survival skill, the more you'll understand how and why it works, and the more you'll understand your own strengths and weaknesses. Many helicopter crew members who have been involved in a survival situation, for example, report that, having ditched their aircraft in the sea, they could not remember how they subsequently

## In this section YOU WILL DISCOVER...

- how keeping **in shape** can keep you **out of trouble...**
- the importance of a **positive mental attitude...**
- that where there's a **will to survive** there's a **way to survive...**
- the difference between a **coping strategy** and an **aggravating factor...**
- how **"show-stoppers"** could **scupper your trip...**
- why an **emergency plan of action** could **save your life...**

escaped from their aircraft and successfully boarded their liferaft. Thanks to their intense training regime, their actions had become instinctive and therefore subconscious.

Whether you're preparing for an overnight camping trip or a year in Africa, the more prepared you are to meet the challenges posed by a particular environment, the more likely you are to be able to cope—both physically and mentally—should you then find yourself confronted with a survival situation.

**It would be foolish** to think that the amount of prior preparation required for an expedition is directly related to the length of the trip or its perceived danger.

**ACCIDENTS CAN HAPPEN** anywhere. One of the most important things you can do to improve your chances of survival is to let people know where you're going and when you'll be back. Leave an itinerary of your trip with family or friends, and arrange a time when you will call to let them know you are safe.

**In many instances**, simply making sure you have a cell phone with you can prevent an accident becoming a major survival incident. In 2007, a professional athlete, out running with her dog in Moab, Utah, slipped on ice, fell approximately 60 ft (18 m), and broke her pelvis. Having left her cell phone in her vehicle, she managed to survive for two nights in the freezing desert before rescuers were finally lead to her by her dog.

**In a separate incident** in 2008, a farm worker in the UK caught his arm in machinery. Unable to attract attention and not having his cell phone with him, he was faced with a stark choice when the machinery caught fire: bleed to death, burn to death, or cut off his own arm with a pocket knife—he chose the latter.

"Never assume that the amount of **prior preparation** required is directly related to the length of a trip or its **perceived danger**"

# GETTING INTO SHAPE

**IN ANY SURVIVAL SITUATION** you're likely to be at your best, both physically and mentally, in the moments before the situation occurs. From that point on, through lack of sleep, food, and water, your situation will deteriorate until your rescue. Being in good physical condition will help you overcome the challenges you'll face in a survival situation.

> **KNOWING YOUR LIMITS**
> Having an idea of how fit you are and knowing how much you are capable of achieving before entering the wilderness means you can set yourself realistic goals—which will help to keep you out of danger.

## THE BENEFITS OF EXERCISE

Over time, exercise induces changes such as weight loss, as well as improved posture, physique, strength, agility, mental alertness, and stamina. These are all vital attributes should you find yourself in a survival situation.

## HOW FIT ARE YOU?

A fit heart pumps blood more slowly and efficiently than an unfit one. The hearts of women, children, and older people beat faster than those of young adult males. Take your pulse first thing in the morning—this is known as the "base rate." As the table below shows, the faster your pulse returns to its base rate after a period of exercise, the fitter you are. Note that < denotes "less than" and > denotes "more than".

*Back: strong back muscles help when you are carrying a heavy backpack*

*Brain: your ability to concentrate for long periods of time improves with increased fitness*

*Heart: improved cardiovascular fitness will enable you to walk greater distances*

*Lower back: strengthening your lower back muscles improves core strength, and your ability to carry heavy loads*

*Calf muscles: lower-leg strength helps on rocky terrain*

*Legs: improved leg strength is a huge benefit when you're on the trail*

*Balance: sure-footedness and confidence are useful qualities on rocky terrain*

| AGE | 20-29 | 30-39 | 40-49 | 50+ |
|---|---|---|---|---|
| **RATING** | **BASE RATE** | | | |
| **MEN** | | | | |
| Good | < 69 | < 71 | < 73 | < 75 |
| Average | 70-85 | 72-87 | 74-89 | 76-91 |
| Poor | > 85 | > 87 | > 89 | > 91 |
| **WOMEN** | | | | |
| Good | < 77 | < 79 | < 81 | < 83 |
| Average | 78-94 | 80-96 | 82-98 | 84-100 |
| Poor | > 94 | > 96 | > 98 | > 100 |

| AGE | 20-29 | 30-39 | 40-49 | 50+ |
|---|---|---|---|---|
| **RATING** | **BEATS AFTER EXERCISE** | | | |
| **MEN** | | | | |
| Good | < 85 | < 87 | < 89 | < 91 |
| Average | 86-101 | 88-102 | 90-105 | 92-107 |
| Poor | > 101 | > 102 | > 105 | > 107 |
| **WOMEN** | | | | |
| Good | < 93 | < 95 | < 97 | < 99 |
| Average | 94-110 | 96-112 | 98-114 | 100-116 |
| Poor | > 110 | > 112 | > 114 | > 116 |

# FIT FOR THE CHALLENGE

Survival fitness is not about trying to run the 100 meters in 10 seconds; it's about stamina and endurance, and about knowing your physical limitations and being able to work with them. It is also about understanding that you may have to push yourself beyond your limits and that having a positive mental attitude is paramount to survival—the mind will often give up long before the body has reached its limit. Bear in mind that every task in a survival situation will sap your energy.

## EXERCISING REGULARLY

Any effective training schedule must include at least three 45-minute sessions per week, with exercises that raise the heartbeat to more than 120 beats per minute.

## STARTING A FITNESS PROGRAM

To spend time in the wilderness with a pack on your back requires a combination of strength and aerobic fitness. Training in the gym before you set off will strengthen your heart, lungs, and leg muscles, and will increase your stamina levels when you are out on the trail.
- Seek expert instruction and guidance wherever possible.
- Start gradually and then build up your routine progressively.
- Never try to work through injuries—rest and seek medical advice.
- Devise a relevant fitness program; there are many websites and organizations that provide you with detailed fitness programs for various levels of specific activities, from training for a trek through the jungle to mountain-biking along the Appalachian Trail.
- Duplicating in training what you'd like to be able to achieve on the trail will allow you to build up reference points about how your body works, and how it copes in different situations. The more you know about how you perform, the better equipped you'll be on the trail.

## WARMING UP AND COOLING DOWN

Time spent warming up and cooling down after exercise will help to improve your endurance levels and will also accelerate the recovery process. Get into the habit of starting and ending your session with a five-minute jog.

# GO FOR A CHECK-UP

It's a sad fact that the majority of us don't have regular medical check-ups. Many people work on the principle that you only need to see a doctor or dentist if something is wrong. However, you should always make sure that you start any adventure or wilderness trek in top condition. Therefore, before you set out, pay a visit to your doctor and dentist and make sure that your body and teeth are in good condition.

## VISIT THE DOCTOR
- Let the doctor know of any ailments that have been a concern to you during the course of the previous year.
- Tell the doctor where you are going and enquire about relevant inoculations or medication that you should be taking with you.

## VISIT THE DENTIST
- Have any problems with your teeth dealt with before you go. Any minor dental problem will almost certainly turn into full-blown toothache when you least want it to.

# USEFUL EXERCISES

If you already get regular exercise, you'll find yourself far more comfortable in a survival situation than your more sedentary counterparts. Any pre-expedition training regime should include plenty of stretching, aerobic exercise, and weight-training.

## STRETCHING YOUR UPPER BODY AND BACK

Regularly stretching your arms, neck, chest, and shoulders will help your body to maintain a strong core. This will be of great use when it comes to activities such as rock climbing or using trekking poles. Undergoing a regular back-stretching routine will loosen the back muscles, making them more flexible and less susceptible to injury, and will increase both the back's range of motion and its endurance.

## STRETCHING YOUR LEGS

Because your leg muscles bear the brunt of the work, leg stiffness is a common complaint at the end of a long day on the trail. Stretching your legs will improve your flexibility, increase blood circulation, and relax your muscles. Concentrate on your calves, quads, and hamstrings.

## AEROBIC EXERCISES

Also called cardiovascular fitness, aerobic fitness refers to the ability of your heart, blood vessels, and lungs to supply oxygen and nutrients to the rest of your body during sustained physical activity. Regular aerobic exercise—such as swimming, jogging, or cycling—will reduce the risk of developing coronary heart disease or high blood pressure, will help you to manage your weight and increase your stamina levels, and will make your heart stronger and more efficient, thus improving blood flow around your body.

## WEIGHT-TRAINING

Increased muscle strength will enhance your ability to perform everyday tasks such as lifting, carrying, and walking. A regular weight-training program will improve your posture, build muscle density around the joints and bones, improve your sense of balance, help your stress management abilities, aid sleep, and reduce the chances of you sustaining an injury. In addition, research has shown that a regular resistance-training program can improve your metabolic rate by up to 15 percent, which will help you shed any unwanted weight at a faster rate.

# MENTAL PREPARATION

**REGARDLESS OF WHETHER** you're backpacking through a remote area, or on a day hike in familiar territory, a situation may arise that changes your circumstances for the worse. Very quickly you move into the unknown, which causes tremendous psychological and emotional stress, known as "psychogenic shock." Understanding this will help you to deal with it better and reduce its impact.

## INDIVIDUAL REACTIONS TO DISASTER

People react to survival situations in different ways, although you can expect to find some common emotional reactions in victims who are experiencing, or have survived, a disaster situation. You may experience one or more of them during or after any survival experience or trauma.

## YOUR RESPONSE TO DISASTER SITUATIONS

Your psychological response to a survival situation is crucial. Statistics show that 95 percent of people who die with psychological trauma die within the first three days. Losing the will to survive—or suffering psychological disorders that prevent you from coping with the physical conditions—is your main concern. If you break down psychologically, your chances of overcoming a situation will be compromised.

## PSYCHOLOGICAL PROGRESSION

It's useful to examine how people are likely to react in a survival situation. Using this knowledge, it's possible to prepare mentally for such eventualities and, in so doing, lessen the impact if the worst should happen to you when out on the trail. Normal psychological reactions to disaster tend to occur in a set pattern of four stages: the pre-impact period, the impact period, the recoil period, and the post-trauma period (see right). Contrary to popular belief, people don't normally panic, although it can be contagious if someone does.

### AGGRAVATING FACTORS

Reactions to disaster can result from a direct blow to the psychological system, such as extreme shock, but they can also be brought on, or aggravated by, other factors. As with all psychological problems, knowing what these aggravating factors are, and attempting to avoid them—or at least recognizing what they might lead to—will maximize your chances of preventing or overcoming the problem. The most common aggravating factors are: hunger, thirst, fatigue, seasickness, and hypothermia.

### HUNGER

Initially, hunger is not a problem, but a long-term lack of food will cause psychological changes to occur. Symptoms include:
- Apathy
- Irritability
- Depression
- Lack of concentration

### THIRST

Thirst is a serious problem, especially for survivors at sea or in the desert, and its effects are more acute than hunger. Agitation is commonplace; other symptoms include:
- Irrational behavior (see box, right)
- Delusions
- Visual hallucinations

### COPING STRATEGIES

There are many things you can do to prepare yourself psychologically for a survival situation—such as learning about what you should expect if the worst were to happen—and to cope better if you find yourself in one. As with all survival skills, prior knowledge is power, and will help you to deal with a survival situation far more successfully. The main areas to think about are: training, motivation, attachment, hope, acceptance, and helping others. Developing coping strategies is an important technique for survival.

### TRAINING

People who are properly prepared, who know their environment and how to use their equipment, and have an understanding of what to expect in a survival situation, will be far more effective if they find themselves in one. Adequate training and practice using your equipment will help you to function effectively at an automatic level. Prior knowledge is key to your survival.

### MOTIVATION

Often known as "the will to survive," motivation involves a refusal to accept death, and to hang on to the belief that you were not meant to die under these conditions. It involves overcoming the emotional and physical discomforts of extreme conditions. Linked to motivation is the ability to establish goals, work out the steps to those goals, and to follow those steps through.

## PANIC

Panic arises from the fear of what might happen rather than what has happened. It tends to occur when people are trapped, or if there is a time limit to their escape.

## HYPERACTIVITY

Hyperactive victims are easily distracted, and are full of chatter, ideas, and often unhelpful suggestions. Sufferers can reach this stage after a state of depression.

## GUILT

Some sufferers feel guilty for surviving, and for not having done enough for others—and some irrationally blame themselves for bringing about the incident.

## DEPRESSION

Depressed people will sit among chaos and debris vacantly gazing and not replying to questions. They're unaware of their situation and unable to help themselves, so risk further injury.

## ANGER

Aggression, anger, and hostility are common reactions to trauma. They're often irrational and may even be directed at the rescuers or medical staff trying to help them.

## SUICIDE

Disaster victims have been known to commit suicide immediately after being rescued, in some cases when they're already safe in the hospital. Victims should be closely monitored.

---

### Pre-impact period

The "pre-impact" period is divided into two stages:
- Threat: danger exists but, though obvious to those who recognize it, those who will not accept it respond with denial and under-activity.
- Warning: threat of danger is now apparent to all; response is now likely to be over-activity.

### Impact Period

This is the life-threatening stage. Statistically, individuals behave in one of three ways:
- 10–20 percent of people are calm and retain full awareness.
- Up to 75 percent of people are stunned, bewildered, and unable to react rationally.
- 10–25 percent exhibit extreme behavior, such as screaming.

### Recoil period

This follows on directly from the impact period; for example, victims may have escaped a sinking ship and are in the liferafts. It can last for up to three days, but generally lasts for around three hours. In most cases, it is characterized by a gradual return to normal reasoning abilities, awareness, and emotional expression.

### Post-trauma period

If the recoil period is not fully successful, individuals may develop psychiatric disorders. The full impact of the incident becomes apparent and a range of emotions—guilt, depression, anxiety, aimlessness, and a feeling of bereavement—may develop. These are often referred to as Post-Traumatic Stress Disorders (PTSD).

---

| FATIGUE | SEASICKNESS | HYPOTHERMIA |
|---|---|---|
| In many cases, physical exhaustion is present from the outset. At other times, it may result from sleep deprivation and the physical hardship endured over time. Most survivors agree that fatigue overwhelms them, but when they want to sleep they can't—they have an inability to relax. Fatigue causes a deterioration in mental and physical performance, followed by a psychological and physical debility. | Seasickness often brings about an overwhelming desire to curl up and die, which in survival situations can easily become a reality. It's important not to give in to this urge. Fight seasickness with the following methods:<br>• Keep a fixed point such as the horizon in sight.<br>• Take small sips of water (not salt water) if you have sufficient supplies—but ration them if you're in a life or death situation. | Hypothermia (see p. 273) produces both physical and psychological effects—the psychological consequences occur early in the condition, and cause:<br>• Loss of concentration<br>• Loss of memory<br>• Motor impairment<br>• Faulty decision-making<br>• Irrational behavior |

### IRRATIONAL BEHAVIOR

Irrational behavior can take many forms. Examples include the earthquake victims who were found collecting flowers instead of helping the injured, and famously, the band of the Titanic, who played while the ship sank rather than trying to save themselves.

---

| ATTACHMENT | HOPE | ACCEPTANCE | HELPING OTHERS |
|---|---|---|---|
| One of the strongest motivating forces for survival is the desire to be reunited with principal figures of attachment in your life. These may include:<br>• Husbands<br>• Wives<br>• Partners<br>• Children<br>• Grandchildren<br>• Close friends | To hope means to entertain ideas that a distressing situation will improve and get better. In any survival situation it's important to cling on to hope, despite information or perceptions to the contrary. Thinking positively will help to ward off psychological trauma. It's often easier to be optimistic in a group situation than it is if you're on your own, as people can support each other. | An inability to accept one's situation or condition leads to frustration, anger, and irrational behavior, and it's important to avoid these feelings in a survival situation. The ability to accept the situation doesn't equate to giving in to it—far from it. Those who have this ability, and know when to be active and when to be passive often have a better chance of long-term survival. | First, monitor your own condition and check that you're really up to the task. Determine who is genuinely disturbed rather than showing "normal" reactions. Psychological first aid is only required for those who are failing to recover. Simple words of comfort and interest will make the majority who are numbed more responsive. Those who are disturbed should be monitored closely. Avoid giving sedatives. |

# PLANNING YOUR JOURNEY

**WHETHER YOUR TRIP** involves a day out with your backpack, or a full expedition over weeks, crossing continents in four-wheel-drive vehicles, you need to plan it very carefully. The plan for your day out won't be as detailed as it would be for the longer expedition, but it's equally important. It's a good idea to have a basic planning outline for your most regular trips, to which you can add supplementary information as your trips become more involved.

## MINIMIZING THE "IF ONLY"

There's no way that you can plan for every eventuality—there are just too many variables—but what you can do is look at the type of trip you intend to take, and ensure that if a situation arises you're not left wishing you'd done something differently. The time to minimize the chances of an "if only" situation is during the planning stage. Look at the potential problems and risks, plan to avoid them, and equip yourself with the knowledge and/or equipment to deal with them if they arise.

> **WARNING!**
> The social customs of a country are not the same all over the world. Many cultural differences stem from ancient cultural or religious pasts, and are taken extremely seriously. While ignoring or breaking some customs may lead only to embarrassment, breaking others can result in a penalty, punishment, or even imprisonment. Cultural differences may require females in your group to dress so that they don't show bare arms or legs, or they may dictate which hand you use to greet someone politely. Always research a country's customs thoroughly when planning your trip.

### THE SIX P'S

Remember the six p's: **P**rior **P**lanning and **P**reparation **P**revents **P**oor **P**erformance. Research has shown that the longer and more complicated the trip is, the less likely there is to be a major "survival" situation. This type of trip is likely to be well organized, and potential problems will have been considered. This means that they can either be avoided, or that there will be mechanisms in place to deal with them. In many ways, simply having a good understanding of how to deal with a situation, and being able to interpret the basic principles of survival, can prevent a minor problem from escalating into a disaster. In a survival situation, it may be your knowledge, combined with your ability to improvise, that determines whether you become a survivor or a statistic.

### ORGANIZATIONAL PRIORITIES

When planning for a trip always start with the most important things—known as the "show-stoppers." These are generally the things that would actually stop the trip from happening in the first place if not organized in advance. If you then work backward from the show-stoppers to items that would simply make the trip more comfortable, most other things will fall into place. The chart on the right lists the things that you definitely cannot do without.

| SHOW-STOPPERS | |
|---|---|
| **MONEY** | ▪ You'll need enough to cover your needs plus extra for emergencies.<br>▪ It must be in the correct currency for the country you are visiting.<br>▪ Ensure your ATM card is set up for use in that particular country.<br>▪ Make sure you have a secure way of storing your money. |
| **PASSPORT** | ▪ Your passport must be valid. If you need to renew it, do so well in advance.<br>▪ Some countries require your passport to be valid for a number of months after your visit.<br>▪ Keep your passport number in several places, such as inside your survival kit.<br>▪ Keep your passport safe, and in a waterproof container, such as a Ziploc bag. |
| **VISA** | ▪ Research the regulations regarding visas relevant to the countries you're traveling to.<br>▪ Find out how to apply, how far in advance you should apply, whether or not you can apply in the country, and what other documents you need.<br>▪ As with your passport, always keep your visa safe, dry, and in good condition. |
| **VACCINATION** | ▪ Check the regulations for the country—many have strict vaccination policies.<br>▪ Ensure you have the vaccinations, and any boosters, within the correct timeframe.<br>▪ Some inoculations last only for six months, so for extended trips you might have to have more while away. This can usually be arranged through local hospitals or clinics. |
| **TICKETS** | ▪ Make sure you have the correct tickets for your journey.<br>▪ Read the tickets and make sure they have the correct names, dates, and locations.<br>▪ Should you need to prove your movements, always keep your tickets in a safe place and never throw them away—often the return journey is included on the same ticket. |
| **INSURANCE** | ▪ It's advisable to get insurance against your trip being cancelled.<br>▪ Ensure that your insurance will cover your medical expenses should the worst happen. You don't have to be climbing Everest—even a twisted or broken ankle when hill-walking could prove to be very expensive if you don't have adequate insurance. |

## YOUR TEAM

If you're embarking on a trip with a group, remember that team dynamics will play an important part in the success, or otherwise, of your trip. Stressful situations—and particularly survival situations—can bring out the best, or the worst, in people. When planning a long trip, it's always a good idea to plan several shorter trips beforehand, to use as practice sessions. These will not only help you decide what equipment to take, and provide you with an opportunity to practice using it, but will also allow team members to assess how they work together as a group. This can help you to organize your team more effectively.

### MIXED-GENDER GROUPS

If the team has both male and female members, it's important to factor this into the planning stage. You'll need to consider sleeping and washing arrangements, who carries what, who is responsible for what, and so on. All this should be planned in detail before you set off. It should also be noted that taking it for granted that the women will cook the meals while the men make the shelters is not the best way to start an expedition.

### MIXED-AGE GROUPS

When planning your trip, remember that different age groups may have different levels of fitness, which will affect the pace of your group. However, what older members may lack in pace, they may make up for in expedition experience.

## PREPARATION THROUGH TRAINING

Training yourself both mentally and physically—and practicing with the equipment you'll be using—may seem like the obvious thing to do, but in many cases the obvious can often get overlooked. You'll get the most out of your trip if you're mentally and physically prepared to a level that means you can operate within your own capabilities and comfort zone. This will allow you to enjoy and appreciate the experience, as opposed to just getting yourself through it.

### TRAINING YOURSELF

Duplicate in training what you intend to do on your trip. Build up your training gradually, over a period of weeks and months, and take into account the following:
- **The environment**: research the weather conditions you'll be facing, and look at the extremes as well as the average. For example, desert areas may be hot during the day, but can drop to below freezing at night.
- **Weight:** increase the amount of weight you carry until you're eventually carrying what you intend to take. This will not only condition you to the weight but also help you to decide just what's important to take and what's not.
- **Distance:** if your trip involves covering a certain distance a day, then train for that distance. This will give you an indication of whether it's achievable and sustainable.
- **Language**: if visiting a country in which your native language is not widely spoken, it will be beneficial if you can learn some useful phrases. Take a phrase book or an electronic translator.

### TRAINING WITH EQUIPMENT

Use your equipment as much as you can, and find out the best way to operate it through practice under realistic conditions (see box, below). This will highlight its strengths and weaknesses, and allow you to determine both its capabilities and your own—the compass may be working perfectly, but practice may highlight the fact that you're not confident enough using it, in which case you'd need to do further training before you set off on your expedition. The wrong time to be trying to find the jack and spare wheel on your rented vehicle is at night, in the rain, with the mosquitoes looking at you as their next free meal. Before you set off, always think about the various skill demands required, and ensure that you're capable of addressing those demands.

### OPERATING UNDER REALISTIC CONDITIONS

When training with new equipment, always practice using it under realistic conditions. For example, if you're going to be using your GPS in cold conditions, can you operate it using the gloves you have selected? If you're pitching a tent, have you got all the necessary components, and can you put it up in the dark and rain?

# EMERGENCY PLAN OF ACTION

**UNFORTUNATELY, EVEN THE MOST** meticulously planned, thoroughly equipped, and best-executed trip can run into difficulties. Unforecasted strong winds could trap you and your kayak on an island overnight, or a sprained ankle could leave you unable to climb down the rocks you climbed up so easily. Each of these survival scenarios are difficult to predict, but could easily happen.

> ## USING YOUR EPA
> An EPA should contain up-to-date information about you as a person. This may change very little over the years, so you may only need to create a standard EPA and just update the details specific to each trip.

## RUNNING INTO PROBLEMS

It's important to make sure that you have done all you can to help yourself, and help any rescue attempt that might take place if you do have any problems. Always remember that there are two sides to any survival or rescue situation: the part that you play and the part that the rescue services play. However, the effectiveness of the rescue services can be greatly increased when they have access to all relevant information—in many cases this arrives too late. It's vital to keep people informed of your intended whereabouts, so that they can raise the alarm if you deviate from your plans.

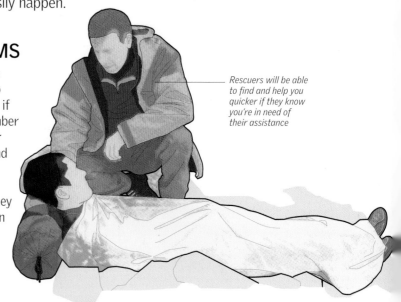

*Rescuers will be able to find and help you quicker if they know you're in need of their assistance*

## WORST-CASE SCENARIO

In the military, every mission that's undertaken, particularly in a theater of conflict, has plans in place for the worst-case scenario. Each part of the mission is meticulously planned, and the team completes a form that states what their basic intention will be should anything happen during the various stages.

### IF THE WORST HAPPENS

Having planned for the worst, should the team find themselves in difficulty, the rescue group will not have to try to second-guess what the team will do—they will have a clear indication of the team's intent and can plan effectively and decisively around this information. The team will be found quicker as a result. It's a good idea to apply this principle to your own trip.

## KEEPING PEOPLE INFORMED

A good way of keeping your friends, family, and the relevant rescue services informed of your whereabouts is to write down the details of your trip, including pertinent itinerary places and dates, so that if you don't reach your destination when planned, the alarm can be raised. Similar to the "worst-case scenario" principle practised by the military (see left), an "emergency plan of action" (EPA) should be prepared by anyone venturing into the great outdoors (see right). Give a copy to your next of kin and group members, and keep a copy on your person. Where applicable, inform local services, such as park and ranger stations, of your intentions. Remember to inform these people when you arrive safely at your destination.

### WRITING AN EMERGENCY PLAN OF ACTION (EPA)

The best way to determine what should be included in your plan is to look at the worst-case scenario you could find yourself in, and ask yourself what information your next of kin would need to know about you and your intentions if they felt they had to raise the alarm. In addition, if you did go missing—particularly in another country—there are many things that the relevant rescue services would need to aid their efforts, for example a recent photograph, your passport details, what equipment you have with you, what languages you can speak, and your skills. The clearer their understanding of you, your abilities, and your intentions, the easier their job will be. In addition, the more information your next of kin have, the more proactive they will feel in your rescue.

## EMERGENCY PLAN OF ACTION FORM

| | | | |
|---|---|---|---|
| **Full name as appears on passport:** *John William Smith* | **Date of birth:** (dd/mm/yy) *05/28/60* | **Height:** *5' 10" (178cm)* **Weight:** *168 pounds (76 kilos)* **Hair color:** *Brown* | |

| | | |
|---|---|---|
| **Passport number:** *2008XXXXX63* **Expires:** *11/03/13* | **Driver's license number:** *JHY280771smit* **Expires:** *12/28/22* | |

| | | |
|---|---|---|
| **Distinguishing marks (scars, tattoos):** *Small scar—center of forehead* *Large scar—right hand, middle finger* *Chinese symbol tattoo—right arm* | **Languages spoken (fluent/basic):** *English—native* *French—basic* *German—basic* | |

| | | |
|---|---|---|
| **Medication:** *Medication—anti-malaria tablets* **Allergies:** *Amoxicillin* | **Swimmer:** *Strong swimmer* **Outdoor skills/experience:** *Attended basic military survival training.* *Attended basic bushcraft course* *Experienced in living outdoors* | |

| | | |
|---|---|---|
| **Next of kin 1:** *Father* *William Smith* *1018 Furlong Avenue* *Brunswick, Maine,* *USA 04555* | **Next of kin 2:** *Brother* *Andrew Smith* *1023 Parkglen* *Ashford, Kent,* *TM24 5HZ* *UK* | |

| | |
|---|---|
| **Tel:** *(001) 55 555 2356* | **Tel :** *(0044) (0)155 555 2357* |

| | |
|---|---|
| **Email:** *willsmith@internet.com* | **Email:** *andrewsmith@internet.com* |

**Trip details:**
*Campsite 1 = Grid ST456654*
*Campsite 2 = Grid ST654987*
*Vehicles: Landrover 1 = white, reg MH55 555*
*Landrover 2 = blue, reg MH56 555*
*Group = Ben Jones, Kim Smith, and myself*
*Day 1: Park Landrover 2 at Campsite 2, and drive in Landrover 1 to Campsite 1*
*Day 2: Follow well-defined path along the Derwent Line Trail, aiming to camp overnight at Grid 4561559*
*Day 3: Continue along the Derwent Line Trail, aiming to be at Campsite 2 by mid-afternoon. Camp overnight at Campsite 2*
*Day 4: Travel in Landrover 2 to campsite 1 and retrieve Landrover 1*

**Foreseeable problems/intentions:**
*Day 1: None*
*Day 2: None but will use Ranger Station 18, grid 555555 (Tel. 666 6666) as an emergency rendezvous point*
*Day 3: None but will use Ranger Station 19, grid 666666 (Tel. 555 5555) as an emergency rendezvous point*
*Day 4: None*

**Communications plan:**
*Will speak to Dad on the morning of Day 1 and try to phone during the trek but am unsure of cell reception once on the trail so don't worry if you hear nothing.*
*Will phone Dad again when we reach campsite 2 on day 3.*

**My mobile:** *07979 555555*
**My email:** *jws@internet.com*
**Alt. No:** *Ben 05555 555555*
**Alt. No:** *Kim 05555 555555*
**Alt. No:** *Campsite 1 555 555 55555*
**Alt. No:** *Campsite 2 555 555 55555*

**Date:** *November 23, 2009*

# KNOW YOUR ENVIRONMENT

**The continued survival** of the human race can be attributed to our ability to adapt to our environment. While we may have lost some of our ancient ancestors' survival skills, we have, in their place, learned new skills as and when they have become necessary. The issue we face today is that the gap between the skills we once had and the skills we now have grows ever wider as we rely more heavily on modern technology. Therefore, when you head off into the wilderness, it is important to fully prepare for the environment.

Before a trip, research how the native inhabitants dress, work, and eat. How they have adapted to their way of life will help you to understand the environment and allow you to select the best gear, adopt the best techniques, and learn the correct skills. This is crucial given that most survival situations arise as a result of a sequence of events that could have been avoided—while you may have no control over the aircraft crashing, for example, you can recognize a change in the weather and choose whether to continue or turn back.

## In this section YOU WILL DISCOVER...

- the difference between **tundra** and **taiga**...
- why you should **step-up** the size of your **survival footprint**...
- the **way to go** when it comes to **snowy peaks** or **swampy creeks**...
- how to avoid **getting lost** in the **permafrost**...
- the best way to **stay at the top** of the **food chain**...
- how to **feel at home** where the tropical **butterflies roam**...
- how a high-visibility **survival suit** could really **get you noticed**...

# The four basic principles of survival are:

protection, location, water, and food. In most survival situations, this is also the order in which you should prioritize them.

**P PROTECTION** You must stay in a condition that allows you to be proactive in your continued survival and rescue. Physically, you should protect yourself against injury, the elements, and wildlife. Mentally, you should protect yourself against emotions that could rob you of the will to live: fear, guilt, despondency, and depression, for example. The best way to achieve this level of protection is to light and maintain a fire. Not only does it offer physical protection against the elements and wildlife, but it also provides a sense of security and familiarity that can help normalize even the most dire situation.

**L LOCATION** Your second priority is to recognize the importance of your location to your chances of survival and rescue. You will usually have two options: stay or go. Your preferred option should be to remain where you are and use anything at your disposal to mark your location to aid rescuers in their efforts to find you. If you can't stay where you are (perhaps because you are in imminent danger) you may have no option but to move to another location that provides either a better chance of survival or rescue, or both. Select a location aid that offers you the best chance of attracting attention in the environment in which you're traveling.

**W WATER** Put simply, water is the essence of life. While you may be able to survive for a few days without it, your ability to function and carry out even simple mental and physical tasks will be dramatically reduced in less than 24 hours. However, if you are injured, if the weather conditions are very hot, and if your workload is particularly heavy, for example, your survival time without water could be reduced to just a few hours. You should learn how to procure water in the particular environment in which you're traveling, and understand the ways in which a lack of water affects you.

**F FOOD** The importance of food is directly related to the length of time you are in a survival situation: the longer the situation lasts, the more important food will become in helping you stay fit and healthy. Even with a moderate workload, going without food for five to seven days will not kill you. You will, of course, feel hungry, you will grow tired, your movements will slow, and your body will lose its ability to repair itself. However, unless you're malnourished before you enter a survival situation, you are unlikely to starve to death within a week. Your body needs water to digest food, so always remember to prioritize water over food.

" We rely so heavily on **modern technology**: water at the **turn of a tap**; heat at the **flick of a switch**; food raised, harvested and **prepared by others** "

# TEMPERATE ENVIRONMENTS

**THE TEMPERATE ZONES** are the two regions between the Tropic of Cancer and Arctic circle, and the Tropic of Capricorn and Antarctic circle. Typified by seasonal variations in climate, conditions can include baking hot summers, freezing cold winters, and rainfall all year round. Landscape features range from forests and snow-covered peaks to grasslands and deserts. Although most temperate regions are highly populated, don't be lulled into a false sense of security—a worst-case scenario can still arise just a few miles from help.

## TEMPERATE FEATURES

Although they contain a wide range of environmental features, the temperate zone's typical feature is forest, ranging from deciduous trees that shed their leaves in fall to coniferous trees that retain their leaves all year round. Grassland predominates where forests have been cleared, while highland areas contain hills and mountains. The abundance of rain means that rivers and lakes are common, and swampy wetlands form in areas with poor drainage.

### WARNING!
Brown bears inhabit extensive wilderness areas in the northern temperate zone, and are the most dangerous temperate animal. The Grizzly, found in North America, is the most likely to attack humans.

**L** *High ground: elevated areas afford a view of your surroundings and may indicate which area offers the best prospects for your survival, or where to go to find rescue*

**P L** *High ground: night-time temperatures are lowest at altitude, so descend to warmer levels before dark. Beware of rock slides and run-off during downpours*

**L** *Tracks: indicators of human activity, tracks may lead to rescue*

**L W F** *Rivers: watercourses may be a way out of the area if you have, or can improvise, a flotation aid or raft (see pp. 106–07). They also provide fresh water for drinking, cooking, and washing, and may contain fish*

## TEMPERATE ESSENTIALS

Climate and terrain can vary widely in temperate areas, so preparation for a range of eventualities is essential:

- Don't underestimate the temperate environment. Although the vast majority of the human race lives in temperate zones, the diversity of terrain and weather means that survival equipment and knowledge must be broad enough to cope with a wide range of situations and conditions.
- Temperate weather can change very quickly, so check the local forecast before you set off, and carry a small AM/FM radio so you can listen to local weather reports.
- Plan a realistic and achievable route, and prepare an EPA (see pp. 24–25). Be ready to re-assess your route during the trip.
- Take clothing for the full range of conditions you may encounter.
- Carry a survival kit (see pp. 60–61), knife, emergency equipment, cell phone, and first-aid kit (see pp. 260–61)—and know how to use them.
- Carry adequate water, and equipment to collect and purify more if necessary.
- Carry some form of basic shelter, even if only going out for the day.
- Always take a map and compass, and consider using a GPS as an aid.

## WHERE TO FIND TEMPERATE AREAS

Deciduous forests are scattered throughout the temperate zones, but the largest occur in eastern North America, western Europe, and east Asia. Extensive coniferous forests are found in the higher latitudes of North America and Eurasia, while grassland is most common in continental interiors.

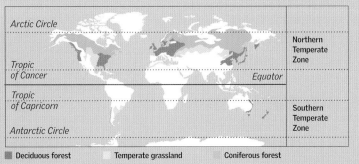

Arctic Circle

Tropic of Cancer

Equator

Tropic of Capricorn

Antarctic Circle

Northern Temperate Zone

Southern Temperate Zone

■ Deciduous forest  □ Temperate grassland  ▨ Coniferous forest

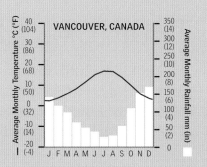

VANCOUVER, CANADA

### TYPICAL CLIMATE

Vancouver lies on the Pacific coast of Canada, and experiences a typical temperate climate of warm summers and cool, wet winters.

## SURVIVING IN TEMPERATE AREAS

Most temperate environments have a relatively mild climate and good natural resources, making them favorable places for long-term survival. Water can be found in most areas, wood for building shelters and lighting fires is usually abundant, and different types of edible plants and animals can be found at different times of year if you know where to look. Potentially the greatest threat is hypothermia (see pp. 272–73), a particular problem in cold, wet and windy conditions, especially in winter and at night, when temperatures tend to fall even further.

### WILDLIFE AND PLANT LIFE

Plant and animal life can be abundant in temperate areas and represents both a valuable food resource and a potential hazard. Shoots and stems, leaves, roots, nuts, or berries of some plants are edible, but only when positive identification—or at the least, the Universal Edibility Test (see p. 206)—is achieved. Small mammals, birds, insects, reptiles, and fish can also be found, but may be difficult to catch and kill, and must be prepared and cooked properly. Wildlife can also pose a threat—snakes, spiders, and scorpions may bite and, though rare, bears, wolves, and cougars may attack if cornered.

P L F **Woodland:** *tree cover affords protection from the elements, and wood for shelter, cooking, and signal fires. It is also a source of edible flora and fauna*

P L **Open ground:** *areas with no vegetation offer a clear view of dangers, and are ideal for deploying location aids, such as signal fires*

P **Running water:** *site your shelter a safe distance from running water. Flooding is a risk, and animals and insects are drawn to water. The noise may also hide the sound of animals or rescuers*

L **Sheltered areas:** *site your shelter on the lee-side of hills, but make sure the hill doesn't interfere with your radio signal. Choose a spot that faces the sun to maximize warmth and light*

### FIND OUT MORE...

P **PROTECTION** Shelters pp. 156–65, 178–81
Fire pp. 118–33, 204–05 **Dangers** pp. 242–49, 300–05

L **LOCATION** Navigation pp. 66–77
Movement pp. 86–89 **Signaling** pp. 236–41

W **WATER** Finding pp. 188–91
Purifying pp. 200–01

F **FOOD** Plants pp. 206–07, 280–81
Animals pp. 208–13, 216–29, 290–99

# TROPICAL ENVIRONMENTS

**THE TROPICAL ZONE** stretches from the Tropic of Cancer to the Tropic of Capricorn, and is centered over the Equator. A range of environmental features occurs in this area depending on the local climate, from lush, humid, biodiverse tropical rain forests to dry, more sparsely vegetated tropical scrub. With adequate preparation and caution you should be able to survive unsupported for extended periods—the jungle holds just as many resources as dangers.

> **WARNING!**
> Mosquitoes are responsible for more fatalities than any other creature in tropical areas. They carry a range of diseases including malaria and yellow fever, which kill millions of people every year.

**W F** *Tropical scrub: water can be found in the rainy season, while animal movements may reveal sources in the dry season. Edible plants and animals can be found*

**L** *Tracks: due to the rapid rate of growth in the rain forest, tracks are likely to be fresh and may lead to rescue. Even remote areas may contain tracks left by loggers, prospectors, or local people*

**P L** *Tropical scrub: provides shade from the sun and materials for fire and shelter, but may be home to dangerous wild animals. Dense vegetation during the rainy season may impede visibility*

## TROPICAL ESSENTIALS

Rain forests contain everything you need to stay alive, so remember the following tips when venturing out:

- While the jungle teems with predatory wildlife (such as big cats, crocodiles, and anacondas) that sees you as part of the food chain, it is the small creatures that can make life miserable. Most animals in the jungle want to avoid you as much as you want to avoid them—making a noise will scare most away.
- High humidity encourages infections, so keep everything covered (sleeves down, gloves on), and wash at every opportunity.
- Always sleep off the ground.
- Boil or treat all water. Some water found in plants can be safe to drink, but if in doubt, and if the water is yellow, milky, or very cloudy, treat before drinking.
- Many plants have defense mechanisms and can emit toxic liquids that may sting or burn—if you can't identify it, leave it alone.
- Dry tinder can be hard to find, so if you come across any, collect it and keep it safe and dry—lighting a fire in a moist, humid environment can be challenging.
- The smoke of a signal fire must penetrate through all the layers of the jungle, so light your fire where the canopy is sparse, such as the bend of a river or a clear-cut area.
- Navigation can be difficult, as you may only be able to see a few yards in front of you. Use dead reckoning—walking a short distance to a recognizable feature on your bearing—or pace-counting (see pp. 72–73).
- Rivers in the jungle usually run downhill to civilization and, eventually, the coast.
- Don't fight the jungle—tune in to its rhythm and work with it rather than against it.

## TROPICAL FEATURES

Tropical rain forest, which occurs within 10 degrees of the Equator, is the predominant environmental feature in the tropics. But there are several other environment types just a few degrees of latitude away.

### VERDANT RAIN FOREST

Tropical rain forests occur in areas with steady year-round temperatures and rainfall. Annual rainfall can reach around 6 1/2–10 ft (2–3 m) and daytime temperatures may reach 90°F (30°C), dropping to 70°F (20°C) during the night. Monsoon (or "seasonal") rain forests occur in areas with a wet and dry season, while montane rain forests, also known as "cloud forests," occur in mountainous areas.

### SCRUB AND SWAMPS

Also known as "thorn forest," tropical scrub consists of low, woody plants with thorns, which usually grow in clusters separated by patches of bare ground (grasses are uncommon). Leaves are shed in the dry season, forming a dense, herbaceous layer in the wet season. Swamps are another common tropical feature, and may consist of fresh or saltwater. Freshwater swamps are found in low-lying, inland areas, and consist of masses of undergrowth, reeds, grasses, occasional short palms, and islands. Saltwater swamps often contain mangroves, and occur in coastal areas that are prone to tidal flooding so are best navigated by boat. Visibility in both types of swamp is poor, and movement is difficult.

## SURVIVING IN THE RAIN FOREST

While natural resources are abundant in the rain forest, the heat, humidity, number of animals, and voracious rate of vegetal growth can make it an uncomfortable place. Water, materials for shelter and fire, and edible plants may all be found, although identification of plants is crucial to avoid poisonous species. Animal life is everywhere, so sleeping platforms must be built off the ground to avoid biting insects, snakes, and spiders. The greatest danger is becoming lost—navigation is difficult due to dense undergrowth at ground level, and rescuers will struggle to find you beneath the thick jungle canopy.

P L W F **Rain forest:** *fuel for cooking and signaling fires and material for shelter may be found, although check for deadfalls and other dangers. Water from rain and rivers, and edible plants and animals can be found*

### FIND OUT MORE...

P **PROTECTION** **Shelters** pp. 158–61, 166–71
**Fire** pp. 118–33, 204–05 **Dangers** pp. 167, 242–49

L **LOCATION** **Navigation** pp. 66–77
**Movement** pp. 106–07 **Signaling** pp. 236–41

W **WATER** **Finding** pp. 192–93
**Purifying** pp. 200–01

F **FOOD** **Plants** pp. 206–07, 284–85
**Animals** pp. 208–13, 224–29, 292–99

**Rain forest emergent layer:** *consists of tall trees around 200 ft (60 m) high that have broken through the canopy*

**Rain forest canopy:** *a uniform layer of trees 60–90 ft (20–30 m) high, whose crowns form a thick canopy that blocks light from the jungle floor*

**Rain forest understory:** *receives 2–15 percent of sunlight, and consists of young trees and herbaceous plants*

**Ground level:** *receives less than two percent of sunlight, and consists of dense ferns, herbaceous plants, fungi, and a thick carpet of leaves*

P L **Swamp:** *hazardous due to wildlife, fast tides, and obstacles to movement, such as submerged vegetation and deep water. Move to dry land as quickly as possible, or use a raft or flotation aid to leave the area*

L W F **Rivers:** *lack of rain forest cover makes rivers a good choice for deploying location aids and being spotted by aerial rescuers, and can be used to leave the area. Also provide water for drinking, cooking, and washing, and fish to eat. Almost all rivers will lead you to civilization*

## WHERE TO FIND TROPICAL AREAS

Tropical rain forests are clustered around the Equator. The largest rain forest areas are found in Central and South America, sub-Saharan Africa, southeast Asia, northern Australia, and several Pacific islands.

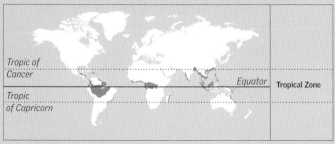

Tropic of Cancer

Equator **Tropical Zone**

Tropic of Capricorn

■ Rain forest areas

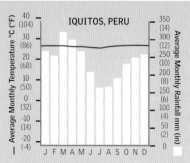

IQUITOS, PERU

Average Monthly Temperature °C (°F)

Average Monthly Rainfall mm (in)

J F M A M J J A S O N D

### TYPICAL CLIMATE

Iquitos sits on the Amazon river in the heart of the Peruvian rain forest. It lies just south of the Equator and has a typical hot, wet tropical climate.

# MOUNTAIN ENVIRONMENTS

**THE MOUNTAIN ENVIRONMENT** is one of the harshest places for humans to survive. Defined as landmasses with a summit above 2,000 ft (600 m), mountains can be very dangerous places due to their elevation and terrain. Lower temperatures and poor weather are more likely at higher altitudes, so there is a significant risk of hypothermia, frostbite, and altitude sickness, while snow, ice, and precipitous terrain present further hazards. Survival may depend on your ability to descend to areas with better prospects of survival and rescue.

**P L** *Mountains: shelter is limited and dangers include unpredictable weather and rock falls. They may require special equipment and knowledge to negotiate*

## MOUNTAIN FEATURES

Above the treeline, mountain terrain is typically barren, featuring bare rocks, gravel, boulders, and snow and ice, which are most extensive during the winter but may persist at high elevations during the summer. At lower levels, coniferous forest is the predominant feature, dissected by streams and rivers fed by snowmelt. Topographical features include scree slopes, cliffs, ravines, boulder fields, snowslopes, and glaciers.

**P L** *Elevated areas: high areas offer good visibility for location aids, but nearby mountains may interfere with communication devices. Rescue at altitude is hazardous—helicopters struggle for lift in the thin air*

**P L** *Scree and cliffs: dangerous and tiring to negotiate. Offer poor protection from the elements. Descend quickly and safely*

**P** *Avalanche-prone slopes: avoid at all costs—the smallest noise or movement can trigger a collapse*

**P L F** *Forest areas: rich in resources. Offer protection from the elements, material for shelters, cooking, fires, and signaling, and edible flora and fauna*

**P** *Shelter: always site your shelter away from areas of avalanche risk, especially if avalanche debris is present*

## ELEVATION CHANGE

Mountains of sufficient height may have vastly different ecosystems at different elevations, due to harsh conditions at high altitude. Plant and animal life varies at different elevations, so the natural resources available for survival will differ according to height. Mixed deciduous trees are common on low slopes and conifers grow at intermediate levels, but thin out to grass, isolated shrubs, moss, and lichen higher up. At the highest levels, high winds, frost, snow, and ice discourage any growth.

**WARNING!**
One of the most dangerous animals in mountain areas is the cougar, also known as the puma, panther, and mountain lion. Found in North and South America, more than 20 percent of attacks are fatal.

**W F** *Streams: usually a clean and safe source of water for drinking, cooking, and washing, and may also contain fish for food. Always treat the water if you have the means. If following water courses downhill in poor visibility, take care. The route could end in a waterfall, with no means of retracing your steps*

**L F** *Watercourses: streams and rivers provide a quick, defined route, and may be navigable if you have, or can improvise, a raft or flotation device (see pp. 106–09)*

# SURVIVING IN THE MOUNTAINS

The prospects for survival are good at lower elevations, where trees provide material for shelter and fire, rivers provide water, and edible plants and animals are likely to be present. At higher elevations vegetation is scarce, so there are fewer options for shelter and food, although water from streams or snow is likely to be available. There may be a risk of avalanche on snow-covered slopes, and crevasses pose a hidden danger in glaciated areas. Cold-related injuries pose the greatest threat (see pp. 270–71).

## HIGH-LEVEL HAZARDS

The primary threats to survival at high altitude are cold-related ailments, the most dangerous of which is hypothermia. This occurs when the body's core temperature falls below 95°F (35°C)—if allowed to drop as low as 86°F (30°C), it can be fatal. Frostbite may also occur in the extremities in freezing or cold and windy weather, and may lead to permanent tissue damage. Altitude sickness, which can cause pulmonary or cerebral edema—and in extreme cases, death— is also a risk above 8,000 ft (2,500 m).

**P L** *Glaciated areas: inhospitable and dangerous, so avoid if possible. Crossing them should never be attempted alone. If in a group, roping up is essential*

**P W** *Snow-covered areas: shelters can be dug from the snow, which can also be melted for water*

---

### FIND OUT MORE...

**P PROTECTION Shelters** pp. 156–65, 178–81
**Fire** pp. 118–33, 204–05 **Dangers** pp. 242–49, 300–01

**L LOCATION Navigation** pp. 66–77
**Movement** pp. 90–91, 94–97 **Signaling** pp. 236–41

**W WATER Finding** pp. 188–91, 194–95
**Purifying** pp. 200–01

**F FOOD Plants** pp. 206–07, 280–81, 286–87
**Animals** pp. 208–13, 216–23, 290–97

---

# MOUNTAIN DISTRIBUTION

Mountains are found on every continent, but the major ranges are the Himalayas and Karakoram in Asia, the Andes in South America, the Rocky Mountains in North America, and the Alps and Pyrenees in Europe.

■ **Mountain ranges**

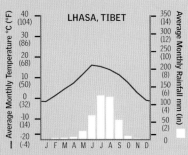

LHASA, TIBET

### TYPICAL CLIMATE

Lhasa, the capital city of Tibet, lies at 11,972 ft (3,649 m) on the Tibetan Plateau, sometimes known as "the roof of the world." The high altitude means that winters are cool, and precipitation is relatively low because it mostly falls as snow, which has just 10 percent of the density of rain.

---

# MOUNTAIN ESSENTIALS

High altitude and lower oxygen levels place higher-than-normal demands on even a fit body, so be prepared. Survival in the mountains is also tough on equipment.

■ Respect nature and err on the side of caution—mountains are unforgiving, and rescue is unlikely to be quick or easy.

■ Plan an achievable and safe route, and prepare an Emergency Plan of Action (see pp. 24–25).

■ Dress in layers (see pp. 46–47). Start a walk lightly dressed (cold) and add or remove layers as necessary.

■ Wear a hat (up to 70 percent of body heat is lost through the head) and gloves—cold fingers will hinder your functions.

■ Tie loose items of clothing (hat, gloves, sunglasses) to your person—a lost glove could result in a lost hand, or life.

■ Take a flashlight—weather changes and unforeseen problems may mean you are on the mountain in low light or darkness.

■ Always carry basic equipment to give adequate protection if forced to camp overnight, such as a bivy sack and sleeping bag.

■ Check avalanche warnings and carry an avalanche transceiver.

■ Contact with snow makes clothing wet and less effective.

■ If moving over snow, make a pair of improvised snow shoes (see pp. 94–95).

# DESERT ENVIRONMENTS

**THE DESERT ENVIRONMENT** is a hostile place for human survival due to temperature extremes and the scarcity—or absence—of water. Most deserts are either hot and dry or cold and dry, and all typically receive less than 10in (250mm) of annual rainfall. They are areas of extremes, where heat exhaustion and hypothermia are threats, and flash floods may rapidly replace dry conditions. A harsh place to survive, the desert should only be entered by those who are prepared.

> **WARNING!**
> Desert areas are home to a range of venomous snakes, including the black mamba of eastern and southern Africa. It is particularly dangerous due to its aggressive nature and highly venomous bite.

## DESERT FEATURES

The popular depiction of a desert is of a dry, sandy landscape with searing skies and temperatures among the highest in the world. Such areas do exist, but the desert environment has far greater diversity, from cold deserts in the polar regions to highlands, grassland, and broken, rocky terrain that contain "wadis" (seasonal stream beds).

### HOT, DRY DESERTS

Temperate and tropical deserts are usually hot and dry due to high daytime temperatures, which leads to low precipitation and high evaporation. There may be months or even years between rainfall, which usually occurs in dramatic bursts but then quickly drains into seasonal stream beds (wadis), or evaporates either in the air or soon after touching the hot ground. Very little rain soaks into the ground, which results in sparse vegetation that has evolved to maximize water, usually via extensive root systems that collect moisture, waxy skin and leaves that prevent water loss, and stems or roots that hold water. At night, in winter, and at higher altitudes, freezing temperatures and frost may occur.

### GRASSLANDS

Known as savanna in tropical areas, grasslands often border desert regions, and experience a similarly dry climate for most of the year. The key difference is that they also experience a wet season, which accounts for the more diverse and extensive vegetation. Temperate grassland features grasses, shrubs, and small pockets of trees, while savanna is typically more varied, with denser tree cover, bushes, and grasses that grow tall during the wet season but die back in periods of drought. Wildlife is more prevalent, including predators. Wildfires may spread during the dry season, and play an important role by destroying dead plant matter and adding fertile ash to the soil.

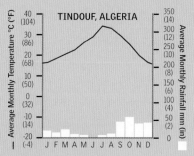

**P L W F** *Oasis: vegetation affords shelter, but animals drawn to the water may pose a threat. Highly visible landmarks, oases are a vital water resource and often contain edible plants and animals*

**W F** *Elevated areas: hills may hold pools of trapped rainwater, and may be home to edible animals*

## WHERE TO FIND DESERT AREAS

Although deserts occur on every continent, the largest hot desert in the world is the Sahara in North Africa, which forms part of a desert band stretching through the Middle East and into south and central Asia.

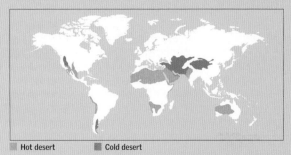

Hot desert ■ Cold desert

**TINDOUF, ALGERIA**

Average Monthly Temperature °C (°F) / Average Monthly Rainfall mm (in)

J F M A M J J A S O N D

### TYPICAL CLIMATE

Tindouf lies in the heart of the Sahara, and experiences a typical hot-desert climate. Precipitation is virtually zero all year round, while temperatures peak in the summer.

# SURVIVING IN THE DESERT

Hostile temperatures and few natural resources limit chances of survival in the desert. Water and shelter are scarce, if not non-existent, edible vegetation is limited, and animals hide from the sun in the day. Wadis, grasslands, and higher ground all hold better prospects. The greatest dangers are dehydration and heat exhaustion (see pp. 272–73), although African savanna areas may be home to large, dangerous mammals. The main killers are big cats, hippos, rhinos, elephants, and crocodiles.

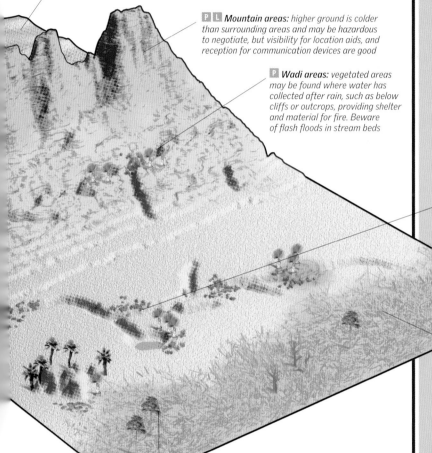

**P L W** *Sand dunes: shelter from the elements is poor, but visibility for location aids and for spotting rescuers is good. Observing converging animal and bird tracks or movements may indicate the direction to a water source.*

**P L** *Mountain areas: higher ground is colder than surrounding areas and may be hazardous to negotiate, but visibility for location aids, and reception for communication devices are good*

**P** *Wadi areas: vegetated areas may be found where water has collected after rain, such as below cliffs or outcrops, providing shelter and material for fire. Beware of flash floods in stream beds*

**P** *Savanna: protection from the elements is limited, although material for building shelters may be found in the wet season. Sunstroke and dehydration are killers, so seek shade during the hottest parts of the day. Beware of snakes or scorpions in shaded areas, big cats and large mammals, and nocturnal animal activity*

## FIND OUT MORE...

**P PROTECTION Shelters** pp. 156–61, 174–75 **Fire** pp. 118–33, 204–05 **Dangers** pp. 242–49, 300–05

**L LOCATION Navigation** pp. 66–77 **Movement** pp. 100–01 **Signaling** pp. 236–41

**W WATER Finding** pp. 192–93 **Purifying** pp. 200–01

**F FOOD Plants** pp. 206–07, 282–83 **Animals** pp. 216–21, 224–29, 292–95

# DESERT ESSENTIALS

Survival in the extreme conditions of the desert is impossible without full preparation. Consider the following:

■ Always prepare an EPA to notify someone of your plans before entering a desert area (see pp. 24–25).

■ Water is life. Do not underestimate your needs, carry extra just in case, and carry equipment to maximize your chances of finding and procuring more (binoculars, surgical tubing, filtration/purification pump) should the worst happen.

■ Ask local people about water sources that may not be marked on maps, such as wells used by Bedouin tribes.

■ If venturing into remote areas, augment your map and compass with a GPS, and consider taking a PLB or satellite phone (see pp. 236–37).

■ If using a vehicle, ensure you carry jacking equipment for use in soft ground, sand mats or ladders for self-recovery, extra water, a shelter, location aids, and any relevant vehicle spares.

**W F** *Wadi areas: rivers flow in wadis during flash floods, and water may be retained below the surface long after the flood has passed. Wadis are also the habitat of edible animals*

**L W F** *Savanna: visibility and reception for communication devices are likely to be good but will be reduced in the wet season when plants growth flourishes. Water sources vary depending on the season*

■ Plan cut-off or safety points into your journey that can be used to divert to in case of an emergency.

■ Ensure you know how to accomplish emergency repairs to your vehicle.

■ Ask local people about known dangers, such as impassable roads, misleading tracks, and soft-sand areas.

■ When using a ladder for self-recovery, tie it to the back of the vehicle so that it's dragged behind once crossed, and can be retrieved when you reach solid ground.

■ If your vehicle breaks down, leave it only if staying is no longer safe or feasible—rescuers will search for it first.

# COLD ENVIRONMENTS

**LOW TEMPERATURES** are a potentially lethal hazard, but as long as you can conserve body heat, survival in the cold is quite possible. The ice-covered Arctic and Antarctic polar regions, sub-polar tundra and taiga, as well as parts of most temperate zones during the winter, can all be classed as cold environments. Wet, windy weather can drive moderately cold temperatures down further, increasing the risk of the most lethal cold-weather condition—hypothermia.

> **WARNING!**
> The largest predatory land mammal on Earth, the polar bear inhabits the Arctic. Attacks are most likely when the bears are hungry, and are usually fatal.

## COLD ENVIRONMENT FEATURES

Outside temperate areas, the typical cold environments are the polar areas, which feature glacial ice sheets and sea ice; tundra, which contains permafrost (permanently frozen soil), small shrubs, mosses, and lichens; and taiga, with extensive conifer forests. Almost half of the northern hemisphere's landmass can be classified as a cold region, due to the influence of cold air masses (see pp. 78–83), while ocean currents and altitude can also have a cooling effect.

### POLAR WASTES

The northern polar area is situated over the Arctic Ocean, so largely consists of sea ice, the extent and depth of which varies throughout the year. Because of the lack of land, melting ice is a serious danger. The southern polar area is located over the continent of Antarctica, and contains the largest glacial ice sheet on Earth. Both areas contain ice shelves—glaciers that have extended over the sea—parts of which break off to form icebergs.

### TUNDRA AND TAIGA

Latitudes that neighbor the polar areas are home to tundra, an environment of permafrost and vegetation that is stunted due to low temperatures. Taiga is located further away from the poles, where temperatures are high enough to support coniferous forests.

**P L** *Mountains: elevated areas give little protection from the elements, but offer good visibility for location aids. They are also ideal points from which to survey your surroundings*

**P** *Taiga: forests provide protection from the elements and materials for shelter and fire, although animal life may pose a threat*

**P L** *Tundra: during the winter, snow cover means that there is little protection from the elements, and movement is difficult without snow shoes or skis*

**P** *Sea ice: dangerous terrain to survive in, sea ice carries risk of exposure, falling through the ice, and polar bears (in nothern polar areas). Your location may depend on the ice flow*

**L W F** *Sea ice: natural resources to assist signaling your location are limited or non-existent. Water may be obtained from snow or ice, and food from fishing*

# SURVIVING IN THE COLD

Natural resources may be scarce in cold environments, so your survival is likely to depend on the equipment and supplies you have with you. Shelters can be dug from the snow to help you stay warm and avoid exposure to freezing temperatures, but material for making fire is limited in polar and tundra areas. Survival is more feasible in the taiga, where wood is available, and fresh water and edible flora and fauna can also be found. The greatest dangers are hypothermia (see pp. 272–73) and—in northern polar areas—polar bears.

## LOW-TEMPERATURE DANGER

Heat loss occurs in several ways, and minimizing it is essential to survival in cold conditions. It's important to avoid over-exertion, since heat is lost through sweating, and to cover your head and wear layered clothing to trap radiated body heat. Heat is also lost through conduction—direct contact between the skin and a cooler surface—particularly when wet, since water conducts heat away from the body 25 times faster than air. For this reason, it's vital to wear insulated and waterproof clothing, and to stay dry. Respiration also involves heat loss—each inhaled breath contains cold air, which is warmed as it passes through the lungs, and laden with moisture when exhaled. Reduce heat loss by covering your nose and mouth with a ski-mask or scarf, or by breathing warmer air next to a fire or in a warm shelter.

**L W F** *Taiga: natural resources are available for making location aids, water sources may be found, and edible flora and fauna are likely to be present*

**W F** *Tundra: snow and ice can be melted in the winter and ground water is present in the summer, although sources are limited. Vegetation increases closer to the treeline*

# COLD ESSENTIALS

The main threats in cold environments are hypothermia and exposure, so ensure you are fully prepared:

■ Dress in loose-fitting layers of clothing (see pp. 46–47), avoid overheating, and ensure your clothing stays dry and clean.

■ If your hands are cold, don't warm them with your breath, which will make them wet—tuck them under your armpits.

■ Regularly check your extremities (face, toes, hands, and ears) for frostnip, the first stage of frostbite (see p. 273).

■ Wind-chill is dangerous, so take shelter from the wind at every opportunity, particularly if you are in a survival situation.

■ Always ensure that your shelter is well ventilated—keep vent holes clear and check regularly, especially when snow falls.

■ Get off the cold ground, snow, or ice—sit on your pack or make a sleeping platform using boughs to avoid losing body heat.

■ If fire is your primary means of warmth, triple the amount of firewood you think you need—you will need enough to last the night.

## FIND OUT MORE...

**P PROTECTION Shelters** pp. 156–65, 178–79
**Fire** pp. 118–33, 204–05 **Dangers** pp. 242–49

**L LOCATION Navigation** pp. 66–67
**Movement** pp. 94–97 **Signaling** pp. 236–41

**W WATER Finding** pp. 194–95
**Purifying** pp. 200–01

**F FOOD Plants** pp. 206–07, 286–87
**Animals** pp. 208–13, 216–23, 290–91, 296–97

# WHERE TO FIND COLD AREAS

The Arctic and Antarctic polar areas are the coldest places on Earth, and are found at the furthest points from the Equator. Tundra exists next to polar regions, and is bordered by taiga, which is found in northern Eurasia and North America.

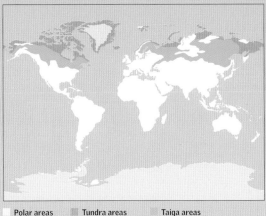

■ Polar areas    ■ Tundra areas    ■ Taiga areas

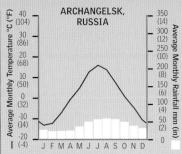

ARCHANGELSK, RUSSIA

## TYPICAL CLIMATE

Archangelsk is a Russian port on the Barents Sea. Located in the taiga zone, it experiences below-zero temperatures for half the year and low precipitation.

# MARINE ENVIRONMENTS

**POTENTIALLY THE MOST HARSH** and challenging of all environments, the sea is unlike any other due to the lack of the most essential requirement for human life—fresh water. Around 70 percent of the Earth's surface is covered by saltwater, ranging from the freezing, wind-torn polar oceans to the warm tropical seas. Winds and currents govern your movement, protection is limited, and natural resources are virtually nil, so reaching land is your best hope for survival.

> **WARNING!**
> There are sharks in every ocean, but those in tropical waters are the most aggressive. Around 20 of the hundreds of species have attacked humans, and the most dangerous types are the great white, tiger, and bull sharks.

## MARINE FEATURES

The marine environment ranges from the coastal margins, which are shallow enough— 650 ft (200 m) or less—to support a huge array of animal and plant life, to the open oceans, the deepest of which plunge to more than 33,000 ft (10,000 m).

### SHELTERED COAST TO OPEN SEA

The coastal margins are home to the majority of ocean life, and include terrestrial areas—the shoreline and intertidal zone—and aquatic—the sea up to the edge of the continental shelf. A variety of environmental features are found, such as sand, rock, and pebble beaches, dunes, cliffs, estuaries, mud flats, mangroves, lagoons, kelp forests, and coral reefs. The open ocean is a more barren environment that supports less life, and is notable for its vast extent, comprising 92 percent of all saltwater. Survival depends on your equipment, supplies, and ingenuity.

### OCEAN CONDITIONS

Your protection and location at sea depends largely on the weather—you may need to deal with anything from exposure to the hot sun, to cold, wet, windy conditions and high seas. Conditions are toughest in the South Atlantic Ocean, where winds (known as the "Roaring Forties") are strong all year round, and sea ice is extensive in the winter. Severe seasonal storms occur: hurricanes in the tropical areas of the western Atlantic, typhoons in the western Pacific. India and Southeast Asia also experience severe weather during the monsoon seasons.

**L W F** *Rocky shoreline: signaling to rescuers may be difficult, and rescuers may not be able to reach you. Water and food will be limited to crabs, shellfish, birds, and eggs*

**P** *Rocky shoreline: difficult to make landfall and to survive on, and poses risk of injury when landing. Progress to safer areas may be difficult or impossible due to cliffs or slippery rocks. Protection from the elements and tides is limited*

**F** *Coastal margins: the majority of ocean life is found near the coasts, and most species live within 650 ft (200 m) of the surface*

## WINDS AND CURRENTS

Winds and currents follow prevailing patterns, so if you know roughly where you are, you can figure out where they'll carry you. With a drift of just 1 knot, a liferaft can move 24 miles (38 km) from its last known position in 24 hours. It may also drift up to 35° either side of the wind, further widening the search area to more than 400 sq miles (1,000 sq km) in the first 24-hour period, and increasing exponentially over time. Conversely, favorable currents can also be used to help you drift to landfall faster.

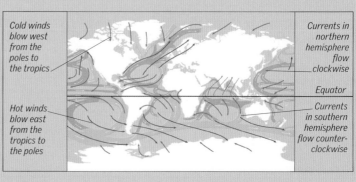

*Cold winds blow west from the poles to the tropics*

*Hot winds blow east from the tropics to the poles*

*Currents in northern hemisphere flow clockwise*

*Equator*

*Currents in southern hemisphere flow counter-clockwise*

— Warm winds    — Cold winds    ▮ Warm currents    Cold currents

**P L** *Beach: above the high-tide mark, beaches may provide protection from wind and rain, and materials for building shelters, lighting fires, and improvising location aids*

**W F** *Beach stream: streams may drain on to beaches, providing water for drinking, cooking, and washing. Edible plants and animals may be present*

**P W F** *Liferaft: increases your chances of survival and rescue, providing protection against the elements and drowning, and containing essential emergency equipment, including water and food. If land is reached, your raft can be used as a ready-made shelter*

**L** *Liferaft: a highly visible location aid, although at the mercy of wind and currents. It may also contain flares*

**P L** *Lifejacket: effective protection against drowning, and also acts as a basic location aid*

**L** *Sea anchor: also known as a "drogue," it reduces drift and maintains stability. It anchors the trailing side of the liferaft to the water and prevents it from overturning, and stops it speeding down the face of swells or waves. Most importantly, it reduces drift, helping to keep you in the same location and increasing your chances of rescue*

## SURVIVING AT SEA

Natural resources in the open ocean are virtually nil, so improvising shelter or locations aids is limited to what you have with you. Seasickness, especially in a small liferaft, can seriously affect your ability to remain both hydrated and motivated. Unless you can reach land, your only drinking water will come from rain or mechanical desalination devices—consuming urine or saltwater will only increase your rate of dehydration. Reaching land or shipping lanes greatly increases your chances of rescue.

## MARINE ESSENTIALS

Your chances of survival at sea will be greatly enhanced by good preparation, so consider the following:

■ Pack sea-survival equipment as if your life depends on it—it might! Other environments allow you to improvise survival and location aids, but not the sea.

■ Take emergency immersion-survival suits. They will protect you against the elements and aid flotation, and their color (high-visibility orange or red) is an aid to location.

■ Always carry a Personal Locator Beacon (PLB), just in case.

■ Take several means of obtaining water, such as a reverse-osmosis pump, which turns saltwater into drinking water, a saltwater desalination kit, a solar still, and rain catchers.

■ Always keep a pre-packed emergency bag handy. It should contain; first aid kit, reverse-osmosis pump, emergency beacon, solar still, water, flares, fishing kit. (see pp. 250).

■ If your vessel sinks, do not abandon it until absolutely necessary. Stay nearby unless it is unsafe to do so—anything that gives you a bigger "survival footprint" will increase your chances of being rescued, and you may be able to retrieve provisions from the vessel.

■ If imminent rescue is unlikely, you will need to ration your water. Consider how much you have, how much can be procured, the chances of seasickness (which leads to dehydration), and the likelihood of being rescued later on.

■ Protect yourself from the elements (sun, wind, cold, heat, and salt) as well as you can—prevention is better than cure.

■ The sea, especially in rough conditions, can sap the will to live quicker than any other environment. Seasickness is literally draining, resulting in lost fluid, energy, and motivation. Take anti-seasickness tablets at the earliest opportunity—even before abandoning ship—so that you can keep them down, and keep taking them as recommended.

### FIND OUT MORE...

**P PROTECTION** Shelters pp. 156–61, 176–77
Fire pp. 118–33, 204–05 Dangers pp. 250–55, 300–01

**L LOCATION** Movement pp. 106–07
Signaling pp. 236–41

**W WATER** Finding pp. 196–97
Treating pp. 200–01

**F FOOD** Plants pp. 206–07, 288–89
Animals pp. 208–13, 224–29, 292–99

# GET THE RIGHT GEAR

**Whether you're equipping yourself** for a lengthy expedition or just a day trip, it's important to choose the correct equipment and clothing. The wrong time to realize that your gear isn't up to the job is when your life depends on it doing what it was designed to do.

When selecting gear, it's always a good idea to work backward from a worst-case-scenario survival situation. Think about what you would need to survive if the worst happened. This is your "first-line" equipment, which you should carry with you at all times. It should enable you to address the basic principles of survival relevant to the environment you are in, and consists of the clothing you would wear and your basic survival equipment—your survival tin and belt-order (see pp. 43, 61).

Once you have organized this basic equipment, you can then decide what pieces of essential gear would make your expedition enjoyable rather than just survivable. This will probably consist of a bivy or tent, a sleeping bag, cooking equipment and food, and something to carry it all in.

## In this section YOU WILL DISCOVER...

- the **meaning** of the term "**bomb-burst gear**"...
- that it's always **good to share** when you're **in a group**...
- which **backpacks** are the **best backpacks** to pack...
- why you should **hike around the house** to **break in your boots...**
- a good reason to take a **three-season tent...**
- how to **sleep** like a **mummy...**
- what **gorp** is and **when** you should **eat it...**

It's at this stage that you should conduct a short trial to check that your chosen gear will fit in your pack and that you can comfortably carry it.

Finally, any spare capacity can be utilized for non-essential "luxury" items, such as an inflatable mattress and pillow, an MP3 player, or a book. Double-check that your gear works and that you know how to use it properly. The more you understand how and why a piece of equipment works, the better able you will be to improvise should it be damaged or lost.

## With each venture into

the wilderness, your confidence in your abilities and that of your equipment will increase. As it does, you may want to explore the world of ultralight camping.

**ULTRALIGHT CAMPING** refers to the careful selection of your three largest items of gear to dramatically reduce the load you have to carry. A standard tent, pack, and sleeping bag have a combined weight of approximately 20 lb (9kg). Ultralight camping has the potential to halve the weight of your "big three."

- Take a hooped bivy instead of a tent and choose a low season-rated sleeping bag (wear your day clothes inside the bag for extra warmth).
- You can then reduce the size of your pack because your tent and sleeping bag are smaller.

**Trekking with less equipment** but still staying safe allows you greater freedom to enjoy the wilderness—carrying less weight puts less strain on your body, enabling you to cover greater distances. Ultralight camping can become addictive and is safe if you use common sense—but never compromise on the quality of equipment. Try:

- Using a hexamine stove to cook food and boil water—you won't have to carry a stove and fuel.
- Taking one pot to cook food and boil water.
- Using natural materials as a mattress.

> The **wrong time** to realize that **your equipment** isn't up to the **task in hand** is when **your life depends** on it doing what it was **designed to do**

# CHOOSING YOUR GEAR

**FORWARD PLANNING IS ESSENTIAL** when you're deciding on what equipment to take on your trip. You'll need to assess your own personal requirements, the likely demands of weather and terrain, and the amount of gear you'll actually be able to transport. With a little forethought, you'll be as well equipped as you can be for any situation.

## PACKING FOR YOUR TRIP

You will first need to weigh up your particular kit requirements against the limitations of your chosen mode of transport (see below). It's then vital to organize and prioritize your gear (see opposite) to ensure that any items you may need in a survival scenario are always close at hand, should the worst happen.

### KEY PACKING TIPS

- Pack your gear in reverse order: the things you want to get to first should be the last things you pack.
- Stash items you may need during the day in side or lid pockets, for easy access.
- Coil and tape long straps so that they aren't a snagging hazard.
- Use a dry bag inside your backpack.
- Ensure that all pockets are fully closed and zipped.
- Air out anything packed wet as soon as you stop for the day.

## HOW MUCH TO PACK

The environment of the region you're traveling to will dictate the type of equipment you will need to take with you, but your proposed mode of transport is the main constraint on the quantity of kit you can take (see chart, right). The more gear you have to carry yourself, the fewer luxuries you can take: the added weight will make traveling uncomfortable, use up too much valuable energy, slow your progress, and also limit the distance you can travel each day. It's also worth considering whether you can reduce the weight and volume of the kit items you're taking (see box, below).

### LIGHTENING THE LOAD

When you're going to be traveling on foot, it's important to get rid of all the excess weight and volume you can, even if it's only by a small amount. The larger and heavier your backpack, the harder you will find the journey. If you have already ruthlessly pared your gear down to the bare essentials, try to reduce the weight or volume of the kit itself. First concentrate on the big three items: tent, sleeping bag, and backpack. Consider using a hooped bivy or tarpaulin rather than a tent; look for a lighter sleeping bag—some can weigh as little as 2lb (0.9 kg); and consider buying a backpack with a lighter frame.

### WEIGHT AND SPACE RESTRICTIONS

| | |
|---|---|
| **ON FOOT** | Backpacks (see pp. 44–45) are available in a wide range of volumes—from 30 liters (a day pack) to 80 liters (suitable for a trip of a week or more). Bear in mind that you'll have to carry whatever gear you take with you, and that the weight of the pack will determine what you're realistically able to achieve each day in terms of distance and activity. Pack only the bare minimum: there's no room for luxuries when traveling on foot. |
| **MOUNTAIN/ TOURING BIKE** | Pannier bags for bicycles are designed to fit on front, rear, or side pannier racks, and are available in a range of shapes, sizes, and capacities (from 5 to 50 liters). Larger bags will provide you with enough space to pack essentials, such as tent, sleeping bag, cooking equipment, and spare clothes, but you'll be restricted by the weight, and also by the need to carry cycle-maintenance gear, such as spare tires, inner tubes, cables, and tools. |
| **MOTORCYCLE** | Side panniers have a capacity of up to 80 liters and tank bags up to 25 liters, and weight is not a major issue. However, you'll need to take extra protective equipment, maintenance tools (including spare tires), and, in some cases, spare fuel, all of which will impact on available space. |
| **PACK ANIMAL** | Ideal for rough terrain, such as mountains or desert, pack animals can carry serious weight. A horse can transport up to 20 percent of its body weight; a camel can carry a weight of up to 990 lb (450 kg)—although 330 lb (150 kg) is more common—but you'll need to factor in the animal's food and water. |
| **VEHICLE** | The size of the vehicle will determine the amount and the weight of gear you can take with you, but you shouldn't have to compromise; extra equipment can be packed in peli boxes—waterproof storage containers with a hard, plastic exterior—that can be strapped to the outside of the vehicle. The main issue will be the weight-versus-fuel ratio: the heavier the vehicle, the more fuel it will use. |
| **CANOE/ KAYAK/BOAT** | Some kayaks and canoes are designed to bear loads of up to 660 lb (300 kg), including the craft's occupant(s), so you should be able to take all of your essential gear, plus a few luxuries. Given your proximity to the water, keeping your gear dry is the main priority. Weight and space restrictions don't apply for larger vessels. |

# PRIORITIZING YOUR KIT

However much gear you decide to take, you should group individual items into one of three categories—first-line, second-line, and third-line—according to their importance to your survival in a worst-case scenario. It's very unlikely that you'll be able to carry all of your equipment all of the time, and in an emergency situation, you may not have time to gather it all together. However, by prioritizing your gear beforehand, you'll have all your essential items on your person, or close enough to grab at a second's notice.

## FIRST-LINE GEAR

Known as "bomb-burst gear" in the military, first-line gear (see right) is your basic survival equipment. If something goes wrong and you have to abandon the bulk of your gear to avoid injury, or death, what you're standing in is all you'll have to help you survive. First-line gear should therefore comprise crucial items of outdoor clothing, along with essential items for navigation and safety. Your bushcraft knife, firesteel, and belt pouch make up your belt order (see pp. 60–61). You'll need to risk-assess your particular situation and adapt your kit priorities accordingly, as conditions change, meaning that your first-line gear may alter as the day progresses. Bear in mind that if a removed layer of clothing goes into your backpack, it's no longer part of your first-line kit.

## SECOND-LINE KIT

Second-line gear is everything you would need to stay safe on a daily basis under normal conditions. It can either be packed in a small day pack, or contained in pouches on a belt, the idea being that you carry it at all times. For example, a climber may decide to leave the bulk of his or her equipment (third-line gear) while attempting to reach the summit of a peak. By proceeding with first- and second-line gear, the climber is sacrificing equipment for weight and speed, but is still safe, as they have the essentials on them. Examples of second-line gear can include:

- A spare set of clothes, a bivy sack, and cordage
- Emergency rations and first-aid kit (see p. 260)
- Hexamine stove (see p. 58–59) and items to make a hot drink
- Matchless fireset (see p. 118), and a metal cup

## THIRD-LINE GEAR

Also known as your "sustainment load," third-line gear is essentially the equipment you need to keep yourself alive and to function for longer periods of time. How much third-line gear you have will ultimately depend on your mode of transport and the amount of equipment you can carry. Examples of third-line gear include:

- A form of shelter—a tent or a tarpaulin
- Cooking utensils, such as a stove or cooking pot
- A backpack
- Food stores
- A sleeping bag and sleeping mat
- Any large water containers or hydration packs
- Wash kit and sanitary items

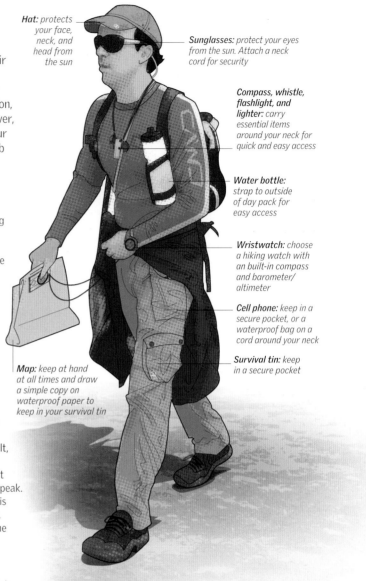

**Hat:** protects your face, neck, and head from the sun

**Sunglasses:** protect your eyes from the sun. Attach a neck cord for security

**Compass, whistle, flashlight, and lighter:** carry essential items around your neck for quick and easy access

**Water bottle:** strap to outside of day pack for easy access

**Wristwatch:** choose a hiking watch with an built-in compass and barometer/altimeter

**Cell phone:** keep in a secure pocket, or a waterproof bag on a cord around your neck

**Survival tin:** keep in a secure pocket

**Map:** keep at hand at all times and draw a simple copy on waterproof paper to keep in your survival tin

## FLASHLIGHTS

A flashlight is a piece of first-line gear, even if you don't intend to be out in the dark, because situations can change unexpectedly. Modern flashlights use LEDs, and are small, lightweight, powerful, and very efficient. Opt for a "hands-free" headlamp and tape a spare set of batteries to your head-band. Also include two miniature Photon (LED) flashlights in your survival kit (see pp. 60–61).

# CHOOSING A BACKPACK

**BACKPACKS ARE DESIGNED** to enable hikers to carry large loads comfortably. They are made from a variety of materials, most of them waterproof. However, you should always use a separate waterproof bag inside your backpack to ensure your sleeping bag and spare clothes are kept dry; they are of little use in a survival situation if they get wet.

> **CARRY ONLY WHAT YOU NEED**
> Regardless of your pack size, you are the one who has to carry it. If in a group, many communal items can be shared. Try not to double up on basics (a party of four does not need four tubes of toothpaste, for example).

## WHAT DO YOU NEED?

Your choice of backpack will depend on a number of factors. How long is your trip? How much do you intend to carry? What type of gear will you be taking with you? The answers to these questions will determine the size of pack—known as the "capacity"—that is right for you. Pack sizes range from 30 liters (a day pack) to 80 liters or more (suitable for trips lasting a week or more).

## BACKPACK FRAMES

If you have chosen a medium- to large-sized pack, you will have to choose between an internal- or an external-frame pack.

## DAY PACK

Day hikers can sometimes find themselves in trouble because they are not carrying the appropriate equipment to protect them from the elements. A day pack provides you with the means to carry essential items such as food, water, maps, compasses, and protection from cold and wet weather on a day trip.

*Elastic cord strapping allows you to attach gear to the outside of the pack*

*Side pouch can be used to carry a water bottle*

## INTERNAL-FRAME PACKS

Internal-frame packs are narrower in profile than their external-frame counterparts and tend to be longer, with either one or two internal compartments and very few pockets on the outside. The frame is integrated within the pack and usually consists of stays or flat bars, about 1 in (25 mm) wide and $\frac{1}{10}$ in (3 mm) thick, made from plastic. Straps on the outside allow you to compress the pack, which prevents the items inside the pack from shifting and throwing you off-balance.

*Additional compartment for quick access to essential items, such as wet-weather gear*

*Compression straps reduce bulk and keep contents of pack in place*

## EXTERNAL-FRAME PACKS

An external frame houses the pack on a lightweight tubing framework. They are great for heavy loads, as the pack sits more squarely on your hips. They are also cooler to carry than internal-frame packs, as the air can circulate between your back and the pack. External-frame packs usually have more pockets on the outside, which allows you to pack your items by category, rather than packing everything into one or two compartments. This makes locating items easier and allows you to unpack only the compartment you need, rather than the entire pack. Chest and waist straps ensure a comfortable fit.

*Outside pockets provide extra storage*

*Extra items can be attached to the frame*

# FITTING A BACKPACK

Once you have chosen a backpack of the right size, design, and features for your trip, you will have to make sure that it's a comfortable fit. You will need someone's help, but here are a few tips for ensuring your new pack sits comfortably on your back.

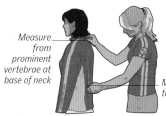

*Measure from prominent vertebrae at base of neck*

*Measure to the top of hip bones*

*Shoulder straps should be snug but arms should still move freely*

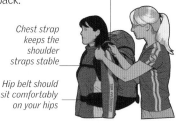

*Load-lifter straps can be tightened to balance weight on shoulders*

*Chest strap keeps the shoulder straps stable*

*Hip belt should sit comfortably on your hips*

**1** First measure your back. The pack you choose should be based on the length of your torso.

**2** Make sure the pack is a comfortable fit, allowing for any extra layers of clothing.

**3** You can now fine-tune the pack's fit by adjusting the shoulder and hip straps.

# PACKING A BACKPACK

Always pack in reverse order: the items you need first should go in last. Heavy items should be placed close to your back to prevent the pack pulling away from your shoulders.

*Use a cloth bag to hold personal items*

*Keep raingear at the top of the pack*

*Store daily essentials in outside pocket*

*Carry your water bottle in an upright and accessible position*

*Use the lower compartment for sleeping bag and mat*

*Secure extra water on outside of pack*

*Strap tent to the bottom of the pack*

## MAKING A SIMPLE PACK FRAME

In a survival situation, having something to carry your gear will be a huge advantage. All you need to make your own improvised backpack is a knife, some wood, some cord, and a waterproof sheet.

*Attach one end of cord to the upper notch*

*Attach both cord ends to the central post*

**1** Cut a light bough about 1 ft (30 cm) below the point where it branches, leaving about 3 ft (1 m) above the fork.

*Trim off any knots from the wood*

**2** Cut notches on all three ends of the bough and tie lengths of cord around the notches to serve as straps to go over your shoulders.

*Attach gear to frame*

**3** Wrap your gear in a groundsheet or waterproof poncho and tie it as high as possible onto the frame on the side opposite the straps.

*Make sure gear is attached securely to the frame*

*Hold straps away from shoulder to avoid chafing*

**4** Don't be tempted to overload your improvised backpack, even though it should be able to support a good weight.

# DRESSING FOR THE OUTDOORS

**MODERN OUTDOOR CLOTHING** is technologically advanced and highly sophisticated. New materials and designs are extremely lightweight, durable, and versatile. To make the most of your gear, choose the fabrics and combinations of clothes most suited to the environment and conditions in which you are traveling.

## LAYERING CLOTHES

The rule of layering is simple: several light layers are better than one heavy layer. Wearing multiple layers gives you flexibility to fine-tune your temperature by taking off or putting on layers to regulate your body heat. Choose fabrics such as wool, fleece, microfleece, and down—all of which are good insulators.

## HOW LAYERING WORKS

Layering is effective because it traps air between the layers of clothes and helps you stay warm in any environment. If you wear the correct layers in the right order, your clothing will move sweat away from your body, keep moisture out, and help to keep you insulated. Wear wicking fabrics, such as polypropylene, in hot and cold weather.

### THE LAYERING SYSTEM

The top (outer) layer repels rain, while dampness is wicked away from the skin by the base layer closest to the skin. The mid-layers insulate the body and help retain warmth.

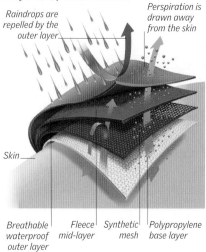

_Raindrops are repelled by the outer layer_

_Perspiration is drawn away from the skin_

_Skin_

_Breathable waterproof outer layer_   _Fleece mid-layer_   _Synthetic mesh_   _Polypropylene base layer_

**REGULATING BODY HEAT**
Don't be tempted to overdress. Sweat can soak you as much as rain, and a sudden change of temperature can leave you vulnerable to hypothermia. Wearing layers helps you to control your body temperature.

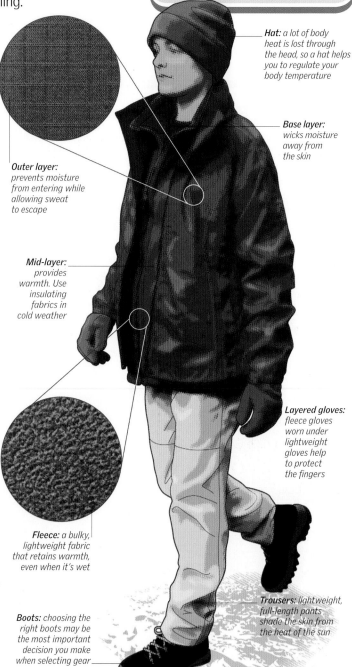

**Outer layer:** _prevents moisture from entering while allowing sweat to escape_

**Hat:** _a lot of body heat is lost through the head, so a hat helps you to regulate your body temperature_

**Base layer:** _wicks moisture away from the skin_

**Mid-layer:** _provides warmth. Use insulating fabrics in cold weather_

**Layered gloves:** _fleece gloves worn under lightweight gloves help to protect the fingers_

**Fleece:** _a bulky, lightweight fabric that retains warmth, even when it's wet_

**Trousers:** _lightweight, full-length pants shade the skin from the heat of the sun_

**Boots:** _choosing the right boots may be the most important decision you make when selecting gear_

# WARM-WEATHER CLOTHING

It's vital to stay as cool as possible in warm weather to avoid heat exhaustion or heat stroke (see p. 272). Too much exposure to direct sunlight can cause sunburn and dehydration, and heat rashes can be exacerbated if sweat is not able to evaporate properly. Choose breathable fabrics that will keep you cool and protect your skin from the sun. Stay hydrated and always wear a hat.

**Desert hat:** *combines the sheltering brim of a baseball cap with the neck protection of a bandana*

**Jacket:** *your outer layer should be a loose-fitting jacket*

**T-shirt:** *choose one made from moisture-wicking fabric, which allows air flow*

**Shorts:** *the legs of convertible pants can be unzipped to make them into shorts*

**Trousers:** *full-length convertible pants protect protect the skin from insects and the effects of sunburn*

# COLD-WEATHER CLOTHING

In cold weather, you need to pay particular attention to your clothing layers. Use a lightweight base layer, which will wick moisture from your skin, several layers of warm, insulating clothing, and an outer shell that's windproof and waterproof. The secret to staying comfortable is to adjust your layers as your body temperature changes. Remove layers as your body temperature rises to avoid sweating.

**Ski mask:** *helps to keep your face warm and protect it from cold winds*

**Jacket:** *filled with down or a synthetic equivalent, a windproof outer layer will help you to stay warm in exposed surroundings*

**Fleece:** *wicking base layers come in several different weights*

**Gloves:** *in cold environments several layers of gloves are more efficient than a single layer. You can add or remove the different layers as required*

**Leggings:** *wicking insulating leggings are worn under waterproof pants*

## WET-WEATHER CLOTHING

Sudden downpours can occur almost anywhere and it is easy to be caught out by them. The best fabrics to wear in such conditions are those that are breathable, waterproof, and allow sweat to escape—the best known of these is Gore-Tex®. Always carry the gear necessary to stay warm and dry, and make sure you can access it quickly if you are caught out— it can be the difference between comfort and misery.

### HOW BREATHABLE WATERPROOF FABRIC WORKS

Breathable waterproof fabric is a laminate of three layers: two layers of nylon on either side of a thin layer of microporous teflon, which contains tiny pores—50 times smaller than the width of a human hair—that keep rain droplets out but allow perspiration (water vapor) to escape.

Microporous teflon

Raindrops repelled

Jacket shell

Perspiration escapes

Jacket lining

*Rain hat: the wide brim stops water from dripping on to your face and down the back of your neck*

*Poncho: an effective waterproof layer, a poncho can be made into a shelter or bed (see pp. 158–59 and 166–67)*

*Waterproof jacket: allows sweat to escape while keeping rain out*

*Waterproof trousers: keep your legs dry in wet conditions*

## SOCKS

Socks are a vital part of your footwear system. Their function is two-fold. Firstly, they cushion the feet and prevent boots from rubbing and causing blisters. Secondly, they keep the feet warm and dry by wicking moisture away from the feet. Note that socks made from breathable waterproof fabric can be worn with regular boots but should not be combined with breathable waterproof boots.

*A good pair of wicking socks helps to prevent blisters*

*Cushioned for extra protection when wearing boots*

*Padded heel for comfort*

### WICKING SOCK

A lightweight inner sock that helps wick moisture away from the skin and reduces friction.

### WALKING SOCK

The thick fabric of the walking sock offers maximum cushioning, comfort, and protection.

### GAITERS

Gaiters are useful, both in temperate areas for keeping the feet and lower pants leg dry, and in polar regions for keeping out snow.

# FOOTWEAR

A number of factors determine which type of footwear is right for you. The first concerns your personal requirements, which include the shape of your feet and the amount of support you need. You also need to consider how far you are traveling and the type of terrain you'll be covering. Then there is cost: footwear varies from the relatively cheap to the extremely costly. Bear in mind that if you intend to spend a lot of time in the wilderness, it pays to invest a little extra in comfortable, sturdy footwear.

## BREAKING IN BOOTS
Your boots and feet should coexist in perfect harmony when you're on the trail. When you buy a pair of boots, wear them around the house and go on short hikes to make sure you have broken them in.

## ANATOMY OF A SOLE
A boot sole has several layers to protect and support your feet. Look for a good tread on the outsole, and for cushioning beneath the heel and toe areas.

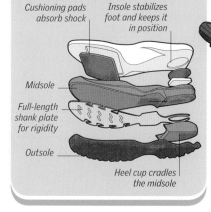

Cushioning pads absorb shock

Insole stabilizes foot and keeps it in position

Midsole

Full-length shank plate for rigidity

Outsole

Heel cup cradles the midsole

Arch straps hold the shoe in place in any terrain

An adjustable fastener ensures a snug fit

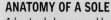

Modern sandal has solidly constructed soles

### SANDALS
Modern sandal designs offer great support, and are extremely comfortable, while offering additional ventilation.

A flexible fabric upper dries quickly when wet and allows the foot to breathe

Shock-absorbing sole gives added comfort on hard terrain

### LIGHTWEIGHT BOOT
Fabric and leather hybrids are increasingly popular because they combine the support and traction of a heavier shoe with the flexibility of a sports shoe, so there is less friction on the foot.

The padded ankle provides comfort and support

Sole provides grip on slippery ground

### HIKING BOOTS
A compromise between weight, durability, and protection produces a good, all-round leather boot with a sole of hard-wearing rubber, such as Vibram®, water-resistant uppers, and valuable support for the ankles.

High uppers keep mud off your pants

Canvas uppers are designed to keep the feet cool

Sole contains wide, deep studs to provide grip on the wet ground

### JUNGLE-TREKKING BOOT
This is a high boot made from rot-proof leather and canvas with a directly molded sole. Breather holes in the instep aid ventilation and help to drain moisture in hot or humid conditions.

Crampons can be added for extra grip on ice and snow

### CLIMBING/HIKING HYBRID BOOT
More flexible than traditional climbing boots, modern hybrid boots are designed to be worn with crampons and to keep the feet warm in very cold environments.

# EXTREME SURVIVAL—IN THE WILDERNESS

## USEFUL EQUIPMENT

- Walking staff
- Pocket chainsaw
- Whistle, flashlight, signal mirror
- Animal deterrent spray
- Water purifiers
- Small AM/FM radio
- Map, compass, GPS
- Survival tin, bushcraft knife
- Cell/satellite phone
- Poncho/bivy sack

**BLAKE STANFIELD, 38, AND HIS 65-YEAR-OLD FATHER,** Neil, endured being trapped beneath river ice, encounters with bears, and four days and nights in the Alaskan wilderness without food. They survived thanks to good survival skills, knowledge of the local area, and an abundance of water and firewood.

Father and son were dropped by floatplane on Friday, June 6, 2003, at a remote point on the Koyukuk River, deep inside Alaska. They planned to spend seven days rafting approximately 90 miles (145 km) to the town of Bettles. The trip had hardly begun when disaster struck—the raft crashed at speed into a massive sheet of ice, throwing the pair into the freezing water. They were both caught by the strong current and pulled under the ice. Somehow Blake was washed ashore, and he used a branch to haul his father to the riverbank.

Blake quickly realized that Neil was close to hypothermia, so used his waterproof lighter to light a fire of sticks and pine needles. Far from rescue, with their supplies lost and no one expecting their return for six days, their prospects looked bleak. With night approaching they built a shelter.

**"THE RAFT CRASHED AT SPEED INTO A MASSIVE SHEET OF ICE"**

The next morning, Blake decided to hike the 65 miles (105 km) to Bettles to get help. On Sunday his progress was brought to a halt by the confluence of two large rivers— the Tinayguk and Koyukuk. However, Blake realized that he had reached a landmark on the flight path of supply planes that frequently flew into the interior, so he built a signal fire and waited. Two days later, a pilot spotted him and radioed his position to a US Army base 200 miles (320 km) away in Fairbanks, then dropped him a two-way radio and supplies. The pilot then continued up the river to find Neil, dropping him a sleeping bag, tent, and supplies, before radioing his position to the Army. Both men were picked up the next day—exhausted, malnourished, and close to hypothermia, but alive.

# WHAT TO DO

**ARE YOU IN DANGER?**

← NO   YES →

If you are in a group, try to help any others who are in danger

Get yourself out of it:
**Elements**—Find or improvise immediate shelter
**Animals**—Avoid confrontation and move away from danger
**Injury**—Stabilize condition and apply first aid

**ASSESS YOUR SITUATION**
*See pages 234–35*

**DOES ANYONE KNOW YOU WILL BE MISSING OR WHERE YOU ARE?**

← NO   YES →

If no one knows you are missing or where you are, you will need to notify people of your plight by any means at your disposal

If you are missed, a rescue party will almost certainly be dispatched to find you

**DO YOU HAVE ANY MEANS OF COMMUNICATION?**

← NO   YES →

You are faced with surviving for an indefinite period—until you are located or you find help

If you have a cell or satellite phone, let someone know your predicament. If your situation is serious enough to be worthy of emergency rescue, and you have a Personal Locator Beacon (PLB), you should consider this option

**CAN YOU SURVIVE WHERE YOU ARE? ***

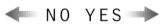

← NO   YES →

If you cannot survive where you are and there are no physical reasons why you should remain, you will have to move to a location that offers a better chance of survival, rescue, or both

Address the Principles of Survival: Protection, Location, Water, Food

**YOU WILL HAVE TO MOVE ****   **YOU SHOULD STAY ****

## DO

- Make an informed decision on the best location to move to—find an elevated position from which to choose a suitable area for survival and rescue
- Regulate your clothing to avoid overheating when moving and hypothermia when static
- Use or improvise a walking staff to help reduce trips and falls
- Improvise shelter when not moving
- Plan your route around potential or known water sources. Filter and purify all water where possible
- Have aids to location accessible while moving and deployed when static

## DON'T

- Ignore your fire—be on constant lookout for dry tinder/kindling and fuel
- Walk faster than the pace of the slowest person in the group
- Be careless when walking downhill—a twisted ankle could prove fatal
- Under or overdress. Start off a walk lightly dressed and add or remove layers as necessary

## DON'T

- Leave food in your campsite as it will be at risk from predators
- Shelter too deep in the woods despite the protection it gives you from elements. Remember: your location aids need to be seen
- Eat unidentified food, as it could exacerbate your situation through illness. Food is not a priority in a short-term situation

## DO

- Check your shelter site before building for natural hazards such as: insects, flooding, rock falls, wild animals, and deadfalls
- Inventory your supplies and ration them
- Keep a fire going: once it's established you can use it to purify water, benefit from the warmth, and signal rescue
- Fill plastic bags or spare clothing with dry foliage and use as a mattress or pillow to insulate you from the cold/damp ground
- If in a group, give everyone something to do, even the children. It will keep them occupied and lessen the worry

\* If you cannot survive where you are, but you also cannot move owing to injury or other factors, you must do everything you can to attract rescue.
\*\* If your situation changes (for instance, you are "moving" to find help, and you find a suitable location in which you can stay and survive) consult the alternative "Do" and "Don'ts."

# SLEEPING SYSTEMS

**REST IS AS ESSENTIAL** for survival as food. A good night's sleep can offset much of the worry and stress of a difficult situation. Making sure your shelter is suitable for the environment you're in, and choosing the right sleeping bag, can be vital factors in survival.

## SLEEPING BAGS

Although there are many different shapes and styles of sleeping bag, the one you choose should have enough padding to keep you warm at night even without a tent. A sleeping bag must never be allowed to get wet, so always keep it inside a waterproof cover, such as the bag's stuff sack or a bivy sack. Always try a sleeping bag before you buy it. If it's too snug, it will be less effective.

### TIPS ON BUYING A SLEEPING BAG

There are many types of bag available. Here are a few things you should consider to ensure you buy the right sleeping bag for you.
- Determine the lowest temperature you're likely to encounter on your trip and choose a bag that will perform at this temperature.
- Synthetic bags are cheaper and easier to clean than down bags, and continue to provide insulation even when wet.
- Down bags are more expensive than synthetic bags, but provide a better warmth-to-weight ratio and last longer.
- A mummy-shaped bag provides better insulation than a rectangular-shaped bag, but has less room to move around in.

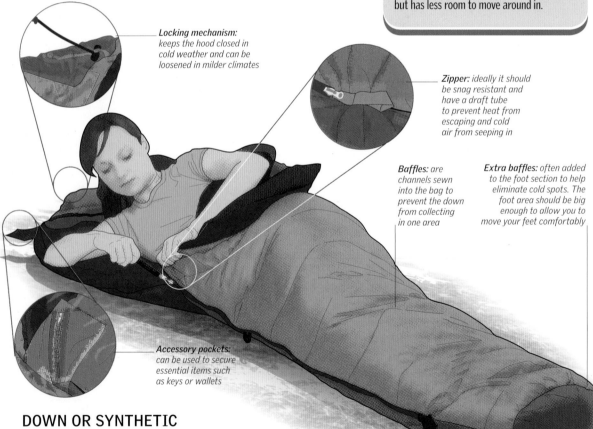

**Locking mechanism:** keeps the hood closed in cold weather and can be loosened in milder climates

**Zipper:** ideally it should be snag resistant and have a draft tube to prevent heat from escaping and cold air from seeping in

**Baffles:** are channels sewn into the bag to prevent the down from collecting in one area

**Extra baffles:** often added to the foot section to help eliminate cold spots. The foot area should be big enough to allow you to move your feet comfortably

**Accessory pockets:** can be used to secure essential items such as keys or wallets

## DOWN OR SYNTHETIC

Sleeping bags are made with either a down or a synthetic filling. Down is made up of highly specialized insulating feathers, normally from ducks or geese, and is unsurpassed when it comes to a warmth-against-weight ratio. However, it is ineffective when wet and can cause an allergic reaction in some people. Synthetic fillings range from simple hollow fibers all the way up to complex fibers designed to mimic the structure of down. They still retain some of their insulating capacity if they get wet.

**Loops:** allow you to attach sleeping bag to the sleeping mat

**Box foot:** creates a mummy shape and is designed to conform to the position of your feet when you're sleeping on your side

## TEMPERATURE RATINGS

Because manufacturers have no standardized way of registering how warm a sleeping bag is, temperature ratings for sleeping bags remain an inexact science. Some manufacturers give a bag both a comfort rating and a survival rating—known as a "season rating.' These give some indication as to how manufacturers expect a sleeping bag to perform.

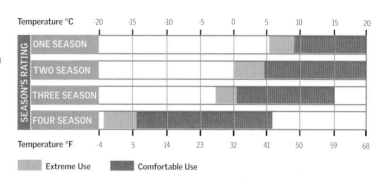

| Temperature °C | -20 | -15 | -10 | -5 | 0 | 5 | 10 | 15 | 20 |
|---|---|---|---|---|---|---|---|---|---|

SEASON'S RATING
- ONE SEASON
- TWO SEASON
- THREE SEASON
- FOUR SEASON

| Temperature °F | -4 | 5 | 14 | 23 | 32 | 41 | 50 | 59 | 68 |
|---|---|---|---|---|---|---|---|---|---|

Extreme Use     Comfortable Use

## CONSTRUCTION

The principle of all sleeping bags is the same: to trap air and prevent its circulation so that the body heats the trapped air and keeps you warm while you sleep. This can be achieved in a number of ways.

### BOXWALL
Used in cold-weather down bags, the filling is contained within box-like sections to minimize bunching.

### SEWN-THROUGH
Filling is in separate oval channels, although heat is still lost through the stitching.

### OFFSET CHANNELS
The filling is laid out in two layers to prevent bunching and heat loss through the stitching.

### SHINGLE
Slanted layers of overlapping fibers that fill with warm air to aid insulation.

### USING YOUR SLEEPING BAG
Before using your sleeping bag, always check inside for spiders and other dangers, and shake it to make sure the filling is distributed evenly. During use, if the bag is too warm, simply unzip it to cool down, or use the bag as a quilt. If it's too cold, either put on some clothing, or use a silk liner or waterproof bivi bag to increase its performance. Always air your sleeping bag well after using it.

## SLEEPING ACCESSORIES

You'll need to get a sleeping mat as well as a sleeping bag to ensure a comfortable, dry night's sleep. Additional gear, such as bivy sacks, sleeping bag liners, and inflatable pillows, will also increase comfort.

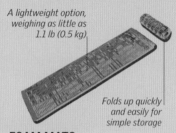

*A lightweight option, weighing as little as 1.1 lb (0.5 kg)*

*Folds up quickly and easily for simple storage*

### FOAM MATS
The lightest and simplest type of mat, foam mats are best used on soft surfaces, such as sand or pine needles.

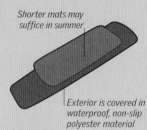

*Shorter mats may suffice in summer*

*Exterior is covered in waterproof, non-slip polyester material*

### AIR MATS
They may be heavier and more expensive than foam mats, but air mats provide superior comfort and thermal insulation.

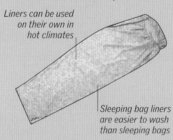

*Liners can be used on their own in hot climates*

*Sleeping bag liners are easier to wash than sleeping bags*

### SLEEPING BAG LINER
Usually made of cotton or silk, sleeping bag liners trap air between your body and the sleeping bag.

*In warmer climates, bivy sacks enable you to sleep outside without a tent*

### BIVY SACKS
A simple waterproof bag that is used over a sleeping bag to keep it dry or used on its own as a shelter.

*Outer layer of pillow is padded for extra comfort*

### INFLATABLE PILLOW
An inflatable pillow adds some luxury to expeditions. Alternatively, fill a stuff sack with spare clothing.

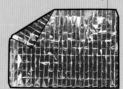

*Foil prevents body heat from escaping and deflects it back to the body*

### SPACE BLANKET
A lightweight foil blanket for use in emergencies, space blankets can also be used as a temporary canopy.

# PORTABLE SHELTERS

Shelter from the elements at night is essential for long-term survival. A variety of products are available to you, depending on the conditions you're about to enter and the amount you're prepared to carry. You can choose from lightweight options, such as hammocks and variations on bivy sacks, and the more traditional alternatives, tents, which are heavier but can accommodate up to eight people.

## USING A HAMMOCK

If you have a hammock you can camp even if the ground is muddy, rocky, or on an incline. The advantage of a hammock is that it's lightweight and can be erected just about anywhere. Modern hammocks provide a shelter and bed solution in one portable package.

*Always use straps to avoid damaging live trees and protect the bark*

*Make sure the tree or upright holding the hammock is strong enough to support it*

*Modern hammocks are designed to enable users to sleep in an almost-flat position*

*Built-in flysheets provide extra protection from the elements*

## USING A TARP TENT

A cross between a tarpaulin and a tent, a tarp tent is a highly versatile, extremely light form of shelter that's capable of withstanding even the most extreme conditions. Groundsheets should be laid out on the ground for added protection, and a suitable sleeping bag is essential. A one-person version can weigh as little as 18½ oz (0.52 kg).

*Some tarp tents come with built-in netting for protection against insects*

*Trekking poles can be used to replace tent poles*

*Guylines give the tarp tent stability*

*A groundsheet provides insulation from the cold, damp ground*

## USING A HOOPED BIVY

The hooped bivy is a waterproof and breathable bivi bag that has been designed to form a one-person shelter. It usually incorporates pegging points and a zippered and hooped entrance that form a small vestibule for your backpack. Many incorporate a heavy-duty groundsheet and can be set up and taken down in a matter of minutes.

*While they may have restricted space, hooped bivys pack small and are extremely lightweight*

*Limited height means you're restricted to a prone position*

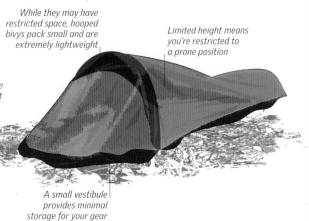

*A small vestibule provides minimal storage for your gear*

# USING A TENT

Tents keep the rain and wind out while retaining warmth. The outer flysheet should be strong, impermeable, taut, and able to withstand high winds. The inner tent—which may be attached to a flysheet—is loose and made of permeable material to minimize condensation but retain heat. The inner and outer parts of the tent must not touch each other; if they do, heat may be lost and condensation may form on the underside of the flysheet, then seep into the tent.

## WARNING!

In some climactic conditions, such as extreme high winds, severe storms, or heavy snow cover, stakes and guylines may not be enough to anchor the tent securely to the ground. This could result in the tent being blown away—and could have severe consequences for the tent's occupants. In such conditions, use extra means—such as rocks or logs—to anchor your tent securely.

## THREE-SEASON TENT

Three-season tents are designed for use in a variety of climates. The inner layer is made of a lightweight material that offers both ventilation and protection against insects. The flysheet—which should extend about 4 in (10 cm) above the ground—and the groundsheet are made of waterproof fabric.

## WINTER TENT

For cold-weather climates, look for a tent that offers extra-strong poles, storm windows, and ample pockets so that you can store your gear inside the tent. However, these extra features increase the tent's weight. The dome shape sheds snow well, and withstands high winds.

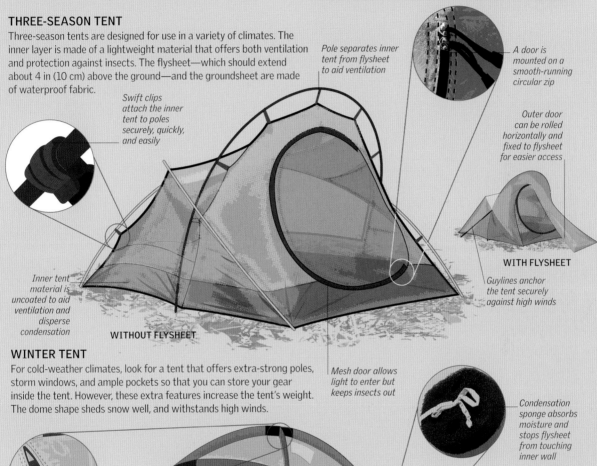

Swift clips attach the inner tent to poles securely, quickly, and easily

Pole separates inner tent from flysheet to aid ventilation

A door is mounted on a smooth-running circular zip

Outer door can be rolled horizontally and fixed to flysheet for easier access

Inner tent material is uncoated to aid ventilation and disperse condensation

**WITHOUT FLYSHEET**

**WITH FLYSHEET**

Guylines anchor the tent securely against high winds

Mesh door allows light to enter but keeps insects out

Condensation sponge absorbs moisture and stops flysheet from touching inner wall

Dome shape prevents heavy accumulation of snow

Ventilation zipper increases air circulation, which helps dry wet gear in poor weather

Fully enclosed pole sleeves provide extra rigidity in poor weather

**WITHOUT FLYSHEET**

Heavy-duty poles provide excellent stability in strong winds

**WITH FLYSHEET**

Vestibule allows occupants to cook without leaving sleeping bag

# EATING ON THE TRAIL

**THE FOOD YOU EAT** determines how efficiently your body will function. This is never more important than when you're undertaking an expedition that will test your physical and mental endurance beyond normal levels.

## FOOD FOR LIFE

Your body requires energy to fuel the chemical and biological reactions that take place within it, and to power your muscles. This, and other nutrients, comes from the food you eat (see below).

### BODY FAT AND SURVIVAL
Being physically fit and active keeps you strong and less prone to injury, but being slightly overweight can actually be an advantage in a survival situation: 1 lb (½ kilo) of body fat converts to roughly 3,500 calories—the amount of energy you would usually expend during an average day.

| TYPES OF NUTRITION | EXAMPLES | BENEFITS |
|---|---|---|
| **CARBOHYDRATE** | • Rice, pasta, bread, and cereals<br>• Fresh and dried fruit<br>• Root vegetables<br>• Chocolate and candy | • Major source of energy, as it converts most readily to glucose, which is your body's preferred source of fuel. |
| **PROTEIN** | • Meat and poultry<br>• Fish, such as tuna and salmon<br>• Eggs and dairy products<br>• Beans, legumes, and seeds | • Essential for growth and repair of muscle tissue.<br>• Increases your stamina and energy levels, and helps you fight fatigue.<br>• Makes you feel satisfied after eating. |
| **FAT** | • Nuts and seeds<br>• Dairy products, such as butter and cheese<br>• Meats, such as bacon and sausage<br>• Cooking oil | • Good source of energy.<br>• Makes you feel satisfied after eating. |
| **FIBER** | • Fresh and dried fruit, especially the skins<br>• Vegetables, beans, and seeds<br>• Whole-grain cereals<br>• Whole-meal bread, whole-meal pasta, and brown rice | • Provides bulk to help your digestion.<br>• Helps to make you feel full. |
| **VITAMINS AND MINERALS** | • Fresh and dried fruit<br>• Green vegetables<br>• Meat and fish<br>• Nuts and seeds | • Essential for growth and the repair of your body's tissues.<br>• Help you to maintain healthy teeth and eyes.<br>• Aids bloodflow and the production of energy. |

## BALANCING YOUR ENERGY LEVELS

You replace the energy that you expend on a daily basis through the food you eat. The energy obtained from food is measured in calories, and you require a certain number of calories each day to remain alive. If you consume too few calories, you will lose weight. However, eating too many calories will lead to weight gain, which can cause long-term health issues. The number of calories you require per day depends on many things, such as your age and level of activity (see right). When you don't replace the energy expended and continue to work, you start to use the energy store contained in your body's fat.

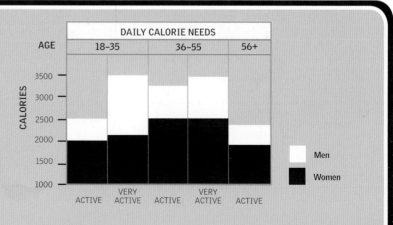

# WILDERNESS DINING

Even if you're only going on a short hike, you should take food with you, such as fruit and chocolate, to replace the energy you're using. For longer expeditions, you'll need to take a number of different foodstuffs—for energy and for variety.

**WARNING!**
In a survival situation, don't eat for the first 24 hours unless to replace expended energy. Ration your food, as digestion uses up water.

| TYPES OF FOOD | EXAMPLES | BENEFITS |
|---|---|---|
| **BREAKFAST CEREALS AND DRIED FRUIT** | ■ Trail mix—also known as "gorp" <br> ■ Muesli or granola <br> ■ Oatmeal <br> ■ Dried fruit | ■ Provide a vital source of carbohydrates, vitamins, and minerals to set you up at the start of the day. <br> ■ Contain dietary fiber to aid digestion. |
| **TRAIL SNACKS** | ■ Cookies and crackers <br> ■ Energy bars and cereal/granola bars <br> ■ Fruits, such as apples, pears, and oranges <br> ■ Nuts and seeds | ■ High in carbohydrates to help you maintain energy levels. <br> ■ Help to keep your hunger pangs at bay between main meals. |
| **HIGH-CALORIE SNACKS** | ■ Dehydrated ice cream <br> ■ Chocolate <br> ■ Hard candies <br> ■ Pudding mixes | ■ Provide a quick boost of energy, when required. <br> ■ Offer a comfort factor, although they are of limited nutritional value. |
| **PRE-PREPARED MAIN MEALS** | ■ Boil-in-the-bag meals—you can buy a wide variety of fully prepared meals, sealed in a foil bag. Cook for five to seven minutes. <br> ■ Freeze-dried and dehydrated meals—simply add boiling water, stir, and wait about five minutes. Extremely lightweight and take up little space. <br> ■ Canned meals—a great variety of them are available, but they are bulky and heavy. | ■ Provide a balanced range of food groups, vitamins, and minerals to help your body to recover and repair itself after the day's exertions. <br> ■ Quick and easy to prepare, and require few utensils. <br> ■ Many require minimal fuel to cook them, or water to rehydrate them. <br> ■ Can be bulked out with beans, legumes, and grains. <br> ■ Smaller cans may have a pull-top to open them. |
| **MEAT, FISH, AND CHEESE** | ■ Canned fish, such as sardines or tuna <br> ■ Cured meats, such as ham, salami, and beef jerky <br> ■ Hard cheese, such as cheddar and parmesan | ■ A great source of proteins and fats. <br> ■ Easy to store and long-lasting, although cans are heavier than other sources of food. |
| **BEANS, LEGUMES, AND GRAINS** | ■ Lentils and dried peas <br> ■ Dried beans and pearl barley <br> ■ Rice and pasta <br> ■ Couscous | ■ Can be used to bulk up main meals and help you to feel full. <br> ■ An important source of carbohydrates. <br> ■ Also provide fiber and protein. |
| **MIXERS** | ■ Flour <br> ■ Salt <br> ■ Suet <br> ■ Sugar | ■ Flour and salt can be used to make dough. <br> ■ Sugar and salt help to make wild food palatable. <br> ■ Suet is an invaluable source of fat that can be used to supplement meals. |
| **FLAVORINGS** | ■ Powdered soup <br> ■ Tomato puree <br> ■ Powdered sauces <br> ■ Gravy cubes | ■ Add flavor and variety to your meals. <br> ■ Especially useful if you're cooking with wild food. |
| **BEVERAGES** | ■ Tea <br> ■ Coffee <br> ■ Chocolate powder <br> ■ Dried milk | ■ Provide warmth and comfort, although they are of limited nutritional value. <br> ■ Chocolate powder is high in carbohydrates. <br> ■ Dried milk is an excellent source of calcium. |

# CAMPING STOVES

**ALTHOUGH NOTHING CAN BEAT** the satisfaction of building your own campfire, the convenience and reliability of purpose-made camping stoves make them an essential piece of cooking equipment, especially in areas where open fires are banned.

## THE BENEFITS OF CAMPING STOVES

Modern camping stoves are very light and collapse down to an incredibly small, compact size. Gas-fueled stoves are by far the most common, but liquid-fueled stoves are also worth considering. Both have their own advantages and disadvantages (see below), but your choice will be dictated by space and weight constraints, the distance you're traveling, and environmental factors. A hexamine stove is a good item to have in a survival situation (see opposite).

## CHOOSING A GAS- OR LIQUID-FUELED STOVE

Gas-fueled stoves are safer, cleaner, lighter, and easier to use than liquid-fueled stoves, but are less economical, and not suitable for low-temperature, high-altitude use. Liquid stoves offer greater stability, fuel versatility and economy, but you need to pump and prime (preheat) them before use, and they are less clean.

### TRANSPORTING FUEL
There are many factors to consider when transporting fuel to make your expedition safer:
- When hiking, pack your fuel container upright in the middle of your backpack, and surround with clothing to protect it from knocks. Make sure you can access it easily when you reach camp. Use similar principles when traveling by other methods.
- Ensure that your fuel bottles look very different from your water bottles to prevent confusion.
- If you're going on a long expedition, check the availability of the fuel, and consider how you will dispose of cylinders safely.

| GAS-FUELED STOVES | | |
|---|---|---|
| **TYPE OF STOVE** | | |
| BUTANE OR ISOBUTENE | PROPANE | BLENDED FUEL |
| **INFORMATION** <br> • Both fuels sold in disposable, pressurized canisters. | • Fuel sold in disposable, pressurized canisters. <br> • Used in most portable stoves and barbecue grills. | • Fuel sold in disposable, pressurized canisters. <br> • Is a mix of butane, propane, and/or isobutene. |
| **PROS** <br> • Lightweight, sealed fuel container. <br> • Butane very efficient and burns at a high temperature. <br> • Isobutene more efficient than butane, and performs better in cold conditions. | • Lightweight, sealed fuel container. <br> • Fuel burns at a very hot, steady heat, and produces an almost sootless flame. <br> • Performs very well in cold conditions. | • Lightweight, sealed fuel container. <br> • Fuel safer than pure propane, and performs better than either pure butane or isobutene in cold conditions. <br> • Isobutene blends give a more efficient flame. |
| **CONS** <br> • Higher cost and lower heat output than liquid fuels. <br> • Fuel efficiency reduced at higher altitudes. <br> • Butane less efficient than isobutene in temperatures below 50°F (10°C). | • Higher cost and lower heat output than liquid fuels. <br> • Fuel efficiency reduced at higher altitudes. <br> • Highly combustible, so less safe than other fuels. | • Higher cost and lower heat output than liquid fuels. <br> • Fuel efficiency reduced at higher altitudes. |

# USING CAMPING STOVES SAFELY

Always take care when storing the fuel and using your stove. Use only the stove manufacturer's recommended fuel, and check all connections and fittings before each and every use. Also:

- Clear the cooking area of dry vegetation and leaves, in case you spill fuel or knock over your stove.
- Place your stove on a level and stable surface.
- Keep naked flames and sparks away from the fuel, especially when filling or refilling the stove. Before refilling, make sure the flame is out and the stove has cooled down.
- Use the cooker in a well-ventilated space. Liquid fuels, in particular, can give off poisonous fumes, such as carbon monoxide, and all cookers also burn vital oxygen.
- Don't use a stove inside your tent. In addition to the risk of poisonous fumes, fire is also a significant danger. A confined space with limited access, your tent can be reduced to ashes in minutes, along with everything inside, and you may not be able to escape in time to protect yourself. Losing your tent and your equipment is bad enough, without you receiving third-degree burns at the same time.
- Don't leave a burning stove unattended. If it topples over, it could easily start a fire. If the stove flame goes out, a spark or naked flame could also ignite the vapors and cause an explosion.

## THE HEXAMINE STOVE

A very useful piece of emergency equipment, the hexamine stove (or hexi-stove) burns solid blocks of hexamethyl-enetetramine (also known as "methenamine"), and folds away compactly. The stove acts as a small windbreak and cooking platform, while the fuel blocks it uses provide a very reliable means of starting a fire in any conditions. The blocks produce a smokeless flame, don't liquefy while burning, and leave no ashes.

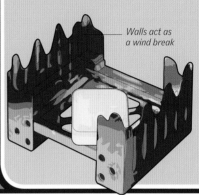

Walls act as
a wind break

## LIQUID-FUELED STOVES

| | WHITE (COLEMAN) FUEL | MULTI-FUEL | DENATURED ALCOHOL | |
|---|---|---|---|---|
| TYPE OF STOVE | | | | |
| INFORMATION | • Fuel sold in disposable canisters. | • Stove can use a variety of fuels, from unleaded gas, kerosene (parrafin), aviation fuel, and white fuel, to diesel—most of which are readily available. | • Fuel sold in disposable plastic containers.<br>• Stove basically consists of a vessel to burn the fuel in, and a windshield that also acts as a cooking platform. | |
| PROS | • Fuel can withstand low temperatures, high altitudes, and most weather conditions.<br>• Produces a clean flame. | • Stove uses a range of fuels.<br>• Fuel is non-pressurized, so can be stowed safely in almost any airtight container.<br>• Stove tends to perform reliably, efficiently, and quickly, producing a hot flame. | • Fuel is non-pressurized, so can be stowed safely in almost any airtight container.<br>• Economical and produces a clean flame.<br>• Stove is lightweight, stable, and safe.<br>• Usually supplied with pots and pans. | |
| CONS | • Stove must be pumped to generate required pressure for use.<br>• Fuel needs to be primed. | • Potential for spillage of flammable fuel.<br>• Stove must be pumped to generate required pressure for use.<br>• Fuel needs to be primed.<br>• Some fuels produce soot and noxious fumes. | • Potential for spillage of flammable fuel.<br>• Stove slower to heat up than other liquid stoves, because it's not pumped.<br>• Flame vulnerable to wind and other environmental conditions. | |

# YOUR SURVIVAL KIT

**A BASIC SURVIVAL KIT** is an essential item to take with you on any outdoor expedition. It should be compact enough to carry on your person at all times, and its contents should address the key principles of survival: protection, location, water, and food.

## EXAMPLE OF A SURVIVAL KIT

Choose a tin with a waterproof seal and locking clasps. While you can buy ready-made kits, you should always adapt the contents, both to your needs and to the environment you'll be in. Ideally, items in the survival kit should be high-quality and multi-purpose—for example, the tin itself could be used as a cup, a small cooking pot, or even a signal mirror. Your kit should contain the following:

LAYERS OF A SURVIVAL TIN

| LAYER 1 | LAYER 2 | LAYER 3 |
|---|---|---|
|  |  | |
| ■ **Blister medical pads and bandages:** useful for minor cuts and blisters. Include a range of bandages (both waterproof and fabric) in a selection of sizes. Waterproof bandages can also be used to mend holes in tents and tarpaulins. | ■ **Antiseptic wipes:** for treating wounds and cleaning bites. Can also be ignited by a spark and used to get a fire going. | ■ **Water purification tablets:** choose from tablets or iodine (but don't use iodine if you're allergic to it, or to shellfish). Water will need to be filtered before being purified. |

| LAYER 6 | LAYER 7 | LAYER 8 |
|---|---|---|
| 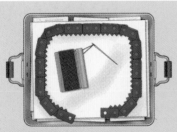 |  |  |
| ■ **Survival saw, or pocket chainsaw:** can be wrapped around the inside of the tin or cut in half, if space is limited.<br>■ **Single-edged razor:** multi-purpose—from skinning an animal to cutting cord. Store in its packaging.<br>■ **Needle and cotton:** use strong, waxed cotton, pre-threaded through the needle. | ■ **Flashlights:** two small Photon (LED) lights—one white and one red—taped in "off" position.<br>■ **Mini multi-tool:** see panel, opposite.<br>■ **Chainsaw handles:** use with pocket chainsaw.<br>■ **High-viz card, signal mirror:** location aids.<br>■ **Compass:** an emergency back-up.<br>■ **Flint, fire steel, tampons:** for starting fires.<br>■ **Snare wire:** for animal traps and lashing. | ■ **Waterproof matches and tinder balls:** for starting fires. Store the matches in a small, resealable plastic bag.<br>■ **Pencil:** sharpened at both ends.<br>■ **Potassium permanganate:** dissolve in water to sterilize water at low concentration, and to clean wounds at a high concentration. Can also be used with sugar to make fire. Store in a waterproof container. |

## CHOOSING A MULTI-TOOL

A useful item to carry with you on your trip, multi-tools are usually designed with a specific task or hobby in mind, and include useful features for survival, such as a small compass, pliers, saw, and various blades. Use one that has quality tools that most suit your needs, with a comfortable grip, and ensure that the blades are lockable to prevent injuries. Carry your multi-tool in a secure pocket, or in a pouch on your belt, and include a miniature version in your survival tin (see below). Bear in mind that your multi-tool should be an addition to, not a replacement for, your bushcraft knife (see p. 146).

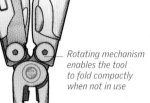

*Other tools, such as scissors, open out from the two "arms" of the multi-tool*

*Rotating mechanism enables the tool to fold compactly when not in use*

*Needle-nose pliers can be used for gripping items, or for cutting wire*

*Close the multi-tool when not using it for safety*

| LAYER 4 | LAYER 5 |
|---|---|
| 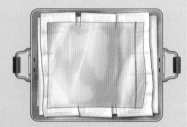 |  |

- **Petroleum jelly:** apply to chapped lips, rashes, and sores. Can also be smeared onto tampons to make them burn longer. Store in a small, resealable plastic bag.

- **Waterproof notepaper:** for drawing maps or leaving messages.
- **Photograph of loved ones:** a psychological incentive in a survival scenario.
- **Credit card:** an effective means of extracting insect stings (see pp. 266–67).
- **Money:** wrapped in cellophane.

| LAYER 9 | TIN LID SEALED WITH TAPE |
|---|---|
|  | 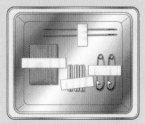 |

- **Non-lubricated condoms:** can be used to carry water, or as a waterproof cover for smaller items, such as your mobile phone.
- **Mini fishing kit:** if you are near water, fish can be easier to catch, prepare, and cook than mammals. Fishing line can be also used for other survival tasks. Should contain a selection of hooks, flies, swivels, and split-shots.

- **Sailmaker's needles:** multi-purpose—can be used as an arrow point, or for mending tents and tarpaulins. Wide eyes are best.
- **Safety pins:** for securing clothing, or mending your sleeping bag or tent.
- **Mini glowsticks (cyalumes):** useful for emergency lighting, and as a location aid.
- **Single-edged razor:** multi-purpose (see Layer 6). Store in its packaging.

## ADDITIONAL USEFUL ITEMS TO INCLUDE

While your survival tin's size may be restrictive, you can always improve your kit with items that can fit on your belt, or in a belt pouch, known as a "belt order." This will form part of your first-line equipment (see p. 43).

- **Space blanket or aluminum foil:** can be used as a signaling device; for shelter; to carry, store, and heat water; or to cook in. Many are dual-sided: one silver, the other green for camouflage, or orange to stand out.
- **Plastic bags:** you can never have too many. Numerous uses—from a water carrier to a transpiration bag.
- **Medicines (such as painkillers and antibiotics):** should not replace your main first-aid kit, but ensures you have some basics if you're separated from your gear.
- **Small candle:** once lit, this will provide a reliable flame that you can build your fire around.
- **Nylon stockings:** can be used for warmth, or as an improvised water filter, mosquito net, or fishing net.
- **Small AM/FM radio:** battery- or solar-powered.
- **Surgical tubing:** enables you to reach water in otherwise inaccessible rock crevices.
- **Fire tin or matchless fire set:** self-contained methods of starting a fire, when no natural fuel is available.

# ON THE TRAIL

# FIND YOUR WAY

**Before you set off** on an expedition, you should have at least a basic understanding of how to read a map and use a compass. Your ability to correctly assess a map of the area you intend to visit will allow you to make informed decisions during your preparation. If you understand the area and terrain, your chances of getting lost will be reduced, and you will be able to continually evaluate your progress and therefore alter your plans as necessary. You will also be able to plan the safest and most appropriate route, and locate water, shelter, and areas that will allow you to use your location aids properly. If you're proficient with a map and compass, you'll have no cause to worry about getting lost or straying off-track and will be free to enjoy your outdoors experience.

In a survival situation, you will be faced with many tough decisions. You may have to decide whether to stay where you are and await rescue or move to an area that offers a better chance of survival and rescue. Your ability to navigate effectively—whether

## In this section YOU WILL DISCOVER...

- how to **use your map** to tell the **lie of the land...**
- that the **path ahead** is as long as a **piece of string...**
- the difference between **eastings** and **northings** and an **ERV** and a **GPS...**
- how a **detour** could be the **most direct route...**
- how to **navigate** using your **hair...**
- why an **anvil of cumulonimbus** is no **fair-weather cloud...**

**The ability** to take a bearing (see pp. 68–71) and navigate using pace counting (see p. 72) could prove to be crucial skills in a survival situation.

**TEST HOW ACCURATELY** you can walk on a set bearing and pace out a set distance by following the exercise below. If you have stayed on your bearings and your pacing has been accurate, you should finish at your starting point. Pick a suitable area where you can walk at least 330ft (100m) in any direction. Don't cheat by heading for your marker! For this exercise to be useful, make sure you follow your bearings and count your paces to navigate.

by using a map and compass or by using natural features—will play a major role in your decision-making process. Whilst a Global Positioning System (GPS) is an excellent aid, it relies on batteries and technology—both of which can fail.

An understanding of weather patterns will also allow you to evaluate conditions and make informed decisions as you travel. The ability to assess your situation and modify your plans means that you will be able to avoid many potential survival situations.

**1** Place a marker on the ground. Dial a bearing onto your compass (110° in our example).

**2** Walk on this bearing, counting your paces until you think you have travelled 100m (330ft), then stop.

**3** Add 120° to your original bearing. Dial this new bearing (230° in our example) onto your compass.

**4** Pace out another 330 ft (100 m) on your new bearing, then stop.

**5** Add another 120° to your latest bearing. Dial a last bearing (350° in our example) onto your compass.

**6** Walk on your final bearing for a further 330 ft (100 m). You should be back at your starting point.

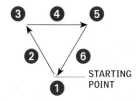

STARTING POINT

Never underestimate the **combined power** of a map, a compass, a GPS unit, and the **skills and knowledge** to use them well—your life may **depend on it**

# MAPS AND MAP-READING

**A MAP IS A TWO-DIMENSIONAL** representation of a three-dimensional area—from a map you can determine distance and height on the ground. If you are able to read a map, and can interpret the information it contains, you can visualize what an area looks like and use these features as landmarks to make navigation easier. Your map is very important, so keep it safe.

## UNDERSTANDING MAPS

Although there are many types of map available—with varying levels of detail and scale—topographic maps are best for hiking. They show important features, such as rivers, roads, railroads, paths, buildings, and forested areas, and also depict the lie of the land through the use of contour lines (see opposite) to represent height.

## THE LEGEND

Topographic maps incorporate a legend, or key, which deciphers the information shown on the map. It's important to familiarize yourself with the symbols used, as this will help you visualize what's being represented on the map more effectively. Some examples are listed below:

### HEIGHTS AND NATURAL FEATURES

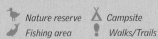

| | |
|---|---|
| Water | Mud |
| Sand; sand and shingle | |

Vertical face/cliff

| Loose rock | Boulders | Outcrop | Scree |
|---|---|---|---|

Coniferous trees

Non-coniferous trees

Managed woodland

Orchard

Scrub

Bracken, heath, or rough grassland

Marsh, reeds, or wetlands

### TOURIST AND RECREATIONAL INFORMATION

Nature reserve

Fishing area

Campsite

Walks/Trails

### THE SCALE

Hiking maps are always drawn to a scale provided in the legend. This is a ratio of how much you would have to enlarge the map to reach actual size. 1:25,000—whereby 4 cm on the map equates to 1 km on the ground (2½ in to 1 mile)—is the most useful level of detail for hikers. A smaller-scale of 1:50,000, for example, will provide a more basic overview of the terrain.

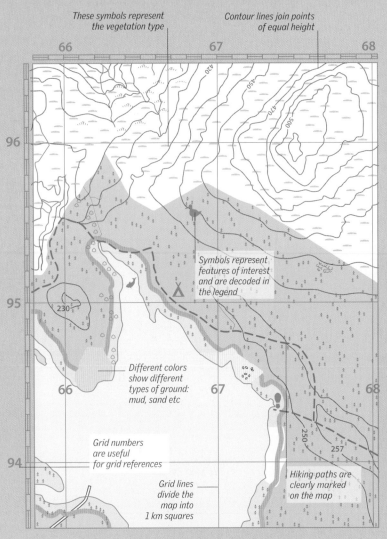

These symbols represent the vegetation type

Contour lines join points of equal height

Symbols represent features of interest and are decoded in the legend

Different colors show different types of ground: mud, sand etc

Grid numbers are useful for grid references

Grid lines divide the map into 1 km squares

Hiking paths are clearly marked on the map

# MEASURING DISTANCE

Maps are drawn to scale so that you can use them to accurately estimate distances on the ground. Being able to measure distance is important because it means you can calculate the most direct—and energy-efficient—route to your destination. In a survival situation, every last bit of energy counts, so the shorter the distance, the better.

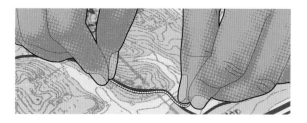

### USING THE GRID LINES

The simplest method of measuring distance on a map is to use the grid lines—on a scale 1:25,000 map each grid square represents 1 km (traveling diagonally across a square, it's approximately 1.5 km). You can also lay a piece of paper between the two points, mark the start and end of your route, and place it underneath the scale line to read the distance.

### USING STRING OR SOLDER

Invariably you will deviate from a straight line and will have to navigate around obstacles or bends. A far better way of measuring distance is therefore to take a piece of string, curve it around your intended route, and transfer it to the scale line. Solder wire (use wire that is lead-free) is even more accurate because it holds its shape on the map and remains flexible.

# CONTOUR LINES

Topographic maps feature lines called contour lines. A contour joins points of equal height above sea level, and allows the topography of the ground to be depicted in detail. The contour interval is specified in the legend—for maps with a 1:25,000 scale you would usually expect to see a 5-meter vertical interval between each line, although for maps of mountainous regions this interval may be 10 meters. The ability to look at the contour lines, and imagine how they translate to the ground, is a skill that takes a little while to acquire, but once mastered will allow you to read a map more proficiently.

### USING CONTOURS

Knowing how steep the ground is will greatly improve your navigational skills, as well as your route-planning (see p. 73). Walking up and down hills uses a lot of energy, so it is far better to follow the contour lines on your map to go around hills instead.

# GRID REFERENCES

Maps contain grid lines, which help you locate a specific point anywhere on a map, using a unique number known as a grid reference. The vertical grid lines are called "eastings," as they increase in value as they travel east on the map. The horizontal lines are called "northings," where these perpendicular lines cross creates the grid.

### WORKING OUT GRID REFERENCES

Use the numbers on the grid lines and apply the easting number first. On a scale 1:25,000 map, where the grid lines are 1 km apart, the shaded area on the grid below would have a four-figure grid reference of 2046, and indicate a grid square that is 1 km by 1 km. To be more accurate, use a six-figure number—mentally divide the square into tenths. The cross would therefore have a grid reference of 185445.

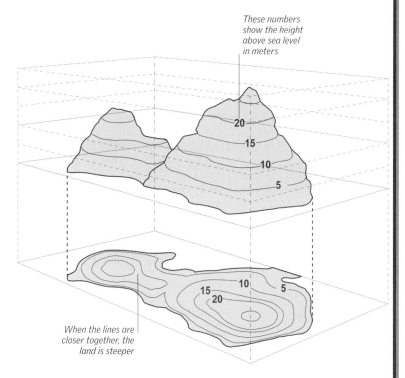

*These numbers show the height above sea level in meters*

*When the lines are closer together, the land is steeper*

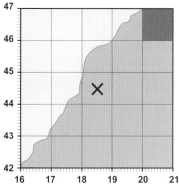

# GET YOUR BEARINGS

**IN ADDITION TO** understanding and reading maps, it's important to know how to orientate your map to the land so you can use it to navigate. It's possible to do this by sight, although in most cases you'll need a more reliable method and for this you should use a compass. Use your compass to determine direction, orientate your map and yourself, take and plot bearings, and navigate.

> **CARDINAL POINTS**
> The four cardinal points of the compass are:
> - North (N)—0°/360°
> - East (E)—90°
> - South (S)—180°
> - West (W)—270°

## HOW A COMPASS WORKS

A compass needle is a magnetized piece of metal that, when allowed to rotate freely, will orientate itself to the North and South magnetic poles. Always hold a compass level.

### STANDARD COMPASS

This standard orienteering Silva compass is a good compass for hiking. It allows you to set your map and work out distances using the printed scale on the base.

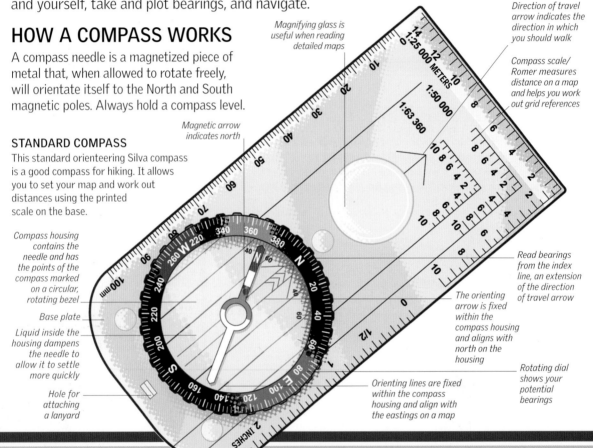

Magnifying glass is useful when reading detailed maps

Direction of travel arrow indicates the direction in which you should walk

Compass scale/ Romer measures distance on a map and helps you work out grid references

Magnetic arrow indicates north

Compass housing contains the needle and has the points of the compass marked on a circular, rotating bezel

Base plate

Liquid inside the housing dampens the needle to allow it to settle more quickly

Hole for attaching a lanyard

Read bearings from the index line, an extension of the direction of travel arrow

The orienting arrow is fixed within the compass housing and aligns with north on the housing

Rotating dial shows your potential bearings

Orienting lines are fixed within the compass housing and align with the eastings on a map

## OTHER TYPES OF COMPASS

There are many different types of compass, ranging from simple button compasses to complex instruments that include features such as sighting mirrors. Use a quality compass that suits your needs, and carry a simpler backup for emergencies.

Only the points of the compass are shown

### BUTTON

The simplest compass available—its small size and basic level of detail makes it ideal as a backup compass.

Non-rotating dial

### FIXED DIAL

As well as the basic points of the compass, degrees and bearings are also shown on the immovable dial.

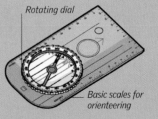

Rotating dial

Basic scales for orienteering

### BASIC ORIENTEERING

With a rotating dial, this has simpler markings than the standard compass above, and is ideal for beginners.

# SETTING YOUR MAP

Walking with your map set allows you to read the ground from the map as you pass over it, and to recognize and predict features as you progress, which means that you'll soon realize if you are heading off course. In some cases, when you have a good view of the terrain around you, and know the approximate area you're in, you can simply rotate your map until the features line up with the corresponding features on the ground. However, using your compass is a far more accurate method.

**1** Rotate the dial so that "N" sits under the index line. Lay your map flat on the ground and ensure there is nothing nearby that could affect your compass (see box below).
■ Lay the compass on the map so its edge runs parallel with a vertical grid line (easting).

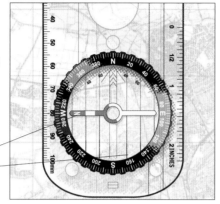

*Needle will not be aligned at present*

*Orienting lines run parallel to the vertical grid lines on your map*

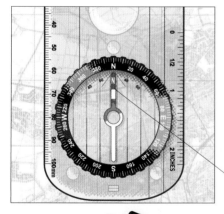

**2** Keeping orienting lines aligned with the grid lines on the map, rotate the entire map until the north magnetic needle on the compass sits inside the orienting arrow. The map is now set to magnetic north and should basically line up with the features that surround you.
■ If magnetic variation in your area is high (+ 5°), compensate accordingly (see right).

*Needle is now aligned*

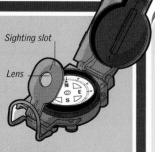

*Sighting slot*

*Lens*

## LENSATIC
The lensatic compass is an excellent instrument for taking very precise navigational measurements.

## TAKING AN ACCURATE READING
Always hold the compass level to allow the needle to rotate easily. A compass is simply a magnetized piece of metal and, as such, is susceptible to interference. To avoid this, never use your compass near:
■ Metal or other magnetized objects
■ Electric currents, such as overhead high-tension power cables
■ Buildings and vehicles—these often contain metal and electricity that might affect the accuracy of your compass readings

# MAGNETIC VARIATION

Map legends refer to north in three ways: "true north," "grid north," and "magnetic north." The angle between magnetic north and grid north is known as "magnetic variation," and is provided in the map legend. True north is the direction of a meridian of longitude that converges on the North Pole. Grid north runs parallel to the vertical grid lines on a map and differs from true north because a map is flat. Magnetic north is the direction indicated by a magnetic compass.

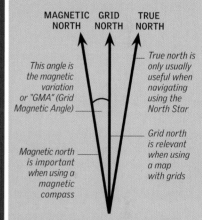

MAGNETIC NORTH   GRID NORTH   TRUE NORTH

*This angle is the magnetic variation or "GMA" (Grid Magnetic Angle)*

*Magnetic north is important when using a magnetic compass*

*True north is only usually useful when navigating using the North Star*

*Grid north is relevant when using a map with grids*

## COMPENSATING FOR VARIATION
When converting a magnetic bearing to a grid bearing, or vice versa, you have to adjust for magnetic variation. When the variation is west, use the phrases "Mag to grid—get rid" or "Grid to mag—add." If the variation is east, the opposite applies.

**1** Check the legend of your map to establish the magnetic variation. This depends on your location, and whether it is east or west of grid north.

**2** If the variation is 0°, there's no magnetic variation affecting the compass, so make no adjustments.

**3** If converting a magnetic bearing to a grid bearing with a 12° west variation, take off the 12°. With an east variation, add it on.

**4** If converting a grid bearing to a magnetic bearing with a 12° west variation, add on the 12°. With an east variation, take it off.

# TAKING BEARINGS

Always give any compass work your full attention. Rushing it, especially when working out bearings, can lead to navigational errors that could, at best, involve more walking and, at worst, get you lost.

## USING A MAP

Using your map to work out the direction in which you need to walk is simple. Use your compass as a protractor to work out your bearing, and then to keep you on track.

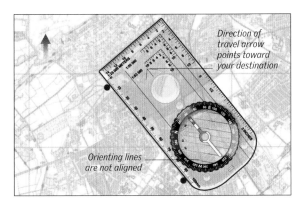

Direction of travel arrow points toward your destination

Orienting lines are not aligned

**1** Lay your map on a flat surface, ensuring that there's nothing nearby to interfere with the compass reading (see box, p. 69).

■ Lay the edge of your compass so that it runs between the point you want to navigate from and the point you want to navigate toward.

■ Ensure that the direction of travel arrow on the compass is pointing in the direction you want to travel on the map.

### BACK BEARING

A back bearing enables you to find your position by taking a bearing from a feature back to you. To do this, take a bearing to a point in the normal way and either add or subtract 180 degrees. You can also read the bearing exactly opposite to the index line. This is useful when working out the bearing from a feature back to you and transferring it to your map (see below).

## USING FEATURES ON THE GROUND

Sometimes you may need to take a bearing to a specific point to navigate toward it. The point may be a feature that you can see at the time but may subsequently lose sight of during your journey because of the terrain. You can also plot that bearing and others on a map in order to work out your own position (see right, and panel, far right).

### TAKING A BEARING ON A FEATURE

Pointing your compass at the feature, hold the base plate steady and rotate the compass housing until the orienting arrow sits directly under the north needle. Read the bearing—this is the magnetic bearing you would walk on to navigate to the feature.

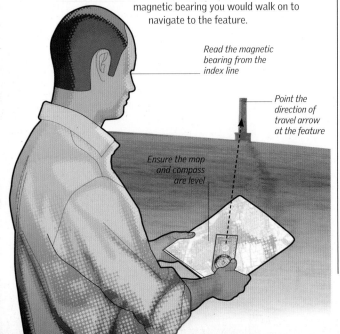

Read the magnetic bearing from the index line

Point the direction of travel arrow at the feature

Ensure the map and compass are level

## TRANSFERRING A MAGNETIC BEARING TO A GRID BEARING

It is important that you know how to transfer a compass bearing from a feature (a magnetic bearing) onto a map (a grid bearing). For this example, imagine that the magnetic variation is 12° west.

■ Take a bearing on your chosen feature (see left). In this example it is 45° magnetic.

■ You want to plot this bearing on your map, which has a grid, so remember the phrase "mag to grid—get rid." You would therefore subtract the magnetic variation (12°) from the magnetic bearing (45°), which equals 33°.

■ Dial this revised bearing into your compass.

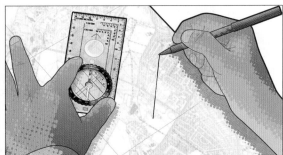

### TRANSFERRING THE BEARING ONTO THE MAP

Place the top left corner of the compass base plate over the feature on your map. Keeping it there, rotate the entire compass until the orienting lines are parallel with the vertical grid lines. Draw a line from the feature down the left side of the base plate to map your bearing.

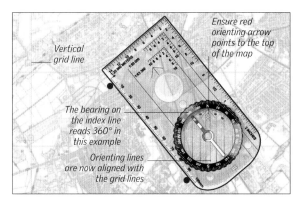

*Vertical grid line*

*Ensure red orienting arrow points to the top of the map*

*The bearing on the index line reads 360° in this example*

*Orienting lines are now aligned with the grid lines*

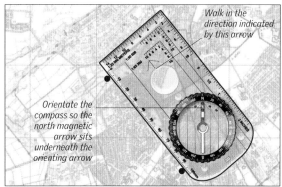

*Walk in the direction indicated by this arrow*

*Orientate the compass so the north magnetic arrow sits underneath the orienting arrow*

**2** Turn the compass housing around until the orienting arrow and the orienting lines within the housing line up with the vertical grid lines on the map. Read the bearing between the two points from the index line on the compass.

■ For this grid bearing to deliver you successfully to your destination, you'll need to convert it to a magnetic bearing by using the magnetic variation information on the map legend (see p. 69). Add or subtract your figure, and adjust your compass accordingly.

**3** In order to walk on this bearing you must now orientate your compass.

■ Hold the compass level and at a height that allows you to comfortably look squarely down on it (close to your chest is a good position).

■ Turn your body until the north end of the compass needle sits inside the orienting arrow. The direction of travel arrow is now pointing exactly in the direction that you need to walk.

# FINDING YOUR POSITION

If you are unsure of your position but can see features on the ground that you also recognize marked on your map, you can take bearings on these features with your compass and transfer them onto your map (see far left, and left) to accurately determine where you are. This process is called "triangulation" (also known as "resection" in military terminology). You'll need to transfer your compass bearings into grid bearings.

### AT A KNOWN FEATURE

If you are at or on a known feature on a map—such as a river, road, or track—and you can see another recognizable feature, you can take a bearing on that feature and mark it on your map. Where that line crosses your known feature is your position. In the example below, you know you are somewhere along the banks of a river and can see a church that you can identify on your map.

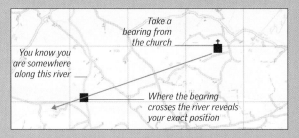

*Take a bearing from the church*

*You know you are somewhere along this river*

*Where the bearing crosses the river reveals your exact position*

## NOT AT A KNOWN FEATURE

If you are not at a known feature, but can see other recognizable features on the ground that you can identify and locate on your map, you can take bearings on these features and transfer them to your map. In order to do this you need two features that are at least 1 km (⁶/₁₀ mile) away and at least 40° apart. After you have transferred both bearings onto your map, the point at which the two lines cross will reveal your exact location. For greater accuracy, plot a third feature onto your map. The lines will cross and form a triangle—your position will be inside this triangle.

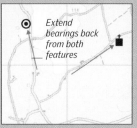

*Extend bearings back from both features*

*Where the two lines cross indicates your location*

**1** Using your compass, take bearings to the features on the ground.

■ Transfer these bearings to back bearings (see box, above left), and draw them on the map from your chosen features.

**2** Extend these lines further over the map until they cross each other.

■ The point at which the lines cross shows your location.

■ If you want to be more accurate, repeat the process with a third feature.

# ROUTE FINDING

**WHETHER YOU ARE PLANNING** to walk a specific route, or are in a survival situation and need to move to a safer area or to one that offers better chances of rescue, being able to study your map and calculate what you can achieve in a certain time can mean the difference between reaching your destination or spending a night in the wilderness.

## CALCULATING DISTANCE

There are several methods of calculating the distance you are walking, and a seasoned hiker will always use at least two of them at any one time.

### PACE COUNTING

Pace counting involves knowing how many paces you take to cover a set distance and then counting them as you travel. It is reasonably accurate. Distances are usually calculated in meters and kilometers, and most people take approximately 60 paces (120 steps) every 100 m. Try any of these methods:

- Cut 10 notches in your walking staff. Move an elastic band down a notch every 100 m.
- Use pace counting beads (a piece of webbing with two sets of beads divided by a central knot). One side contains nine beads to count off every 100 m, and the other has four beads to count off kilometers.
- Place 10 small pebbles in your pocket. Every time you cover 100 m, transfer a pebble to the other pocket.

### NAISMAITH'S RULE

Naismaith's rule takes into account distance and topography, and is used for estimating the duration of hikes.

- Allow one hour for every 3 miles (5 km) you will travel
- Add 30 minutes for every 985 ft (300 m) you will climb
- Subtract 10 minutes for every 985 ft (300 m) you will descend. However, for very steep slopes you should add 10 minutes for every 985 ft (300 m) you will descend

### ROUTE PLANNING

Break your route down into small sections. This will focus your navigation and make the overall distance seem less daunting. If you're in a group, designate an emergency rendezvous (ERV) point within each section—if someone gets separated you should all head there. If you can, include water sources and a safety point, such as a campsite, on your route.

*When the elastic band reaches the bottom notch you have covered 1 km*

### USING CUT-OFF FEATURES

Use your map to choose some key features on your route, and calculate the distance between these. As you pass them, check them off mentally in your head or physically mark your progress on the map. You'll then be able to keep track of the distance you have traveled when you reach each one.

### EXPERIENCE

As you gain experience you will be able to build up an idea of how long it takes you to cover a particular terrain. Naismaith's Rule (see left) is an excellent starting point, but there is no substitute for picking fixed distances on your map and timing yourself over that distance. You will eventually be able to build up a frame of reference.

# NAVIGATION TECHNIQUES

When navigating across land, you're less likely to get lost if you take direct bearings from one feature to another. Unfortunately this may not always be possible; obstacles such as lakes and swamps may be directly in your path and it may be easier to walk around some features rather than walk over or through them.

**PRINCIPLES OF NAVIGATION**

You will never get lost if you know:
- Where you started from
- What bearing or course you have been traveling on
- How far you have traveled

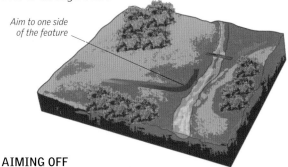

*Aim to one side of the feature*

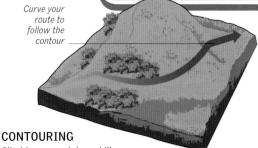

*Curve your route to follow the contour*

## AIMING OFF

It's easy to find yourself slightly off-course after a while. If you were aiming for a small footbridge over a stream and didn't arrive exactly at the bridge, you would need to guess whether to turn left or right to reach it. By deliberately aiming off to one side (also called "deliberate off-set") you can guarantee this direction.

## CONTOURING

Climbing up and down hills can expend a lot of energy and may not be the most effective method of navigating a particular terrain. Instead, use a technique called "contour navigation." This involves walking at the same height around a feature, which will conserve energy.

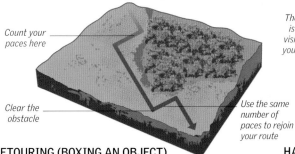

*Count your paces here*

*Clear the obstacle*

*Use the same number of paces to rejoin your route*

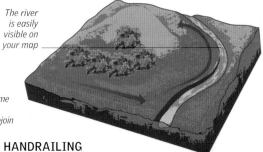

*The river is easily visible on your map*

## DETOURING (BOXING AN OBJECT)

If an obstacle makes a straight-line bearing impossible, use your compass to calculate four 90° turns, which you will then need to walk on to pass the obstacle. Count your paces on the first and third detours to return to your original, intended route as accurately as possible.

## HANDRAILING

Following long linear features that run in the general direction of your travel—such as rivers, roads, or paths—can be an effective way of navigating. Because you use the features rather than your compass, navigation becomes simpler, as the features are usually easy to follow. A slight detour toward one can be worthwhile.

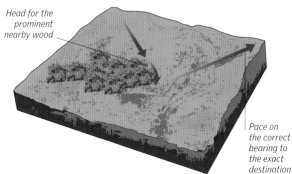

*Head for the prominent nearby wood*

*Pace on the correct bearing to the exact destination*

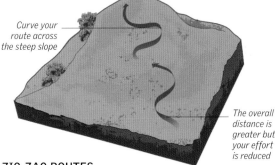

*Curve your route across the steep slope*

*The overall distance is greater but your effort is reduced*

## STAND OFF/ATTACK POINT

Useful when navigating to a specific point that may be difficult to locate, this technique involves aiming initially for a nearby prominent feature. Calculate a distance and bearing from it and use pacing to accurately locate the specific point. If you fail to find it, simply return to the prominent feature and start again.

## ZIG-ZAG ROUTES

You may have no alternative but to climb a steep slope and this can be exhausting. However, if you choose a zig-zag route up the slope you can reduce the effort required to achieve the climb. This will dramatically reduce the strain on your legs, ankles, lungs, and heart. It is also effective when walking down steep slopes.

# NAVIGATING WITHOUT A COMPASS

**IF YOU DON'T HAVE A COMPASS** you can use a few simple items from your survival kit to determine direction and enable you to navigate reasonably accurately. Advances in technology have also made satellite-navigation aids more readily available.

> ## TOOLS AND MATERIALS
> You will need an improvised needle or razor blade, plus one of the following:
> - Knife
> - Hair
> - Silk
> - Magnet
> - Battery and wire; paper and tape

## IMPROVISING A COMPASS

It's relatively simple to make an improvised compass using a piece of magnetized ferrous metal. How accurate your compass is depends on the materials you have available to you and your own ingenuity.

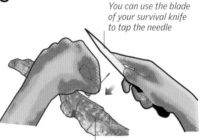

You can use the blade of your survival knife to tap the needle

Stroke the needle through your hair

## SOURCING AND MAGNETIZING THE NEEDLE

If you have a compass but it's damaged, you may still be able to use the needle from it, which will already be magnetized. If this is unusable, you'll need to find a piece of ferrous metal to magnetize. Suitable items you could use include:

- A needle from your survival tin or sewing kit
- A paperclip, opened up and straightened out
- A razor blade from your survival kit
- A small nail or straightened staple taken from a fence

Once you have your improvised needle, you will need to magnetize it. The smaller and thinner the needle is, the easier this will be. Use one of the methods shown here.

Tap the needle into hard wood to heighten the effect, but make sure it doesn't become embedded

### THE TAPPING METHOD

Align the needle as close to the north-south line as you can determine, hold the needle at an angle of 45 degrees, and gently tap the end of it with another piece of metal. Lightly tapping it into a hard piece of wood will increase the effect.

### USING YOUR HAIR

Hold the sharp end of the needle perpendicular to your head and—taking care not to hurt yourself—stroke the needle in one direction through your hair, using careful and deliberate strokes. Repeat until the needle is magnetized.

## ALLOWING THE NEEDLE TO FLOAT FREELY

Once you have made your improvised needle using one of the methods above, you need to find a way to allow it to turn freely so that it is able to indicate direction. Take care to protect your needle from elements such as the wind, which will affect its movement.

### SUSPENSION METHOD

The advantage of the suspension method is that the equipment is portable and can be reused. It works best with a magnetized razor blade, which will balance well. Attach the magnetized blade to a cotton thread and suspend it inside a plastic bottle. If the bottle's neck is not wide enough to fit the blade through, remove the base of the bottle instead.

The bottle protects the compass from the elements

Use the hole in the blade to attach the cotton

### FLOATING METHOD

In a sheltered place, float the needle on the surface of some water—a puddle or a small non-magnetic container filled with water, for example. Balance the needle on a small, dry leaf (or piece of paper, piece of bark, blade of grass, or inside a shortened straw).

Use a puddle in a sheltered area

The needle will rotate, settle, and align itself

The leaf enables the needle to float on the surface of the water

## PRINCIPLES OF MAGNETIZING

In general, the longer you work on the needle the stronger the magnetization will be and the longer it will last. To tell when it is magnetized sufficiently, hold the needle up against another metal object—if it is attracted to the metal and has enough strength to hold itself against it then it will be strong enough. Once the needle is magnetized you will need to allow it to float freely (see below), and then determine which end points north by using natural aids, such as the sun (see pp. 76–77). Mark the north end of the needle with a pen or a small scratch.

## USING ELECTRICITY

The most effective way to magnetize a needle is to pass a small electrical current around it. Use a battery and insulated wire; alternatively, use brass snare wire from your survival kit and insulate it using something non-conductive, such as paper.

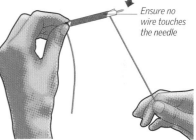

**1** Wrap the needle in a small piece of paper, which will insulate it from the electrical current.

*Cover the full length of the needle with paper*

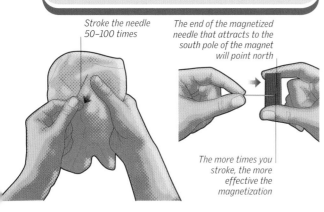

*Stroke the needle 50–100 times*

*The end of the magnetized needle that attracts to the south pole of the magnet will point north*

*The more times you stroke, the more effective the magnetization*

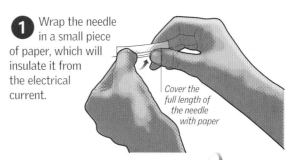

**2** Wrap the wire tightly around the full length of the insulated needle.

*Ensure no wire touches the needle*

### USING SILK

This works on a similar principle to the hair method but is more effective. If you have anything made from silk, such as a sleeping bag liner or thermal clothing, stroke the needle repeatedly in one direction against the silk.

### USING A MAGNET

Stroke the magnet along the length of the needle repeatedly in one direction. It's a good idea to carry a magnet with you at all times, although you should never keep it near your compass as it will affect its accuracy.

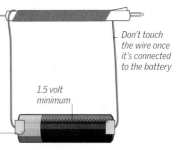

**3** Attach the wire to the battery until battery starts to get warm—this indicates the process is complete.

*Don't touch the wire once it's connected to the battery*

*1.5 volt minimum*

*Attach the wire using some tape*

# USING GPS TECHNOLOGY

A Global Positioning System (GPS) is a hand-held unit that uses 24 orbiting satellites to triangulate your position on the Earth's surface to within meters. A GPS will allow you to work out straight-line distances and bearings to and from points, but unless it incorporates mapping it will not show you the best way to get there or take into account hazards on your route. Use it in conjunction with your map and compass.

### TAKING EFFECTIVE GPS READINGS

A GPS needs to have a clear view of the sky. Anything that obstructs its signal, such as tall buildings or heavy tree canopy, will reduce its ability to lock onto satellites.

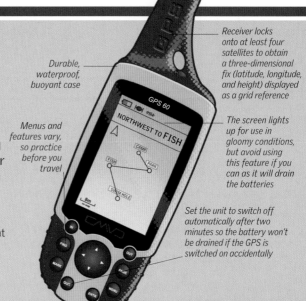

*Durable, waterproof, buoyant case*

*Menus and features vary, so practice before you travel*

*Receiver locks onto at least four satellites to obtain a three-dimensional fix (latitude, longitude, and height) displayed as a grid reference*

*The screen lights up for use in gloomy conditions, but avoid using this feature if you can as it will drain the batteries*

*Set the unit to switch off automatically after two minutes so the battery won't be drained if the GPS is switched on accidentally*

# NATURAL NAVIGATION

**IF YOU HAVE LOST** or damaged your compass and don't have the materials necessary to make an improvised version, use natural indicators to determine direction. The east-west rotation of the Earth means that you can orientate yourself according to the position of the sun, moon, and stars. All you need are some very basic materials and these simple techniques.

## USING THE SUN

When visible, the sun is the clearest natural signpost to the four cardinal points (north, south, east, and west). It rises approximately in the east and sets approximately in the west and, at midday, is due south in the northern hemisphere and due north in the southern hemisphere. Use the sun's course across the sky to determine direction and approximate the time.

> **SHADOW STICK BASICS**
> Use a shadow stick to determine direction and time anywhere between the Arctic (66.5°N) and Antarctic Circles (66.5°S).
> ■ In the northern hemisphere the shadow of the stick will be on the north side of the east-west line
> ■ In the southern hemisphere the reverse is true: the shadow of the stick will be on the south side of the east-west line.
> ■ When the shadow is at its shortest, it is midday.

## ORIENTATION

Tracking the movement of the sun across the sky using a shadow stick will provide an indication of its direction of travel. The sun moves from east to west at 15° an hour.

**1** Drive a stick into a piece of level round, and ensure it's as upright as possible.

**2** Place a stone at the tip of the stick's shadow.

**3** Wait three hours and place a second stone at the new position of the shadow's tip.

*The stick should be approximately 3 ft (1 m) high*

*A line linking the two stones will point east-west*

*Place the first stone on the line of the first shadow*

*Place the second stone on the line of the second shadow*

E

W

*A line at 90 degrees to the east-west line will point north-south*

N

**4** Draw a line between the stones to find east-west; the first stone will be at due west and the second at due east.

**5** To find north-south, mark a line at 90° to the east-west line.

## TELLING THE TIME

Once you have established the east-west and north-south lines, you can turn the shadow-stick apparatus into a sundial, to give an approximate idea of the time.

**1** Place the stick at the intersection of the north-south and east-west lines

*Move the shadow stick into the correct position on the ground*

**2** Tie a piece of cord to the stick. Attach a smaller stick to the other end of the cord and use it to draw an 180-degree arc between the two marker stones.

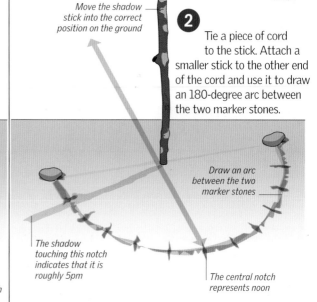

*Draw an arc between the two marker stones*

*The shadow touching this notch indicates that it is roughly 5pm*

*The central notch represents noon*

**3** Divide the arc into 12 equal sections and mark each division with a notch. The notches represent one hour of time, from 6am to 6pm with noon at the middle notch.

# USING THE STARS

It's possible to orientate yourself by spotting certain recognizable stars. In the northern hemisphere, Polaris is located above due north on the horizon, from which you can determine east, west, and south. Find it by locating the Plow (also known as the Big Dipper). In the southern hemisphere, you can work out the approximate position of south on the horizon by finding the Southern Cross.

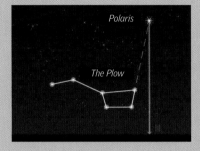

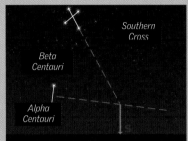

### NORTHERN HEMISPHERE

Find the Plow and project a line from the top of the two stars that form its front. Follow this line until you find Polaris, which is located approximately four times the distance from the Plow as the distance between its two front stars.

### SOUTHERN HEMISPHERE

Project a line from the longer axis of the Southern Cross until you find a dark area of sky. Project a second line at 90° from the mid-point between two bright stars in the Centaurus constellation. Due south is below the point where these lines meet.

# USING THE MOON

Reflecting the light of the sun, the moon rises in the east and sets in the west, so can be used for orientation. A shadow stick will work on a cloudless, full-moon night.

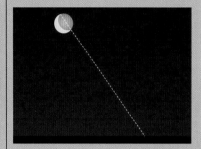

### CRESCENT MOON

Although not an entirely accurate method, a line vectored between two horns of a crescent (quarter) moon will lead to a point that is approximately south on the horizon in the northern hemisphere, and roughly north in the southern hemisphere.

# USING AN ANALOG WATCH

If you can see the sun, you can use an analog watch as a protractor to determine an approximate direction. Ensure it is set to the correct local time and that you have taken daylight savings (DST) into account. If you don't have a watch but know the time, simply draw a watch face on a piece of paper, marking 12 o'clock and the hour hand. This method is increasingly less effective as you near the Equator.

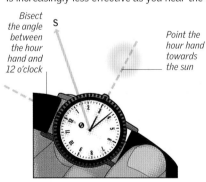

### NORTHERN HEMISPHERE

In the northern hemisphere the cardinal point nearest to the sun is south. Point the hour hand of your watch at the sun and bisect the angle between the hour hand and 12 o'clock. This will be due south.

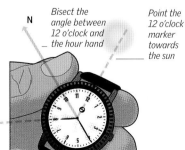

### SOUTHERN HEMISPHERE

In the southern hemisphere, the cardinal point nearest to the sun is north. Point the 12 o'clock marker on your watch at the sun and bisect the angle between 12 o'clock and the hour hand on the watch. This will be due north.

# NATURAL SIGNPOSTS

Nature responds to the elements in a range of ways, some of which can be studied for orientation tips. This is useful if you know the predominant wind direction of an area.

### TREES AND PLANTS

- Windswept trees point away from the wind.
- Tree growth is most lush on the side that faces the sun (south in the northern hemisphere, north in the southern hemisphere).
- Some plants, such as the barrel cacti, twist toward the sun as they grow.
- Moss and lichen grow out of direct sunlight, on the shady side of rocks or trees.

### ANIMALS AND INSECTS

- In very windy areas, small animals and birds tend to nest or burrow on the lee-side of hills.
- Spiders spin webs out of the wind, so an area with a lot of broken webs could indicate a recent change of wind direction, away from the dominant wind.

### SNOW AND ICE

- In powder-snow conditions, snow "dunes" often form parallel to the prevailing wind.
- Frost erosion is most severe on slopes facing the sun (south in the northern hemisphere, north in the southern hemisphere).

# HOW WEATHER WORKS

**CHANGES IN THE WEATHER** can have a significant effect on your expedition—or chances of survival if something goes wrong—so it's important to be as prepared as possible for all the conditions you might face. Check the weather report for the days ahead thoroughly, and pack and wear appropriate clothing. If the weather forecast is so bad that it could make traveling or navigation difficult, rethink your plans.

## UNDERSTANDING THE WEATHER

Weather is created by the movement of air currents, the moisture content of the air, and the meeting of warm and cold fronts. Looking at weather maps before you leave for your trip will help you track these elements. You'll then need to use your understanding to forecast the effects of these movements on the ground.

### READING WEATHER CHARTS

It can be helpful to compare weather charts with regular topographic land maps. Just as the gradient is steeper where contour lines appear closer together on land maps, the wind is stronger where isobar contours appear closer together on weather charts.

> **WHAT IS WEATHER?**
> The term "weather" relates to current conditions on the ground—such as the temperature, and whether or not it is windy or raining—while "climate" refers to a region's conditions over a longer period of time. Changes in the weather are caused by alterations in air pressure and temperature. Extreme weather, such as a hurricane, occurs when these changes are more marked than usual. Weather is monitored by meteorologists, and very accurate predictions can be made. However, weather can still cause surprises, so always prepare for all possible scenarios when packing or dressing for an expedition.

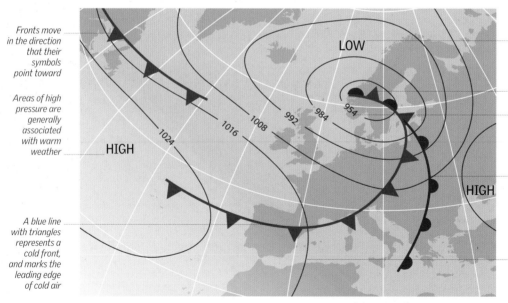

Fronts move in the direction that their symbols point toward

Areas of high pressure are generally associated with warm weather

A blue line with triangles represents a cold front, and marks the leading edge of cold air

Areas of low pressure are associated with cooler weather

Occluded fronts are fronts where two air masses merge

The lower the value of the central pressure, the more severe the wind and rain

A red line with semi-circles represents a warm front, and marks the leading edge of warm air

Isobars join areas where the air pressure is the same

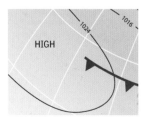

**HIGH PRESSURE**
Under conditions of high pressure, air descends in a spiral formation, and warms. The water vapor does not condense into clouds and we would expect to observe fairly clear skies.

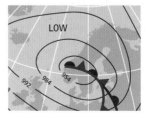

**LOW PRESSURE**
Under conditions of low pressure, air spirals upward—parallel to the center of the isobars—and cools. The air condenses to form clouds, and skies are usually overcast.

## GLOBAL CIRCULATION

Warm air from the equator rises and moves toward the poles in each hemisphere. As it cools it descends and travels back toward the equator. Because of the Earth's rotation, three separate cells of circulating air in each hemisphere develop, which produce predictable wind and pressure patterns.

## AIR MASSES

Large bodies of air with a particular temperature and humidity help weather forecasters predict the forthcoming weather and are known as air masses. They are largely defined by the area that they originated from. In general, northerly winds are colder than southerly winds, and air that has tracked over the sea ("maritime air mass") accumulates moisture and is more cloudy than air that has tracked over the land ("continental air mass"). The boundaries between tropical and polar air become warm and cold fronts.

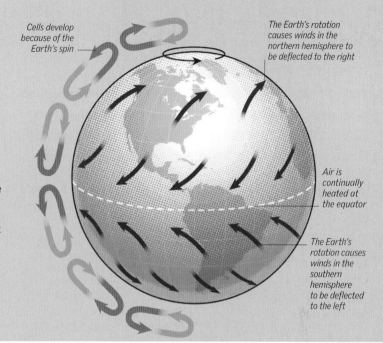

*Cells develop because of the Earth's spin*

*The Earth's rotation causes winds in the northern hemisphere to be deflected to the right*

*Air is continually heated at the equator*

*The Earth's rotation causes winds in the southern hemisphere to be deflected to the left*

## ON THE GROUND

As a weather system travels over the ground, it changes in predictable ways. Knowing how the system will progress is an important part of interpreting your weather map or forecast.

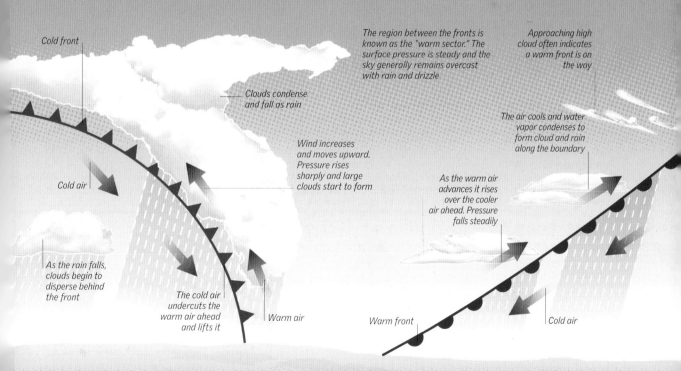

*Cold front*

*The region between the fronts is known as the "warm sector." The surface pressure is steady and the sky generally remains overcast with rain and drizzle*

*Approaching high cloud often indicates a warm front is on the way*

*Clouds condense and fall as rain*

*Cold air*

*The air cools and water vapor condenses to form cloud and rain along the boundary*

*Wind increases and moves upward. Pressure rises sharply and large clouds start to form*

*As the warm air advances it rises over the cooler air ahead. Pressure falls steadily*

*As the rain falls, clouds begin to disperse behind the front*

*The cold air undercuts the warm air ahead and lifts it*

*Warm air*

*Warm front*

*Cold air*

# WEATHER PHENOMENA

**LOOKING AT THE CLOUDS** can help you to read approaching weather, which is invaluable when you're on the move with no access to weather forecasts or charts. Knowing how to recognize a storm cloud, for example, will ensure that you have enough warning to seek shelter or to change into appropriate clothing. If low cloud threatens to impair your visibility, use your compass to navigate and proceed with caution.

## READING THE CLOUDS

Clouds are condensing masses of water vapor that provide precipitation and reflect solar radiation. They are categorized by height—into low, medium, and high clouds—and further defined by their shape. The shape of a cloud is determined by the way in which warm air rises, and is an indicator of the air stability.

> **HOW CLOUDS FORM**
> Clouds form by a cooling process. This process can be compared to breathing on cold glass, when condensation appears because invisible water vapor in your breath, cooled to a temperature known as the "dew point," condenses into its visible liquid state. Clouds form in a very similar way. Air temperature falls at an average rate of two degrees celcius per 1,000 ft (300 m). When air containing moisture—perhaps because it has travelled over sea—reaches the height at which it meets its dew point temperature, the water vapor condenses to form visible cloud.

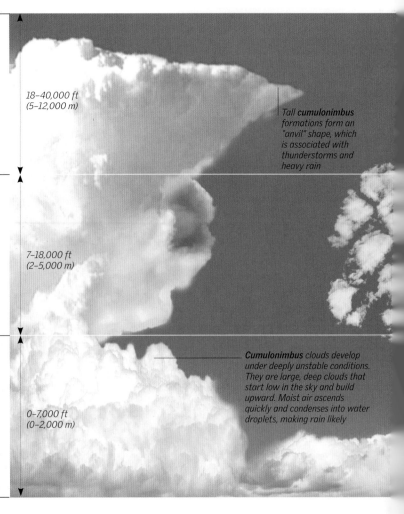

### HIGH CLOUDS

Fair-weather clouds are white and high in the sky. If there are no clouds, expect excellent conditions. Blankets of high cloud progressively invading the sky can signify the onset of bad weather. High clouds include:

- Anvil of cumulonimbus
- Cirrus
- Cirrustratus

18–40,000 ft
(5–12,000 m)

*Tall **cumulonimbus** formations form an "anvil" shape, which is associated with thunderstorms and heavy rain*

### MEDIUM CLOUDS

Thick layers of medium-layer cloud give heavy, persistent rain, especially if the clouds are dark and gray. The clouds you are most likely to see at this level are:

- Altocumulus
- Nimbostratus
- Altostratus

7–18,000 ft
(2–5,000 m)

### LOW CLOUDS

Low clouds have clearly defined edges and can indicate whether rain will fall in short downpours (cumulus) or persistently (stratus). Common clouds are:

- Cumulonimbus
- Stratus
- Stratocumulus
- Cumulus

0–7,000 ft
(0–2,000 m)

*__Cumulonimbus__ clouds develop under deeply unstable conditions. They are large, deep clouds that start low in the sky and build upward. Moist air ascends quickly and condenses into water droplets, making rain likely*

# WEATHER RISKS

The weather can have a massive impact on your trip, bringing with it added dangers. It can affect your visibility levels, and the safety of the ground you're hiking over. In a survival situation, the temperature, and whether or not it's raining, can have a huge effect on your chances.

**WARNING!**
Never shelter under a solitary tree during a lightning storm—get in your vehicle if possible or find low ground.

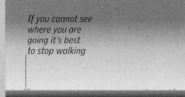

*If you cannot see where you are going it's best to stop walking*

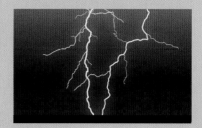

## HEAVY RAIN
If heavy rain falls quickly, the ground may become saturated, slippery, or flood. Seek shelter or proceed cautiously in waterproof clothing.

## FOG
Essentially a cloud in contact with the ground, fog reduces visibility, so beware of dangerous terrain, especially on mountains.

## LIGHTNING
Lightning is an atmospheric discharge of electricity—it will strike the first object it encounters on its route to earth, so avoid high, exposed places.

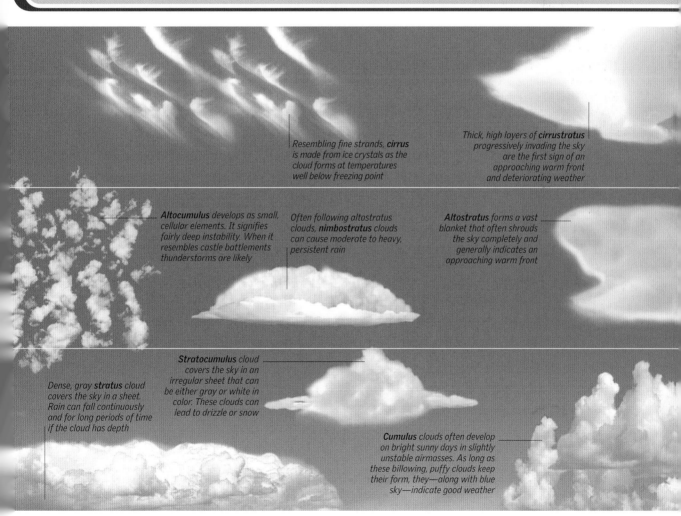

*Resembling fine strands, **cirrus** is made from ice crystals as the cloud forms at temperatures well below freezing point*

*Thick, high layers of **cirrustratus** progressively invading the sky are the first sign of an approaching warm front and deteriorating weather*

*__Altocumulus__ develops as small, cellular elements. It signifies fairly deep instability. When it resembles castle battlements thunderstorms are likely*

*Often following altostratus clouds, **nimbostratus** clouds can cause moderate to heavy, persistent rain*

*__Altostratus__ forms a vast blanket that often shrouds the sky completely and generally indicates an approaching warm front*

*__Stratocumulus__ cloud covers the sky in an irregular sheet that can be either gray or white in color. These clouds can lead to drizzle or snow*

*Dense, gray **stratus** cloud covers the sky in a sheet. Rain can fall continuously and for long periods of time if the cloud has depth*

*__Cumulus__ clouds often develop on bright sunny days in slightly unstable airmasses. As long as these billowing, puffy clouds keep their form, they—along with blue sky—indicate good weather*

# UNDERSTANDING LOCAL WEATHER

**WEATHER IS AFFECTED**—and can be predicted—by the local geography surrounding you. High ground forces air to rise and cool, and the relative temperatures of land and sea produce predictable effects.

## REGIONAL EFFECTS

It helps to understand how these predictable weather patterns occur in various geographic areas. They may influence your decisions when on the trail.

### THE FOHN EFFECT

The leeward side of high ground is warmer and more sheltered than the windward side. Air rises as it travels over obstacles and, if the air contains moisture, the water vapor condenses to form cloud once cooled to a certain level. The air loses water at the summit, then descends and warms on the leeward side.

*Air cools as it rises at a rate of 37 °F (3 °C) per 1000 ft (300 m)*

*Air cools at 35 °F (1.5 °C) per 1000 ft (300 m)*

*Water vapor falls as rain at the summit*

*Dry air descends and warms at a rate of 37 °F (3 °C) per 1000 ft (300 m)*

## ANABATIC AND KATABATIC WINDS

Winds that flow up and down slopes during certain atmospheric conditions are known as "anabatic" and "katabatic." They typically occur in mountainous regions.

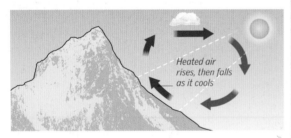

*Heated air rises, then falls as it cools*

### ANABATIC WINDS

During the day, the surface of sloping terrain heats up. The air rises and creates a gentle upslope breeze. Anabatic winds are lighter than katabatic winds because they act against gravity.

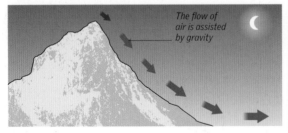

*The flow of air is assisted by gravity*

### KATABATIC WINDS

Katabatic winds form on clear nights with a light breeze. Air in contact with the ground cools and its density increases, causing it to flow down the slopes of the hillside.

## SEA AND LAND BREEZES

Sea breezes often develop along coastlines on clear sunny days, whereas land breezes tend to develop along coastlines on cloudless nights.

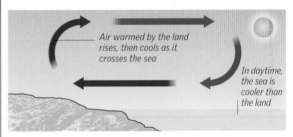

*Air warmed by the land rises, then cools as it crosses the sea*

*In daytime, the sea is cooler than the land*

### SEA BREEZE

Warm air rises over land during the afternoon, drawing in cool air to replace it along the coast. The result of this coastal air circulation by day is a wind that blows from sea to land.

*As the air passes over the land it cools*

*At night the sea is warmer than the land*

### LAND BREEZE

At night, the sea becomes comparatively warmer and air begins to rise. Air from the neighboring land is drawn toward the sea. The result is a wind that blows from land to sea.

# NATURAL WEATHER FORECASTERS

These natural indicators are based on observation and can be useful if you have no alternative means of predicting the weather.

## LOOKING AT THE SKY

■ If the sky is red at dawn there is moisture in the air and a potential storm ahead. A red sky at night often indicates good weather to come.
■ A rainbow usually indicates good weather is on the way, or a light shower.

## PLANTS AND FLOWERS

■ The scent of plants and flowers is often stronger before rain.
■ Certain flowers, such as Scarlet Pimpernel and Morning Glory, are said to close up if bad weather is on the way.
■ Pine cones are one of the best natural forecasters—their scales absorb moisture in the air and close up if wet weather is approaching, and unfurl in dry air.

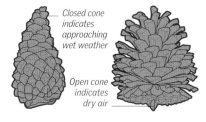

Closed cone indicates approaching wet weather

Open cone indicates dry air

## WATCHING ANIMALS

■ Animals migrating from high to low areas may indicate that a storm is on the way.
■ Cows often lie down before it rains.
■ Wool reacts to moisture in the air by swelling and straightening. It shrivels in dry weather conditions.
■ Humans can also sense atmospheric change—some people suffer headaches before a thunderstorm.

### CHANGING WEATHER

Watch out for alterations in the wind direction or strength as this may lead to a change in the weather. A dry, steady wind that changes direction or decreases in strength often indicates that rain is on its way.

# THE BEAUFORT SCALE

Providing visual references for the effects of wind speed on land and at sea, the Beaufort Scale was designed by Sir Francis Beaufort in 1805. It provides a simple way of estimating wind speeds without the need for equipment, and is still in common usage today. The scale ranges from calm to hurricane, and is numbered from zero to 12.

| BEAUFORT NUMBER | WIND DESCRIPTION | WIND SPEED KPH (MPH) | WIND EFFECT ON LAND AND AT SEA |
|---|---|---|---|
| 0 | Calm | 0 (0) | Smoke rises vertically. Sea like a mirror. |
| 1 | Light air | 1–3 (1–2) | Smoke drifts gently. Sea ripples like scales. |
| 2 | Light breeze | 4–11 (3–7) | Leaves rustle. Wind felt on skin. Small wavelets. |
| 3 | Gentle breeze | 12–19 (8–12) | Leaves and twigs move. Large wavelets with scattered whitecaps. |
| 4 | Moderate breeze | 20–29 (13–18) | Small branches move. Small waves with frequent whitecaps. |
| 5 | Fresh wind | 30–39 (19–24) | Small trees begin to sway. Moderate waves with some foam and spray. |
| 6 | Strong wind | 40–50 (25–31) | Umbrella usage is difficult. Large waves of 10 ft (3 m) with some spray. |
| 7 | Near gale | 51–61 (32–38) | Whole trees sway. Sea heaps up and foam begins to streak. |
| 8 | Gale | 62–74 (39–46) | Walking is difficult. Moderately high waves of more than 18 ft (5 m). |
| 9 | Severe gale | 75–87 (47–54) | Damage to roofs. High waves with toppling crests. |
| 10 | Storm | 88–101 (55–63) | Trees uprooted or broken off. Very high waves and sea surface appears white. |
| 11 | Severe storm | 102–119 (64–74) | Houses damaged. Exceptionally high waves of more than 38 ft (11 m). |
| 12 | Hurricane | More than 120 (More than 75) | Buildings destroyed. Huge waves of more than 46 ft (14 m). |

# MAKE A MOVE

**While some survival situations** are simply unavoidable, many are entered into because basic techniques relevant to a particular mode of transport have not been followed correctly. This could be due to a lack of knowledge, a loss of concentration, an individual's over-confident belief in his or her own equipment or skills, or as a result of sheer recklessness. Therefore, before you venture into an unfamiliar environment, make sure that you carefully research the type of terrain you will be encountering and investigate the best method of traveling safely and efficiently across it. Knowing the correct techniques for scrambling up a mountain or walking down a steep hillside, for example, could mean the difference between an enjoyable day out and a life-threatening survival situation arising from a fractured ankle in a remote location. Equally, being able to regain control of your vehicle after it has entered a skid could quite simply save your life. Thoroughly researching the terrain will also allow you to select the correct

## In this section YOU WILL DISCOVER...

■ how to make a **paddle** (so you're never **up a creek** without one)...

■ the difference between your **finger shelf** and your **hand jam...**

■ how to **pull** your own **pulk** and **scramble** over **scree...**

■ when to **blaze a trail** or **ski without skis...**

■ how to tell your **front-wheel skid** from your **skidoo...**

■ when to let the **camel train** take the **strain...**

■ how **chewing gum** can stop that **sinking feeling...**

**A walking staff** is one of the simplest yet most important survival aids you will ever need. It's the first piece of equipment to improvise should you find yourself in a survival situation.

**THE "SURVIVOR'S THIRD LEG"**—as a walking staff is also known—increases your ability to support yourself by allowing you to have two points of contact with the ground at any one time. This will reduce the chance of you slipping— a crucial factor given that your ability to walk is your main means of rescue; reduce your mobility and you seriously reduce your ability to survive.

**A versatile tool**, your survivor's third leg can be employed in many different survival situations. Among its many uses, it can be employed to:

- Support you as you walk
- Protect your face when you're walking through thickets or gorse
- Check for adequate support when crossing marshy ground
- Test the ground ahead for obstructions
- Check the depth of water when you're crossing streams and rivers
- Protect you against wild animals
- Form a ridgepole for your shelter
- Help you with your pace counting
- Spear fish or catch game
- Dig up roots or plants

equipment and most appropriate clothing, and enable you to familiarize yourself with the survival techniques relevant to a particular environment.

Whether you're planning to travel on foot, by boat, on horseback, in a 4WD vehicle, or by boat, you must consider not only your own capabilities and those of other members of your team, but also the capabilities of your equipment. Remember, pushing anything beyond its limits—whether that be a person, an animal, or a vehicle—will invariably lead to it failing.

" Your ability to walk may be your **primary means of rescue**; reduce your mobility and you dramatically reduce your **chances of survival** "

# TRAVELING ON FOOT

**HIKING IS A GREAT WAY** to explore wilderness terrain. It's important to have a decent level of fitness before you set out, and to wear and carry appropriate clothing and equipment. Hiking requires basic skills—using the correct techniques will help you move more efficiently, and ensure that your trip is safe.

## BASIC WALKING SKILLS

Aim for a slow, even pace that can be maintained for the duration of the hike by all members of the group. A good way to maintain this pace is to develop a hiking rhythm. Take regular rest breaks and, if you're walking in a group, ensure everyone knows the route.

## UPHILL TECHNIQUES

When traveling uphill, lean forward slightly, maintain your momentum but shorten your stride. When pushing upward, keep your feet flat on the ground.

- Carry a walking staff for support as you ascend.
- Move your legs forward from the hips.

*Make sure your backback fits properly for comfort*

*Swing your arms for momentum and balance*

*Break in new boots before long hikes to avoid blisters*

*Deep tread grips the ground and reduces slipping*

*Lean backwards slightly*

## DOWNHILL TECHNIQUES

Walking downhill can place a lot of strain on your thighs, knees, and ankles, especially when you're carrying a heavy backpack. Be careful not to lose control or gather too much speed.

- Use your arms for balance.
- Maintain a steady rhythm.

## WALKING AT NIGHT

Unless you're in the desert and it's cooler to move in darkness, avoid walking at night because of the added risks posed by navigational difficulties, and predators that hunt at night. If there's no alternative, try the following:

- Use your flashlight or improvise a torch by setting alight some birch bark or similar.
- If this isn't possible and you've time, close your eyes for 20 minutes to allow them to adjust to night vision.
- Use your walking stick or pole to feel in front of you for obstacles, tripping hazards, or sudden drops in the ground.
- Keep your pace slow and deliberate, and check your compass regularly.

# NEGOTIATING DIFFICULT GROUND

One of the most challenging terrains to hike over is "scree," a mass of small rocks that slides underfoot making uphill and downhill travel difficult. The slippery nature of the surface can make progress slow, and care should be taken to avoid falling and injuring yourself. Hiking on scree is hard work, but using the correct techniques will help you to advance confidently, efficiently, and safely.

## TRAVERSING SCREE

Choose a zig-zag route and look for a path that contains similar-sized rocks. Walk sideways across the slope, taking small steps and testing rocks for stability before placing your full weight on them.

*Rocks at the edge of the slope are likely to be larger and more stable*

## ASCENDING SCREE

Tread carefully, kicking your toes into the slope and testing the step before transferring your weight to that leg. Alternatively, walk with your feet splayed, placing your weight on the inside of each foot.

## DESCENDING SCREE

"Screeing" downhill combines sliding with slow-motion jogging. When you have the technique it can be great fun, but avoid larger rocks to prevent ankle injuries.

# TRAIL MARKERS

Your map and compass should be your primary method of navigation, but keep an eye out for trail markers, or "blazes," during your hike.

*Trails are coded using colors or symbols*

*Arrows indicate direction*

## ROCKS

Trail blazes painted onto rocks and boulders are especially common in rocky terrain. They may be low on the ground so look carefully.

## SIGNPOSTS

Made from wood, metal, or plastic, these signposts are particularly useful in areas where there are few rocks or trees on which to blaze.

*Stacks should be visible from a distance*

*The same sign may indicate several trails*

## CAIRNS

Piles of rocks, known as "cairns," are designed to be visible in thick fog. Their size can vary from a few rocks to a large stack of boulders.

## DIRECTIONAL SIGNS

When reading markers, look out for painted arrows or variations in the blazing, such as a bend. This indicates a change of direction in the trail.

*Face the direction of travel*

*Knees are your center of gravity*

*Stay as upright as possible*

*Use your arms for balance*

*Use your arms to break your fall*

*Keep your knees bent as if you're skiing downhill*

**1** Ensuring the scree is fine and deep, use gentle hops to launch yourself down the slope. Keep balanced and let gravity do the hard work.

**2** As you build up momentum and rhythm, dig your heels into the slope and slide a short distance with each step, avoiding leaning forward.

**3** If you lose your balance temporarily, use your arms to steady yourself, relax your knees, and continue your descent.

# CROSSING RIVERS

**RIVER CROSSINGS ARE DANGEROUS** and should be avoided unless absolutely necessary. In a survival situation, once you are cold and wet—which can lead to hypothermia—it is hard to get warm and dry. Always check your map for routes around the river, and choose the safest available crossing point.

## CROSSING SAFELY

Before you get into the water, make sure you have a change of clothes or means of getting dry on the other side. In cold conditions, collect everything you need to get a fire going (tinder, kindling, and dry wood), and keep this dry as you cross.

## CHOOSING YOUR CROSSING POINT

Walking upstream generally leads to shallower water, but be aware that even shallow water can have strong currents, as can water that looks calm on the surface. Always check for bridges further up- or downstream.

**WADING BASICS**
Wear footwear when wading to protect your feet from rocks and other dangers. Remove pants to keep them dry and decrease resistance in the water. Use a walking staff for added support.

Trees on the opposite bank provide shelter from the wind after exiting the water

Exposed rocks can be dangerous if you slip onto them

Avoid crossing on the outside of bends where water flows faster

Watch out for unusual variations in the flow of the water—there may be rocks beneath

Always assess how fast-moving the water is, and use your walking staff to assess depth

Look for shallow banks, as they make entering and exiting the water easier

This gravel shoal can be a good halfway point, but be aware of fast-flowing water chanelled around it

Cross downstream of debris or fallen trees, as it is easy to get caught up and dragged under the water

# WADING WITH OTHERS

Crossing in a group is safer than crossing alone. Linking your arms together creates a stronger, more stable structure against the current and provides backup for anyone who falls. Loosen the straps of your backpack, and place only one arm through them, so you can release the pack quickly if you fall.

**WARNING!**
Never cross white water, or rivers that have flooded. In these situations it is safer not to cross at all than to risk injury.

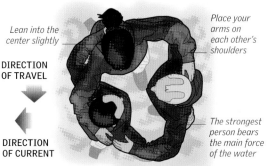

*Lean into the center slightly*

*Place your arms on each other's shoulders*

DIRECTION OF TRAVEL

DIRECTION OF CURRENT

*The strongest person bears the main force of the water*

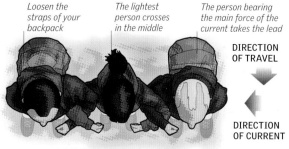

*Loosen the straps of your backpack*

*The lightest person crosses in the middle*

*The person bearing the main force of the current takes the lead*

DIRECTION OF TRAVEL

DIRECTION OF CURRENT

## CROSSING IN A HUDDLE

Positioning the strongest person upstream, with the others providing stability and support, link your arms tightly and take short, deliberate steps across the river.

## CROSSING IN A LINE

Keeping well balanced, cross the river perpendicular to the current. Move slowly and position each step carefully to avoid being swept away by the force of the water.

# WADING ALONE

Wading across a river alone is not ideal, but if you have no option then your walking staff or "survivor's third leg" (see p. 72)—or simply any long stout stick—will provide additional support and balance. Use it as a probe to alert you to any sudden changes of depth in the river bed.

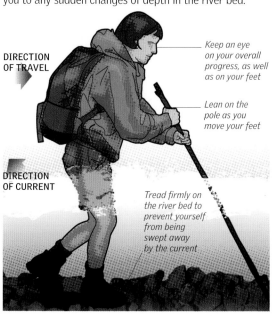

DIRECTION OF TRAVEL

*Keep an eye on your overall progress, as well as on your feet*

*Lean on the pole as you move your feet*

DIRECTION OF CURRENT

*Tread firmly on the river bed to prevent yourself from being swept away by the current*

## USING A WALKING STAFF

Facing the current, walk diagonally across the river, placing each foot down firmly and deliberately, and leaning on your walking staff for support. Your feet and your staff are your three points of contact—keep at least two of them in contact with the river bed at all times.

# CROSSING WITH ROPES

Using ropes is a good option for dangerous crossings, but they can get tangled, and drag you under the water. Always aim for the easiest and safest option—using ropes is complicated and should be your last resort.

*Safety rope is attached to a tree*

*Each rope is paid out by a person on the bank*

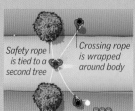

*Safety rope is tied to a second tree*

*Crossing rope is wrapped around body*

**1** A "safety" rope is tied to a tree and then carried across by the strongest person, who also takes a "crossing" rope with a carabina tied centrally.

**2** The safety rope is tied to a tree and the carabina clipped to the safety rope. The carabina is pulled back and fixed to the next person to cross.

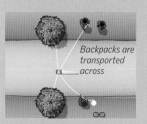

*Backpacks are transported across*

*The last person to cross is supported by the others*

**3** He or she crosses upstream of the safety rope, holding it for support. Backpacks can be clipped to the carabina and transported, too.

**4** The final person unties the safety rope from the tree, wraps it around his or her body, and wades across, supported by the others.

# SCRAMBLING AND CLIMBING

**CLIMBING WITHOUT ROPES** is known as "scrambling." As with roped techniques, the idea is to maintain three points of contact with the rock at all times—either two feet and one hand or both hands and one foot. Your legs should power the climb, with your arms used predominantly for balance. Proceed carefully, making sure you are always balanced and confident of your next move.

**WARNING!**
Climbing is a dangerous activity that should only be considered as a last resort. Ideally, plan ahead using your map to find a way around the obstacle.

## HAND AND FOOT HOLDS

When planning your route, choose your hand and foot holds carefully. Don't reach too far, and test each hold for stability before using it to support your weight.

### EDGES
For very small footholds, place the inside edge of your foot in the hold in the rock to take the pressure off your toes.

### FINGER SHELVES
Curl your fingers over the rock for a secure fingerhold. The larger the fingerhold, the more secure it will be.

### LARGE POCKETS
Placing your foot securely within the pocket, balance yourself so both your arms and legs take the strain.

### SIDE PULLS
Side pulls can be used to maintain balance or to pull yourself across the rock. Grip the rock tightly.

### PROTRUSIONS
If possible, place the entire sole of your foot on the protrusion. If only the ball of your foot will fit, keep your heel low.

### HAND JAMS
Insert your hand into the crack, push your thumb into your palm, arch your hand, and wedge it tightly inside.

## BASIC CLIMBING TECHNIQUES

Always climb within your capabilities. It's important not to take any risks, as it's far safer to descend and start the climb again than to chance a fall. Before you start to climb, plan the easiest and safest route.

## SCRAMBLING

When moving across the rock you will need to combine a variety of techniques to negotiate different obstacles. Always plan your moves several steps in advance, and keep three points of contact with the rock at all times.

*Take the weight of your backpack into account when moving*

*Always ensure you can move back down if you can't move up*

## MANTELLING

The mantelling technique is used to climb overhangs in the rock. Use your lead ankle and then your knee to lever your body up over the obstacle. It's a physically challenging technique, but useful.

*Lift your ankle onto the shelf, followed by your knee*

*Lean your weight on your elbows until you are ready to push up with your arms*

*Supporting leg*

## CHIMNEYING

To climb up the inside of large rock clefts, or "chimneys," use the chimneying technique. To ascend, move your back and hands up the wall, and push and follow with your legs. It's easy to get stuck at the top so plan your exit route carefully.

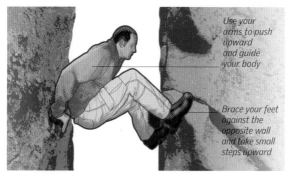

*Use your arms to push upward and guide your body*

*Brace your feet against the opposite wall and take small steps upward*

### STRADDLING

If the chimney is relatively wide, you may need to alter your body position to straddle the gap. With a leg and arm on each wall, inch yourself up the rock using your legs to push your body upward.

*Use your arms to steady yourself*

*Wear shoes or boots with a good grip*

## CLIMBING WITH EQUIPMENT

The advantages of climbing with ropes cannot be underestimated as far as safety is concerned, although a lot of specialized equipment is required. As well as ropes, helmets, and harnesses, climbers can also use screws to secure themselves to the rock as they progress each stage.

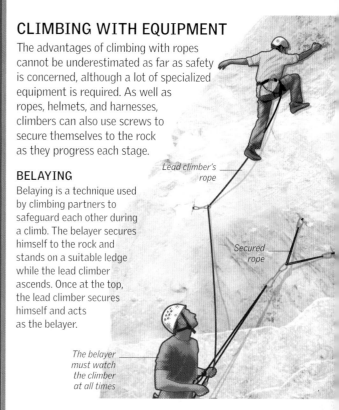

*Lead climber's rope*

*Secured rope*

### BELAYING

Belaying is a technique used by climbing partners to safeguard each other during a climb. The belayer secures himself to the rock and stands on a suitable ledge while the lead climber ascends. Once at the top, the lead climber secures himself and acts as the belayer.

*The belayer must watch the climber at all times*

## ICE CLIMBING

Ice climbers utilize similar techniques to rock climbers, although they carry ice axes and wear crampons on their feet, to help them grip the ice.

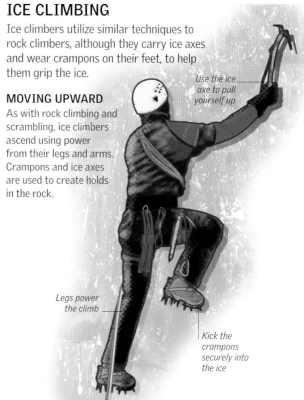

*Use the ice axe to pull yourself up*

### MOVING UPWARD

As with rock climbing and scrambling, ice climbers ascend using power from their legs and arms. Crampons and ice axes are used to create holds in the rock.

*Legs power the climb*

*Kick the crampons securely into the ice*

# EXTREME SURVIVAL— IN THE MOUNTAINS

## USEFUL EQUIPMENT

- Two-way radio
- Avalanche beacon and probe
- Waterproof clothing
- Spare clothing layers
- Collapsible shovel
- Climbing equipment, if needed
- Signal flares
- Map, compass, GPS
- Survival tin, bushcraft knife
- Cell/satellite phone
- Poncho/bivy sack

**STEVEN GREEN, 32, AN EXPERIENCED HILL WALKER** from Dumfries, Scotland, spent four nights lying on a remote mountainside after a life-threatening fall. Suffering from a broken jaw and fractured skull, he survived via a combination of good preparation, quick thinking, and improvisation.

On Thursday, October 7, 1999, Steven set out alone for a trek in the hills of Wester Ross in the northwest Highlands of Scotland. He was well equipped with, among other things, a cell phone, bivy sack, pita bread, and water—and had taken the wise precaution (or so he thought) of informing his girlfriend of his intended route.

Following an all-day trek and an overnight camp, he was descending the mountain on Friday when he slipped on wet grass and fell down a waterfall, coming to rest in the shallow, rocky riverbed. He knew he would not survive for long in the cold water so, despite being in intense pain, he crawled to the relative safety of the bank, then wisely got

**"HE SLIPPED ON WET GRASS AND FELL DOWN A WATERFALL"**

into his bivy sack for warmth and waited. He sustained himself by eating pita bread, which he softened in water because he couldn't chew. His phone was damaged in the fall so he was unable to call for help. When he failed to return home on time, the alarm was raised by Steven's girlfriend, but she had forgotten to write down his intended route so no one knew his exact location.

Steven experienced a further four days and nights of exposure while local and RAF rescue teams and search-and-rescue dogs combed the mountains for him. As the days passed they feared the worst, but when they located Steven on Tuesday morning— after finding his car and, inside it, his route map—they found him in good spirits. At hospital Steven was diagnosed with a fractured skull, broken jaw, missing front teeth, cuts and bruises, and a leg injury—but he was alive.

# WHAT TO DO

## ARE YOU IN DANGER?

 NO YES

If you are in a group, try to help any others who are in danger

Get yourself out of it:
**Elements**—Find or improvise immediate shelter
**Animals**—Avoid confrontation and move away from danger
**Injury**—Stabilize condition and apply first aid

## ASSESS YOUR SITUATION
*See pages 234–35*

## DOES ANYONE KNOW YOU WILL BE MISSING OR WHERE YOU ARE?

 NO YES

If no one knows you are missing or where you are, you will need to notify people of your plight by any means at your disposal

If you are missed, a rescue party will almost certainly be dispatched to find you

## DO YOU HAVE ANY MEANS OF COMMUNICATION?

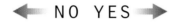 NO YES

You are faced with surviving for an indefinite period—until you are located or you find help

If you have a cell or satellite phone, let someone know your predicament. If your situation is serious enough to be worthy of emergency rescue, and you have a Personal Locator Beacon (PLB), you should consider this option

## CAN YOU SURVIVE WHERE YOU ARE? *

 NO YES

If you cannot survive where you are and there are no physical reasons why you should remain, you will have to move to a location that offers a better chance of survival, rescue, or both

Address the Principles of Survival: Protection, Location, Water, Food

### YOU WILL HAVE TO MOVE **

### YOU SHOULD STAY **

## DO

- Keep all clothing dry and clean
- Collect drinking water from fast-moving streams; filter and disinfect if you have the means
- Be on constant lookout for signs of cold-related injuries such as frostnip, frostbite, and hypothermia
- Regulate your clothing to avoid overheating when moving and hypothermia when static
- Use a walking staff to aid safe movement
- Watch the weather closely and be prepared to change your plans at short notice—mountain climates are highly unpredictable
- Improvise shelter when not on the move

## DON'T

- Descend hills in a careless manner; zig-zagging across hills is less tiring and puts less strain on leg muscles
- Travel at too fast a pace—high altitude equals less air and this will place greater demands on even a fit person
- Sweat too much, as the moisture will chill you further
- Ignore any opportunities to collect dry tinder/kindling

## DON'T

- Allow your extremities to get too cold as those areas are most susceptible to frostbite
- Overlook the dangers of carbon monoxide poisoning in cramped shelter. Don't let candles, stoves, or fires burn all night
- Breathe on your hands to warm them up: you are exhaling warm air that you will have to replace with cold

## DO

- Select a shelter site that offers protection from the elements. Build it no bigger than it needs to be
- Fill plastic bags or spare clothing with dry foliage and use as a mattress or pillow to insulate you from the cold, damp ground
- Deploy all your aids to location and prepare for immediate use
- Check upstream for the quality of your water source
- Light a fire and (if in a group) take turns tending it to keep it going all night
- Continually re-assess your situation and adapt your actions as necessary.
- Be constantly alert for signs of rescue

* If you cannot survive where you are, but you also cannot move owing to injury or other factors, you must do everything you can to attract rescue.
** If your situation changes (for instance, you are "moving" to find help, and you find a suitable location in which you can stay and survive) consult the alternative "Do" and "Don'ts."

# MOVING OVER SNOW

**PREPARATION IS ESSENTIAL** when hiking over frozen terrain. Not only must you be physically fit—the conditions make for slow, exhausting progress—but you must also have the right equipment and know how to use it. Wearing snowshoes or skis, and breathable and layered clothing to regulate your temperature, is essential. With the correct techniques you can hike safely and enjoy the surroundings.

## WARNING!
Walking over deep snow without snowshoes is called "post-holing" and should be avoided unless absolutely necessary. Sinking into the snow will leave you exhausted and very wet, which in cold conditions can quickly lead to hypothermia. The exertion can also cause sweating and a dangerous reduction in your body temperature when you stop.

## SNOW AND ICE
Knowing how to deal with different types of snow and ice is invaluable when hiking over frozen terrain.

### DEEP SNOW
■ If in a group, walk in single file and take turns at the front: the most strenuous position, as you're creating the path.
■ Avoid rocks—in spring, they absorb heat and the snow above becomes unstable.

### FROZEN CRUST
■ Use a walking staff to test the snow ahead. An ice crust above deep snow may take your weight, but progress carefully.
■ Later in the day you may come across melted depressions, called "sun cups." Cross on the rims to avoid sinking into the snow.

### SLOPES
■ Kick firmly into the slope and test your weight before ascending. When descending, you can use a technique called "boot skiing" (skiing without your skis).
■ Choose your route based on the conditions: travel in straight lines if you are able to, or in zig-zags if the terrain is steep.

### ICE
■ Always progress carefully, using your walking staff to test the ice, especially over rivers and lakes. If in a group, rope yourselves together for safety.
■ Wear crampons for extra grip. On very steep slopes, use your ice ax to cut steps.
■ Use your ice ax to halt a fall by turning to face the slope and digging it into the ice.

### GLACIERS
■ Never attempt to cross glaciers without a guide—glaciers require specialized skills.

## WAYS OF TRAVELING
When traveling over snow, your main aim is to get to your destination as safely as possible, without expending too much energy or losing too much body heat. Methods range from improvised snowshoes to motor vehicles.

### USING SNOWSHOES AND SKIS
Snowshoes and skis are an effective way of traveling over snow. They work by spreading your body weight over a larger surface area, which enables you to walk on the surface of the snow rather than sink into it. Always set off cold, as you'll warm up quickly, and add or remove layers as required.

Ski mask protects your eyes from glare

Wear a backpack to keep both arms free

The shoe's ability to pivot reduces drag and improves maneuverability

Wear breathable clothing so you don't overheat

Waterproof pants or gaiters keep your legs dry

Snowshoes stop you from sinking into the snow

Ski poles can be used to test the snow ahead

# MAKING IMPROVISED SNOWSHOES

If you don't have any pre-manufactured snowshoes—for example, in a survival situation—you can make some very simple shoes to help you negotiate the snow more effectively, using your knife, some green wood, and cordage. They may take time to build, but will save time and effort in the long run.

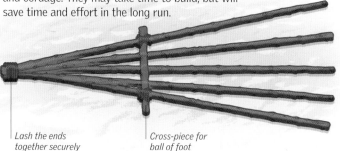

*Lash the ends together securely*

*Cross-piece for ball of foot*

**1** Cut five lengths of green wood. They should be as thick as your thumb and the same length as the distance from your foot to your armpit. Cut three shorter lengths for the cross-pieces.
- Lash the ends of the five longer pieces together securely using cordage.
- Calculate where the ball of your foot will be positioned on the shoe and lash a cross-piece across the five lengths. Ensure the shoe will balance.

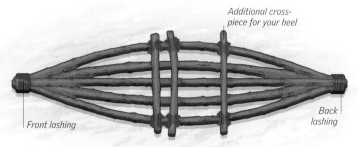

*Additional cross-piece for your heel*

*Front lashing*

*Back lashing*

**2** Lash the five loose lengths of wood together at the back of the shoe. It's important to make this lashing as secure as possible.
- Fix the second cross-piece roughly 2 in (5 cm) behind the first.
- Lash the third cross-piece where your heel will rest.
- Repeat steps 1 and 2 to make a second shoe before progressing to step 3.

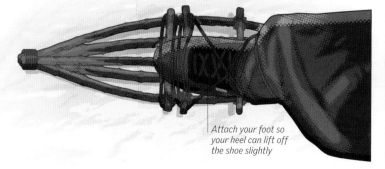

*Attach your foot so your heel can lift off the shoe slightly*

**3** Place your foot on top of the snow shoe, ensuring that the ball of your foot sits directly over the front cross-piece and that your heel is positioned on the back cross-piece.
- Tie your boot to the snow shoe using whatever cordage you have, but ensure the heel is allowed to remain free to pivot. Repeat for the other foot.

## ALTERNATIVE METHODS

These alternative methods will also spread your weight on the snow. If you have no gaiters, tie plastic bags around the bottom of your legs to keep them dry.

### USING BRANCHES

Ideal for short distances, a simple way to get you out of deep snow and to a road or track is to attach branches to your feet using cordage. Select a tree, such as pine, that has strong, close branches.

*Use cordage to tie the front of your boot to the bough*

*Ensure the back of your foot can lift slightly as you walk*

### USING SAPLINGS

You will need branches that have some flexibility. Gently bend the longest branch into a teardrop shape and lash the two ends together. Heating the saplings over a fire will make them easier to bend.

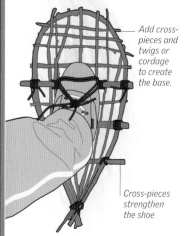

*Add cross-pieces and twigs or cordage to create the base.*

*Cross-pieces strengthen the shoe*

# MAKING A SLED

If you find yourself in a survival situation with heavy equipment to carry over snow, making a simple sled or "pulk" (see panel, right) will help you transport it more efficiently. You could also build one to transport an injured person or small child. You can make your sled as large or as small as you need, providing you follow these basic principles.

**TOOLS AND MATERIALS**
- Survival saw or pocket chainsaw
- Knife
- Cordage
- Forked branch (for bulk of sled)
- Two branches (for bracing pieces)
- Sticks (for cross-pieces)

**1** Using a short saw or penknife, cut a forked branch to form the base of the sled.
- Tie the two ends of the fork to the main branch with cord. This creates tension and forces the branches to curve and act as runners.

*Lash the bracing piece to the main branch*

*Attach the cord to the main branch using a slip knot (see p. 142)*

*Attach the cord to the end of the fork using a taut line hitch (see p. 145)*

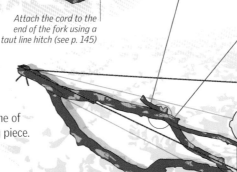

**2** Lash an additional branch to one of the runners to create a bracing piece.
- Repeat on the other side.
- The bracing pieces strengthen the branches and prevent any cord from touching the ground—if it does, it will wear out quickly and disintegrate once the sled is on the move.

*Adding bracing pieces creates a support for the carrying platform*

## ANIMAL POWER

Huskies, or sled dogs, are ideal for transporting people and equipment across winter terrain. Because of their thick coat they can endure very low temperatures, and their large, furred feet allow them to move quickly over snow. Huskies work well as a team and can pull heavy loads easily and efficiently.

## TRAVELING WITH DOGS

Although huskies are easy to care for and relatively simple to handle, you should not undertake an expedition with dogs unless you are traveling with an expert or have first undergone extensive training. The same goes for all expeditions in snowy terrain.

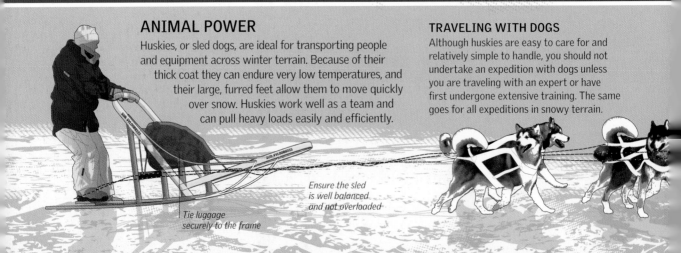

*Ensure the sled is well balanced and not overloaded*

*Tie luggage securely to the frame*

# HUMAN POWER

Pulling your equipment behind you using a pulk is an extremely efficient way of moving over snow. Pulks are small, low-slung toboggans, typically made from lightweight plastic, and come in many different sizes.

## TRAVELING WITH A PULK

Although pulks are the most efficient method of carrying heavy loads over snow using human power, they can be hard work, especially in softer snow. Wear breathable clothing to allow excess body heat to escape. Know how to release your harness quickly in an emergency. If you are in a group, one person can be harnessed to the rear of the pulk to act as a brakeman when going downhill.

*Attach the pulk to your body using a harness*

**WARNING!**
Take care when travelling down slopes, as the pulk can easily pick up speed and become difficult to control if you have no brakeman.

*A pulk can be used to carry equipment or a person*

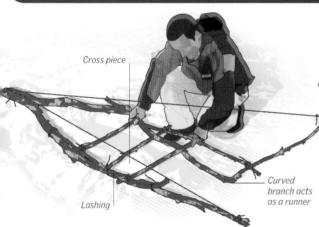

*Cross piece*

*Lashing*

*Curved branch acts as a runner*

**3** Lay sticks across both bracing pieces and lash them together. These cross-pieces strengthen the structure.
- You can use as many sticks as you can find, but three or four should suffice.
- These cross-pieces will also form the main carrying platform of your sled.

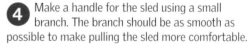

*Tie the handle securely so it can take the strain*

*Tie luggage tightly to the sled*

**4** Make a handle for the sled using a small branch. The branch should be as smooth as possible to make pulling the sled more comfortable.
- Attach the handle to the front of the sled using a long piece of cord.

# MOTOR POWER

Snowmobiles are practical and quick, and have revolutionized arctic travel. They are easier to handle than huskies, and can reach relatively high speeds. However, although you can cover great distances in short periods of time, if anything goes wrong you may be far from help. Always carry survival equipment when you travel.

*Linking the dogs together helps them to power forward in unison*

*Harnesses allow the dogs to pull comfortably*

## BEFORE YOU GO

Prior to a snowmobile trip, regardless of distance, it is vital to check your vehicle maintenance and ensure that you have sufficient fuel for the trip. Plan your route carefully and inform someone of your plans so that they can raise the alarm if you don't reach your destination when planned. Dress warmly, wear goggles or a ski mask to reduce glare, and drive safely.

# USING PACK ANIMALS

**PACK ANIMALS CAN BE USED** to transport heavy loads when hiking over wilderness terrain. Ideally suited to carrying substantial loads, they can cover great distances in areas where vehicles would struggle. When you are organized, and know how to care for the animals, traveling with pack animals can be very rewarding.

## LOADING THE ANIMAL

Stand on level ground, making sure that the animal has all four legs placed firmly on the ground. Before placing the loaded panniers onto the animal, lift them to ensure they are well balanced. Rearrange if one is lighter. You may need to hobble or blindfold the animal to keep it still while loading.

## ANIMAL WELFARE

Remember to transport food, water, and supplies for the animal as well as for yourself. Their welfare is paramount, so treat them well.

### PACKING TIPS
- Know the capabilities of your animal, and what weight they can safely carry over the necessary distance.
- Before loading the animal, groom it well and check for sores or ticks.
- Place heavier items at the bottom of your panniers and lighter items at the top.

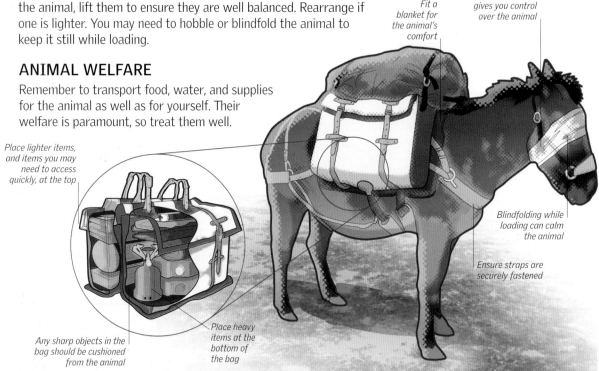

Fit a blanket for the animal's comfort

A headcollar gives you control over the animal

Place lighter items, and items you may need to access quickly, at the top

Blindfolding while loading can calm the animal

Ensure straps are securely fastened

Any sharp objects in the bag should be cushioned from the animal

Place heavy items at the bottom of the bag

## PACK TRAINS

Roping animals together on the trail is standard practice when traveling with more than one animal. When tying them together, ensure the ropes are long enough to allow the animals to walk comfortably, and short enough to prevent tripping.

### THE PEOPLE

Appoint a driver to lead the group and take control of navigation. You will need sufficient people to control and care for the animals.

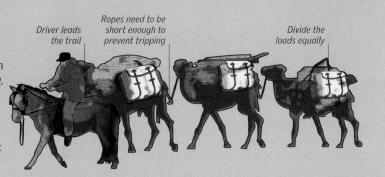

Driver leads the trail

Ropes need to be short enough to prevent tripping

Divide the loads equally

# USING PACK ANIMALS TO SURVIVE

In an emergency situation, your priorities change significantly when using pack animals. Unpack the panniers and remove any heavy items not essential for survival. If necessary, you can climb on and ride to safety or, in a worst-case scenario, your animal can be used for food.

## CARRYING INJURED PEOPLE

If a member of your group is injured, build a makeshift stretcher (see pp. 278–79) and use the animal to drag him or her to safety.

Strap the stretcher securely to the animal

Try to make the patient as comfortable as possible

**WARNING!**
Do not attempt to use pack animals without expert help or extensive training. The animals require a lot of care, and you will need to organize your days meticulously.

# CHOOSING YOUR ANIMAL

The availability of pack animals depends on the region you are traveling in. Within any region, your choice of animal should take into account the load you are expecting them to carry, the distance you require them to travel, and the terrain you plan to cross. However, remember that individual animals' abilities can vary depending on their age and size.

| ANIMAL | REGION | AVERAGE LOAD | ADVANTAGES | DISADVANTAGES |
|---|---|---|---|---|
| Horse | Worldwide | ▪ 175–240 lb (80–110 kg)<br>▪ 20 percent of body weight | ▪ Easy to train, with a good temperament<br>▪ Strong<br>▪ Can tolerate heat<br>▪ Can manage steep terrain | ▪ Require grooming<br>▪ Can stray from camp if not securely tethered |
| Mule | Eurasia, Americas | ▪ 120–180 lb (55–80 kg)<br>▪ 20 percent of body weight | ▪ Will stick by a mare closely—this can be used to keep them moving and to keep them within the camp at night<br>▪ Very hardy and can manage steep terrain | ▪ Young mules can be easily startled, so good training is essential<br>▪ Stubborn |
| Husky | Arctic | ▪ 85lb (40kg)<br>▪ 7 dogs can pull 600lb (270 kg) | ▪ Hardy—can cope well with snow and cold conditions<br>▪ Can travel fast | ▪ Need a lot of fresh meat, which must be carried<br>▪ Prone to fight among themselves |
| Camel | Central Asia, North Africa, Australia | ▪ 198–308 lb (90–140 kg)<br>▪ 30 percent of body weight | ▪ Versatile on different terrains<br>▪ Can drink up to a quarter of its body weight and then go without water for several days | ▪ Strong-willed and difficult to control<br>▪ Violent—can spit and bite |
| Llama | Andes | ▪ 77–123 lb (35–55 kg)<br>▪ 25–30 percent of body weight | ▪ Minimal environmental impact<br>▪ Travels well at high altitudes on difficult and steep terrain | ▪ Makes horses and mules nervous<br>▪ Can be difficult to control if poorly trained |
| Elephant (Indian) | South Asia | ▪ 1,650–2,750 lb (750–1,250 kg)<br>▪ 25 percent of body weight | ▪ Can carry very heavy loads<br>▪ Can manage steep terrain | ▪ Slow-moving<br>▪ Requires large amounts of food and water<br>▪ Takes time to train |
| Ox | Eurasia, Americas | ▪ 300–450 lb (135–205 kg)<br>▪ 30 percent of body weight | ▪ Hardworking<br>▪ Very strong<br>▪ Surefooted and can manage steep terrain | ▪ Slow-moving<br>▪ Stubborn |

# FOUR-WHEEL DRIVING

**A FOUR-WHEEL-DRIVE (4WD)** vehicle can cover large areas of difficult terrain that would be inaccessible in a 2WD vehicle. With an experienced driver, most 4WD vehicles can tackle deep mud, water, snow, ice, and sand.

## CHOOSING YOUR VEHICLE

When choosing your vehicle it's important to consider what you'll be using it for. Large vehicles have more internal space than smaller ones, but may find it harder to negotiate very rough ground without getting stuck. Similarly, very powerful vehicles can cross almost any terrain but use a lot of fuel, so may not be a viable option for long-term expeditions.

### EXPEDITION CHECKLIST
- Check your map and inform others of your route and intended timeframe.
- Ensure the vehicle is fit for the journey, with all necessary spares. Check the fuel, oil, water, brakes, and hydraulic fluids, and check that there are no leaks.
- Inspect the tire treads, wheel nuts, lights, and steering arms.
- Always carry spare water, wheel(s), and fuel, as well as survival equipment, sand ladders, a 12v heavy-duty tire inflator, winching strap, and first aid kit.

Roof rack with high sides is advisable

Use a winching mechanism if the vehicle gets stuck

Load must be evenly distributed and tied down securely

Always carry a spare wheel

A high axle ensures good ground clearance

## GENERAL DRIVING TECHNIQUES

Four-wheel-drive vehicles enable you to manually switch between two-wheel-drive, for driving on roads, and four-wheel-drive, for low-traction conditions, such as on soft ground. The difference is the number of wheels powered by the engine at any one time.

### WARNING!
Don't hook your thumbs around the steering wheel when driving over rough terrain. Hitting a rut can jerk the wheel and break them.

### CHOOSING A ROUTE

When unsure about the conditions immediately ahead, walk the route first, checking for potential problems and obstacles. Where necessary, mark the route you have walked and follow these markers when you drive. Ask yourself whether you really need to go that way and, if so, which route is best to avoid getting stuck. And, if you do get stuck, what are your options for self-recovery or escape?

### WHEN TO ENGAGE 4WD

Engaging 4WD uses up a lot of fuel and should not be used on hard roads because of the risk of damaging tires and gears. Always choose the four-wheel-drive option on difficult terrain. It allows you to travel in a very low gear and gives the vehicle a far superior traction. Just before starting to cross the rough ground, stop the vehicle and engage the four-wheel-drive.

### DRIVING AS A TEAM

Driving off-road over rough terrain is both mentally and physically tiring. Take regular breaks and share the driving if in a group. You should always have at least two people in the vehicle:

- A driver—who takes responsibility for powering and steering the vehicle.
- A spotter—who takes responsibility for navigation and helps the driver pick a good route across the terrain. This may involve getting out of the vehicle and guiding the driver across a difficult section of ground.

# DRIVING OVER DIFFICULT TERRAIN

A 4WD vehicle handles difficult terrain well because all four wheels can be powered by the engine at any one time (gas engines are generally more powerful, but diesel engines last longer and work well at low speeds). Using a few simple techniques, you will find that you are able to drive over terrain—and to places—that would otherwise be inaccessible. Always remember that the principle behind 4WD is to reduce the chances of you getting stuck—not to allow you to go further until you do get stuck.

## MAXIMUM TRACTION

Your vehicle's traction on soft surfaces can be improved by lowering your tire pressure slightly. As a guide, place a brick $\frac{1}{2}$in (1 cm) away from the side of a rear tire on flat ground, deflate the tire until it touches the brick, measure this pressure, and apply to all four tires. Make sure you can reinflate them.

## DRIVING ON SAND

In soft sand the tires tend to move the sand from the front of the tire to the rear of the tire. If forward movement is halted for even a few seconds the wheel can dig itself into a hole. To prevent this, continually steer from side to side, so that the tire steers out of its own ruts. Avoid rapid changes in speed.

## MUDDY TRACKS

Driving in mud requires concentration and the ability to adapt your driving to suit the conditions. In deep mud, use wide tires or lower the tire pressure slightly; however, if there is a hard surface below the mud this will make things worse. Steering outside existing track ruts is most likely to ensure the best traction.

Apply plenty of engine power

Lower your tire pressure slightly

Deep tread helps the vehicle to grip the track

## DRIVING ON SNOW AND ICE

Snow and ice require very smooth driving methods. Apply gradual pressure to the accelerator and brakes to avoid wheel spin, use low gears, especially when traveling downhill, and avoid changing gears unnecessarily. Using snow chains will increase traction, and you should practice fitting them before you need them.

## CROSSING WATER

Always walk your route before driving across water. If the water seems too deep or the current too fast, don't attempt the crossing. It's important to drive at the correct speed—too fast will send water everywhere, but driving too slowly may flood the engine bay.

Snow chains give tires additional traction

Fit drain plugs if applicable

The water level should not rise above the top of your wheels

# RECOVERY FROM SOFT GROUND

Although using the correct techniques will certainly improve your chances of crossing soft ground successfully, it's important to know what to do if you do get stuck. Ideally you should never set out on a driving expedition with fewer than two vehicles. A second vehicle can be used for winching, dealing with breakdowns, or driving for help.

### EQUIPMENT LIST
- Winching mechanism and strap
- Cable or tow rope
- Spare tire (inflated)
- Shovel and saw
- Sleeping bag or blanket
- Branches or stakes
- Sand ladders or mats

## BASIC RECOVERY TECHNIQUES

When you get stuck, it's tempting to keep trying to aggressively free your vehicle. However, churning up what solid ground is left—and digging yourself into deeper ruts—will only make things more difficult in the long run. Stop, evaluate your options (reversing or pushing, digging, using branches, and winching), and calmly decide how best to achieve your aim. Don't act in haste—an ill-thought-out plan could leave you in more trouble than you were in originally.

### REVERSING OR PUSHING

If you can't free the vehicle using four-wheel drive, try alternating between reversing and driving forward in first gear.
- If this has no effect, ask the passengers to get out and push while you drive forward.
- If you are making the situation worse, stop immediately and try an alternative solution.

*Push as hard as you can*

*Try not to make the holes any deeper*

*Dig the exhaust and chassis free if they are also stuck*

### DIGGING

If reversing and pushing don't work, the next step toward freeing your vehicle is to dig down in front of the wheels in an attempt to create a slope that you can then drive up.
- Dig out the sand in front of each tire to create an upward slope
- Drive very gently up the slope. Avoid revving the engine as this can cause the wheels to spin and lose their grip on the ground.

*Dig a slope in front of all four wheels*

### USING BRANCHES

If the vehicle still won't move, place branches, wooden planks, sand ladders, or blankets—in fact, anything that will increase your traction—in front of the wheels. The idea is to give the tires something to grip, and it should get you moving fairly quickly.
- Without revving the engine too much, gently ease the vehicle forward onto the branches or other material.
- Maintain a slow, steady speed and continue until you are back on firmer ground.
- Once clear, remember to stop and pick up your equipment, and remove any obstacles from the track.

*Place branches in front of the wheels*

# WINCHING

If none of the basic techniques work, and your vehicle is still stuck, it's time to consider winching. Use a cable attached to an electric-powered winching mechanism to pull the vehicle out of the hole via a strong anchor point. You can winch to another vehicle if you're traveling in convoy, although you do run the risk of both vehicles getting stuck. When winching, take time to assess your options—using a natural anchor point is the easiest method and should be your first approach.

## NATURAL ANCHOR POINTS

Trees, rocks, roots, or deadfalls can all be used as anchor points. When using a tree, always place the strap or cable near the ground, and use a winch strap where possible to avoid damaging the tree. If the tree looks as if it may not be able to provide the required support, tie the tree to others in the vicinity. If you intend to use rocks, ensure they are large enough and firmly embedded in the ground.

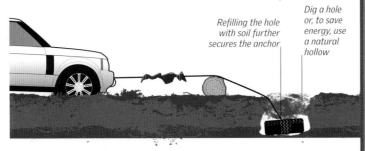

*Place a blanket over the cable to help reduce whiplash if the cable breaks*

*Use a log or rock to provide an angle for the winch*

## BURIED ANCHOR POINTS

If there are no natural anchor points, you can construct an improvised anchor by burying objects such as logs or a spare wheel. Dig a hole in the ground that's at least 3 ft (1 m) deep, attach your winch cable to your improvised anchor, then bury the anchor in the hole. Refill the hole to secure it. If you're using a tire, use the tire lever behind your spare wheel as an attachment point for the cable.

*Refilling the hole with soil further secures the anchor*

*Dig a hole or, to save energy, use a natural hollow*

## WINCHING TO A STAKE

A series of long stakes in the ground can also provide an improvised anchor point. You will need a long, sturdy main stake—to which the winch cable is attached—and a series of supporting stakes, lashed together for additional strength. Push the stakes securely into the ground at a slight angle. Be careful not to stand near the stakes when winching, in case they come loose.

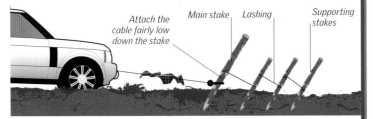

*Attach the cable fairly low down the stake*

*Main stake*  *Lashing*  *Supporting stakes*

# EMERGENCY ACTION

Knowing what to do in certain emergency situations will help you stay calm if the worst happens.

## FRONT SKIDS

The term "skid" covers any kind of slide in which the wheels fail to grip the road. In a front skid—also called an "understeer"—the front wheels fail to turn when you steer so the vehicle continues to travel forward.
- Steer in the direction of the skid but be careful not to oversteer. If you're on ice and skidding straight, step on the clutch or shift to neutral.
- Once you have gained control, correct your course and continue driving. Consult your driver's manual if you have anti-lock brakes.

## REAR SKIDS

In a rear skid, the back wheels lose control and the vehicle rotates more than usual and can spin.
- Steer in the direction of the skid but face toward where you want to travel.
- Once facing in the right direction, bring the steering wheel back to the center and continue to steer, regardless of what the rear is doing, until you have gained total control.

## BRAKE FAILURE

Before setting out on a drive, always check to see whether there is brake fluid leaking from the vehicle. If so, don't travel. If the brakes fail when on the move, do the following:
- Without turning off the engine, shift down the gears to reduce speed while maintaining control.
- Once the vehicle reaches a speed of less than 25 mph (40 kph) apply the handbrake, keeping a firm grip on the steering wheel.

## ACCELERATOR MALFUNCTION

If the accelerator sticks and your engine will not slow down, you can decelerate by putting the vehicle into neutral and applying the brakes.
- If it's safe to do so, switch off the engine, but you'll lose functions like power steering and lights.
- Steer safely to a stop. If possible, avoid using the handbrake as this may cause a skid—although it may be necessary if you need to avoid a collision.

# KAYAKING AND CANOEING

**TRAVELING IN A KAYAK OR CANOE** is a good way of negotiating river systems and open water. With your equipment safely stowed in your boat, expeditions can range from short day trips to year-long adventures.

*Double-bladed paddle increases stroke rate*

*Rudder aids control*

*Lifejacket provides flotation*

## KAYAKING

Kayaks are an extremely efficient method of water transport, especially on open sea, rivers, and lakes. Their narrow design and light frame make them easy to maneuver.

*Spray deck keeps you dry and stops the kayak filling with water*

*Water-tight hatch ensures equipment is kept dry.*

## CAPSIZING IN A KAYAK

Capsizing is an almost inevitable part of kayaking in rough water. The "wet exit"—slipping out of the kayak completely while still holding on to it—is sometimes the only option, but wherever possible use an eskimo roll instead.

*Closed deck conceals space for your legs and rudder pedals*

### ESKIMO ROLL

Mastering the eskimo roll enables you to avoid getting your legs wet and having to climb back in your kayak. With practice, it should become one fluid movement.

*Handling toggle allows you to drag the kayak easily*

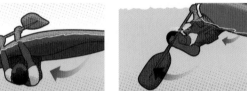

**1** From the upside-down position, twist your body to the side of the kayak.
■ Gripping your paddle, firmly push your arms out of the water, then rest them on the side of the kayak.

**2** With your head near the surface, sweep your body and paddle away from the side of the kayak.
■ At the same time, flick your hip away to start the rotation of the kayak.

**3** Continue the hip flick until the kayak returns to an upright position in the water.
■ Straighten your back so you are sitting upright again, and continue to paddle your course.

### WARNING!
■ Always wear a lifejacket. Empty water bottles in your pockets can be used as makeshift flotation devices in an emergency.
■ In a survival situation, never leave your kayak or canoe unless it is life-threatening not to do so. A kayak is highly visible, especially from the air, and is far more likely to be spotted first by rescuers.

## BASIC PADDLING SKILLS

Kayak paddles have two blades that sweep alternately through the water, propelling the kayak forward. To steer, paddle on the opposite side to the direction in which you want to go. Some kayaks have a foot-operated rudder.

**CATCH**
Place your lead blade firmly in the water so that it enters near to your feet.

*Lead blade enters the water near your feet*

**BRACE**
Rotate your torso and lead blade in preparation for the propulsive stroke.

*The power comes from your torso*

**STROKE**
Sweep your lead blade firmly through the water to propel the kayak forward.

*Keep your grip loose on the following arm*

**TRANSITION**
As the blade exits the water, repeat the catch on the other side and continue paddling.

*The transition should be as smooth as possible*

# CANOEING

As with kayaks, canoes can hold one or two people with equipment, and are powered by the body from a seated position. They are generally wider than kayaks, however, and their decks are open. Canoe paddles have one blade as opposed to two.

*Tie your gear securely to the canoe*

*Unlike kayaks, canoes usually have raised seats*

## TANDEM CANOEING

In a tandem canoe, one person should sit at the front and one at the back. Each person paddles on either side—swap sides regularly to avoid muscle fatigue and strain. The person at the back generally controls the steering, using his or her paddle like a rudder.

## CAPSIZING IN A CANOE

Because canoes are open and fill with water easily when you capsize, your greatest challenge is emptying this water out when the canoe is righted. If traveling alone, always carry a pump, or head for shallower water so you can lift the canoe and tip the water out.

### CANOE-OVER-CANOE RESCUE

If you are traveling with another canoe and are far from shallow water, the best option is the canoe-over-canoe rescue. The capsized canoe is rotated upside-down and pushed onto the rescue vessel, which empties the water out. The people on the rescue craft then rotate the canoe back to an upright position and return it to the water.

*One person in the water supports the rescue canoe*

*Turn the canoe upside down to empty the water out*

*One person in the water pushes the capsized canoe over the rescue canoe*

## KAYAKING AND CANOEING TIPS

- Research your route and weather conditions thoroughly.
- Don't overload the boat, and ensure it's well balanced.
- Carry a high-volume pump so you can rescue yourself when alone.
- If watertight bulkheads are not fitted on your kayak, use airbags to add buoyancy and reduce the amount of water that can enter a compartment.
- Use waterproof dry bags to keep your kit dry.
- Clip valuables onto the boat or yourself. If they don't float, attach a float to them so they won't sink if they fall in the water.
- Carry waterproof material and bungee cord to repair blown hatches.
- Never enter a cave alone, or without head protection.
- Fit a leash to your paddle and attach it to the craft. If you then have to perform a rescue you can throw it in the water and keep both arms free.
- Chewing gum is great for the short-term repair of small holes in the craft, as is black masking tape and plumber's repair tape.

## BASIC PADDLING SKILLS

When canoeing solo, use a "switch" style of paddling to ensure your canoe travels in a straight line—if the canoe starts to veer off course, switch sides.

### CATCH

Sit in the middle of the canoe, ensuring that it's well balanced. Reach forward and thrust the blade into the water.

*Paddle enters the water at the front of the canoe*

### DOWN STROKE

Drive the paddle swiftly and firmly down into the water so that it assumes a vertical position.

*Use strong arm motions*

### PULL STROKE

Firmly pull the paddle blade backward through the water. This will propel the canoe forward.

*Paddle generates forward momentum*

### REPEAT STROKE

Lift the blade out of the water toward the rear of the canoe and return to the starting position to repeat the stroke.

*Paddle leaves the water at the rear*

# BUILDING A RAFT

**IF VENTURING INTO** the wilderness, it is useful to know how to build an improvised raft or flotation aid. You may find that a major water obstacle lies between you and rescue, or you may be in an area in which dense undergrowth makes cross-country travel difficult but river travel relatively easy. However, in a survival situation you are unlikely to have a lifejacket, so assess the risks carefully.

**WARNING!**
Apart from the brushwood raft (below), most improvised rafts will float half-submerged, so you'll be constantly sitting or kneeling in water. This could lead to hypothermia in certain conditions, so build an additional raised platform if necessary.

**TOOLS AND MATERIALS**
- Knife or small saw
- Poncho, shelter sheet, or tarpaulin
- Long sticks, brushwood, and thatch
- Cordage

## MAKING A BRUSHWOOD RAFT

If you have a poncho, shelter sheet, or tarpaulin, you can construct a brushwood raft. This is a one-man raft, but if built correctly will keep you completely out of the water. Build it as close to the water as possible so you don't have to carry it far.

**1** Construct your raft near a suitable launching place.
- Lay your poncho on the ground to determine the size of the finished raft. Make sure there's enough material to come up the sides and gather on top.

**2** Peg out sticks to form an oval shape, the size and shape of your intended raft.
- Interlace brushwood and thatch tightly through the sticks to form the sides of the raft. The tighter you weave the brushwood, the stronger the body of the raft will be, and the better it will float. The height of the brushwood will also determine how high the raft sits in the water.

**3** Form a sitting platform by pushing a selection of long poles or sticks through the sides of woven brushwood. Weave the sticks under and over each other as much as you can to create a stable structure.
- Using your knife or a small saw, trim the sticks to size so that they don't protrude from the sides.
- Remove the pegs from around the brushwood.

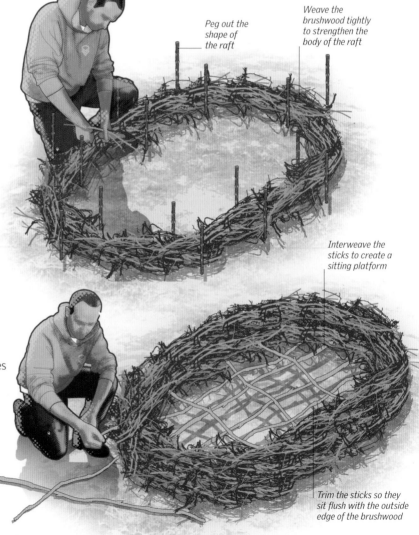

Peg out the shape of the raft

Weave the brushwood tightly to strengthen the body of the raft

Interweave the sticks to create a sitting platform

Trim the sticks so they sit flush with the outside edge of the brushwood

# MAKING A PADDLE

In most cases, you can use the current of the river for momentum rather than having to paddle, and your walking staff to maneuver the raft. However, where there is no current you will have to provide the propulsion yourself, and will need to improvise some form of paddle.

**1** Find a suitable length of green wood to form the handle. This should be as wide as possible but still comfortable to grip.
- In the end of the wood, make a split long enough to form the paddle face.
- Collect smaller branches and insert one of them into the split. Lash into place.

**2** Continue to force smaller branches into the split, lashing each one as you progress until you have a sufficient paddle area.
- Securely lash the two open splits of the handle together.
- To make the paddle more rigid, lash the ends together.

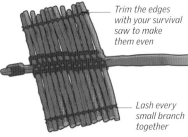

*The length of the split determines the size of the paddle face*

*Lash above the split to stop it splitting further*

*The first small stick forms the top of the paddle*

*Trim the edges with your survival saw to make them even*

*Lash every small branch together*

**4** Slide your poncho underneath the raft to form a waterproof seal.
- Push the poncho hood through to the inside and tie its neck securely to ensure it's completely water tight.
- Pull the poncho up the sides of the raft and lash securely across the top.

**5** Fill the space underneath the sitting platform with natural materials, such as additional brushwood, grass, or moss. You could also use any item that would aid buoyancy—such as empty plastic bottles or waterproof bags filled with air and tied off.
- Drag or push the raft into the water, checking to see whether it floats in shallower water before loading your equipment and climbing aboard.

*Add extra foliage to increase buoyancy and stability of raft*

# ALTERNATIVE RAFTS

Use whatever materials are available to you to make your raft. Look out for logs, bamboo, and discarded oil drums, as they are naturally buoyant materials that can be used to make an effective raft.

## LOG RAFT

To make a log raft, use dry wood—ideally standing deadwood—as this will float higher in the water. Cut notches in the logs to allow the cross-pieces to sit snugly.

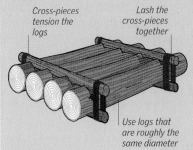

*Cross-pieces tension the logs*

*Lash the cross-pieces together*

*Use logs that are roughly the same diameter*

## BAMBOO RAFT

Bamboo is made up of hollow compartmentalized sections, which means it is ideal for raft-making. Bamboo rafts are much lighter than log rafts.

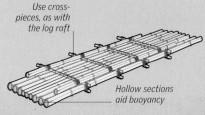

*Use cross-pieces, as with the log raft*

*Hollow sections aid buoyancy*

## DRUM RAFT

If oil drums are available, they make ideal rafts. Always take care when handling chemical drums, as they may once have contained toxins.

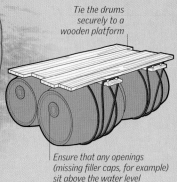

*Tie the drums securely to a wooden platform*

*Ensure that any openings (missing filler caps, for example) sit above the water level*

# SWIMMING

**WHEN THE WATER IS TOO DEEP** to wade and you don't have the materials to build a raft, you may need to swim to negotiate a water obstacle. Before you get into the water, plan how you will get warm and dry when you get out. Making a float will help to keep clothing and equipment dry.

## SURVIVAL SWIMMING

Unless you need to cross rocky ground to enter the water, remove your boots and most of your clothing to reduce drag and keep them dry. Place them either in a waterproof survival bag or in an improvised poncho float (see opposite) and float them across.

### SWIMMING ACROSS RIVERS

Choose a safe place to cross (see p. 88), and plan where you will exit the water.

■ Take the current into account as you are likely to drift downstream slightly.

■ Lower yourself in gently—never jump or dive into the water.

■ If the water is cold, gently immerse yourself until your body has recovered from the initial shock.

### THE CROSSING

Choosing a stroke you feel comfortable with (and that will expend the least energy), swim across your route with your float in one arm.

> **WARNING!**
> As with any survival activity involving water, try to avoid getting wet—find a way around the obstacle if possible, or find shallower water to wade across. The cold water increases your risk of hypothermia so ensure you have the necessary equipment for building a fire. Never enter water where there are likely to be dangers such as crocodiles or hippos.

*Tie the neck of the bag tightly to keep water out*

*Kick your legs to push yourself across the river*

*Use one arm to propel yourself through the water*

*A waterproof survival bag will keep backpacks dry and aid buoyancy*

### SWIMMING DOWN RIVERS

Avoid swimming up or down rivers—walking the route instead is far safer. However, if you accidentally fall in and find yourself traveling downstream in fast-moving water, there are ways of protecting yourself until you reach safety.

### DEFENSIVE SWIMMING

The aim of defensive swimming is to adopt a position that keeps you as safe as possible and prevents your feet from becoming ensnared in rocks, which, in a strong current, could push you under the water. Assume the defensive swimming position until you reach shallow water, and can stand up and climb onto the bank.

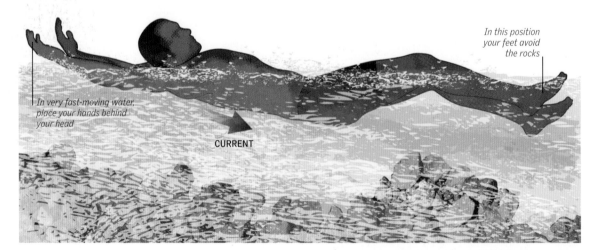

*In this position your feet avoid the rocks*

*In very fast-moving water, place your hands behind your head*

CURRENT

## SWIMMING STROKES

It's important to know what the different swimming strokes are, although you're unlikely to stick to them strictly in a survival situation. If you're a confident swimmer, always choose the stroke that will use the least amount of energy, such as breaststroke. If you're less experienced you should avoid getting in the water unless in a life-or-death situation.

### DOG PADDLE

An easy stroke suitable for less confident swimmers, this involves simply paddling forward with your arms and legs. When you paddle with your left arm, kick with your right leg and vice versa.

### FRONT CRAWL

Also known as "freestyle," front crawl uses a lot of energy so is not the best stroke for a normal survival situation. However, you can build up a lot of speed, which may sometimes be required.

### BREAST STROKE

This is perhaps the most common stroke for crossing rivers. Your arm and leg movements should be made simultaneously and smoothly. It is a good option if you're pulling a float.

### BACK STROKE

If you know the water is safe, this stroke can be a good choice, as it uses little energy. However, not being able to see where you're going can be a disadvantage, especially in rocky areas.

## MAKING A PONCHO FLOAT

Constructing a poncho float will keep your belongings dry and provide limited flotation as you cross the river. If you don't have a poncho, use any large piece of waterproof material.

**1** Push your poncho hood to the inner side, and tightly secure its neck with the drawstrings or cordage.
■ Lay the poncho on the ground with the inner side facing upward.
■ Place your gear on top.

*Lay the sheet on flat ground*

**2** Bring one side of the poncho up and over the equipment that is piled together in the middle.
■ Repeat with the other three sides to create a rectangular parcel.
■ Fold the corners, and ensure that they won't allow water to enter the float.

*Fold each side of the poncho over your equipment*

**3** Wrap carefully to make it watertight.
■ At this point, if you have a second poncho, repeat from step one, placing the float face down on top of the second sheet and wrapping again.
■ If available, place brushwood inside the float for added buoyancy.

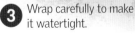
*Tuck the corners in neatly*

**4** Tie ropes, bootlaces, vines, or improvised cordage around the float to secure it.
■ As you enter the water, gently lower the float in with you. Pull it along as you cross the river.

*Float is now waterproof*

*Tie the cordage tightly*

# CAMP CRAFT

# CAMP ESSENTIALS

**Whether you intend** to remain where you are and wait for rescue, move to a safer area and await rescue there, or walk out of the survival situation yourself, you're probably going to need to select a site on which to put up a shelter. This could be for just a single night or for a longer-term stay.

A sound understanding of what constitutes a good location will allow you to address the basic principles of survival. For example, a well-selected site will help keep you safe from danger while still allowing you to deploy your location aids effectively. It should also provide you with adequate materials for building a shelter and a fire, and offer an accessible supply of water, both for drinking and for hygiene.

A well-organized site will not only give you a sense of purpose and order, but will also provide a safe environment for yourself and your equipment. Designating an area for storing equipment and tools, for example, will help prevent vital items from being lost and will reduce the likelihood of you or members of your team being injured.

## In this section YOU WILL DISCOVER...

- how to **make a shower** before you **take a shower...**
- why **keeping clean** is good for both **body and soul...**
- how to work up a **lather** with **wood ash...**
- when a **thatched screen** could **protect your modesty...**
- what turns a **hard candy** into a **firestarter...**
- the **difference** between **cattails** and **fire dogs...**

A fire is an integral part of any campsite. It can be used for warmth, for purifying water, for cooking, for signaling to potential rescuers, for protection against wild animals, and for providing light when darkness falls. It also provides a sense of security. The psychological effects of being able to start a fire in a survival situation should never be underestimated; neither should the psychological effects of *not* being able to start one. Even in a survival situation, a simple camp can give a sense of normality and "home."

**You can produce** a spark—and therefore light a fire—by using a device such as a firesteel or a ranger's flint and steel (see p. 127).

**A FIRESTEEL COMPRISES** two main parts: the material that will produce the spark (usually a rod made from ferrocerium or magnesium alloy) and a sharp striker device (usually a knife blade or short piece of hacksaw blade). When the striker is drawn over the rod, a spark is produced.

**To control the spark** created by these two moving parts, follow the method outlined below. It will allow you to direct the spark accurately, and reduce the chance of you knocking and scattering your tinder. This can be a problem if you hold the rod next to the tinder and strike down into it—especially if you are cold, wet, and tired and your hands are shaking.

1. Place the rod in the center of the tinder. Then position your striker onto the rod. Lock the hand holding the striker into position.

2. Pull the rod up and away from the tinder, drawing it against the striker. By drawing away from the tinder you avoid the danger of disrupting or scattering it.

3. To direct the sparks, alter the angle at which you pull the rod up and away.

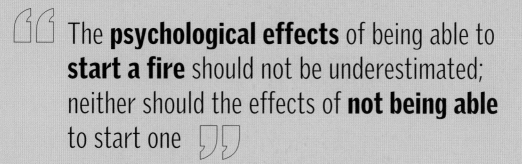

The **psychological effects** of being able to **start a fire** should not be underestimated; neither should the effects of **not being able** to start one

# ORGANIZING YOUR SITE

**WHERE YOU CHOOSE** to set up your shelter depends on the environment, but always take into account the four principles of survival: protection, location, water, and food. First, make sure there are no obvious dangers, and that you're able to signal for rescue. If possible, select a location close to a water source.

*Pitch your camp near a source of wood for shelter and for fuel*

*Select a place for a latrine that's downwind of the camp and downstream from the water source (see p. 117)*

*If predators are in your area, hang unused food in a bag 10 ft (3 m) off the ground and 3 ft (1 m) away from the trunk or branches of a tree*

## SITE FEATURES

Once you're happy with your chosen site—and confident it doesn't hold any forseeable dangers—you can organize the area to accommodate your needs, and to make your time in camp easier and more efficient.

## CAMP ADMINISTRATION

Whether you're in a group or on your own, it's important to organize your site, and quickly establish disciplines and routines to ensure camp safety and to reduce the risk of accidents. Designate specific areas—for storing equipment, firewood, cooking, and sleeping—and specific routines for when you do things (see panel, right).

*When you take off your boots, prop them upside down on a stick to ensure nothing crawls inside. Never put them too close to a fire to dry*

*Assign an open area for location aids, such as a large "V", and as a potential landing site for a rescue helicopter (see pp. 236–41)*

*Create a safe area for cutting wood. Use a tree stump as a platform for cutting and chopping*

*Collect and cut the fuel you need before it gets dark and keep it dry in an upright stack*

*If heavy rain is likely, reduce the risk of flooding by digging a small run-off trench around your shelter and diverting water away downhill*

*Locate a nearby water source, but check the water upstream for contamination, such as dead animals*

*Build three signal fires (see pp. 238–39) on open ground if you can*

## ASSESSING YOUR ENVIRONMENT

You need to protect yourself from injury, threats, and risks, so have a good look around your campsite and assess it for any potential dangers, such as animals, unstable rocks or trees, and the likelihood of flooding.

### ANIMALS

Look out for signs of animals, especially near water. If possible, pitch your camp against a rock face so it can only be approached from one direction. Keep a fire going all night. If you're in a group, organize a watch system. Keep things to hand that you can make a noise with to scare off prowling predators. Don't camp close to standing water where insects, such as mosquitoes, swarm.

### WIND AND FLASH FLOODS

Position the entrance to your shelter at an angle to the wind. Gullies run the risk of flash floods or avalanches; inside river bends are prone to erosion and floods; and a river might burst its banks on an outside bend during a heavy downpour.

### STANDING DEADWOOD

These are dead trees that haven't yet fallen. Heavy wind, or the weight of rain or snow, can make them fall. This is the best type of wood for kindling and fire fuel (see p. 121).

### DEADFALLS

These are dangerous branches that have broken off a tree, but haven't yet fallen to the ground. Some trees, such as beech, ash, and yew, drop their branches without warning.

### ROCKFALLS AND ICE FALLS

If you camp next to rocks, check for cracks and fissures. Fires below them can cause rockfalls. When it's cold, ice sheets can suddenly fall from the rocks.

## CAMP TIMETABLE

In most cases, when you arrive at an area in which you intend to remain for a while (known as "going static"), start planning your activities by working back from a cut-off time—usually when it gets dark.

### THREE HOURS UNTIL DARK

You arrive in the area. Drink water, stow what is no longer needed (map, compass, and so on), and change from wet clothing, but keep one set of clothes dry at all times. Scout the area for the most suitable campsite.

### THEN...

Start pitching your camp. Build your shelter, including bedding. Gather tinder, kindling, and fuel and make a safe firebase and reflector. Collect water and forage for food. Prepare all aids to location (for both night and day).

### ONE HOUR UNTIL DARK

During twilight, finish organizing the site and see to your personal needs—wash, use the latrine, and check your equipment. If you're in a group, make sure everyone knows where the emergency equipment is and who has been designated each task (lighting the signal fire, shining the flashlight, blowing the whistle). Set up a watch system for the fire.

## WHERE NOT TO CAMP

- Don't set up your shelter on sloping, poorly drained ground.
- Don't pitch your camp too close to water because of the risk of flooding and the presence of insects and animals.
- Avoid camping near noisy water sources, such as waterfalls, because they mask any other sounds that could alert you to the presence of threats, such as wild animals, or even possible rescue, such as a helicopter or emergency whistles.

# STAYING CLEAN

**PERSONAL HYGIENE IN THE FIELD** is an important element of protection. Keeping yourself clean and healthy helps to ensure that your body is working at its most efficient and reduces the risk of illness. How you feel physically also has a direct impact on how you feel psychologically. It's a state of mind: if you let your personal hygiene slip, it's just a matter of time before everything else starts to follow.

## CLEAN CLOTHING
The condition of your clothing and equipment can affect your state of mind. If your clothing is dirty and unkempt, your attitude to survival will lack discipline. Try to keep your clothing clean and in good repair.

## HYGIENE CHECKLIST

Personal hygiene is about keeping clean and healthy, so develop a daily routine that ensures you correctly use personal protection aids (tablets, insect repellents, sunblock), and safely handle food, water, and cooking and eating utensils. Keep your clothes clean, and attend to your bodily functions (see opposite).

### HAIR
You don't need to shampoo your hair—let it make its own oils and minerals and establish a natural balance. Wash out incidental smells, such as fire smoke, with hot or cold water.

### SCALP
Check your head for insects and bites every morning and night. Local knowledge will help—for example, look for ticks if you are in a wooded area populated by deer.

### EYES
Wear sunglasses or a hat to protect your eyes from bright sunlight and snow glare. Rinse your eyes with water twice a day to protect against infections like conjunctivitis.

### EARS
Carefully check your ears for foreign objects with a clean, wet finger, especially if you're sleeping rough on the ground.

### TEETH AND GUMS
Use clean fingers to rub your teeth and gums, or make a toothpaste from baking soda, or a mouthwash from salt and water.

### BODY
Every two days wash your armpits, crotch, hands, feet, and toes with running water to keep fungal infections at bay.

## MAKING A SHOWER

Standing under a shower can work wonders for your spirit—it removes accumulated dirt and sweat and makes your body feel refreshed. An improvised shower is quick and easy to make from a metal or a plastic container.

**1** Turn the container upside down on a flat surface.
- Punch holes in the bottom with the bradawl on your penknife or the point of your knife.

*Bradawl*

*Make hole in rim*

**2** Make a hole about 1 in (2.5 cm) down from the rim of the container.
- Make a matching hole on the opposite side of the container.

*Cordage*

**3** Smooth out any rough edges around the two holes.
- Thread a piece of cordage more than 2 ft (60 cm) long through the two holes.

*Overhand knot*

**4** Pull the cord through until you have the same length—about 1 ft (30 cm)—on either side.
- Tie the two strands together with an overhand knot (see p. 143).

# BODILY FUNCTIONS

In a genuine survival situation, you don't eat as much food as usual and your toilet functions—particularly with regards to solid waste—will reduce dramatically after a day or so. Nevertheless, it's important to maintain a routine, especially if you are in a group.

## IN TRANSIT

If you're moving every day or so, it's not worth making a latrine, so just attend to your bodily functions as follows:
- **Urination:** choose a tree away from the water source and downwind of the camp.
- **Defecation:** dig a hole at the base of a tree, fill the hole afterward, and mark it with stones or two crossed sticks. Clean yourself (but don't use the hand you eat with) with toilet paper, leaves, or grass, then running water. Wash your hands and fingernails. Burn or bury used toilet paper.
- **Menstruation:** if you don't have tampons or sanitary napkins towels, use something cotton and washable, or even sphagnum moss. Burn or bury whatever you have used.

# GOING STATIC

If you're going static by staying in one place for more than a few days, build a latrine downwind of your camp, and downhill and away from your water source. Dig a deep trench, either next to or between two trees, and make a seat from two poles. Cover the deposits with sand or soil to reduce the smell and keep flies away. When you leave, dismantle the latrine, fill the trench, and mark the area with stones or crossed sticks.

*A thatched screen can be erected for privacy*

*Tie a pole at the back of the two trees to lean against when you use the latrine*

*Cover each deposit with soil or sand and fill in the hole completely when you decamp*

*Attach two poles either side of the trees to use as seating*

*Bowed sapling*

*Use water warmed over the fire or leave water for washing to warm in the sun.*

**5** Hook the shower over a bowed sapling or a low branch.
- Pour water into the container to test the flow of the shower. If the water runs too quickly, put leaves in the bottom to slow it.

# LATHERING UP

Camping soap is a concentrated antibacterial liquid soap that can be used without water. Decant a little into a small container, such as an old 35mm film container, and it will last for weeks. Alternatively, you can make soap from natural materials.

## MAKING SOAP

You can make natural soap from various sources that contain a substance called saponin, which —when mixed with water—has a cleaning effect.
- **Birch leaves:** Select young leaves and place them in a container (even a plastic bag will do). Add some cold water, then add some hot or boiling water (whichever your container can handle without melting). Agitate the mixture—this allows the saponin in the leaves to dissolve into a natural soap.
- **Soapwort:** Agitate soapwort roots in water until they foam up. Let the light foam settle before using it to wash yourself and your clothes.
- **Horse chestnut:** Dip horse chestnut leaves in warm or hot water then remove. Squeeze the leaves in your hand to produce saponin.
- **Wood ash:** Mix wood ash with water. Don't use this method too often, as it can dry out your skin.

# MAKING FIRE

**THE ABILITY TO MAKE** and maintain a fire can be a significant psychological factor between determining whether you do all you can to survive or just give up. Fire gives you a sense of "being," and, like a shelter, it can transform a clearing under a tree into a "home."

## A PORTABLE KIT

It's important to gather all your materials before you start—not only your tinder, kindling, and fuel, but also your means of lighting a fire. This involves a fair amount of organization, so a portable kit that keeps it all in one place is much more convenient.

### FIRE PRECAUTIONS

If you intend to have a fire in front of your shelter, bear in mind some basic rules:

■ Don't build the fire too close to the shelter as it may get out of control or a spark may blow into the shelter and ignite it.

■ Make sure you have fully extinguished your fire before you decamp and leave the site. Pour water (if you have enough) onto the fire and the immediate surrounding area, or use damp soil, sand, or earth.

## COMPONENTS OF FIRE

Three crucial components—oxygen, heat, and fuel—need to be present in order for a fire to start and be sustained. Although you don't have any control over the resulting chemical reaction, known as combustion, you can develop the skill of lighting a fire. The key is to achieve the best balance between the components. If your fire isn't going well, get back to basics and ask yourself which one of the components is working against you.

### OXYGEN

Although oxygen is vital for combustion to happen, it's all too easy to prevent it from getting to the flame by smothering the fire with too much wood. If your initial fire looks as though it's dying, try fanning it with your hand or a map to create a draft that feeds oxygen to the fire.

### HEAT

Heat is essential for igniting the fuel. In most cases this heat can be generated either by a spark (such as flint and steel), by a chemical reaction and friction (such as matches or potassium permanganate), or by friction alone (such as a bow drill). (See pp. 126–27 and pp. 130–33.)

### FUEL

Once the fire gets going, you need to have fuel to burn (see pp. 120–21). You should start with small, dry pieces of fuel that will catch the flame and generate enough heat to then burn increasingly large pieces of fuel.

## MATCHLESS FIRESET TIN

Working on the principle of "Don't make things any harder than they need be," this matchless fireset, designed for the military, contains a one stop solution to getting a fire going—regardless of the weather conditions.

### INSIDE THE TIN

The small tin, which is waterproof when taped, contains everything you need to produce a fire: a sparking device, tinder, kindling, and fuel. Hexamine from the fuel blocks is scraped onto cotton wool, then a spark from the flint and steel ignites the cotton wool long enough for the fuel blocks to light.

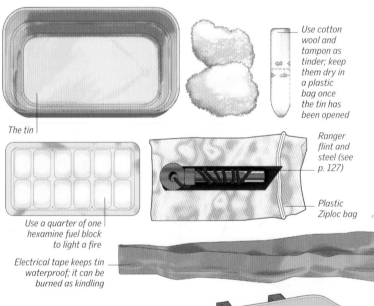

*The tin*

*Use cotton wool and tampon as tinder; keep them dry in a plastic bag once the tin has been opened*

*Ranger flint and steel (see p. 127)*

*Plastic Ziploc bag*

*Use a quarter of one hexamine fuel block to light a fire*

*Electrical tape keeps tin waterproof; it can be burned as kindling*

### USING THE TIN

You can use the tin itself to boil water. Raise the tin 1 in (2.5 cm) off the ground with two sticks and light a quarter of a hexamine fuel block underneath. After a while, the water boils so you can have a potentially life-saving drink.

# PREPARING BEFOREHAND

More than any other survival task, starting a fire needs good prior preparation. If you don't have the correct materials and in sufficient quantities, you will probably fail in your attempts to start a fire. Preparing the ground, your materials, and your equipment will usually make firelighting much easier and more likely to succeed.

## CHOOSING YOUR GROUND

You need to be careful when selecting the place in which you intend to start your fire. Clear the ground before building your fire. Never light a fire directly on the ground and watch that your fire doesn't spread or burn out of control.

> ### KEY POINTS TO REMEMBER
> ■ Carry some form of firelighter with you at all times.
> ■ Practice your skills before you need them—in different conditions and using different materials. You'll soon learn what works and what doesn't.
> ■ Collect tinder as soon as you enter the forest. If it's wet, dry it in your pockets against your warm body.
> ■ Collect everything you need to get a fire going, then multiply it by ten. If you're in a dire situation, you may have only one or two chances of getting a fire going before you either run out of matches or tinder, or you suffer from exhaustion or hypothermia.

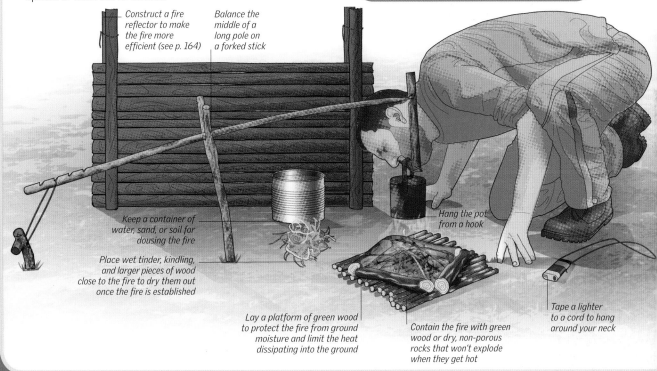

Construct a fire reflector to make the fire more efficient (see p. 164)

Balance the middle of a long pole on a forked stick

Keep a container of water, sand, or soil for dousing the fire

Place wet tinder, kindling, and larger pieces of wood close to the fire to dry them out once the fire is established

Lay a platform of green wood to protect the fire from ground moisture and limit the heat dissipating into the ground

Hang the pot from a hook

Contain the fire with green wood or dry, non-porous rocks that won't explode when they get hot

Tape a lighter to a cord to hang around your neck

## CAMP FIRE DO'S

■ Make sure you have enough wood close by to fuel your fire. Carrying wood to your fire uses energy, which may be at a premium in a survival situation.

■ Rake the area around the spot where you intend to start the fire and brush away leaves or anything else that may ignite and start a forest fire.

■ Check the ground for tree roots. Your fire could set an exposed root alight, or even one just under the surface. Once a root starts to burn underground, the heat works its way along the root and could start a forest fire.

■ If you're trying to get rescued, choose a spot for the fire where passing vehicles and aircraft can see it.

## CAMP FIRE DON'TS

■ Don't use your hands as a rake to clear the ground, because you may get bitten by an insect or a snake. Use your feet or a branch instead.

■ Don't build a fire next to old logs or fallen trees, as they may catch fire. They may not look alight but they can smolder for several days and a heavy breeze could subsequently fan the embers and start a blaze.

■ Don't build your fire under an overhanging branch, or leaves, as the heat from the fire can soon dry them out and then set them alight.

■ Don't position your fire so that the wind affects the way the fire burns, or blows smoke or flames into your shelter.

# THE ELEMENTS OF FIRE

**THE THREE MATERIAL ELEMENTS** you need to build a fire are tinder, kindling, and fuel. They must be dry and collected in sufficient quantities. A well-made feather stick effectively provides tinder, kindling, and fuel on one piece of wood—and it needs only a spark to set it alight.

## EMERGENCY TINDER
Carry tinder, such as a tampon or cotton wool balls, in a 35mm film canister or a Ziploc bag in your emergency kit. For each fire, use some cotton wool and a small piece of tampon. Cotton wool balls smeared with petroleum jelly make a flame last ten times longer.

## MAKING A FEATHER STICK

Between four and six well-made feather sticks provide enough combustible material to get a fire going. Keep a few already made and packed away to use in an emergency. The best feather sticks are made from standing dead wood, but just about any type of dry wood will do. If you use small, dead branches that have snapped off a tree, remove the bark first.

**1** Choose the side of a stick with an even grain and no knots. Work on a hard, flat surface to stop the stick slipping.
- Lay the blade flat on the stick and run it all the way down without cutting into the wood—do this ten times. This gives you a feel for the wood and how your knife moves over it.

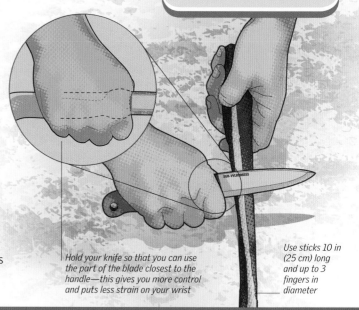

*Hold your knife so that you can use the part of the blade closest to the handle—this gives you more control and puts less strain on your wrist*

*Use sticks 10 in (25 cm) long and up to 3 fingers in diameter*

## TINDER
The first element you use to make a fire is dry, combustible material called tinder. You may have tinder in your equipment (see pp. 122–23), or you may need to find natural or other man-made sources. The key to success is to experiment with what's around you before you actually need it. Make sure it's dry—leave it in the sun if it's damp. When you use some tinder, replace it at the earliest opportunity.

### TYPES OF TINDER
**Natural sources:** Feather sticks (see above), shavings from the outside of a bamboo stem, bark shavings, fine wood dust, pine pitch, plant and animal down, powdered dung, and fire dog (a charred stick). Also, birch bark (silver birch bark can be lit even when it's wet), clematis, honeysuckle, cattail, dry grass, dead and dry moss, and some fungi. The best tinder for friction methods of firelighting (see pp. 130–33) is tree bark, dry grass, fungi, lichen, plant roots, fibers, and down.
**Man-made sources:** Cotton wool balls, tampons, char cloth, fire tin (see p. 123), lint, tissue paper, camera film, strips of rubber, and candle wick.

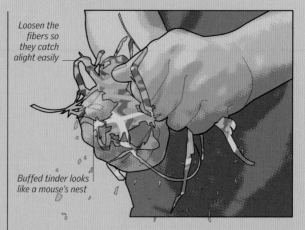

*Loosen the fibers so they catch alight easily*

*Buffed tinder looks like a mouse's nest*

### TINDER BUNDLE
A good way to prepare your tinder to take a spark or a coal is to make it into a tinder bundle. Vigorously tease, rub, and pull the fibers with your fingers until it becomes a ball the size of a grapefruit. Push the finest, most combustible material into the interior of the ball. Try mixing up your tinder to make it more effective—for example, dry grass, birch bark, and cattail.

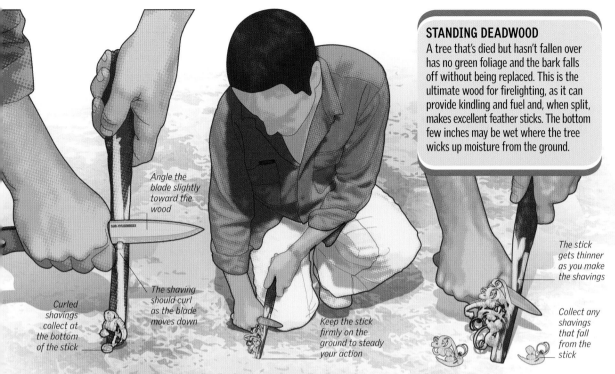

Angle the blade slightly toward the wood

Curled shavings collect at the bottom of the stick

The shaving should curl as the blade moves down

Keep the stick firmly on the ground to steady your action

The stick gets thinner as you make the shavings

Collect any shavings that fall from the stick

**2** Now tilt the angle of the blade slightly toward the wood.
- Keeping a part at the top of the wood to use as a handle, run the blade down the wood to cut a shaving.
- Stop just before the bottom so that the shaving stays attached to the stick.

**3** Turn the stick slightly and run the knife down the edge created in step 2 to create a second shaving. Turn the stick again and repeat, working around the stick.
- Try to get a rhythm going, and put your body behind the cutting action.

**4** Once you have mastered the technique, continue to feather the rest of the stick.
- When you've finished you will have a thin stick with curled shavings still attached, and ready for use as kindling.

## KINDLING

Kindling is the second material element of firelighting and, when dry, is added to burning tinder. Kindling can be as thin as a match or as thick as a finger. You should be able to snap it with your hands. If it doesn't break with a crack then it's probably not completely dry. If it's damp, remove the outer bark (this retains most of the moisture) and break the kindling down into small sticks 6 in (15 cm) long.

### TYPES OF KINDLING
- Soft-wood twigs are very combustible, while wood with flammable resin, such as pine, burns hot and long.
- You can use some types of tinder as kindling—for example, bark, palm leaves, pine needles, grass, ground lichens, and ferns—but you will need larger quantities for kindling than you needed for tinder.

*Strip off the bark with your knife*

## FUEL

Initially, your fire needs constant tending, but once it can sustain itself for five minutes it's established and you can add increasingly larger fuel to create a good heart—a bed of hot coals that sustains the fire with minimum effort on your part. The fuel should be about as thick as your wrist or forearm. At first, use dry fuel split into sticks that catch alight easily. Add green (live) wood and larger logs (whole or split) later, once when the fire is established. In wet conditions, build your fire under cover to keep off the rain.

### TYPES OF FUEL
- Hard woods from mainly deciduous trees (such as oak, maple, ash, beech, and birch) burn hot and long, produce good coals, and are more efficient. But they are hard to get going.
- Soft woods from conifers (such as pine, fir, and spruce) are easier to light as they can contain resin, but burn faster and produce less heat than hard woods. They also make more smoke.
- Peat is found on well-drained moorland and can be cut with a knife. However, it needs a good air supply.
- Charcoal is lightweight, smokeless, and burns hot.
- Dried animal droppings provide a good smokeless fuel.

# CHAR CLOTH AND FIRE CAN

**BEFORE SETTING OFF ON A TRIP,** add either some char cloth or a fire can to your backpack. These excellent forms of tinder are reliable and potentially life-saving. Alternatively, you can take some mayasticks. Char cloth is very easy to make, so keep some dry in your emergency fire kit or lining the bottom of your survival kit (see pp. 60–61).

> **TOOLS AND MATERIALS**
> - A can with a tight-fitting lid, such as a small shoe-polish can
> - Nail
> - 100 percent cotton cloth
> - Knife or scissors
> - Spark or flame

## MAKING CHAR CLOTH

Char cloth is cotton cloth that's been combusted in the absence of oxygen (pyrolysis). It's lightweight, takes up almost no space, and produces an ember from even a weak spark extremely well. Char cloth works only when it's completely dry, so keep it in a watertight container.

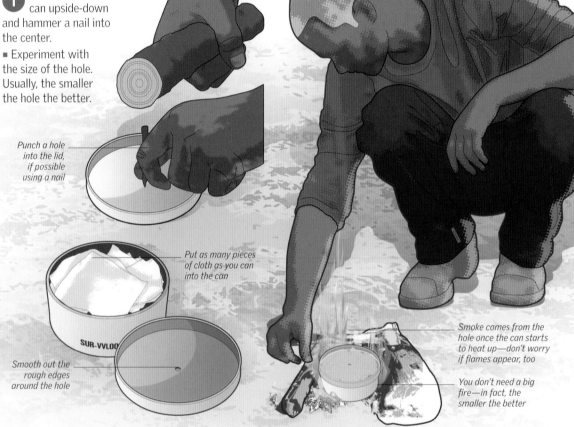

**1** Turn the lid of a can upside-down and hammer a nail into the center.
- Experiment with the size of the hole. Usually, the smaller the hole the better.

*Punch a hole into the lid, if possible using a nail*

*Put as many pieces of cloth as you can into the can*

SUR-VVL00

*Smooth out the rough edges around the hole*

*Smoke comes from the hole once the can starts to heat up—don't worry if flames appear, too*

*You don't need a big fire—in fact, the smaller the better*

**2** Cut 100 percent cotton cloth into pieces that fit into the can without folding.
- Vary the sizes of the pieces so they don't just stack flatly on top of each other, but at the same time don't squash them in.
- Securely place the lid on the can.

**3** Place the can on a fire to burn off all the oxygen inside the can, or place it on top of some good coals scraped to the side of your camp fire.
- When the smoke stops the process is complete.
- Safely remove the can from the fire.
- Don't open the can until it's cool.

# MAKING A FIRE CAN

You can use a fire can to start a stubborn fire when conditions are less than perfect, or to boil water, do some basic cooking, or warm your hands on a cold day. Once lit, a fire can burns for hours with a concentrated, controllable flame that produces no smoke. When it starts to fail, you can either replenish the existing cardboard with more wax or replace the cardboard and start again.

> **TOOLS AND MATERIALS**
> - A can with a tight-fitting lid, such as a small shoe-polish tin
> - Cardboard (ribbed or plain)
> - Candle and a match or lighter
> - Knife or scissors

*The extra ⅙ in (4 mm) of cardboard will burn down slightly and act as a wick*

*Angle the candle so that the flame melts the wax rather than just burning into air*

*The can becomes hot so don't touch it*

**1** Cut out a long, thin piece of cardboard that's ⅙ in (4 mm) wider than the depth of your can.
- If it's ribbed, cut it across the grain.
- Roll it tightly along its length until the roll just fits inside the can.

**2** Light your candle and let the melting wax drop into the can.
- Let the wax soak the cardboard and fill up the can—it's a slow process.
- Stop when the wax nears the top.
- Allow the wax to harden.

**3** When the can has cooled down, hold it at an angle and light the top of the cardboard with the candle.
- The flame should be concentrated and spread across the top of the can.

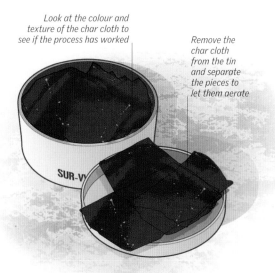

*Look at the colour and texture of the char cloth to see if the process has worked*

*Remove the char cloth from the tin and separate the pieces to let them aerate*

**4** Once the tin has cooled down, remove the lid and examine the charred cloth.
- The cloth should be completely black and have a semi-rigid, but softish texture. If it's fawn or brown, put it back on the fire and leave for longer.
- Cloth that's brittle and crumbles is of no use.
- Check the cloth works by striking a spark on to a piece; the spark should create a small red ember.

# FIRE WADS AND MAYASTICKS

Fire wads are rolled strips of newspaper soaked in a fuel. Once dry, they make handy waterproof tinder. Mayasticks are pieces of resinous fatwood from the highlands of Mexico and Guatemala. The pieces are easy to light, even when wet, and generate a hot flame.

### MAKING FIRE WADS AND MAYASTICKS

- To make fire wads, tightly roll strips of newspaper into a tube 4 in (10 cm) long and tie them with cord. Soak them in melted wax and allow to dry. Light the center with a match.
- To light a mayastick, cut a little sliver of wood with your knife and lift it from the surface of the stick. When a little resin seeps out, set it alight with a flint and steel (see p. 127).

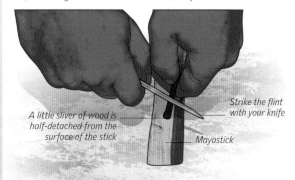

*A little sliver of wood is half-detached from the surface of the stick*

*Strike the flint with your knife*

*Mayastick*

# TYPES OF FIRE

**ONCE YOU HAVE COLLECTED** your tinder, kindling, and fuel, and made sure it's dry and ready at hand, you can set about making your fire. There are many different types of fire to choose from, depending on what you need the fire for (see below). Before you start to build your fire, make sure you have prepared the ground so that everything is safe (see pp. 118–19).

## CHOOSING A FIRE

If you have a choice of fuel, as well as time to invest in building a specific type of fire, look at the choices below and determine which one is likely to suit your immediate needs.

- Your primary consideration should be the function of the fire: warmth is probably your most urgent requirement, but other uses include cooking, signaling (see pp. 238–39), drying wet clothing, and disposing of waste. You may want a particular type of fire because it lasts all night.
- Consider the availability of the components you need to build the fire—for example, the right fuel and the best ground. A rule of thumb is to estimate how much you think you'll need, then double it.

### FIRE ESSENTIALS

There's plenty of advice surrounding the pros and cons of making fires, but three general tips will help:
- Never make things any harder than they need to be. Choose a fire that requires the least effort for the maximum gain.
- It is more efficient to build a small fire and sit close to it, than to build a large fire and sit far away from it.
- If all your wood appears wet, remove the bark and split the wood—the center will usually be dry.
- Once the fire is established, place damp tinder, kindling, and larger pieces of wood close to the fire to dry out. Keep watch on them so that they don't dry out to the point where they catch fire!

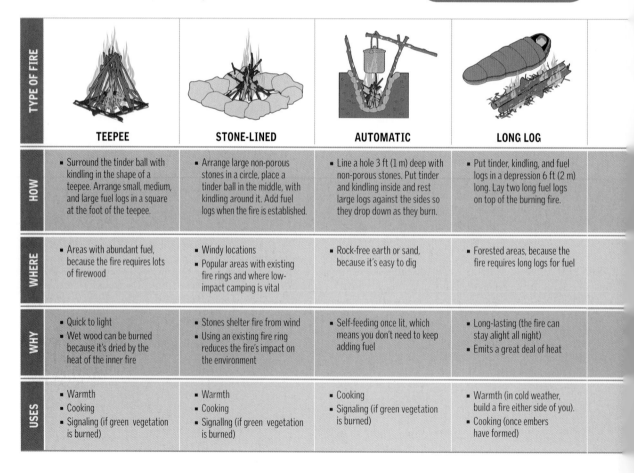

| TYPE OF FIRE | TEEPEE | STONE-LINED | AUTOMATIC | LONG LOG |
|---|---|---|---|---|
| **HOW** | ▪ Surround the tinder ball with kindling in the shape of a teepee. Arrange small, medium, and large fuel logs in a square at the foot of the teepee. | ▪ Arrange large non-porous stones in a circle, place a tinder ball in the middle, with kindling around it. Add fuel logs when the fire is established. | ▪ Line a hole 3 ft (1 m) deep with non-porous stones. Put tinder and kindling inside and rest large logs against the sides so they drop down as they burn. | ▪ Put tinder, kindling, and fuel logs in a depression 6 ft (2 m) long. Lay two long fuel logs on top of the burning fire. |
| **WHERE** | ▪ Areas with abundant fuel, because the fire requires lots of firewood | ▪ Windy locations<br>▪ Popular areas with existing fire rings and where low-impact camping is vital | ▪ Rock-free earth or sand, because it's easy to dig | ▪ Forested areas, because the fire requires long logs for fuel |
| **WHY** | ▪ Quick to light<br>▪ Wet wood can be burned because it's dried by the heat of the inner fire | ▪ Stones shelter fire from wind<br>▪ Using an existing fire ring reduces the fire's impact on the environment | ▪ Self-feeding once lit, which means you don't need to keep adding fuel | ▪ Long-lasting (the fire can stay alight all night)<br>▪ Emits a great deal of heat |
| **USES** | ▪ Warmth<br>▪ Cooking<br>▪ Signaling (if green vegetation is burned) | ▪ Warmth<br>▪ Cooking<br>▪ Signaling (if green vegetation is burned) | ▪ Cooking<br>▪ Signaling (if green vegetation is burned) | ▪ Warmth (in cold weather, build a fire either side of you).<br>▪ Cooking (once embers have formed) |

# LIGHT YOUR FIRE

There are numerous ways to build a fire and get one going, and everyone has their favorite. The following example is a tried-and-trusted method that's versatile and works well in a variety of conditions.

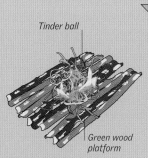

*Tinder ball*

*Green wood platform*

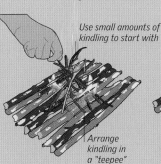

*Use small amounts of kindling to start with*

*Arrange kindling in a "teepee"*

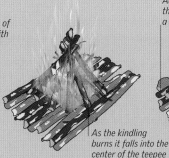

*As the kindling burns it falls into the center of the teepee*

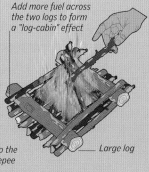

*Add more fuel across the two logs to form a "log-cabin" effect*

*Large log*

**1** Place your tinder ball (see p. 120) on a platform composed of green wood.
- Light the tinder with your chosen method (see pp. 126–27) and let it catch.

**2** Gently lay kindling by the tinder ball.
- Build a kindling "teepee", as this lets the fire breathe where the heat is strongest.
- Feather sticks also make ideal kindling (see p. 120).

**3** As the kindling catches fire and the flames grow, add larger pieces of kindling.
- Continue to add kindling, gradually building up to split logs (see p. 148).

**4** The fire is established when you can leave it alone for five minutes without it going out.
- Then lay a large log on the wind-facing side and one on the other side.

| | SNAKE HOLE | STAR-SHAPED | HUNTER | DAKOTA HOLE | TYPE OF FIRE |
|---|---|---|---|---|---|
| **HOW** | - Create a hole in the side of a bank and a chimney up through the earth. Light a fire inside using any fuel. | - Build a fire from tinder, kindling, and fuel.<br>- Arrange four logs so they meet in the middle.<br>- Push logs in as they burn. | - Make a fire out of tinder, kindling, and any type of fuel. Place two long logs either side of the fire in a V-shape. | - Dig a large hole for the fire and a slightly smaller hole for the chimney, with a tunnel linking the two. Use small logs as fuel and cook at ground level. | |
| **WHERE** | - Windy locations<br>- Rock-free earth or sand bank | - Forested areas, because of the logs the fire needs | - Cold or windy locations | - Anywhere you can dig a hole, because the fire requires very little fuel once established | |
| **WHY** | - Chimney creates a draft, giving a high-temperature fire<br>- Sheltered from the elements | - Long-lasting<br>- Good embers for cooking | - Hardwood logs shelter the fire from the wind<br>- Produces a great deal of heat | - Concentrated heat<br>- Flames are below ground so fire is hidden | |
| **USES** | - Warmth<br>- Cooking<br>- Waste disposal | - Cooking—balance a pot on the logs<br>- Heating water | - Warmth<br>- Cooking | - Cooking<br>- Keeping warm<br>- Drying wet clothing | |

# MAKING SPARKS AND FLAMES

**LIGHTING TINDER IS THE FIRST STAGE** of making a fire. Matches and lighters do this instantly, but there are a number of ways to create a spark that you can then use to coax your tinder into a flame. This is relatively easy when everything is dry, but with patience and persistence it is also possible when conditions are bad.

## IGNITION DEVICES

There are various ingenious methods of creating that all-important spark or flame to ignite your fire. If you don't have matches or a lighter, you'll need to use another device, such as a flint and steel. You can also improvise by using an external energy source, such as:

- Focusing the sun's heat with a magnifying glass or beverage can.
- Making sparks with a battery.
- Creating a chemical reaction using potassium permanganate.

## STRIKING A MATCH

It may seem simple enough, but there's a way of striking a match—known as "commando style"—that reliably produces a flame in all kinds of conditions.

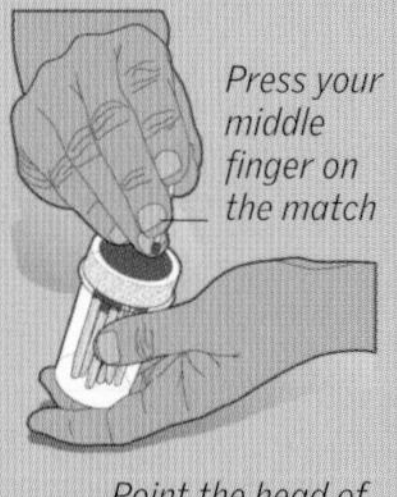
Press your middle finger on the match

**1** Hold the box in one hand and a match between the thumb and first two fingers of the other.
- Strike the match firmly away from you.

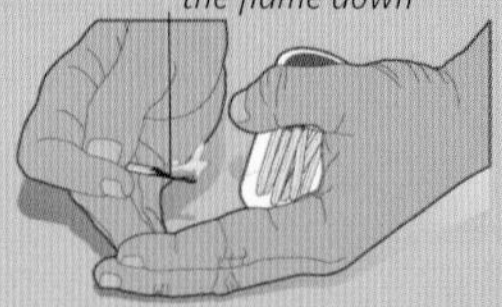
Point the head of the flame down

**2** When the match lights, immediately cup your hands to protect the flame.
- Let the flame burn a little way along the stem before using it to light the tinder.

| TYPE OF DEVICE | MATCHES/LIGHTERS | MAGNIFYING GLASS | BEVERAGE CAN | BATTERY |
|---|---|---|---|---|
| | 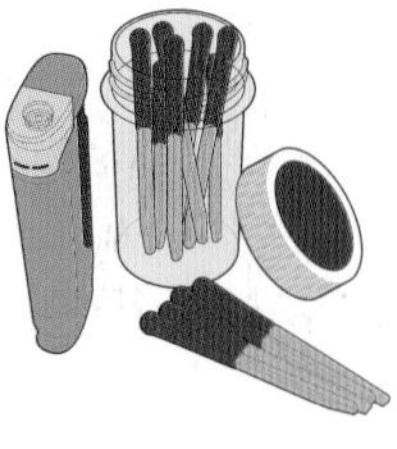 | 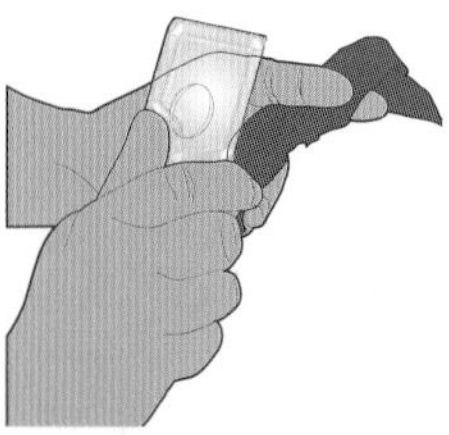 | 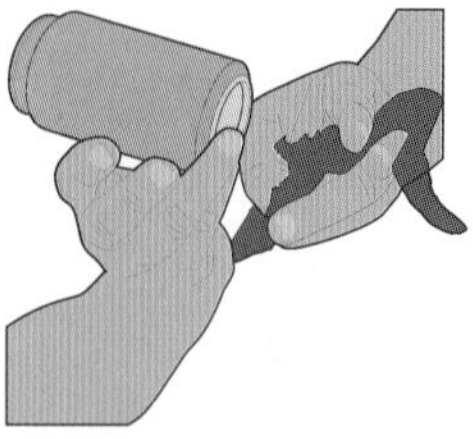 | 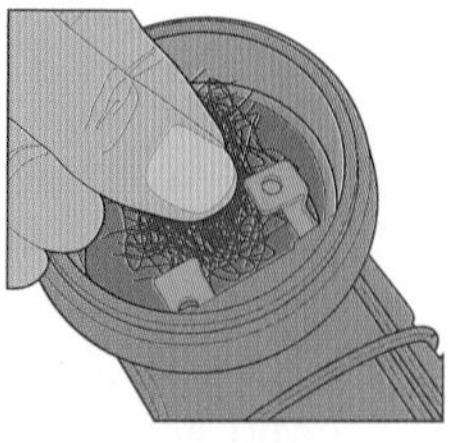 |
| GEAR | ▪ Waterproof box of matches.<br>▪ Cigarette lighter taped to a piece of cord around your neck.<br>▪ Dry tinder | ▪ Magnifying glass<br>▪ Dry tinder | ▪ Empty beverage can<br>▪ Dry tinder | ▪ Flashlight and its battery<br>▪ Wire or wire wool<br>▪ Dry tinder |
| WHAT TO DO | ▪ To light a match "commando style," strike it away from you on the box and then cup it in your hands (see above). | ▪ With the magnifying glass, focus bright sunlight onto some dry tinder and create a hot spot. Hold the magnifying glass steady until the tinder catches alight. | ▪ Polish the bottom of the can (see Signal mirror, p. 245).<br>▪ Catch bright sunlight on the shiny surface and reflect it onto tinder to create a hot spot. Hold the can steady until the tinder catches alight. | ▪ Lay the wire across the battery terminals to create some sparks.<br>▪ Remove the bulb from the flashlight and place wire wool over the terminal. Switch on the flashlight to create sparks. |
| COMMENTS | ▪ Waterproof matches are usually just standard matches that have been coated with wax and varnish.<br>▪ Always have a lighter around your neck on a piece of cord. | ▪ When you choose a compass, make sure it has a magnifying glass incorporated into it (for reading the details on maps).<br>▪ You can also use the lens in reading spectacles. | ▪ You'll need to practice this technique so that you can rely on it in a survival situation. | ▪ The thinner the wire the better this will work, especially with lower voltage batteries (1.5v).<br>▪ Use this method for a short period only, otherwise you will drain the battery. |

# CREATING A CHEMICAL FLAME

Potassium permanganate is an extremely useful item to have in your survival kit, because you can use the chemical not only to sterilize water and wounds, but also to create a spark to light a fire. You will need some sugar to make it work, so use some from your survival rations or crush a hard candy.

> **WARNING!**
> Potassium permanganate is a strong oxidizer that can, when mixed with certain chemicals, create an explosive mixture. It can also stain your clothes and skin.

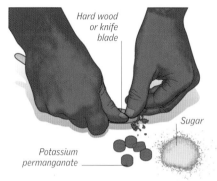

Hard wood or knife blade

Sugar

Potassium permanganate

Press firmly with your knife

Drag the knife along the surface

**1** On a hard surface, such as a flat piece of wood or rock, crush some potassium permanganate. Have an equal amount of sugar ready.

**2** Mix the ingredients. With the back of your knife, push down on the mixture and drag it along the hard surface to create friction.

**3** Continue to push down and drag your blade until you get a spark.
- The flame dies down quickly so have your tinder at the ready.

| | FIRESTEEL | FLINT AND STEEL | ONE-HANDED STRIKER | POTASSIUM PERMANGANATE |
|---|---|---|---|---|
| **TYPE OF DEVICE** | | | | |
| **GEAR** | - Ferrocerium firesteel<br>- Metal striker<br>- Dry tinder | - Magnesium-alloy rod<br>- Steel striker (usually a short piece of hacksaw blade)<br>- Dry tinder | - A magnesium-alloy rod and steel device that can be operated using only one hand<br>- Dry tinder | - Potassium permanganate<br>- Sugar<br>- Knife<br>- Dry tinder |
| **WHAT TO DO** | - Hold striker next to the tinder.<br>- Place the firesteel under the striker, directly on to the tinder.<br>- Draw the firesteel back across the striker to direct the sparks onto the tinder. The firesteel moves, not the striker. | - Follow instructions for the firesteel (left). | - Place the flint rod in the tinder.<br>- Press the thumb button onto the rod and push the handle down the length of the rod.<br>- Pushing harder creates greater friction, which leads to a more intense spark. | - Mix potassium permanganate and sugar in equal amounts on a hard surface.<br>- Press down on the mixture with your knife and drag the blade along to create a spark (see above). |
| **COMMENTS** | - Lasts for about 12,000 strikes.<br>- Temperature reaches 3,000°C.<br>- Works in all weathers and at any altitude. | - There are many variations and kits; one has a magnesium block for the holder and the striker shaves slivers of magnesium into the tinder to help with ignition. | - Works in all weathers.<br>- Has a safety feature that prevents accidental use.<br>- Designed for fighter pilots, who may injure an arm or hand after ejecting. | - You can also mix a small amount of potassium permanganate with glycol or antifreeze. Quickly wrap in paper and put on the ground. **Warning:** stand well clear as the combustion can be sudden and dangerous. |

# EXTREME SURVIVAL— IN THE DESERT

## USEFUL EQUIPMENT
- Personal Locator Beacon (PLB)
- Sunglasses and sunscreen
- Cotton scarf or hat
- Signal mirror and signal flares
- Map, compass, GPS
- Survival tin, bushcraft knife
- Cell/satellite phone
- Poncho/bivy sack

**DESPITE A LACK OF SURVIVAL KNOWLEDGE,** a party of five survived searing temperatures, dehydration, hunger, and the threat of animal attack for six days when their plane crashed in the Kalahari Desert in Botswana.

On Wednesday, March 1, 2000, Carl du Plessis and three associates—Mike and Lynette Nikolic, and Nebojea Graorac—set off on a business flight from the capital of Botswana, Gaborone, bound for Maun, a popular tourist town in the north of the country. However, the aircraft developed engine trouble during the flight and was forced to crash-land. Critically, radio contact was lost, so no distress call was emitted before the plane went down. The pilot and all four passengers on board suffered burns during the crash and subsequent fire, but two sustained even more serious injuries—Lynette Nikolic damaged her spine and left arm, and Graorac suffered a punctured lung.

**"CRITICALLY, RADIO CONTACT WAS LOST, SO NO DISTRESS CALL WAS EMITTED BEFORE THE PLANE WENT DOWN"**

The following morning, Du Plessis and pilot Costa Marcandonatos decided to walk the estimated four days to Maun to find help. Their plan was misguided from the start—Maun was actually around some 190 miles (300 km) to the west, and other settlements to the east were much closer. They attempted to navigate by the sun but, lacking a machete, couldn't penetrate the dense bush. They were forced to follow elephant tracks to find watering holes, meeting elephants on one occasion, and heard the roar of lions at night. By Saturday they had walked 56 miles (90 km), but their zig-zag route had taken them only 20 miles (30 km) from the crash site.

Despite their mistakes, they stumbled upon a manned hunting lodge the following day. After their initial efforts to radio the authorities had failed, a helicopter finally reached the crash site on Monday, March 6, airlifting the casualties to hospital for emergency treatment six days after the crash.

# WHAT TO DO

### ARE YOU IN DANGER?

 **← NO   YES →**

If you are in a group, try to help any others who are in danger

Get yourself out of it:
**Sun/Heat**—Find or improvise immediate shelter
**Animals**—Avoid confrontation and move away from danger
**Injury**—Stabilize condition and apply first aid

### ASSESS YOUR SITUATION
*See pages 234–35*

### DOES ANYONE KNOW YOU WILL BE MISSING OR WHERE YOU ARE?

 **← NO   YES →**

If no one knows you are missing r where you are, you will need to notify people of your plight by any means at your disposal

If you are missed, a rescue party will almost certainly be dispatched to find you

### DO YOU HAVE ANY MEANS OF COMMUNICATION?

 **← NO   YES →**

You are faced with surviving for an indefinite period—until you are located or you find help

If you have a cell or satellite phone, let someone know your predicament. If your situation is serious enough to be worthy of emergency rescue, and you have a Personal Locator Beacon (PLB), you should consider this option

### CAN YOU SURVIVE WHERE YOU ARE? *

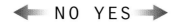 **← NO   YES →**

If you cannot survive where you are and there are no physical reasons why you should remain, you will have to move to a location that offers either a better chance of survival, rescue, or both

Address the Principles of Survival: Protection, Location, Water, Food

**YOU WILL HAVE TO MOVE ****   **YOU SHOULD STAY ****

## DO

- Make an informed decision on the best location to move to
- Leave clear indications of your intent (written messages or signs) if abandoning a vehicle
- Have aids to location accessible while moving and deployed when static
- Protect yourself against glare from the sun and windburn
- Seek or improvise shelter when not moving and seize all opportunities to collect fuel for a fire—deserts get cold at night
- Be on constant lookout for signs of water or civilization—such as green vegetation, converging animal/human tracks, or circling birds

## DON'T

- Sit directly on the hot ground when you stop
- Travel during the hottest part of the day
- Take risks—a twisted ankle caused by running down a sand dune could be fatal
- Force the pace—travel at the speed of the slowest person in the group
- Shelter in dry river beds, because of the potential risk of flash floods

## DON'T

- Leave a broken down vehicle unless absolutely necessary—it's easier to see and is what rescuers will be looking for
- Waste energy unnecessarily—be idle unless there is something that requires doing
- Ignore your fire—use anything that burns (wood, vehicle tires) to generate heat and smoke

## DO

- Seek or improvise shade and work during the coolest part of the day/night. A shelter dug even 6 in (15 cm) below ground level will provide a much cooler place to rest
- Ration sweat, not your water; you require around 1¾ pints (1 liter) per hour in temps above 100°F (38°C), half of this if it's cooler
- Continually re-assess your water situation and options for augmenting your supplies
- Leave everything out overnight that could collect dew so you can drink it
- Prepare all of your aids to location for immediate use. Be constantly alert for signs of rescue

---

\* If you cannot survive where you are, but you also cannot move owing to injury or other factors, you must do everything you can to attract rescue.
\*\* If your situation changes (for instance, you are "moving" to find help, and you find a suitable location in which you can stay and survive) consult the alternative "Do" and "Don'ts."

# FIRE BY FRICTION

**THIS METHOD USES PRIMITIVE EQUIPMENT**, such as a bow drill, and requires knowledge, skill, practice, the correct wood, time, and effort. However, once learned it's possibly the most rewarding of all survival skills. Your first fire created from a coal produced by a fireset that you have made yourself will be a fire you will never forget. In a genuine survival situation, however, you would always start a fire with the quickest and easiest method available.

## TOOLS AND MATERIALS
- Cordage such as para cord, fishing line, shoelaces, or bailing twine
- Wood
- Knife
- Bradawl (optional)

## THE FOUR SKILLS
There are many ways to make fire by friction, including a hand drill, bamboo fire saw (see p. 133), and bow drill. Each has its own advantages, depending on the materials available and your practical skills. Regardless of the method, however, there are four main elements to producing fire by friction—each a skill on its own:
- Identifying and procuring the correct types of wood.
- Manufacturing the individual pieces that make the fireset.
- Using the fireset to produce a coal.
- Nurturing the coal into a flame.

## MAKING A BOW DRILL

The bow drill set is one of the most efficient methods of making fire by friction. Try to find the right type of wood for each part, especially the drill and hearth board (see Testing Wood, opposite).

**1** To make the bow, cut a stick to the same length as the distance between your armpit and your fingertip.
- Cut a notch (or make a hole with a bradawl) near each end.
- Tie cord with an arbor knot (see pp. 142–43) to one notch and with half hitches (see pp. 144–45) to the other. Leave only enough slack to wrap around your finger.

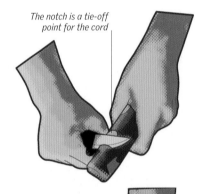

*The notch is a tie-off point for the cord*

*Shape the end that fits into the hearth board to a bluntness that maximizes friction*

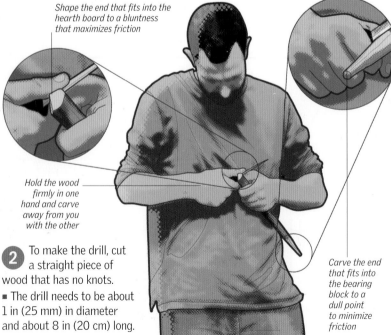

*Make a notch with the point of your knife in the middle of the block*

*Hold the wood firmly in one hand and carve away from you with the other*

**2** To make the drill, cut a straight piece of wood that has no knots.
- The drill needs to be about 1 in (25 mm) in diameter and about 8 in (20 cm) long.

*Carve the end that fits into the bearing block to a dull point to minimize friction*

**3** Make the bearing block from a piece of hard wood about 3–4 in (7.5–10 cm) across.
- Cut it to a length of 4–5 in (12–15 cm), split it in two, and make a notch in it.
- The drill's dull point fits into the notch, while you hold the block when you are bowing (see p. 132).

## TESTING WOOD

Standing deadwood is ideal for the drill and hearth board as it's dry. Soft deadwood is easier to use than hard deadwood, but if you can't tell the difference, use these tests.

### THUMBNAIL TEST

Cut through the bark of a branch, exposing a patch of wood beneath. If you dent this wood easily with your thumbnail, it's a soft wood. If you can only make a small impression, then it's a hard wood.

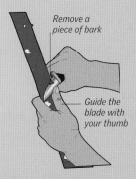

Remove a piece of bark

Guide the blade with your thumb

Try to dent the wood with your nail

**1** Hold your knife at a slight angle to the wood. Push it with a thumb on top of the blade.

**2** Press your thumbnail at an angle of 90 degrees to the wood in the exposed patch.

### CHAR TEST

Each type of wood produces a distinctive char and coal. Some, such as hazel and lime, make a coal easily but the fireset will wear out quickly. The char test helps you discover which woods make a good coal. Drill into a softwood hearth board until it smokes, continue for five seconds and then stop. Look at the char produced:
- If it's like a fine powder it will probably produce a coal.
- If it's coarse, or appears to disintegrate into nothing, it probably won't make a coal.

**4** Make the hearth board from a flat piece of wood about 1 in (25 mm) thick. You may have to split some wood to get what you need.
- Hold your drill so that it sits about ²/₅ in (10 mm) from the edge of the board.
- Mark this point with your knife and notch out a small hole to help the drill get started.

Use the tip of your knife to make a hole

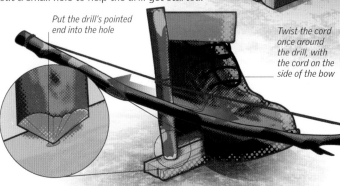

Put the drill's pointed end into the hole

Twist the cord once around the drill, with the cord on the side of the bow

**5** Set up the bow, drill, and bearing block (see also p. 132) and bow the drill into the hole in the hearth board until the hole is as wide as the drill. Don't go all the way through.

Make the V about an eighth of the circumference of the hole

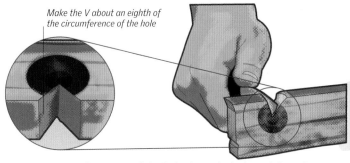

**6** Cut a V to the center of the hole through the hearth board. The bottom of this V is where the char collects and the ember forms in the ember pan (see p. 132).

## THE FINISHED FIRESET

The bow drill set works best when the drill and hearth board are made from the same wood, because both parts then wear down evenly. This may not always be possible, so experiment with different woods.
- Good woods to start with are sycamore, hazel, ivy, lime, willow, and sotol (not found in Europe).
- Also useful are alder, birch, cedar, pine, spruce, maple, oak, and poplar.

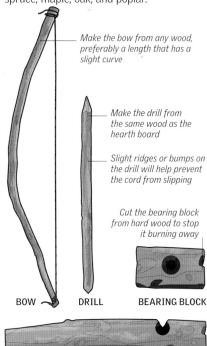

Make the bow from any wood, preferably a length that has a slight curve

Make the drill from the same wood as the hearth board

Slight ridges or bumps on the drill will help prevent the cord from slipping

Cut the bearing block from hard wood to stop it burning away

BOW  DRILL  BEARING BLOCK

HEARTH BOARD  Make the hearth board from wood that heats up and ignites easily

# USING A BOW DRILL

Before you use a bow drill, have your dry tinder bundle, kindling, and fuel beside you. Until you become proficient at using a drill, you will use lots of energy, so beware of overheating and dehydration. Turning a coal into a fire is a skill in itself, so use every opportunity to practice making tinder bundles and lighting them with a small coal from your camp fire.

## TOOLS AND MATERIALS

- Bow drill set (see pp. 130–31)
- Thin, dry piece of bark to use as an ember pan
- Buffed tinder, kindling, and fuel

## GETTING INTO POSITION

Place the ember pan on a flat, dry surface and align it with the V on the hearth board. Rest one foot on the board. Loop the bow cord once around the drill, starting on the inside. Insert the drill into the hole on the hearth board, slot the block on top (with a green leaf in the notch for lubrication), and lock your wrist into your shin as support. Kneel on the other leg and bear down on the block.

**1** Hold the bow horizontal to the ground and parallel to your body.

- Lean slightly forward to apply downward pressure to the drill and back to reduce it.
- Start bowing slowly, using the full length of the bow. Aim for an even, flowing rhythm.
- Breathing steadily as you bow, gradually increase speed and pressure until smoke appears. Vigorously bow with maximum effort ten more times—this usually produces a coal in the ember pan.

*Keep your head as still as you can above the bow*

*Bear down on the block with the weight of your body*

*Use your arm for bowing, not to bear down on the block*

*If the drill slips, move your grip further along the bow to increase the tension in the string*

*Steady the hearth board with your foot*

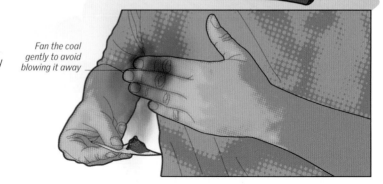

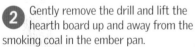

*Keep the drill upright as you bow*

*As the drill turns, friction heats the wood*

*A pile of black ash will collect on the ember pan*

**2** Gently remove the drill and lift the hearth board up and away from the smoking coal in the ember pan.

- If the coal is sticking to the board, gently tap the board with your knife to loosen it.
- Carefully lift the ember pan off the ground and hold it in the air to see if the coal is glowing.
- If the coal in the ember is just smoking, and not glowing, then gently fan it with your hand until you see it glow.

*Fan the coal gently to avoid blowing it away*

**3** Gently transfer the glowing coal into your tinder bundle.

- The coal must touch the tinder to transfer its heat, so squeeze the tinder around the coal, but don't crush it or starve it of oxygen.

*Tip the coal off the ember pan and into the center of the tinder bundle*

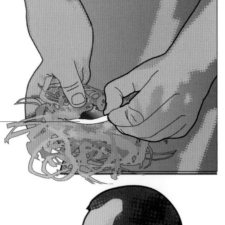

*Hold the tinder bundle away from your face (turn your back to the wind if there is any)*

*Air from your breath or the breeze helps with combustion*

*Don't blow too hard*

*Hold the tinder bundle up, but not too close to your face*

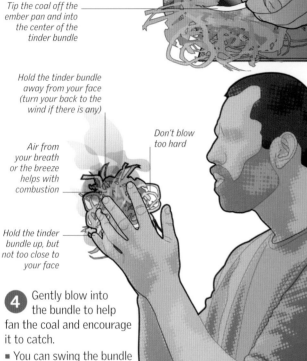

**4** Gently blow into the bundle to help fan the coal and encourage it to catch.

- You can swing the bundle down and back up in between breaths to let dry air fan the coal.
- Continue as the amount of smoke increases and eventually the bundle will burst into flames.

**5** Don't throw the burning bundle on the ground, just calmly place it where you intend to have your fire. Start building the fire around the bundle (see pp. 124–25).

*Place kindling over the top of the burning tinder bundle*

*Once the kindling is set alight, you can add some fuel*

# BAMBOO FIRE SAW

This friction method uses a saw technique to light tinder collected from scraping the outside of the bamboo with your knife.

## MAKING THE FIRE SAW

You need a bamboo section 18 in (45 cm) long. Split it lengthways into two equal pieces.

**1** Sharpen the edge of the first piece with your knife and then cut a V-shaped notch in the outside middle of the second piece.

**2** Hold tinder over the notch in the second piece of bamboo with another bamboo strip that's snapped but not fully broken.

- Kneel down and brace the sharpened piece of bamboo vertically between the ground and your stomach (place a pad on your stomach for comfort).
- Place the notch and tinder over the sharp edge of the first piece, and rub the second piece up and down in a rhythmic movement.

*Lean over the top of the fire saw*

*Rub the saw up and down*

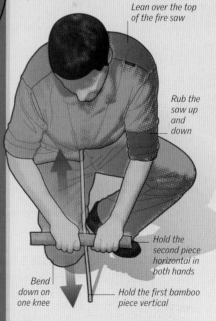

*Hold the second piece horizontal in both hands*

*Bend down on one knee*

*Hold the first bamboo piece vertical*

**3** When the friction produces lots of smoke, continue for 20 strokes more and you should have a coal.

# MANUAL SKILLS

**Learning skills that you can use** in the wilderness is always a "work in progress." Having taught thousands of students over several years, I am yet to conduct a course in which I didn't learn a new skill. For example, this could be a more efficient way to erect a shelter, how to tie a new knot, or the best way to carry out a task more safely and efficiently.

In the military, we invariably teach students how to accomplish a particular task using only the most basic gear. By learning how to perform a task using the absolute basic equipment, they will be able to understand the important elements of the task and will have no choice but to get them right in order to succeed. This in turn helps students to appreciate how and why certain techniques do and don't work, and gives them an opportunity to use their improvisational skills to modify basic techniques in order to get the most out of them. Knowing the correct method of using a knife, for example, will not only improve safety on an expedition, but will also mean that only the minimum

## In this section YOU WILL DISCOVER...

- the merits of a **hank** in **your pocket**...
- how to strip a **nettle stem** and not **get stung**...
- when **to twist** and when **to roll**...
- how to tell a **working end** from a **standing end**...
- the uses of a **sheet bend** or a **Siberian hitch**...
- the **difference** between a **parang** and a **kukri**...
- how to **fell a tree** with a **thumping stick**...

**If you give someone** with little understanding of knots a length of cord and ask them to complete a task, they will invariably use the whole length of cord. If, however, you teach someone two simple knots and set them the same task, they will invariably use only the necessary amount of cord.

**USING THE BEST KNOT,** lashing, or hitch for a particular task means that you will use cord more efficiently and, therefore, ensure that your supply will go further. In a survival situation, where you may be moving every day, you need to be able to use the same pieces of cordage day after day.

- Use knots that don't require cutting and that can be untied quickly and easily (trying to undo a knot with cold, wet hands in the dark, and when you are tired and miserable, can be an emotional experience that usually ends in frustration and several pieces of cut cordage).
- Before you set off into the wilderness, learn a few basic knots, such as the Siberian hitch and the taut-line hitch, which are great for rigging a simple poncho shelter.
- Practice these knots until you can tie—and untie—them with your eyes closed.
- If you are trekking in a cold environment, practice tying them wearing gloves.

amount of valuable energy is being used to complete a task. Equally, knowing how to tie a few simple knots, which can be used in the majority of survival situations, will allow you to use whatever cordage you have in the most efficient way possible.

If you find yourself in a survival situation with more than the most basic gear, life will be much easier. However, the ability to improvise what you need when you don't have it could mean the difference between continued survival and despair.

" The **ability** to **improvise** what you **need** when you **don't have it** can mean the **difference** between **continued survival** and **despair** "

# MAN-MADE CORDAGE

**A VITAL PIECE OF SURVIVAL EQUIPMENT**, man-made cordage is one of those small items that has many uses: building a shelter, repairing equipment and clothing, making traps and nets, and producing fire by friction using a bow drill. Always pack plenty.

## PACKING CORDAGE

Before you set off on your travels, check how much cordage you will need. Make sure you pack it in two places—in your backpack and on your person, in case you get separated from your pack. Make sure, too, that the needle you pack in your survival kit has an eye big enough for the inner strands of the cordage.

## PARACORD

Parachute cord, or "paracord," is a type of cordage originally developed for the rigging lines of parachutes and then adopted as the standard utility cordage by most of the world's military forces. It is a lightweight, nylon rope composed of 32 braided strands. Each strand contains a number of smaller threads that can also be used. In most situations, paracord is a very good option because it's readily available, strong, and packs down small.

## SURVIVAL TIP

Green is the ideal color for military paracord as it remains camouflaged. In a survival situation, red is best because it stands out—it's easier to find if you drop it and can be used as an aid to location. Don't pack just one very long piece of paracord (150ft/30m, for example). It's much better to cut the paracord into 30 ft (10 m) lengths and tie each of them into a coil called a hank (see opposite and below).

### TEN HANKS

A hank can fit in the palm of your hand. It takes up very little room so you can easily stuff up to 10 of them into your pack and pockets, and leave them there until you need them.

### USING CORDAGE

It is vital that you use your limited supply of cordage as efficiently as possible.
- Use only the minimum cordage that is absolutely necessary to accomplish each task.
- Use simple, strong knots that, if possible, can be released without cutting. This leaves the cordage intact for the next task.

*Each braid of paracord is composed of several useful inner threads*

*When they are cut, the ends of the braids can unravel*

*Paracord is a kernmantle rope with an interior core (the kern) surrounded by a woven exterior sheath (mantle)*

*The outer sheath is designed to optimize strength, durability, and flexibility*

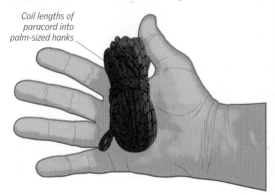

*Coil lengths of paracord into palm-sized hanks*

# TYING A HANK

It's best to keep your cordage in a hank—you can untie it when you need a piece and retie it to store it again. Tying a hank is straightforward and soon becomes second nature, because you'll do it again and again.

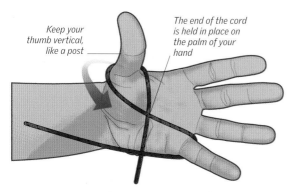

Keep your thumb vertical, like a post

The end of the cord is held in place on the palm of your hand

**1** Hold out your hand (you can use either hand) with the thumb and the fingers spread.

■ Lay the end of the cord on your palm, then loop the cord in a figure-eight around your thumb and little finger.

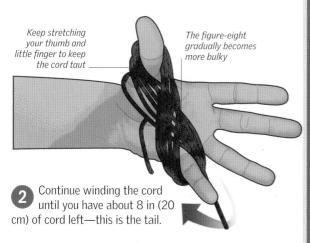

Keep stretching your thumb and little finger to keep the cord taut

The figure-eight gradually becomes more bulky

**2** Continue winding the cord until you have about 8 in (20 cm) of cord left—this is the tail.

Release hitch knot

Seal the end

**3** Take the hanked cordage off your thumb and little finger.

■ Secure the hank by tying the tail around it with a release hitch knot (see p. 143).

## OTHER TYPES OF CORDAGE

In a survival situation you may have to improvise and use other types of cordage, especially if you didn't bring any paracord with you or have run out. Before you start making it from natural materials (see pp. 138–41), see what else you might have that would be quicker and easier to adapt.

### SHOELACES

The normal laces of shoes and boots are often strong enough to use as cord. However, the members of many military units, who are limited to the amount of equipment they can stow or carry, replace their bootlaces with paracord. They use twice as much as they need and wrap the extra length around the top of their boots before tying it. This gives them a ready supply of extra cordage that they can cut off as needed. You can easily do the same—but never sacrifice all the cordage you are using as shoelaces as you'll need to make sure you can still walk comfortably.

### BELTS, CLOTHING, AND HATS

You can cut any type of belt, whatever it's made of (leather, canvas, and so on) into strips to use as cordage. You can cut clothing into strips, too. However, you don't have to destroy a shirt completely: start at the bottom hem and cut 1 in (2.5 cm) strips all the way round. You can even use your hat—a 1 in (2.5 cm) strip from the brim of a jungle hat is just over 3 ft (1 m) long. Better still, coil paracord around the crown of your hat and stitch it in place (just the front and the back).

### RAIDING YOUR KIT

You may have other items in your equipment that you could use as cordage, such as guylines from tents or draw cords from clothing or sleeping bags. Dental floss, especially the waxed type, is extremely strong and can be used effectively for lashing or sewing. If you have a vehicle, you probably have a towrope; take a part of it and unravel the rope into smaller pieces of cordage.

### BE A SCAVENGER

Few places are untouched by modern man. Even in remote areas you'll come across discarded items from the "civilized world"—from plastic bottles to bailing twine. In a situation where improvisation could be the difference between life and death, collect anything you could use to your advantage.

### SEALING PARACORD

Paracord can be awkward to use because its ends, if left unprotected, eventually unravel. Try to seal the ends after you have cut them by holding a flame next to them until they melt. Be careful, as the melted nylon can drip and burn.

# NATURAL CORDAGE

**IF YOU DON'T HAVE** any man-made cordage, you may be able to make a natural substitute. Use the roots and stems of plants to produce improvised rope for erecting shelters, and use sinew from the tendons of larger animals for strong whipping and sewing.

> **WARNING!**
> Take extreme care when you collect and work with plant fibers, especially removing plants such as green ferns from the ground. Bending a stem at its base and pulling it up can expose fibers that are razor-sharp. Cut the plant with a knife or wear gloves. The juice of some plants can irritate the skin, so wash your hands when you've finished.

## PREPARING NETTLE FIBERS

Old stinging nettles or wood nettles with long stems have the most fibers. Wearing gloves (or with your hands covered), strip the leaves from the nettles by grasping the stem at the base and pulling your clenched fist up the full length of the stem.

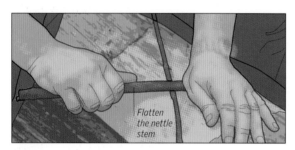

*Flatten the nettle stem*

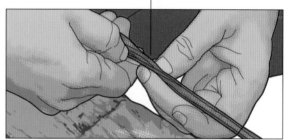

*Open the flattened nettle stem to form a long strip*

**1** Sit astride a log and lay a nettle stem in front of you. Roll a smooth, rounded stick backward and forward on the stem, pressing down hard.
- Continue rolling until the whole stem is crushed.

**2** Tease open the crushed tissue along the whole length of the stem of the nettle with your thumbnail. This exposes the spongy pith within.

## CHOOSING YOUR RAW MATERIALS

Many kinds of raw material can be used to make natural cordage, from bark and roots to stems and sinews. Search your immediate environment first to see what can be used—you may not have to look too far.

| | BARK | ROOTS |
|---|---|---|
| **FACTS** | ▪ Tree trunks have layers between the bark and heartwood called the "cambium" layers, which are best for cordage. | ▪ Many tree roots make good cordage and lashings, but evergreen trees, such as pine, fir, spruce, and cedar, work best. |
| **FINDING** | ▪ The bark of trees such as willow and linden make good cordage.<br>▪ Use other types of bark, such as clematis or honeysuckle, as they break from the tree or vine. | ▪ Look for new roots near the surface of the soil; these are flexible. Cut slightly thicker roots than you need, as you have to remove the bark. Remove only a few roots from each tree and repair any damage you do to the topsoil. |
| **PREPARING** | ▪ Strip the bark from a dead tree, then beat it to loosen the inner cambium fibers.<br>▪ Pull off the cambium fibers in long strips. Use them as they are (clematis and honeysuckle), or braid them into stronger lengths. | ▪ Cut a slit along the root. Peel the bark and let the bare root dry and shrink before splitting in half or into quarters.<br>▪ Keep the bark for tinder or kindling. You could also put it on a fire to produce smoke that keeps away flies. |

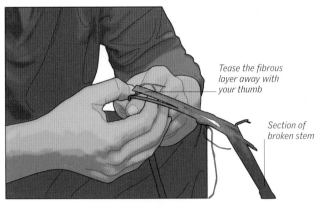

Tease the fibrous layer away with your thumb

Section of broken stem

**3** Bend the stem in the middle of its length. When you bend it, the inner pith will break away from the outer skin, making it easy for you to separate them.

## MAKING CORDAGE FROM PLANTS

To begin with, you must have access to enough quantities of the plant. Don't start making cordage with the only plant in the area. There should also be some basic characteristics present in order for plant material to work well as cordage.

■ The fibers need to be long enough. If you have to splice them together to make workable lengths, you will weaken the line.

■ If you're braiding pieces together to make a stronger line, use rougher fibers, as they will bite together better. Shiny or smooth fibers tend to unravel easily.

■ The fibers need to be strong. Pull on them to see how much strain they take before breaking. They also need to be pliable enough so they don't break when you bend and tie them.

**4** Carefully peel the outer skin from the inner pith.

■ With the finger and thumb of one hand, gently pull the layer outward, while pushing down on it with the thumb of the other hand.

■ You'll be left with long fibrous strips of outer skin, which you can make into short bindings or natural cordage (see p. 140).

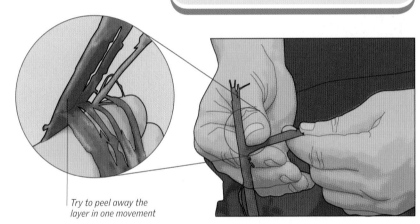

Try to peel away the layer in one movement

| | WITHIES | LEAVES | SINEW |
|---|---|---|---|
| **FACTS** | ■ The strong, flexible stems of willow, birch, ash, and hazel are called "withies" and are used for thatching and in gardening.<br>■ Withies make useful and robust lashing and are best used in spring or summer. | ■ The leaves of many plants, such as the lily family, agave, and sisal hemp, contain useful fibers. | ■ Animal sinew makes strong and versatile cordage—some sinews can support the weight of a man.<br>■ Sinew has been used to bind arrow heads to shafts and to sew together everyday clothing, such as leather and mukluks. |
| **FINDING** | ■ Choose a young sapling or branch that's long and flexible. The fewer the stems or branches the better, as they will need to be removed. | ■ To find out if the leaves of a plant contain useful fibers, simply tear a leaf apart to see if it breaks into stringy layers. | ■ Sinews are the tendons connecting bone to muscle. The largest are on both sides of the spinal column, running parallel to it.<br>■ Shorter lengths can be taken from the calves of the hind legs. |
| **PREPARING** | ■ Remove stems or branches. Grasp the wand at the base and twist until the fibers break, working your way to the tip. Bend the wand into an S-shape and crank the middle of the wand to loosen the fibers. Then cut the wand from the tree and use the withies. | ■ Soak the leaves in water to make the inner layers swell and burst. Bacteria work on the cell tissue, separating it from the fibers.<br>■ Rinse the fibers in fresh water to stop further bacterial decay and then dry them. | ■ Take a tendon from an animal's body, remove its outer sheath, then clean it and let it dry. Separate the dried fibers and use them as individual threads, or splice or braid them together to form stronger cords. You can soften dried sinew with water or saliva. |

# MAKING NATURAL CORDAGE

Once you have prepared a sufficient quantity of fibers, it's best to let them dry before using them—hang them up in the sun or near a fire. In a survival situation, you can use them before drying. Twisting or rolling the fibers are the two main methods of making natural cordage. As with most survival tasks, practice makes perfect.

> **TOOLS AND MATERIALS**
> Enough prepared natural fibers (see pp. 138–39) to give you the length of cordage that you require

## TWISTED CORDAGE

Start your first length of cordage toward one end, not in the middle, to prevent all the subsequent splices from coinciding at the same point. This provides strength, as each splice is a potential weak point. If they are thin enough, the twisted cordage fibers can then be plaited to create a thicker cord that's even stronger.

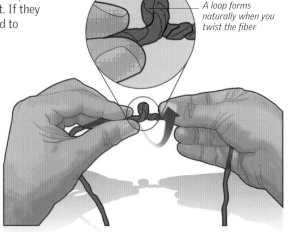

*A loop forms naturally when you twist the fiber*

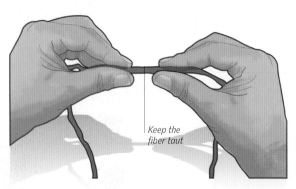

*Keep the fiber taut*

**1** Grip the first length of fiber a third of the way along its length between your left thumb and forefinger.
- Grasp the fiber with the thumb and forefinger of your right hand 1 in (3 cm) from your left.

**2** Twist the fiber with your right hand until a tight loop is formed.
- Keeping the tension in the cord, inch your left thumb and forefinger forward and clamp down on the loop.

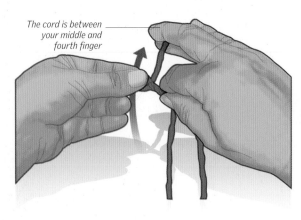

*The cord is between your middle and fourth finger*

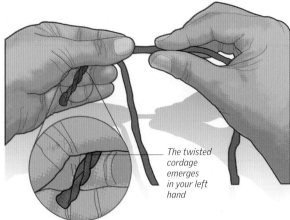

*The twisted cordage emerges in your left hand*

**4** Sweep the middle and fourth fingers of your right hand upward, pulling the left-hand cord under the captive piece.
- Inch your left thumb and forefinger forward, and clamp down on the new twist.

**5** Now that the new twist is clamped by your left hand, you can release your right thumb and forefinger, letting the lower cord fall.
- Grip the upper cord 1 in (3 cm) from your left fingers with your right thumb and forefinger.

## SIMPLE ALTERNATIVE TWIST

You need to start with two fibers of different lengths so that when you splice on additional lengths the splices are staggered. Start by tying one end of one fiber with one end of the other.

- Clamp tied ends in your left thumb and forefinger and the two tails in your right thumb and forefinger about 2 in (5 cm) down.
- Roll both fibers between your fingers away from you for one complete roll. Repeat this until you have about 3 in (7.5 cm) of rolled fibers, then clamp them in your right thumb and forefinger.
- Release your left thumb and forefinger and the rolled fibers will naturally twist together to form a strand of cordage.
- Repeat the process until you have enough for your needs.

## ROLLED CORDAGE

This method of rolling cordage, which is also known as the "pygmy roll," is easier to do if you're sitting down. As with the simple alternative twist (see left), you need to start with two fibers of different lengths and tie one end of one fiber to one end of the other.

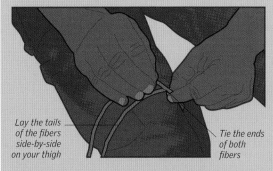

Lay the tails of the fibers side-by-side on your thigh

Tie the ends of both fibers

**1** Hold the tied ends between the thumb and forefinger of your left hand.
- Lay the two tails of the fibers on your right thigh.

Keep the fingers together

The fibers are twisted but remain separate

**2** Use the flat palm of your right hand to roll both fibers simultaneously away from you. You may find it easier to use the flat of your fingers.
- At the end of the roll, clamp the fibers down onto your thigh with the tips of your fingers.

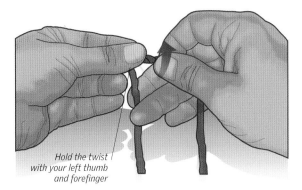

Hold the twist with your left thumb and forefinger

**3** Move your right hand back so that 1 in (3 cm) of cord is visible and apply another twist.
- At the same time reach forward with the middle and fourth fingers of your right hand and grasp the cord hanging from your left fingers.

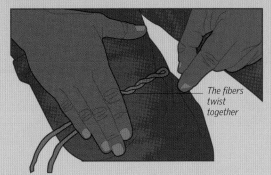

The fibers twist together

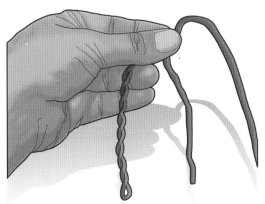

**6** Repeat Steps 3, 4, and 5 as you work your way along the length of cord.
- To splice in an extra length, overlap the new piece 2 in (6 cm) along the existing fiber and twist the two together between your left thumb and forefinger. Then continue with the process as before.

**3** Release your left thumb and forefinger and the rolled fibers will naturally twist together to form a strand of cordage.
- Repeat the process, splicing in more cordage as required.

# TYING KNOTS

**THERE ARE HUNDREDS** of different types of knot in existence, but by practicing the handful of straightforward knots shown here and overleaf, you should be able to accomplish most survival tasks. Start by tying each knot in the situation you expect to use it—for example, erecting a poncho shelter—and then practice it at least 20 times.

> **THE ENDS OF A LINE**
> The end of a rope or line that takes the most active part in knot tying is the working end. The other end is called the standing end—it's more passive, as the knot is tied around it.

## SLIP KNOT

A slip knot is a good example of a simple knot that has many practical uses in survival situations.

*Hold the working end between your right thumb and forefinger*

*Hold the standing end between your left thumb and forefinger*

**1** Twist the standing line over the working line to form a loop.
- Hold the loop between your left thumb and forefinger.

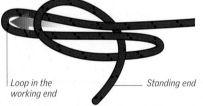

*Loop in the working end*     *Standing end*

**2** Make a loop with the working end and pass it into the first loop.
- Collect the second loop with your left thumb and forefinger and pull it through.

*Pull to tighten the loop*

*Pull to loosen the loop*

**3** Gather both ends in your right thumb and forefinger and pull them away from the loop in your left hand.
- Put the loop over whatever you want to secure—for example, a button-tie on your bivy sack—and pull the knot tight.

## ARBOR KNOT

This all-purpose knot has several survival uses. When erecting a poncho or a tarp (see Chapter Four), it can be used as a tie-off knot to secure one end of a line to a fixed point, such as a tree or peg, where no adjustment is required. It can also be used as a lashing to secure two poles together—for example, in an A-frame shelter (see p. 164)—with just one turn of cordage.

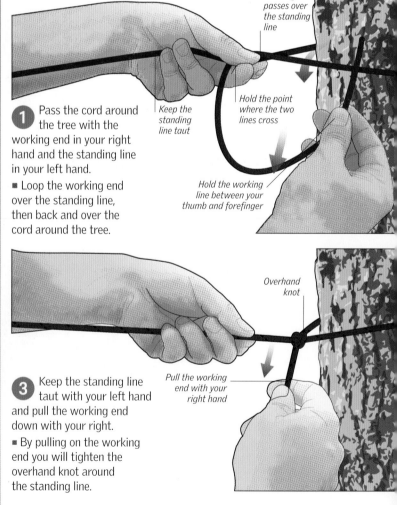

*Working line passes over the standing line*

*Keep the standing line taut*

*Hold the point where the two lines cross*

*Hold the working line between your thumb and forefinger*

**1** Pass the cord around the tree with the working end in your right hand and the standing line in your left hand.
- Loop the working end over the standing line, then back and over the cord around the tree.

*Overhand knot*

**3** Keep the standing line taut with your left hand and pull the working end down with your right.
- By pulling on the working end you will tighten the overhand knot around the standing line.

*Pull the working end with your right hand*

## OVERHAND KNOTS

An overhand knot is the first part of the knot you use to tie the laces on your shoes. One overhand knot tied around another forms a stop knot or they can be tied as a double overhand knot around a fixture.

### OVERHAND KNOT

Twist the left line over the right to form a loop. Hold it with your right thumb and forefinger.

■ Pass the working end through the loop with your left forefinger and thumb and pull both ends to tighten.

### DOUBLE OVERHAND KNOT

Follow the sequence for the overhand knot (left), but pass the working end through the loop twice before pulling the two ends.

■ A stop knot used at the end of a line can stop the line from slipping.

*Tie an overhand knot around the standing line*

**2** Pass the working end around the standing line, and then over itself to form an overhand loop.

■ Pass the free end up through the loop. (You have now tied an overhand knot around the standing line—see above, Step 1).

*Pull hard on the standing line to lock the two knots together*

*Pull to unlock*

*Two single overhand knots tightly locked*

**4** Tie another overhand knot in the working end as close to the first knot as possible.

■ Once the two knots are locked together, give the standing line a sharp tug.

## DOUBLE CHAIN FASTENING KNOT

This knot securely attaches the free end of a line to a fixture, particularly when weight is involved and you don't want the knot to slip or come loose.

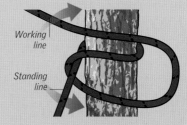

*Working line*

*Standing line*

**1** Loop the working end around the fixture, such as a tree or pole.

■ Pass the working end over and around the standing line.

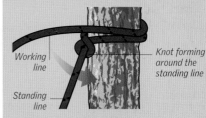

*Working line*

*Standing line*

*Knot forming around the standing line*

**2** Pass the working end back around the fixture and then bring it back under the standing line.

*Working line goes around the fixture*

*Standing line*

*Working line goes over the standing line*

**3** Pass the working end over the top and around the standing line again, and once more around the fixture.

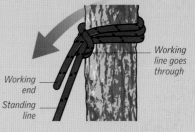

*Working end*

*Standing line*

*Working line goes through*

**4** As you bring round the working line, thread it underneath itself to complete the knot.

■ Lock the knot neatly into position.

## DOUBLE SHEET BEND

The sheet bend, also known as the "weaver's hitch," is an extremely useful survival knot as it securely ties together two ropes. Double sheet bends are even more secure and are recommended for tying ropes of different thickness. In this instance you use the thinner of the two ropes to tie the knot.

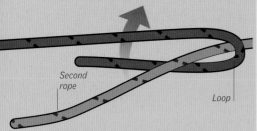

*Second rope*

*Loop*

**1** Start with two ropes and form a loop in the working end of one of them.

■ Pass the end of the second rope through the loop.

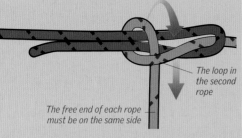

*The loop in the second rope*

*The free end of each rope must be on the same side*

**2** Pass the free end of the second rope first under, then up and over the loop. Pass the end through the new loop you have created.

■ To finish a single sheet bend, pull the standing end of each rope to tighten it.

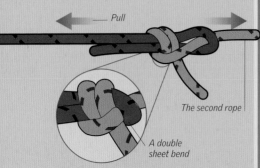

*Pull*

*The second rope*

*A double sheet bend*

**3** To tie a double sheet bend, pass the free end of the second rope through the loop (as in step 2) again.

■ Tighten the knot as before by pulling the free end of each rope.

## SIBERIAN HITCH

This knot, which is also known as the "Evenk knot," is good for attaching a rope to a fixture—for example, when securing a ridgeline to a tree for a poncho shelter (see p. 158).

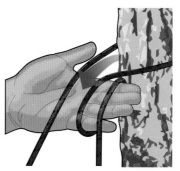

**1** Pass the cord around the tree with the working line in your right hand and the standing line in your left hand.

**2** Lay the standing line on the palm of your left hand.

■ Loop the working line one and a half times around your fingers.

*Hook your thumb into the loop*

**3** Bring your left hand under the standing line.

■ Turn the palm of your hand so that one loop twists over another.

**4** Hold the working end in your right thumb and forefinger.

■ Bring the loop that is around your left fingers over the standing line.

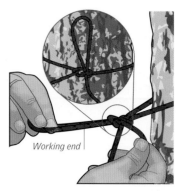

*Working end*

**5** Pinch the working line with the fingers of your left hand.

■ Pull it up through the loop to tighten the knot on itself.

**6** Pull the working end again, to tighten the knot around the tree.

■ To free the knot, pull the end of the standing line.

# TAUT LINE HITCH

This knot is widely used in survival and outdoor activities because it can be adjusted to increase or decrease the tension in a fixed line—for example, a guide rope on a tent or a mooring on a boat in tidal waters.

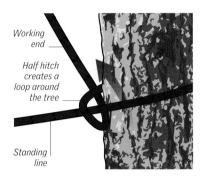

*Working end*

*Half hitch creates a loop around the tree*

*Standing line*

**1** Attach the standing line to an anchor point, such as a tent, and pass the working line around a tree.
- Tie a half hitch (see below) with the working end around the standing line.

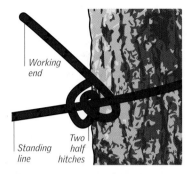

*Working end*

*Standing line*

*Two half hitches*

**2** Tie another half hitch next to the first one, so that the two half hitches sit side by side around the standing line.
- Don't tighten the half hitches yet.

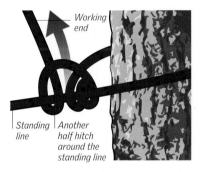

*Working end*

*Standing line*

*Another half hitch around the standing line*

**3** Pass the working end under the standing line and back through the new loop it created (but outside of the loops in Steps 1 and 2).

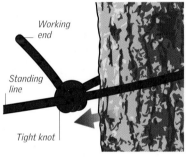

*Working end*

*Standing line*

*Tight knot*

**4** Tighten the knot by pulling both the lines.
- Pull the knot further from the anchor point to increase the tension.

# QUICK KNOT RELEASE

You can dismantle a tent or free a boat from its mooring more quickly by finishing off the taut line hitch (see left) with a quick-release knot.

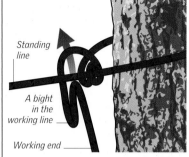

*Standing line*

*A bight in the working line*

*Working end*

**1** Repeat Step 3 of the taut line hitch (see left), but this time make a loop, known as a "bight," in the working line and pass it—rather than just the end—through the loop.

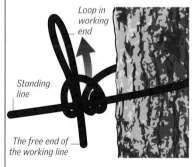

*Loop in working end*

*Standing line*

*The free end of the working line*

**2** Tighten the knot as in Step 4 (see left).
- Leave the working end free so you can pull it quickly to release the knot.

# HALF HITCH

The half hitch is a simple knot that forms the basis for other knots (see taut line hitch, above). It's not a secure knot and, when used alone, it tends to slip. You can double or treble the knot to remedy this. Two half hitches under tension can be difficult to undo without cutting the cord, especially after a few days, if the knot has dried out after being wet.

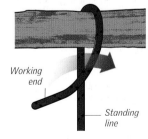

*Working end*

*Standing line*

**1** Pass the cord around the fixture, such as a bar or tree.
- Pass the working end around the standing line and back through the loop.

*The knot is not secure*

*Working end*

**2** Hold the standing line and push the half hitch knot toward the fixture to tighten it.
- Repeat the sequence and tie another half hitch.

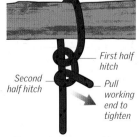

*Second half hitch*

*First half hitch*

*Pull working end to tighten*

**3** Push the second knot tight to the first hitch knot for more security.
- If you need to, finish off the working end with an overhand knot (see p. 143).

# USING CUTTING TOOLS

**ANYONE VENTURING INTO THE WILDERNESS** should carry some kind of knife, preferably a bushcraft knife. It's probably the most important survival tool after knowledge. Although a good knife will help you through many survival situations, look at the environment you are traveling to and choose your cutting tools according to their potential uses—for example, you may need a saw as well as a knife.

**WARNING!**
If you drop a bushcraft knife, never attempt to catch it because there's a very good chance you will lose your fingers!

## BUSHCRAFT KNIFE

An experienced person can accomplish most survival skills, such as making feather sticks (see pp. 120–21), with a quality bushcraft knife. This type of cutting tool has a number of crucial features that will stand you in good stead in every situation.

*A firesteel that fits into your sheath means that, as long as you have your knife, you can also get a fire going*

*Fitted leather sheath holds the knife securely*

*Attachment point for a wrist lanyard*

*The handle is comfortable to hold and work for extended periods. Avoid ribbed, rubber handles*

*Blades that extend through to the end of the handle (full tang) have no weak points*

*Sharpened blade ends near the handle – working close to the handle puts less strain on your wrist*

*Blade is ³⁄₁₆ in (4 mm) thick and made of stainless or high-carbon steel*

*The guard is a ridge in the handle that reduces the chance of your hand slipping on to the blade*

## LARGE KNIVES

All over the world, people living primitive lives have two essential items: a cooking pot and a large working blade, either a parang or machete.

■ Parangs and machetes are similar types of knife. The parang is associated with the Malay people and there are many varieties available. Machetes are more common—you can still see machetes being used in Africa today that were made 40 years ago from old Landrover suspension springs! The kukri is a similar knife used by the Ghurkas of Nepal.

■ A parang or machete blade is about 18–20 in (45–50 cm) long and is used primarily for cutting and slashing but, like the ax, can be used for intricate work.

■ Always wear a wrist lanyard when using a machete, parang, or kukri—and pay attention to what you are doing.

KUKRI

MACHETE/PARANG

### KNIFE KNOW-HOW

■ A bushcraft knife is used primarily for carving, cutting, and splitting small logs. If you need to chop large logs, use either a machete or a saw.

■ A knife doesn't need to be longer than 8–9 in (20–22.5 cm).

■ Don't use a knife with a serrated edge when working with wood, as the serrations make it hard to use the part of the blade closest to the handle (essential for making feather sticks, etc).

■ Keep your knife safe when not in use. Clean and dry the blade and return it to its sheath.

■ Wear your sheath on your belt or around your neck on a lanyard. Belt sheaths may be high (the handle is above the belt) or low (the handle is below the belt, which allows you to sit down without the handle poking you in the side).

# SHARPENING A KNIFE

It's very important to keep the blade of your knife sharp. Blunt blades are dangerous because they are likely to bounce or slip off the wood you're working on. Also, blades that have completely lost their cutting edge are very difficult to sharpen.

## SHARPENING STONES

Keep a good sharpening stone at home to ensure you always set out with a knife that is sharp.

- In the field, carry a smaller, lightweight device for quickly re-sharpening a blade that is beginning to lose its edge.
- There is a good range of small sharpening stones (medium one side, fine the other) that fit into a neat leather pouch.
- Small automatic sharpeners are available to buy that use two sets of ceramic stones to sharpen a knife pulled between them.

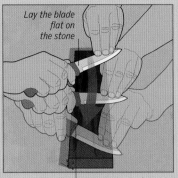

*Lay the blade flat on the stone*

*Raise the back of the blade to lay the edge on the stone*

**1** Hold the knife in a forehand grip, with the blade pointing away from you. Support the tip of the blade with the thumb and fingers of your other hand.

- Push the knife so the full blade arcs over the stone in one sweep.
- Lift the blade and return to the start, repeating the action 6–8 times.

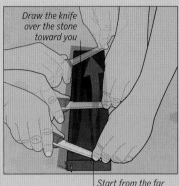

*Draw the knife over the stone toward you*

*Start from the far end of the stone*

**2** Repeat the sequence for the other side of the blade, but reversing the crucial elements.

- Hold the knife with a backhand grip, with the blade pointing toward you at the far end of the stone.
- Pull the knife in an arc over the stone in one draw. Lift and return to the start, repeating the action 6–8 times.

# WORKING WITH YOUR KNIFE

The way you hold your bushcraft knife can help you accomplish a variety of cutting tasks easily and safely. There are several essential grips, including the forehand, backhand, and chest lever. In most cases, you need to grip the handle firmly at the end nearest the blade so that you can cut with the part of the blade nearest the handle.

## SAFELY PASSING A KNIFE

A group may only have one good knife for everybody to use, so you'll need to pass it to each other frequently. Pass the knife handle first, with the blade up. This simple and safe method is easily learned and can be adopted by everyone.

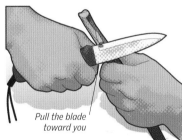

*Pull the blade toward you*

## FOREHAND GRIP

This grip is the most natural and the one most often used. It allows your back and arm to provide the power and strength, while your wrist provides the control. Placing one or both thumbs on the back of the blade allows you additional control for finer, more detailed work. Make sure the blade is facing down. Otherwise you are likely to give yourself a serious cut.

*Steady the blade with one or both thumbs*

## BACKHAND GRIP

This is the same as the forehand grip, except the blade faces up toward you. You can use it when you want to see and control exactly where the blade is going, or when you're cutting something and a follow-through would injure you—for example, when sharpening a stick.

## CHEST LEVER

This is an extremely effective technique in which you hold the knife in a backhand grip and use the muscles of your arm and chest to provide power and strength. You can cut close to your body while your wrists control the cutting action.

*Work the wood with the part of the blade nearest the handle*

# TREE-FELLING WITH A BLADE

For shelters and fuel, the largest tree you are likely to cut down will be about 4 in (10 cm) in diameter. For anything larger you'd need an ax, but for smaller ones use a saw (see pp. 150–51). If you don't have a saw, use the blade of your bushcraft knife or a machete or parang. Whichever blade you use, keep its lanyard around your wrist.

**1** Figure out the lean of the tree and start your first cut on the opposite side. This stops your blade jamming in the cut as the tree leans further.

■ Hit the top of the blade with a thumping stick (club).

■ Move the blade about 5/8 in (15 mm) to one side of the first cut, and then angle the blade at 45 degrees toward the first cut.

■ Continue to alternate this action from side to side, cutting a V into the wood.

> **WARNING!**
> Ensure your blade is sharp. Keep what you're cutting between you and the blade, with the blade pointing away.

*Your thumping stick is 18 in (45 cm) long and 3 in (7.5 cm) thick*

*The way the tree leans is the direction in which it will fall when you cut it*

*As you progress, the cut will open with the weight of the tree*

*Place the blade of your knife at 45 degrees to the surface of the tree*

*Choose the smallest tree that will provide you with the wood you need*

*Strike the back of your knife blade into the wood*

# SPLITTING FIREWOOD

When you split wood into fuel for a fire, use the largest blade you have, work on a solid surface, and avoid wood that has large knots as these prevent the blade from making a clean cut.

> **SAFE WORKING AREA**
> Chop wood in a safe area that other people won't wander into and where there are no snagging hazards or objects to impede your swing and knock your knife off-target.

## LARGE LOGS

If you only have a bushcraft knife to work with, and you need to split large logs into smaller pieces, the following method works well.

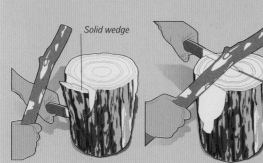

*Solid wedge*

*Hit the wedge hard with your stick until it sinks into the log*

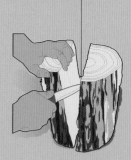

*Even wet wood will be dry in the center*

**1** Hit the back of your knife with a stick and cut a solid wedge from the side of the log.

**2** Use your knife and a thumping stick to start the initial cut across the top of the log.

**3** Hit the wedge into the initial cut. Keep doing this until the log splits. Use more wedges if you need to.

**4** If the log does not split completely, force it open with your hands or pry it with your blade.

*Make a V-shaped cut in the side of the tree trunk*

**2** Work the cut around the tree until you've almost reached the middle from every direction except from below.

■ If you try to cut completely through the wood from one side it will get increasingly difficult as the blade goes deeper.

**3** Once the cuts are deep enough to weaken the wood, you will be able to snap the tree in two.

■ Take care that the tree doesn't fall on your feet.

## SMALL LOGS

Splitting a small log can be more tricky than splitting a large log, because it's difficult to balance it safely while you hit the blade with your thumping stick.

**1** Place the log on a solid surface and put your knife in the middle of the end of the log you're about to chop.

■ Hit the back of the blade firmly with your stick.

*Put the blade in the wood so you can steady the log*

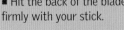

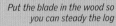

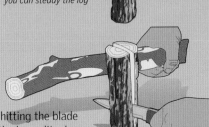

**2** Keep hitting the blade until the log splits down the middle. Split each piece again to quarter the wood.

**4** To trim the branches from the fallen tree, start at the bottom and work your way to the top. This allows you a clear, short swing for your thumping stick.

■ Keep the tree between you and the blade, and trim each branch in the direction of its growth.

■ If you're using a machete, you don't need a thumping stick, as the heavy blade has enough momentum of its own.

*If you're trimming on the ground, lay the tree on a flat, solid surface*

*Give yourself a clear swing and make sure the blade cannot harm you if it slips*

# USING A SAW

A saw is much better than a bushcraft knife for larger jobs, such as preparing logs for a fire or cutting down the poles needed to build a shelter. There are several types of pocket saw available that are lightweight and take up very little room in your backpack or survival tin.

## USING A POCKET CHAINSAW

Using a pocket chainsaw to cut down a small tree is safe and not especially hard work. You can use the same saw to trim the branches and then cut the wood into manageable sections.

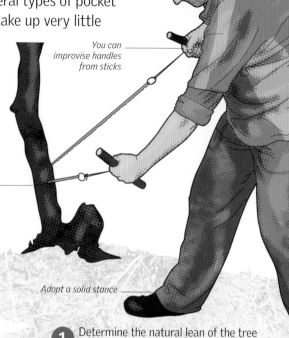

*You can improvise handles from sticks*

*Insert a wedge to prevent the saw jamming*

*Adopt a solid stance*

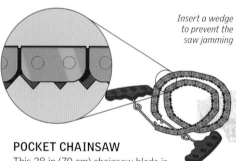

**POCKET CHAINSAW**
This 28 in (70 cm) chainsaw blade is compact and has attachment rings and handles. It can cut through a (3 in (7.5 cm) diameter tree in under 10 seconds.

**1** Determine the natural lean of the tree and start to saw on the opposite side.
- Pull the saw back and forth.
- Knock a wedge in behind the saw when halfway through to stop the tree from jamming the blade.

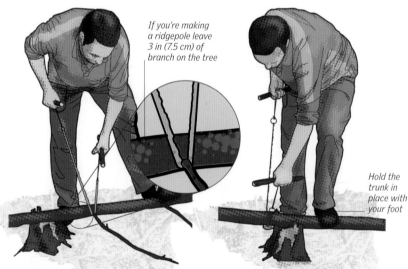

*If you're making a ridgepole leave 3 in (7.5 cm) of branch on the tree*

*Hold the trunk in place with your foot*

**2** Slow down when the saw has nearly cut through the tree.
- Allow the weight of the tree to snap the cut and break it in two.

**3** Use the same back-and-forth rhythm to trim the branches.
- Clear the branches away as you trim them from the tree.

**4** Saw the trimmed trunk into a measured section.
- When you're halfway through, prop up the trunk to make sawing easier.

## FOLDING SAWS

Folding saws are strong, light, and convenient. Some, such as the Sandvik Laplander, have a serrated blade that folds into the handle (see right). Others, such as the backpacker's (see below), can be dismantled for stowing.

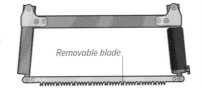

The blade opens and closes at a hinge

FOLDING SAW

### BACKPACKER'S FOLDING SAW

These saws are generally lightweight and strong, but are not as effective as the pocket chainsaw. If space is tight, then you can pack only the blade and improvise a bow saw, using natural materials found in the woods.

Removable blade

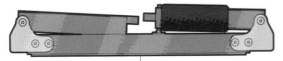

The tension frame and saw blade can usually be taken apart and stowed safely

BACKPACKER'S FOLDING SAW

## COMMANDO SAW

This saw takes up very little space and consists of a serrated wire blade with a swivel ring at each end. It's a useful piece of survival equipment, although it tends to snag and snap easily unless you keep it completely straight. You can easily convert it into an improvised bow saw, and, with a little more effort, make it into a very effective tension saw.

COMMANDO SAW

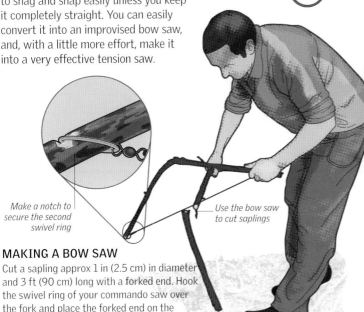

Make a notch to secure the second swivel ring

Use the bow saw to cut saplings

### MAKING A BOW SAW

Cut a sapling approx 1 in (2.5 cm) in diameter and 3 ft (90 cm) long with a forked end. Hook the swivel ring of your commando saw over the fork and place the forked end on the ground. Ease the sapling into the other ring and make a notch for the ring to fit in.

## IF YOU HAVE NO TOOLS

Even without any cutting tools, it's still possible to safely break wood down to size. The answer is snapping—or even burning—the wood. Don't be tempted to stand branches and sticks against a log or rock and then stamp on them in the middle. In a genuine survival situation your feet are your only means of transportation so don't do anything that risks injuring them.

### SNAPPING THE WOOD

You need to limit the size of wood you're trying to break—don't try to snap branches that are too broad. Use wood that's dead, because green living wood just bends and refuses to break completely.

■ Find two trees that are 1–2 ft (30–60 cm) apart—or a tree with two trunks close together—to use as a fulcrum for the wood. Place the wood in the fulcrum.

■ Adopt a firm and steady stance and, with one foot in front of the other, pull the wood toward you until it breaks. Pulling toward you keeps your center of gravity over your spread feet, while pushing away from you causes you to stumble forward when the wood breaks.

Hold firmly on to the piece of wood

Place the wood between two trees—one is a stop or buffer, the other is a leverage point

### BURNING THE WOOD

If you have a fire going, place the wood on the fire where you want it to break. Leave it on the fire until it burns all the way through. Alternatively, when it has burned halfway through, use the snapping method described above—but don't work on the wood while it's still burning or hot.

# TAKING SHELTER

# TAKING SHELTER

**A shelter is your primary means** of protection in a survival situation. It can be somewhere to simply keep dry during a sudden downpour or a place to spend several nights while out in the wilds. It's important, therefore, that you understand how to correctly construct your shelter. After all, its effectiveness could mean the difference between relative comfort and abject misery!

In a survival situation, it's important to play a proactive role in your own continued survival and rescue. You can only achieve this effectively if you're in a good condition—both physically and mentally. A day or night spent exposed to the elements will determine how well or how badly you perform the next day. A restless and uncomfortable night, for example, will lead to sleep deprivation, which can make you moody, irritable, and easily frustrated. This in turn can lead to a lack of concentration and irrational thinking—none of which are helpful in a survival situation.

Cold nights spent in the wilderness seem to last longer than they should, so time spent ensuring that you can

## In this section YOU WILL DISCOVER...

- when to **lie low** in a hollow or **camp in a cave...**
- how to **modify** your **poncho** to put up a **shelter...**
- the difference between a **bothy** and a **bivy...**
- how to **bed down** with **duck down** or **wake up** in a **wickiup...**
- the **importance** of using your **noggins** to **secure** your shelter...
- how to **configure** your **fig leaves** to keep out the **rain...**

**On any expedition**, you should aim to carry equipment—such as a basic bivy or a tarpaulin –that could be used to form a shelter should you need to protect yourself from the elements.

**A SPACE BLANKET**, however, is quite simply an essential piece of gear—if you pack nothing else, make sure you carry one and keep it with you at all times. Space blankets pack down very small and are available with one side silver (to reflect heat) and one side bright orange (to aid location). No matter what environment you're exploring, a space blanket can offer you immediate protection from the elements.

**With a little ingenuity**, a space blanket can also be converted into a basic shelter. You will find instructions on how to build a variety of shelters throughout this chapter, but always remember the following general tips, too:

- First look for natural sheltering places
- Look out for hazards such as signs of flooding
- Construct your shelter well before nightfall
- Clear the ground before you start to build
- Position the entrance at right angles to the wind
- Build for the worst possible weather conditions
- Make sure your shelter is sturdy and secure
- Don't over-exert yourself as you build
- Raise your sleeping area off the ground
- If on a slope, sleep with your head higher than your feet

always enjoy as warm, dry, safe, and comfortable a night as possible is rarely wasted.

With shelter-building—as with other areas of survival—you should always apply the principle of expending the least amount of energy for the maximum amount of gain. This could mean simply exploiting the options nature has already provided, such as caves or hollows. Finally, plan for the worst conditions—it may be sunny when you build your shelter but pouring with rain at three in the morning!

The **effectiveness of a shelter** can mean the difference between relative comfort and **abject misery**

# HOLLOWS AND CAVES

**IF YOU DON'T HAVE** a shelter of your own, look for shelter opportunities that nature has already provided for you, such as a cave or a natural hollow in the ground. However, avoid natural hollows in low-lying areas that may flood and, if you're on a slope, keep well away from hollows exposed to run-off water.

## BEDDING

Cover the floor of a shelter with some form of bedding to prevent your body from losing heat to the cold ground through conduction. After all the energy you've used to build the shelter, why waste it on an uncomfortable night? Use the driest materials you can find (see list below).

### MAKE YOURSELF COMFORTABLE

Here are some ideas to help you enjoy a good night's sleep in your shelter:
- Collect twice as much bedding as you think you need: 6 in (15 cm) of holly, for example, compresses to about 2 in (5 cm) after you've been lying on it for a while.
- Place logs around the bedded area to stop the bedding from shifting and spreading.
- If the ground slopes, sleep with your head higher than your feet.

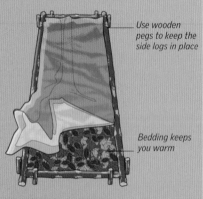

Use wooden pegs to keep the side logs in place

Bedding keeps you warm

### BEDDING MATERIALS

- Feathers, such as duck and goose down, are the best bedding as they retain warmth but not moisture.
- You're unlikely to find enough feathers, so also try pine and spruce boughs, dry leaves, moss, bracken, grasses, and holly (cover it to prevent it from pricking you).

## NATURAL HOLLOWS

A hollow that may be too shallow to sit in can still provide shelter from the wind if you lie in it—and, with a basic roof, keep you dry too.

A digging stick is a sturdy piece of wood with a pointed end

**1** If the hollow isn't deep enough to lie in, remove some soil with a digging stick.
- Beware wet soil, as it could be prone to flooding.
- If the ground is too hard to dig, build up the sides with logs for extra depth.
- Lay bedding material on the ground before continuing.

Lay a log on top of the cross poles and along the length of the hollow

Make sure the poles are resting firmly on the side of the hollow

**2** With your saw, cut a number of sturdy poles or branches (see pp. 150–51) that are long enough to place across the hollow to create a supporting roof.
- Cut a thicker, longer log and place it across the poles. This will create height and slope for a pitched roof. Make sure the log isn't too heavy.

## TAKING SHELTER IN CAVES

Caves are ready-made shelters that are usually dry and secure. There are some dangers, including animals, poor air quality, and water. Many caves are outlets for streams or are connected to pools. Don't go any further in than you can see, as there may be hidden drops, slippery surfaces, and crevasses. Avoid old and disused mines, as they may be prone to collapse.

### ANIMAL DANGERS

Many animals, such as bears, bats, insects, spiders, and snakes, shelter in caves, so check the ground around the entrance and inside for signs of tracks and nests. Vampire bats can be dangerous as they are known to carry rabies. Bat droppings (guano) form a thick layer on the ground and, in large quantities, can be highly combustible.

### POOR AIR QUALITY

If a cave makes you feel light-headed or nauseous, leave at once because the air may be foul due to excess carbon dioxide. Other warning signs are an increased pulse and breathing rate. If a flame starts to dim, or turn blue, leave the cave immediately—this may not be a sign of excess carbon dioxide but a lack of oxygen, which can be worse.

### LIGHTING FIRES

If you build a fire at the front of a cave the smoke can blow back inside and the fire can block your exit if it gets too big. Build a fire toward the rear of the cave, but make sure that there is a sufficient flow of air for the smoke to escape. You can erect a small fire reflector or make a pile of rocks at the entrance to reflect heat back into the cave.

## COASTAL CAVES

Coastal caves share the same dangers as any other cave, but they are also subject to the tides, which can rise very quickly—in some areas they can advance hundreds of yards in a matter of minutes.

### THE DANGERS OF COASTAL CAVES

When you're assessing a coastal cave, look out for the following warning signs of flooding during high tide:

- A line of seaweed, driftwood, or flotsam and jetsam—either in the cave or further back on the beach either side of the entrance.
- A damp or wet smell. The cave may even look wet if the tide has recently gone out.
- Rock pools in the cave or in front of it.

*Air currents take the smoke out of the cave*

*A pile of rocks at the entrance helps retain heat in the cave*

*Use fuel that doesn't produce too much smoke*

**3** Place shorter branches, sticks, or poles over the top of the log and cross branches to create the pitched roof.
- Pack these materials tightly together and make sure they're firmly in position.

*Lay a covering of short branches on the roof*

*The space between the support and pitched roof will help retain the heat generated inside the shelter*

*The height and slope allow water to run off the pitched roof, rather than seep through*

**4** Leave an entrance at one end of the shelter with enough space to get in and out without disturbing the roof.
- Ensure the entrance doesn't face the wind—an angle of 90 degrees to the wind is best.
- Insulate the pitched roof with as much foliage as possible.
- Start the final insulation layer at the ground, working up to the top of the roof to create an overlap for rainwater to run off.
- In wet conditions secure your ponch or space blanket over the top.

*The entrance should allow air to circulate in the shelter*

# USE-ANYWHERE SHELTERS

**WITH A PONCHO OR BIVY SACK** (see pp. 160–61), you can make a shelter for use in any environment and in any conditions. You can also adapt any type of material—a survival space blanket, ground sheet, or tarpaulin—in the same way.

(see pp. 160–61)

### TOOLS AND MATERIALS
- Poncho, bivy sack, groundsheet, space blanket, or tarpaulin
- Cordage or elastic bungees
- Pegs; stick or pole
- Rock or log for hammering
- Survival knife or penknife

## ONE-POLE PONCHO

This shelter is very quick and easy to erect and take down—useful when energy levels are low or when you just want to get out of the rain. If you need to be rescued, put the most visible color on the outside to increase the chance of being spotted.

**1** Cut three 2 ft (60 cm) lengths of cordage and one 6 ft (2 m) length.
- Tie the shorter lengths into loops using an overhand knot (see p. 143).
- Tie the long length to one corner with a Siberian hitch knot (see p. 144).
- Fasten the cordage loops to the corner grommets.

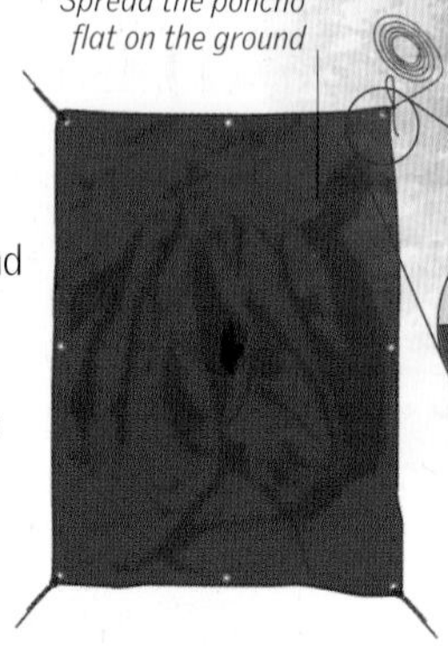

*Spread the poncho flat on the ground*

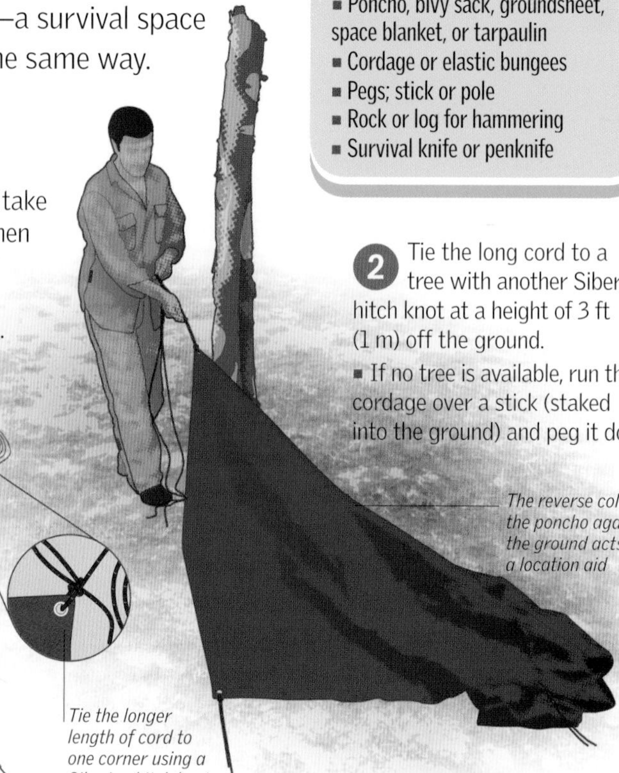

*Tie the longer length of cord to one corner using a Siberian hitch knot*

**2** Tie the long cord to a tree with another Siberian hitch knot at a height of 3 ft (1 m) off the ground.
- If no tree is available, run the cordage over a stick (staked into the ground) and peg it down.

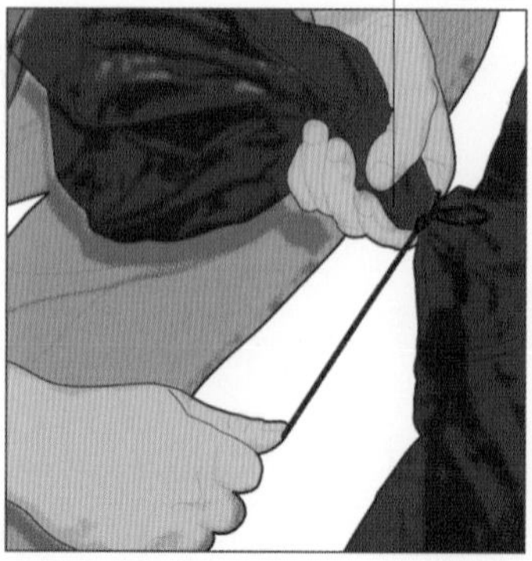

*The reverse color of the poncho against the ground acts as a location aid*

*Make sure the top of the stick in the poncho is secure*

**3** Place one end of a 3-ft (1-m) long stick in the hood of the poncho.
- Seal the hood by tying a simple knot.
- Wind several turns of cordage around the knot and secure it with an arbor knot (see p. 142).

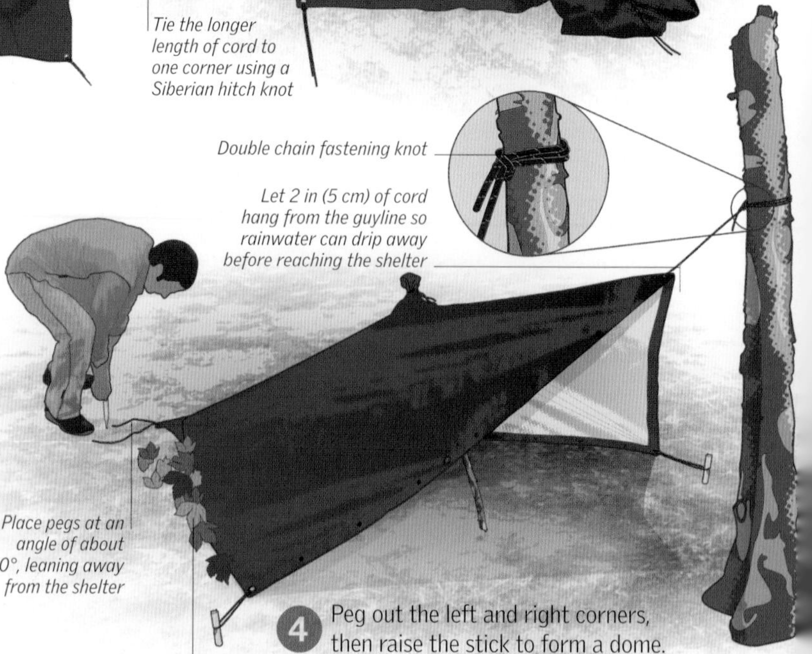

*Double chain fastening knot*

*Let 2 in (5 cm) of cord hang from the guyline so rainwater can drip away before reaching the shelter*

*Place pegs at an angle of about 40°, leaning away from the shelter*

*Pile leaves around the edges of the shelter to keep out the wind*

**4** Peg out the left and right corners, then raise the stick to form a dome.
- Pull the rear corner taut and peg it out to add tension, making the structure rigid.
- To enter the shelter, curl your body around the center pole.

# CORDED A-FRAME

This poncho A-frame creates a tentlike shelter between two trees. If you have enough cordage, a single ridgeline can be tied between the trees; if not, use two cordage loops, as shown below. Alternatively, you can use a ridgepole at the same height.

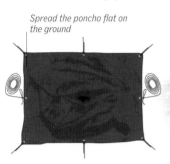

*Spread the poncho flat on the ground*

*Tie one of the longer cords to a tree using a double chain fastening knot*

**1** Find two trees 2 ft (60 cm) further apart than the length of your poncho.

■ Attach cordage loops 1 ft (30 cm) long to each grommet on the longer sides of your poncho and 3-ft (1-m) loops to the end ones.

■ Tie a knot around the hood to seal it.

**2** Tie the end of one of the longer cords to a tree with a double chain fastening knot (see p. 143) at a height of 3 ft (1 m).

■ Tie the other long cord to the second tree with a taut line hitch knot (see p. 145) and adjust the hitch to pull it tight.

*Raise the hood to prevent water from pooling*

**3** Peg the middle loop of each side to pull the poncho taut. Peg out the four remaining loops, pulling tight as you go.

■ If you have enough cordage, raise the hood by tying it either to a second horizontal line or to a vertical line passed over a branch above.

■ Place long boughs along each side of the shelter, with shorter boughs at each end to hold in bedding material.

**NEED TO KNOW**
■ Block one end of the shelter with branches, boughs, and mulch to help retain heat.
■ If your material has no grommets, use button ties instead (see p. 161).

## TENT PEGS

You can make your own tent pegs and then either reuse them or replace them with new ones when necessary. Discard old pegs that naturally decompose over time.

### MAKING TENT PEGS

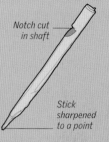

*Notch cut in shaft*
*Stick sharpened to a point*

■ Pegs should be about 9i n (22.5 cm) long and 1 in (2.5 cm) in diameter. Anything less will either snap under pressure or pull out in high winds.
■ Cut wood for the pegs from green trees.
■ Don't use wood from the ground as it will be in some stage of decay.
■ Dry out new pegs slowly over the embers of a fire to harden them. Remove them when they're a light brown color. Wet wood sounds deep and dull when you tap it; as it dries the sound gets higher and crisper.
■ Never drive a peg in with your foot. Use a stone or a heavy stick instead. If you misjudge it, the peg may stab you through the ankle or pierce your boot and even your foot.

## ALTERNATIVE DESIGN

If you're in a group and you each have a poncho, you can clip two ponchos together and use one as a built-in floor.

### USING TWO PONCHOS

First clip the poppers of both ponchos on their two long sides to form a tube. The top one is the A-frame, the bottom one the groundsheet.
■ Pack all your bedding material under the bottom poncho and hold it in place by laying branches at either end.
■ Assemble the shelter with the top poncho in the same way as the single poncho version.

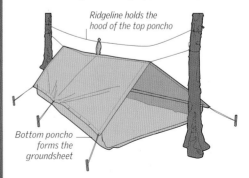

*Ridgeline holds the hood of the top poncho*
*Bottom poncho forms the groundsheet*

# BIVY PUP TENT

A bivy sack is a lightweight, waterproof cover for a sleeping bag and is made out of a breathable material that cuts down condensation. It's an essential component of ultralight camping (see p. 52) and can very easily be turned into a single-person pup tent. The advantage of making a tent from the bivy sack is that, in wet conditions, the rain runs off the side and doesn't seep to the inside as quickly as it does when the bag is flat on the ground.

> **TOOLS AND MATERIALS**
> - Bivy sack
> - Saplings
> - Button ties
> - Wooden pegs
> - Cordage and knife
> - Rock or log for hammering

**1** Lay the bivy sack flat on the ground where you intend to set it up.
- If you have the flap of the hood on top it will form a door that hangs down. However, if the flap is on the bottom you can tie it up as a door.
- Attach a button tie (see panel, opposite) with a loop to each of the bottom corners of the bivy sack.
- Peg the button-tie loops into the ground.

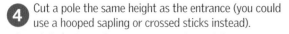

*Attach a button tie to the middle seam of the bivy sack, about 18 in (45 cm) from the bottom*

**2** Attach a button tie with a long length of cordage to the center of the bivy sack's opening and hold it up.
- Pull down the right and left sides of the opening and place a button tie and loop where they meet the ground.
- Peg out the button-tie loops into the ground.

*Hold up the button tie to see how high the entrance can be*

**4** Cut a pole the same height as the entrance (you could use a hooped sapling or crossed sticks instead).
- Stand the pole at the entrance, run the middle button-tie cord over the top, and peg out the cord tightly.
- Readjust all the pegs to ensure tight and even tension.

*Make sure the cord sits squarely on top of the pole*

**5** When you want to get into the bivy pup tent, simply remove the opening pole and climb in feet first.
- Make sure you avoid the long cord as you wriggle in.

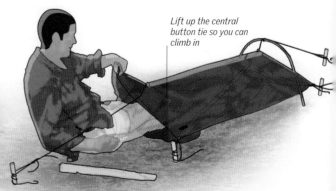

*Lift up the central button tie so you can climb in*

## OTHER SHELTERS

There are other temporary shelters you can erect by adapting the techniques, tools, and materials outlined for both the use-anywhere shelter and the bivy pup tent. Which shelter you choose depends on whether you have a poncho, tarpaulin, or bothy bag.

### HOOPED SHELTER

If there are saplings or soft wood trees, you can form three hoops and peg out your poncho over them.

### TARPAULIN

Attach one side of the tarp to a line between two trees and peg the other end down to the ground at an angle.

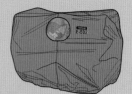

### BOTHY BAG

A bothy bag, or storm shelter, is a large, light, nylon bag that protects one or two people from the elements.

---

**3** Place a hooped sapling (or two crossed sticks) over the bottom of the bivy sack.

■ Attach the button tie that's 18 in (45 cm) from the foot of the bivy sack to the hoop to raise it and provide more space for your feet.

■ Tightly peg out the cord from the hoop.

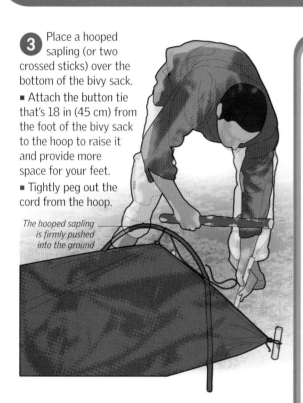

*The hooped sapling is firmly pushed into the ground*

**6** After you have climbed in, replace the pole under the long cord.

■ Use the hood of the bivy sack as a door and open and close as necessary.

*Be sure to replace the pole in a vertical position with the cord squarely on top*

## MAKING A BUTTON TIE

Button ties provide a simple, secure fastening for staking out ponchos and tarpaulins that have no loops or grommets to which you could attach a line. As you don't have to cut holes in the material, it remains waterproof and less prone to ripping.

**1** Encase a small, round, smooth stone (or similar) in material to form a "button". Prepare cord, with the open loop of a slip knot (see p. 142) at one end.

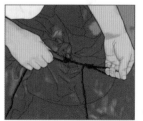

**2** Place the open loop of the slip knot over the neck of the button and pull it tight.

**3** At the other end of the cord make a simple loop to place over your shelter pegs.

# FOREST SHELTERS

**IF YOU FIND YOURSELF** in a survival situation in a temperate forest without a poncho, bivy sack, or tarp, you can make a shelter from natural materials. For example, you can construct a lean-to or an A-frame, or simply adapt a fallen tree. A forest lean-to is easier for a group to build because you can share the workload and don't have to use up too much precious energy.

> ### TOOLS AND MATERIALS
> - Poles and stakes
> - Saw and knife
> - Cordage
> - Saplings
> - Foliage for the roof covering

## BUILDING A FOREST LEAN-TO

A lean-to has a sloping roof that leans against a horizontal ridgepole. It works best on a flat area between two trees or vertical supports secured firmly into the ground. If you're building a lean-to for a group, ask everyone to lie down next to each other and add an additional 6 in (15 cm) per person—this will establish how wide the shelter needs to be.

## BUILDING IN A FOREST

Temperate forests, whether they consist of deciduous or coniferous trees or both, provide many opportunities for finding or building a shelter. Expend the least amount of energy for the most amount of protection—first see what nature can provide before building a shelter yourself.

### POINTS TO REMEMBER

If you do need to make a shelter in a forest, here are some tips:
- Select a place close to water but away from water hazards, such as flooding, animals, and insects.
- Before you start, check for hazards such as deadfalls (sudden branch falls), rockfalls, and flash floods.
- Select a place that gives you maximum protection from the elements and with all the materials you need nearby.
- Collect everything you need before you start building and before it gets dark.
- Make sure your aids to location can be seen or activated quickly (signal fires, heliograph, flares, radio signals).
- Think safety: if possible, wear gloves to clear leaves and debris from the ground to protect you from spiders and snakes.
- Layer down your clothing as you work to prevent overheating.
- Make your shelter as waterproof as you can and ensure your bedding raises you at least 4 in (10 cm) off the ground.

*Make the ridgepole longer than the distance between the trees*

*A log raises the foot of the shelter to give more room for your feet*

*Secure log in place with pegs driven into the ground*

*Lash each support pole (noggin) to the ridgepole and to the tree*

**1** Place the ridgepole against the trees at the height you require and lash it with an arbor knot (see p. 142) to both trees.
- Place a support pole (noggin) under the ridgepole and lash to the trees.
- Firmly peg a log where you want the foot of the shelter to be.

*Criss-cross more saplings over the roof poles*

*Lay the covering from foot to ridgepole to help the rain run off*

**4** Apply the covering to the woven skeleton of the roof and walls. How much you apply depends on the weather you're experiencing.
- Lay large materials—for example, pine or fir boughs, large leaves, clumps of moss—as a base to stop smaller materials from falling through.

# TREE SHELTERS

The branches, roots, or trunk of a fallen tree can make a basic shelter. Make sure the tree is safe before you use it, as a further fall could injure you. Dead trees are probably dry, so don't light a fire under them. Check the base of the tree for snakes, spiders, and nests of insects.

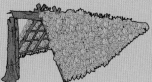

### BROKEN BRANCHES
A branch that has snapped from a tree trunk but hasn't yet fallen makes a good ridgepole. Prop smaller branches and roofing material up against it.

### UPTURNED ROOTS
The base of an uprooted tree can give good protection from the elements. Make sure it's safe and won't flood if it rains, then add boughs and foliage.

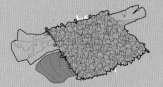

### FALLEN TRUNK
Lay sticks or branches against a fallen trunk to form a pitched roof. Weave saplings across them and cover with bark, turf, moss, leaves, and mulch.

*Roof poles should be at least as long as the shelter needs to be*

*Side stakes along either side of the shelter form walls*

*Lay the saplings horizontally, then criss-cross with diagonal saplings*

**2** Place five roof poles evenly along the ridgepole so that they slope back to the foot of the lean-to.
- Keep the outside poles between the trees to stop them moving outward.
- Lash each roof pole to the ridgepole.
- Hammer in side stakes alongside the outside poles.

**3** Weave saplings in and out through the roof poles, working across and down from the ridgepole.
- Alternate the weave of each row of saplings, first horizontally and then diagonally.
- Weave smaller saplings through the side stakes to form walls.

*Bank the final covering against the walls to help the insulation*

*Erect a sturdy fire reflector (see p. 164) around the front of the shelter*

**5** With everyone in the same lean-to shelter you need to light and tend only one fire.
- Layer the inside floor with dry material to form bedding.
- Establish a watch system during the night to ensure that the fire is maintained and controlled.

*Place a pole between the trees to keep the bedding in place*

# FOREST A-FRAME

A-frames can take several hours to build, but if you're staying in one place for a few days it may be worth expending the energy. One-person A-frames are relatively simple to construct and are easy to keep warm. They can be adapted into multi-person shelters to accommodate groups of people.

### TOOLS AND MATERIALS
- Poles of various lengths
- Saplings
- Knife
- Saw (or ax)
- Cordage
- Covering for walls—such as pine boughs, leaves, and moss

*The long, sturdy ridgepole needs to be at least 3 ft (1 m) longer than you*

*Put the bare side of the ridgepole on the inside of the shelter*

*Rest side poles against branch stubs*

*Tie ridgepole and A-poles together with an arbor knot (see p. 142)*

*Make sure the pole is firmly in the ground*

*Ensure each pole has a stable footing*

*Tie a pole to the "A" to form the head end*

**1** Smooth one side of the ridgepole with your knife, leaving one side bare and one with branch stubs.
- Hammer two poles into the ground to form an "A".
- Rest one end of the ridgepole on top of the "A" and the other end on the ground.

**2** Lay a series of poles against the branch stubs on the ridgepole. These will be of decreasing height as you work your way from front (the "A") to back (the ground).
- At each junction, rest the side poles against the stubs or tie them to the ridgepole with an arbor knot (see p. 142).

# FIRE REFLECTOR

A fire radiates heat in all directions—up, down, and 360 degrees around. A fire reflector makes a fire more efficient as it directs heat into your shelter.

Construct your reflector so that you can build a fire about 3 ft (1 m) from the entrance to your shelter. You can sit in the entrance and tend the fire at arms' length—any closer and you would be too hot and the shelter might catch fire; any further away and you lose too much heat. An L-shaped end to the reflector will retain more heat.

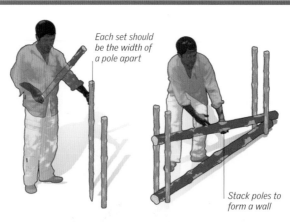

*Each set should be the width of a pole apart*

*Stack poles to form a wall*

*Finish the stack when it reaches the height you require*

**1** Check the air flow will be across the proposed reflector (to disperse smoke).
- Hammer two poles into the ground. Put a second set in at poles' length apart.

**2** If the fire is going to be close to the reflector, use green wood to prevent the heat setting it on fire.
- Put poles between the sets to form a wall.

**3** Tie the top of the upright poles together.
- Make sure the wall is as long as the shelter's entrance to retain heat and keep out wind and rain.

## ALTERNATIVE SHELTERS

Two other options are a front-opening A-frame and a one-person lean-to. For the former, secure a ridgepole or line to a tree at the height you want the entrance to be, then adapt the forest A-frame (see opposite). For the latter, tie the ridgepole to two forked sticks hammered into the ground and apply a cover similar to the forest lean-to (see pp. 162–63).

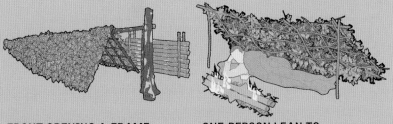

### FRONT OPENING A-FRAME

Wedge a noggin under the ridgepole and lash it to the tree with an arbor knot to take some of the weight. Build a fire reflector to the side with the prevailing wind.

### ONE-PERSON LEAN-TO

A small one-person lean-to, together with a long log fire built in front, provides you with a warm, dry, and comfortable shelter for an overnight stay.

*Alternate the weave of saplings between one row and the next*

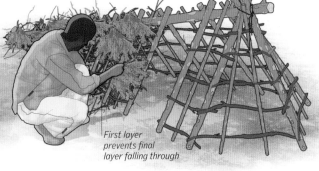

*First layer prevents final layer falling through*

**3** Weave four or five rows of saplings horizontally through the side poles to make the walls into a strong framework for the covering.

■ Leave an entrance in the side near the front. Make sure it's large enough for you to sit inside comfortably.

**4** Cover the framework with a thick layer of natural material, such as pine boughs, small branches, and sturdy twigs. Weave the materials into a "thatch".

■ On each side, work your way gradually from the back of the shelter to the front, and from the bottom to the top.

### NEED TO KNOW

Build your shelter so that the wind blows across the front of it at a slight angle, rather than into it. This maintains its effectiveness and prevents smoke entering from the fire. If the shelter backs on to the wind, there's a risk the wind will blow around it and curl into the entrance.

*The covered walls provide protection from the wind and the rain*

**5** Cover the first layer with leaves, moss, and mulch, starting from the ground and working up to the ridgepole.

■ Build a fire reflector (see opposite) in front of the entrance to help direct heat towards you.

■ Stow your equipment and pack in the front of the shelter.

*Build a fire in front of the reflector*

# TROPICAL SHELTERS

**TROPICAL RAIN FORESTS CAN BE** the easiest environments for building shelters because of the wealth of available materials. Once you've found a suitable location just decide what type of shelter you need. The most important thing is to raise the shelter off the ground. Make it as comfortable as you can, because quality sleep is important.

**TOOLS AND MATERIALS**
- Poncho fitted with press-studs
- Cordage
- Long, heavy poles or wide bamboo stalks
- Spacer bars
- Knife, saw, machete, or parang
- Needle
- Strong, waxed, cotton thread

## MODIFIED PONCHO BED

Most ponchos have press-studs to allow you to clip up the edges or to clip two ponchos together. They also have grommet holes that you can use as lashing points. Here, a poncho is modified into a tropical bed.

*Slide a pole down each side of the poncho "tube"*

*Make the poles at least 3 ft (1 m) longer than your poncho*

*The spacer bar fork fits around the pole*

*Keep poncho as taut as possible*

*A simple knot keeps the grommets together*

*Make sure that the length of pole sticking out from either end is equal*

**1** Clip the press-studs of the two sides of your poncho together to form a kind of "tube".
- Tie the grommets on the clipped side with pieces of cordage so that the press-studs don't come undone.

**2** Cut two strong support poles that can take your weight.
- Insert the two support poles inside the "tube" of your poncho, one down each side.

**3** Cut two "spacer bars" that will fit perpendicularly across the support poles or, if you can find them, cut poles with a natural fork in them.
- Tie the spacer bars into position using an arbor knot (see p. 142).

## HAMMOCKS

Many types of hammock are designed for the kind of hot weather you get in the tropics, and are often fitted with mosquito nets. In fact, hammocks make the best overnight shelter, as long as you can find two trees the right distance apart. The Hennessy hammock is a good choice because it packs down small.

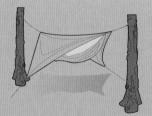
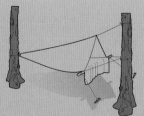
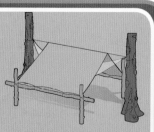

**HENNESSY HAMMOCK**
This ultralight, quick-drying hammock is both easy to set up and comfortable to sleep in (see p. 54). It's equipped with a self-closing door.

**PARACHUTE SHELTER**
Fold the panels of a parachute into a triangle. Lash a spacer bar to the opening and peg it out. Tie off the apex of the triangle further up the tree.

**HAMMOCK AND TARP**
Tie a ridgeline above the hammock. Drape the tarp over the line and anchor it on either side to a horizontal pole tied to two uprights.

## ALTERNATIVE METHODS

You can easily modify other forms of sheeting, such as a tarpaulin, shelter sheet, and groundsheet. You will need a decent needle and plenty of strong, waxed, cotton thread (see Survival kits, pp. 60–61). There are two methods, which you can do either on the trail or as part of your prior preparation. Adding spacer bars keeps the poles apart and the sleeping platform tight. Both of these methods produce an excellent emergency stretcher.

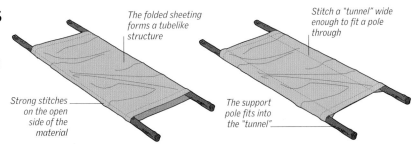

*The folded sheeting forms a tubelike structure*

*Strong stitches on the open side of the material*

*Stitch a "tunnel" wide enough to fit a pole through*

*The support pole fits into the "tunnel"*

### METHOD ONE

Lay the material on the ground and fold it once to create a wide "tube." Stitch the length of the open sides and then insert a pole along each side of the tube.

### METHOD TWO

Fold the sheet and stitch a "tunnel" along both sides just wide enough to take a pole that will support your weight. Push the support poles through the tunnels.

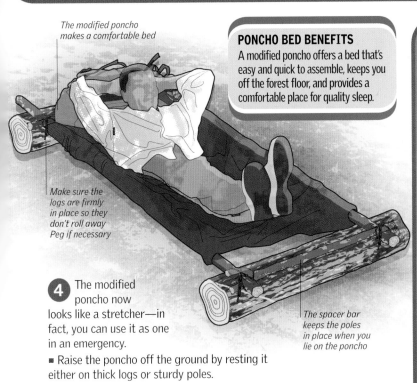

*The modified poncho makes a comfortable bed*

*Make sure the logs are firmly in place so they don't roll away Peg if necessary*

**4** The modified poncho now looks like a stretcher—in fact, you can use it as one in an emergency.

- Raise the poncho off the ground by resting it either on thick logs or sturdy poles.

*The spacer bar keeps the poles in place when you lie on the poncho*

### PONCHO BED BENEFITS

A modified poncho offers a bed that's easy and quick to assemble, keeps you off the forest floor, and provides a comfortable place for quality sleep.

## ALTERNATIVE DESIGN

If you have a second poncho, shelter sheet, or tarp you can create a shelter to keep the rain off your modified poncho (see also Corded A-frame, p. 159).

- Tie a ridgeline between two trees and hang the poncho, sheet, or tarp over the top of it.
- If you're using a second poncho, tie its hood to another ridgeline.
- Peg out the four corners of poncho, sheet, or tarpaulin.

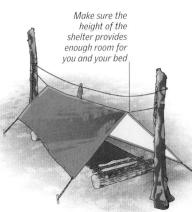

*Make sure the height of the shelter provides enough room for you and your bed*

## BUILDING IN THE JUNGLE

Shelters in the rain forest need to be quick to erect, just big enough for your needs, and safe from animals.

### CHECKLIST

If you're thinking about building a shelter in a tropical forest, the following tips may help you:

- Check for hazards such as deadfalls (sudden branch falls)—a major cause of injuries during military jungle training.
- You'll need a sharp cutting tool—ideally a parang or machete, but a decent bushcraft knife or small ax will suffice.
- Clear the ground around your shelter to deter animals. Use a makeshift brush, never your bare hands, to avoid being bitten by snakes or spiders.
- Build your shelter far enough off the ground to avoid being bothered by insects, snakes, or any other animals—particularly those that move around at night.
- Start building your shelter well before darkness sets in, which, in tropical zones, usually happens very quickly. Using a large knife in reduced light or by the light of a flashlight can be very dangerous.
- Work at a rate that you can manage. Humid conditions can very quickly lead to dehydration and heat-related injuries such as heat stress and heat stroke. Your body tries to keep itself cool by sweating, so don't work too fast, drink water frequently, and take regular breaks.
- Make your shelter secure—you don't want to make repairs at night.
- Inside your shelter use a full mosquito net and a mosquito head-net.
- A fire will deter insects and animals.

# JUNGLE A-FRAME

An A-frame is relatively easy to make. If you have a poncho, tarpaulin, shelter sheet, groundsheet, or another type of sheet, you'll need to modify it first to make it into a bed (see pp. 166–67). If you do not have a poncho, lay branches across the poles to form a sleeping platform.

**1** Cut seven long poles that will take your weight. Tie two poles together with an arbor knot (see p. 142) to form an "A" and tie the joint to a tree or branch of a tree (as shown).

*The angle formed by the "A" determines how far down the legs the platform will sit*

**2** Tie two more poles together to form an "A" for the other end.
- Position these in line with the first "A".
- The distance between the two "A"s needs to be at least 2 ft (60 cm) longer than your height.

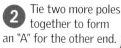

*Make sure the poles are wedged firmly into the ground*

*Check the junctions are securely tied*

**3** Put a ridgepole on top of the two "A"s.
- Tie this to both junctions for extra stability.

*Use an arbor knot (see p. 142) to secure the poles at the top of each "A"*

**4** Position both poles of your poncho bed (see p. 166) on the outside of the A-frame.
- Move the poles down the outside of the frame legs until the sheet is taut.

*The poles of the modified poncho settle into position*

*Tie the poles of the modified poncho to the legs of the A-frame for extra stability*

**5** Place a tarpaulin or shelter sheet over the ridgepole.
- Securely tie a guyline to each corner with a Siberian hitch (see p. 144).
- Run each guyline to a peg or tree and secure it with a taut line hitch (see p. 145).

*Make the tarp or sheet tight by adjusting the taut line hitches*

**TOOLS AND MATERIALS**
- Long poles and ridgepole
- Cordage and pegs
- Knife, saw, machete, or parang
- Modified poncho bed
- Tarpaulin, groundsheet, poncho, or shelter sheet

# BAMBOO LEAN-TO

If you can find enough bamboo you can make a type of lean-to shelter. Find a spot close to the bamboo supply to reduce the amount you have to carry. If you need a raised sleeping platform, adapt the method used for the jungle hut (see p. 174).

**TOOLS AND MATERIALS**
- Thick wooden poles and bamboo poles
- Knife, saw, machete, or parang
- Cordage and pegs
- Poncho and tarpaulin (if you have them)

*Use a thick piece of wood as a hammer*

*Wood with bark is easier to lash than bamboo*

*The ridgepole sits on top of the noggin*

*A ridgepole at hip height will let you get in and out easily*

*Rest a ridgepole on the back posts and tie it to them*

*Make one back post slightly higher than the other*

**1** Cut four thick, wooden support posts.
- Hammer two posts into the ground, wide enough to let you lie lengthways between them.

**2** Tie a noggin to each post for support. Make sure they are level and at the height you need for an entrance.
- Place a wooden ridgepole on top of the noggins and tie it to the posts.

**3** Make two short, forked back posts to give the shelter a sloped roof.
- Align them with the front posts and far enough back so the roof is wide enough to shelter you.
- Hammer them into the ground and tie a second ridgepole to them.

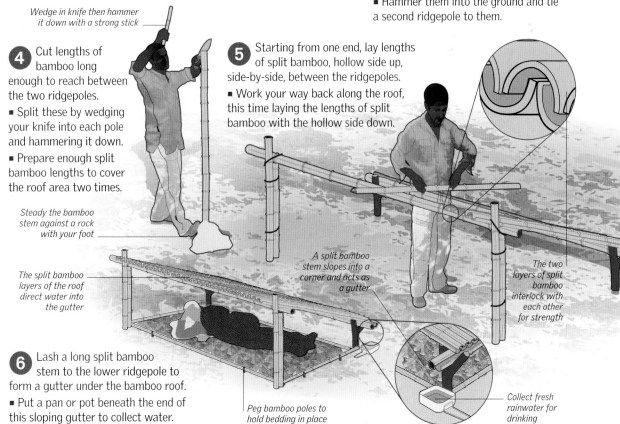

*Wedge in knife then hammer it down with a strong stick*

**4** Cut lengths of bamboo long enough to reach between the two ridgepoles.
- Split these by wedging your knife into each pole and hammering it down.
- Prepare enough split bamboo lengths to cover the roof area two times.

*Steady the bamboo stem against a rock with your foot*

**5** Starting from one end, lay lengths of split bamboo, hollow side up, side-by-side, between the ridgepoles.
- Work your way back along the roof, this time laying the lengths of split bamboo with the hollow side down.

*The split bamboo layers of the roof direct water into the gutter*

*A split bamboo stem slopes into a corner and acts as a gutter*

*The two layers of split bamboo interlock with each other for strength*

**6** Lash a long split bamboo stem to the lower ridgepole to form a gutter under the bamboo roof.
- Put a pan or pot beneath the end of this sloping gutter to collect water.

*Peg bamboo poles to hold bedding in place*

*Collect fresh rainwater for drinking*

# JUNGLE HUT

With a little extra effort you can make a more permanent and substantial shelter than a jungle A-frame. The raised apex roof of a jungle hut allows you to sit on the platform in relative comfort. This method uses a framework of four posts, but using two trees instead of two of the poles would make it more rigid.

> **TOOLS AND MATERIALS**
> - Strong posts and poles
> - Branches for platform
> - Knife, saw, machete, or parang
> - Digging tool
> - Broad leaves for thatching the roof

**1** Dig four strong posts into the ground to form a rectangle at least 1 ft (30 cm) longer and wider than yourself.

*Roof supports are secured in position with an arbor knot (see p. 142)*

*Horizontal pole fits into a notch*

*Use a digging tool to loosen the soil*

*Support noggin*

*Pole is at least 1m (3ft) from the ground*

*Tie each branch to the poles beneath*

**2** With your knife or saw, cut a notch into each post deep enough to fit the curve of the horizontal pole.
- Wedge the four horizontal poles into their notches and secure the junction using an arbor knot (see p. 142).
- Lash a noggin to each post to support the poles.

**3** Lay a row of stripped branches side-by-side across the horizontal poles to form a raised floor.
- To make the roof supports, cut a notch on the inside of each post about 3 ft (1 m) higher than the platform.
- Tie a pole into the notches on the posts.

# THATCHING LEAVES

By taking advantage of the shapes of some tropical leaves, you can make a substantial, long-lasting roof or walls. The bigger and broader leaves involve less work. If you use rattan palm leaves you can create an alternating interweave that gives a tighter thatch than the overlapping method described above.

### RATTAN LEAVES

The rattan palm has leaves that are composed of rows of smaller leaflets. You can split the leaves in two and hang the halves in layers on the framework of your roof. Alternatively, you can use them whole, by folding the leaflets from one side and individually weaving them with leaflets from the other side.

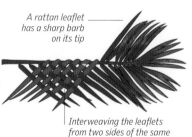

*A rattan leaflet has a sharp barb on its tip*

*Interweaving the leaflets from two sides of the same leaf creates a tight mesh*

### LONG, BROAD LEAVES

Many tropical plants have long, broad leaves that are good for thatching. These include some banyan figs, rubber plants, and types of banana. Arrange these leaves side-by-side on the poles of your roof frame, tuck them over the pole, and sew them into position with strips of vine. The tips of the leaves in one row point down over the leaves of the row underneath.

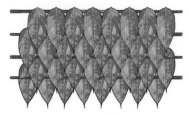

# ALTERNATIVE SHELTERS

Wickiups are found in various forms around the world and are adapted as local needs and materials dictate. For example, Native Americans made them as temporary shelters in the plains, where they were also known as teepees. The pygmies of the rain forest used saplings to form a hemisphere that, once covered with natural material, created a warm, dry shelter.

An opening at the top of the wickiup allows air to circulate

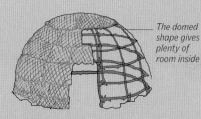

The domed shape gives plenty of room inside

## WICKIUP

The wickiup is a cluster of straight poles that are lashed together at the top, with an interwoven framework that's covered with animal hides or grass.

## PYGMY HUT

The domed pygmy hut is made from a circle of bent saplings or limber poles secured firmly in the ground, then lashed and thatched with natural materials.

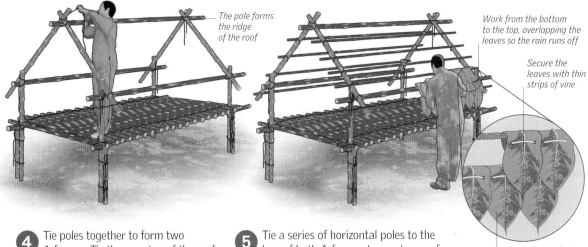

The pole forms the ridge of the roof

Work from the bottom to the top, overlapping the leaves so the rain runs off

Secure the leaves with thin strips of vine

Hang leaves with tips pointing down and shiny side up

**4** Tie poles together to form two A-frames. Tie these on top of the roof support poles at each end of the framework.
■ Place a ridgepole across the apex of the two A-frames and tie it in place.

**5** Tie a series of horizontal poles to the legs of both A-frames to create a roof.
■ Cover the roof with big, broad leaves (such as palm or banana) by folding them over the horizontal roof poles.

## THREE-LOBED LEAVES

Leaves with three lobes, such as the familiar fig leaf, can simply be hooked over the poles of your roof with the stem pointing upward. On each row of leaves you need to hang the left and right lobes either behind the pole or in front of it in an alternating pattern. The middle lobe then hangs down over two leaves on the row underneath.

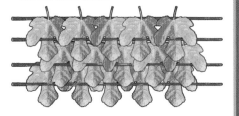

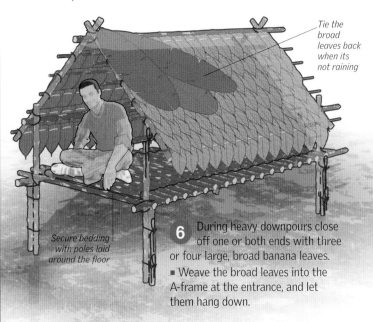

Tie the broad leaves back when its not raining

Secure bedding with poles laid around the floor

**6** During heavy downpours close off one or both ends with three or four large, broad banana leaves.
■ Weave the broad leaves into the A-frame at the entrance, and let them hang down.

# EXTREME SURVIVAL— IN THE JUNGLE

## USEFUL EQUIPMENT

- Machete/parang
- Tarpaulin/shelter sheet
- Hammock and mosquito net
- Insect repellant
- Signal flares and whistle
- Flashlight and batteries
- First-aid kit
- Map, compass, GPS
- Survival tin, bushcraft knife
- Cell/satellite phone
- Poncho/bivy sack

**FRENCHMEN GUILHEM NAYRAL AND LOÏC PILLOIS** lost their way on a 78 mile (125 km) trek through virgin rain forest in French Guiana. They survived for 51 days in the jungle by drinking rainwater and eating palm seeds, snakes, and insects—although Nayral narrowly escaped death after eating a poisonous spider.

The pair set off from the Grand Kanori rapids on the Approuague River on Wednesday, February 14, 2007, bound for Saül, a former mining village at the center of the country. They planned to spend 12 days hiking, and carried sufficient food supplies, a compass and map, machete, a tarpaulin, and two hammocks. They soon found that the going was tough—some days it would take several hours of hacking through vines to hike just one mile. On the morning of February 26, when Nayral and Pillois had been due to reach Saül, the pair found themselves far from civilization and in unexpected terrain.

Knowing that a search operation would be launched, they set up camp and waited to be rescued. They built a shelter and divided the tasks—Nayral in charge of food and Pillois the fire, which was kept alight constantly to attract rescuers. They had abundant water from rainfall, but were reduced to scavenging for palm seeds, beetles, snakes, frogs, and spiders.

**"THE PAIR FOUND THEMSELVES FAR FROM CIVILIZATION AND IN UNEXPECTED TERRAIN"**

Occasionally, helicopters passed overhead, but failed to spot them through the dense canopy of foliage. After waiting for three weeks, the pair decided to abandon camp and trek west toward Saül. After another week of trekking for just three hours a day, unknowingly just 3 miles (5 km) from Saül, Nayral was incapacitated after eating a still-poisonous half-cooked spider. With no choice but to leave his companion behind, Pillois pushed on and reached Saül, returning with a helicopter to rescue Nayral—dehydrated, with intestinal poisoning, and plagued by parasites—on April 5, 51 days after beginning his trek.

# WHAT TO DO

**ARE YOU IN DANGER?**

← N O   Y E S →

If you are in a group, try to help any others who are in danger

Get yourself out of it:
**Sun/Heat/Humidity**—Slow down to the pace of the jungle. Find or improvise immediate shelter
**Animals**—Only six percent of snakes are poisonous but everything in the jungle will try to protect itself
**Injury**—Stabilize condition and apply first aid

**ASSESS YOUR SITUATION**
*See pages 234–35*

**DOES ANYONE KNOW YOU WILL BE MISSING OR WHERE YOU ARE?**

← N O   Y E S →

If no one knows you are missing or where you are, you will need to notify people of your plight by any means at your disposal

If you are missed, a rescue party will almost certainly be dispatched to find you

**DO YOU HAVE ANY MEANS OF COMMUNICATION?**

← N O   Y E S →

You are faced with surviving for an indefinite period—until you are located or you find help

If you have a cell or satellite phone, let someone know your predicament. If your situation is serious enough to be worthy of emergency rescue, and you have a Personal Locator Beacon (PLB), you should consider this option

**CAN YOU SURVIVE WHERE YOU ARE? ***

← N O   Y E S →

If you cannot survive where you are and there are no physical reasons why you should remain, you will have to move to a location that offers a better chance of survival, rescue, or both

Address the Principles of Survival: Protection, Location, Water, Food

**YOU WILL HAVE TO MOVE ****

**YOU SHOULD STAY ****

## DO

- Make an informed decision on the best location to move to
- Use line of sight to navigate on your bearing, as visibility may be less than 33 ft (10 m)
- Improvise shelter when not moving, and sleep off the ground, clear of the damp floor and animals
- Be on constant lookout for dry tinder and fuel
- Follow water courses downstream. Transport in the jungle relies on rivers, so settlements are most likely to be found alongside rivers
- Step onto logs so that you can see what is on the other side, rather than stepping straight over onto an unseen snake

## DON'T

- Use your hands to clear undergrowth—a machete or walking staff is better suited
- Drink untreated water—boil or treat all of your water before drinking
- Leave it too late in the day to stop and make camp—three hours before sunset is recommended
- Keep too quiet. Make a noise as you progress to warn animals for your approach

## DON'T

- Let the oppressive nature of the jungle overwhelm you. Slow down to its pace, don't fight against it
- Let your firewood get damp—store dry tinder and split or quarter wood to get to the dry inner core
- Eat what you cannot identify as edible—this could result in you becoming so ill that you cannot function

## DO

- Select a shelter site where you can sleep off the ground and where your location aids will be most effective
- Use a mosquito net if you have one; if not, put damp foliage on your fire to repel insects, or cover exposed skin with mud
- Deploy all your aids to location and prepare them for immediate use. Be constantly alert for signs of rescue
- Keep your flesh covered despite the heat—the high humidity encourages infections. Also wash at every opportunity
- Keep a fire going—it aids location and wards off insects

* If you cannot survive where you are, but you also cannot move owing to injury or other factors, you must do everything you can to attract rescue.
** If your situation changes (for instance, you are "moving" to find help, and you find a suitable location in which you can stay and survive) consult the alternative "Do" and "Don'ts."

# DESERT SHELTERS

**IF YOU'RE PLANNING A TRIP** into the desert, take something you can use to improvise an immediate shelter from the sun—for example, a shelter sheet, tarpaulin, poncho, space blanket, or even a couple of pieces of parachute material that will pack down into almost nothing. You can either build a shelter called a "scrape" in a natural hollow or erect a quick shelter above the ground using your poncho.

## BUILDING IN THE DESERT

Erecting a natural shelter in the desert is a challenge because of the heat and potential lack of materials, so try to find a site that's shaded by a tree or shrub.

### POINTS TO REMEMBER

The following tips will help you deal with the extremes of temperature:

- Never try to build your shelter during the hottest part of the day.
- Ration your sweat and not your water. Avoid exerting yourself. If you start to sweat then stop what you're doing and take a break in the shade (30 minutes under an unfolded map or a space blanket and have a drink). If in a group, share the work.
- Don't leave it until the last minute to find a suitable location for your shelter. Make the decision early and plan accordingly.
- Never build a shelter in a low-lying area, dry river bed, or wadi as they are potentially at risk of flash floods.
- Avoid the top of large, isolated hills or mountains because of the danger from lightning and extreme winds.
- Try to set up your shelter on a small rise, where the temperature can be as much as 10 degrees warmer at night (cold air sinks).
- Ensure the opening faces north in the Northern Hemisphere and south in the Southern Hemisphere so the sun doesn't shine directly in during the day.
- Try to dig down to create a depression, as the ground is cooler below the surface.
- Build your shelter for the worst possible conditions and not the conditions at the time. Desert weather can change very quickly and dramatically, and the ferocious winds will rip apart any shelter that is not secure.
- If your shelter sheet has a shiny side, make sure it faces up to reflect heat and act as an aid to location from above.

## DESERT SCRAPE

If you have cord, you can dig a scrape and use the cord to peg out the sheet above the scrape. If you don't have cord the sheet will have to be held in place by other means, such as soil, sand, or rocks. With all layered desert shelters try to maintain tautness and separation between the layers.

## CORDLESS SCRAPE

If you don't have enough cord to peg out a sheet, you can make a scrape by either digging down or building up the sides with rocks or sand mounds placed at regular intervals. Anchor your sheet with rocks.

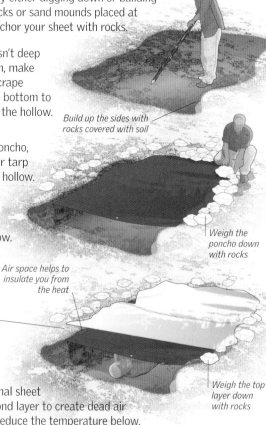

**1** If the hollow isn't deep enough to lie in, make a digging tool and scrape out the soil from the bottom to build up the sides of the hollow.

*Build up the sides with rocks covered with soil*

**2** Spread your poncho, shelter sheet or tarp across the top of the hollow.
- Make sure the edges of the material overlap the sides of the hollow.

*Weigh the poncho down with rocks*

*Air space helps to insulate you from the heat*

*Make a gap of at least 6 in (5 cm) between the layers*

**3** Use an additional sheet to make a second layer to create dead air space that helps to reduce the temperature below.
- If you only have one piece of material to use as cover, try to double it over to create the two layers.

*Weigh the top layer down with rocks*

# QUICK SHELTER

If you can't find a hollow, erect a poncho shelter (see pp. 158–59) in a place that keeps you cool during the day—for example, under existing shade, such as trees or bushes, or at the top of a slight rise in order to benefit from any cool breeze.

**1** Find a site beside a tree or secure a post next to where you want the shelter's opening to be.

■ Rig a ridgeline to the tree or post, and peg your poncho over it to form a shelter.

■ Repeat with a second poncho, shelter sheet, or space blanket to create a separate layer.

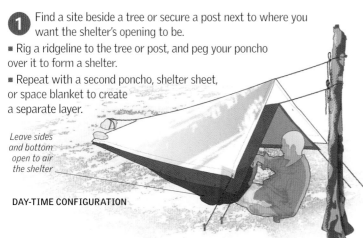

Leave sides and bottom open to air the shelter

**DAY-TIME CONFIGURATION**

**2** At night, de-rig the outer shelter and use it as a sleeping cover for warmth.

■ Prevent heat escaping by securing the sides and bottom with rocks, stones, shingle, or sand.

■ Sleep on some bedding if possible.

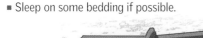

Weigh down with rocks or sand to keep the heat in

**NIGHT-TIME CONFIGURATION**

# PARA SCRAPE

If you have cordage you can tie your sheet to four posts. If you haven't got enough cordage for four, use your backpack or a pile of stones instead.

■ Prepare the depression or hollow as for a cordless scrape (see left).

■ Use trees if available, or improvise posts from wood, piles of stones, or your backpack.

■ Tie the sheet to the trees or the posts above the depression, leaving a gap for air to flow over.

■ Create a second layer at least 6 in (15 cm) above the first.

■ If foliage is available, place it between the layers to maintain separation.

# SUN PROTECTION

You should always carry immediate protection against the sun. You may be able to create shade using something you've brought, such as a trekking umbrella, tent, or space blanket.

Material may be used as an aid to location

## TREKKING UMBRELLA

A small, lightweight umbrella protects against sun, wind, and rain, creates cool shade, and doubles as a walking stick. Some have reflective material, or a flashlight in the handle.

Twigs and branches help to raise the shelter

## SPACE BLANKET

This should be part of your basic survival equipment and will afford immediate relief from the sun. Remember that it's almost impossible to pack a space blanket to its original size once it's unpacked.

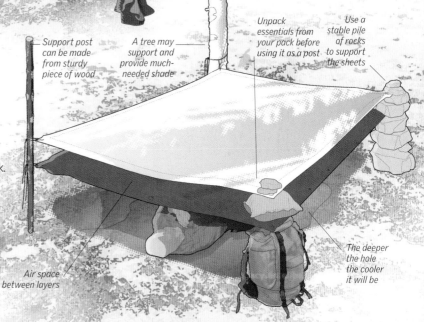

Support post can be made from sturdy piece of wood

A tree may support and provide much-needed shade

Unpack essentials from your pack before using it as a post

Use a stable pile of rocks to support the sheets

Air space between layers

The deeper the hole the cooler it will be

# SHORELINE SHELTERS

**IF YOU FIND YOURSELF** in a survival situation, and can make your way to a shoreline or beach, it may offer you particular benefits. Rescue is more likely here than further inland as your aids to location work better in open areas, people are more likely to live on the coasts, and useful flotsam washes up twice daily on even the remotest of beaches.

## DRIFTWOOD SHELTER

If there's enough driftwood around on the shoreline, you can use it to make a variety of shelters covered in this chapter. A hole-in-the-ground driftwood shelter offers simple protection, but may need continued attention if the sand is very fine or gets wet.

### BESIDE THE WATER

Shorelines vary with the environment—from tropical beaches, where sleeping out under the stars is not a problem, to rugged coasts in higher latitudes, where spending a night unprotected from the elements would be suicidal.

### POINTS TO REMEMBER

If you intend to spend a night on a shoreline, exposed to the elements, the following tips may help you:
- Build the shelter above the highest high-tide mark on a seashore (see opposite) and above the highest watermark on a river or lake beach. If in doubt, move slightly further inland, where the protection may be better and materials more easily available.
- Try to establish what the weather's going to do by looking at the sky, watching the water, or detecting changes in the wind (see pp. 82–83).
- Plan for the worst, or at least have a back-up location should things not work out.
- Check the area for insects, such as midges, mosquitoes, gnats, and horseflies.
- Look for signs of wildlife, such as crabs and even turtles as sources of food.
- Finish your shelter and collect water and firewood before it gets dark.
- Beware the effects of sun and windburn, even on overcast days.
- Utilize driftwood and other building materials. Remember, any wood that's been in the sea is likely to be very heavy.

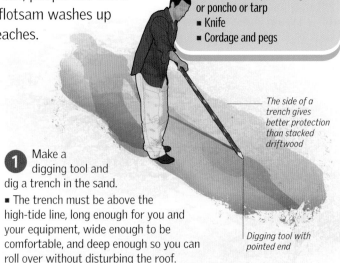

**TOOLS AND MATERIALS**
- Digging tool
- Driftwood and/or rocks
- Broad-leaved plants or grass, or poncho or tarp
- Knife
- Cordage and pegs

*The side of a trench gives better protection than stacked driftwood*

**1** Make a digging tool and dig a trench in the sand.
- The trench must be above the high-tide line, long enough for you and your equipment, wide enough to be comfortable, and deep enough so you can roll over without disturbing the roof.

*Digging tool with pointed end*

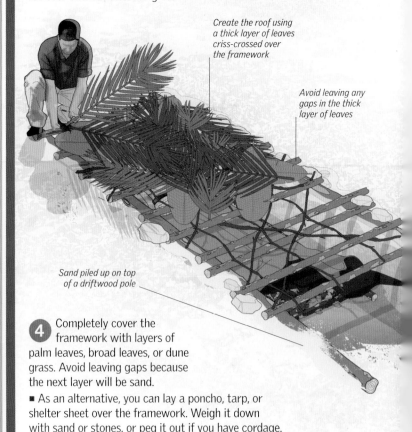

*Create the roof using a thick layer of leaves criss-crossed over the framework*

*Avoid leaving any gaps in the thick layer of leaves*

*Sand piled up on top of a driftwood pole*

**4** Completely cover the framework with layers of palm leaves, broad leaves, or dune grass. Avoid leaving gaps because the next layer will be sand.
- As an alternative, you can lay a poncho, tarp, or shelter sheet over the framework. Weigh it down with sand or stones, or peg it out if you have cordage.

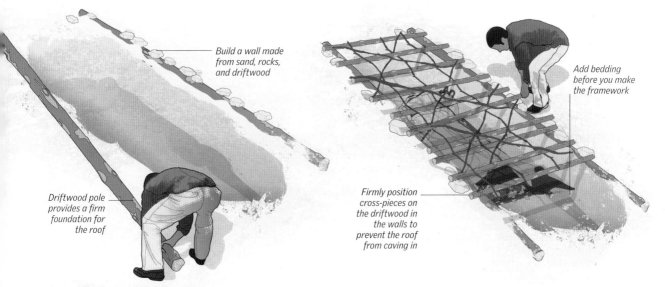

*Build a wall made from sand, rocks, and driftwood*

*Driftwood pole provides a firm foundation for the roof*

*Add bedding before you make the framework*

*Firmly position cross-pieces on the driftwood in the walls to prevent the roof from caving in*

**2** Find two pieces of driftwood that are as long as your trench. Several shorter pieces in a line will work equally well if you can't find long pieces.
- Place the driftwood beside the trench and pile on sand and rocks to build up the height of the walls.

**3** Place pieces of driftwood across the trench to form the framework of a basic roof.
- Weave smaller pieces of driftwood into the framework, making sure they sit firmly on the driftwood in the walls.

**5** Once you have covered the framework sufficiently, finish the shelter with a thick layer of sand or soil.
- The more cover you put on the roof, the more protected from the elements you will be. However, take care not to put so much weight on it that it collapses.

*Sand insulates the shelter, and protects you from the elements*

*Bedding material is essential for keeping warm at night*

### USING A LIFERAFT AS SHELTER
Remember, if you have abandoned ship in a liferaft, it can be used as a ready-made immediate shelter—even on land.

## ON THE BEACH
The best place for a shelter is the landward side of the backshore: you can watch the sea, your daily fire can be seen from the sea, and you can see your shelter as you scavenge along the beach. In bad weather, however, the landward side of the dune crest is the best place.

### PARTS OF A BEACH
A beach is shaped by the tides and the berm (a natural ridge) consists of deposits of the materials that make up the changing shoreline (sand, shingle, shale, and so on).
- At the top of the berm is a crest. A slope, or face, leads down from the crest to the water. At the very bottom of the face there may be a trough.
- The storm beach extends inland and this is where the wind and storms blow small particles of sand.
- Dunes form where the wind creates larger deposits of sand behind the beach.
- Longshore bars (sandbanks) may lie further out to sea and are formed where the waves first start to break.

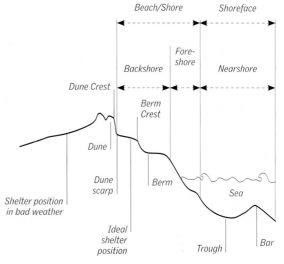

# SNOW SHELTERS

**THE TYPE OF SNOW SHELTER** you can build depends on the kind of snow, the equipment you have, and the opportunities offered by the environment—for example, wooded areas are usually better than open areas because they provide protection and natural materials. You could build a snow trench, snow cave, tree pit, snow ledge, or a quinzhee.

> **TOOLS AND MATERIALS**
> - Boughs and branches
> - Bedding
> - Long pole
> - Spade or pan for shovelling snow
> - Long knife or saw
> - Knife (or other long blade)
> - Tarpaulin or shelter sheet

## COMPACTED SNOW TRENCH

If the snow is compact enough, and if you have a long knife or snow saw, you can cut out blocks of snow to form a trench and then use the blocks to form an apex roof. This design requires a lot of effort and a bit of practice, but gives you a solid shelter with some additional height.

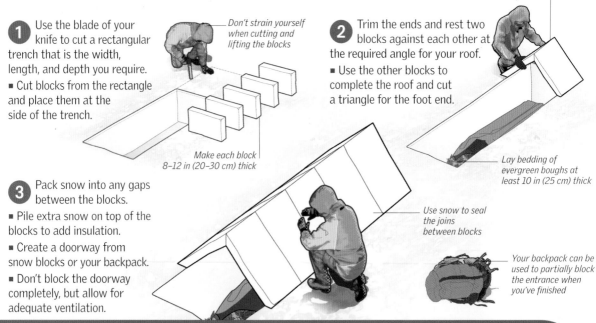

**1** Use the blade of your knife to cut a rectangular trench that is the width, length, and depth you require.
- Cut blocks from the rectangle and place them at the side of the trench.

*Don't strain yourself when cutting and lifting the blocks*

*Make each block 8–12 in (20–30 cm) thick*

**2** Trim the ends and rest two blocks against each other at the required angle for your roof.
- Use the other blocks to complete the roof and cut a triangle for the foot end.

*Carefully balance and fit the trimmed blocks, starting at the foot end*

*Lay bedding of evergreen boughs at least 10 in (25 cm) thick*

**3** Pack snow into any gaps between the blocks.
- Pile extra snow on top of the blocks to add insulation.
- Create a doorway from snow blocks or your backpack.
- Don't block the doorway completely, but allow for adequate ventilation.

*Use snow to seal the joins between blocks*

*Your backpack can be used to partially block the entrance when you've finished*

## BUILDING SNOW SHELTERS

Study the snow around you to determine whether it's compacted or uncompacted before you start.

### POINTS TO REMEMBER

The following tips may help if you intend to build and stay in a snow shelter:
- Make a shelter that's just big enough for you and your equipment. Don't spend hours building a shelter for only one night: do the least amount of work for the maximum amount of protection.

- If you need to peg out guylines in the snow, tie a short stick 6–12 in (15–30 cm) long to a line or cordage and bury it in the snow. Compact the snow down on top and, when the snow sinters (hardens), your peg will be held secure.
- Snow is an excellent insulator. Fresh, uncompacted snow is typically 90–95 percent trapped air. Since the air barely moves, the snow can keep you warm and dry if used correctly.
- Check your site for hazards, such as snowdrifts, freezing winds, avalanche, cornice collapse, and big animals.

- Create ventilation holes—make one near the ground to let fresh air in and one at the top to let air escape. Check the holes are clear every 1–2 hours.
- Keep tools inside the shelter in case you have to dig your way out.
- If you leave the shelter, mark the entrance. Take basic survival equipment with you: it's better to have and not need than to need and not have.
- Brush snow off your equipment and clothing before entering the shelter.
- Tie all vital equipment to yourself so that you can't accidentally drop and lose it in deep snow.

## FOUND SHELTERS

If you're lucky you may find a tree that has space under it so you don't have to dig a trench. For example, under a low bough or in a tree pit—an area where a heavy and deep snowfall has built up around a tree, leaving little or no snow under the lower branches. Use your walking stick to check the depth of the snow, and also to check for pockets of air.

*Keep fire controlled so it doesn't melt snow above*

### LOW BOUGH

Find an evergreen tree with a large branch lying on top of the snow. Dig down from the leeward side, excavate a pit, insulate the floor with boughs, and make sure you have adequate ventilation.

### TREE PIT

Test the snow around a tree that has large, low, snowbound branches. Little or no resistance indicates a pit. Dig from the leeward side, place boughs on the floor, and ventilate the pit.

## FIGHTER TRENCH

If the snow is soft, a fighter trench is quick and easy to build. In an emergency, you can even make a trench by kicking out the soft snow. First, find a location that protects you from the elements as much as possible, then test the depth of the snow with your walking stick or a pole.

**1** Using a spade or pan, or by simply kicking away the snow, clear a trench large enough for you and your equipment.
- Allow at least enough depth for you to be able to roll over in your sleep without disturbing the roof.

*If you can, dig down through the soft snow to the ground*

### WARMING AND COOLING TIPS

Whether you're building a shelter or resting inside it, the following tips may help you stay at the right temperature:
- Remove layers of clothing as you work, perhaps to your base layers with a waterproof layer on top. Keep clothing dry so that when you stop working you can put it on again.
- Keep shelters at a constant temperature. If snow melts and then re-freezes, it stops insulating.
- Avoid heating your shelter too much. Even a candle flame can raise the temperature inside by four degrees.

*Add bedding before making the roof*

**2** Create a framework of branches and boughs across the trench.
- Make sure you have enough roofing material on top to stop the snow from penetrating through.

*A shelter sheet or tarp makes an extra insulating layer*

*Inside a trench you only have enough space to lie down*

**3** If you have a shelter sheet or tarpaulin, place it on top of the framework to form an extra insulating layer.
- Alternatively, you can use it to cover your bedding.

**4** Cover the framework with at least 12 in (30 cm) of snow to act as insulation.
- Dig a small pit at the entrance to allow easy access.
- At the entrance, you can make a small, controlled fire on a green log base.

# QUINZHEE

A quinzhee is a dome-shaped shelter made by hollowing out a pile of settled snow. It's an overnight shelter that is easier to construct than the more permanent igloo ("igloo" means "home"), which is made from cut blocks of snow and requires skill and knowledge. You can't stand up in a quinzhee, but you can sit upright or just curl up.

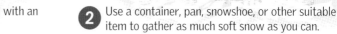

*Scoop up the snow with a pan and throw it on top of the core*

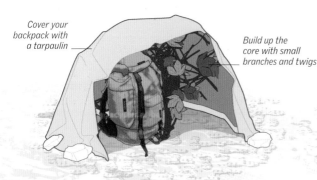

*Cover your backpack with a tarpaulin*

*Build up the core with small branches and twigs*

**1** Find a relatively flat area that's covered with an abundance of snow.

- Mark a circle for your quinzhee, including walls that will be about 10 in (25 cm) thick, and stamp down the snow.
- Use your backpack and boughs or leaves covered with a tarpaulin to form the core of the shelter. Site the doorway at 90 degrees to the prevailing wind.

**2** Use a container, pan, snowshoe, or other suitable item to gather as much soft snow as you can.

- Pile snow on the shelter's core to form a dome of the required height. Build up layers of snow until you have a covering of at least 10 in (25 cm), smoothing out each layer as you go.

*Never use your hands to smooth out the snow*

*Mark each guide-stick at about 12–18 in (30–45 cm) before inserting it into the snow*

*Scoop up snow into a small mound to form the entrance*

**3** Smooth out the snow on the dome and leave it to sinter (harden) for 1–3 hours, depending on the type of snow and the ambient temperature.

- Keep active during this waiting period, particularly if it's windy: collect wood, build a fire (away from the quinzhee), and prepare yourself for the night.

**4** To get an even thickness in the roof and walls, push guide-sticks of equal length through the snow toward the center of the dome.

- Build a small compact mound in front of the dome.

# SNOW CAVE

A snow cave provides good protection but it takes a lot of work. Suitable locations might be compact snow on the lee side of a hill or an established snowdrift with a firm crust. Avoid snow that's newly fallen, powdery, loose, or shallow and uneven. The cave should be high enough to sit up in and deep enough for you and your equipment. Locate the entrance 45 degrees downwind to keep it free of drift.

### BUILDING THE CAVE

- Dig a tunnel 3 ft (1 m) long into the snow bank, then excavate a cave on two levels. The lowest is the tunnel, while the other is a ledge at least 2 ft (70 cm) higher, and wide enough to sleep on.
- Create an arched ceiling to give the cave more support. Make it at least 18 in (45 cm) thick so it can take the weight of heavy snow.
- Mark the area with boughs to warn people where the shelter is.
- Insulate the sleeping ledge with plenty of natural material.
- Make at least one ventilation hole in the roof, but not facing into the wind.

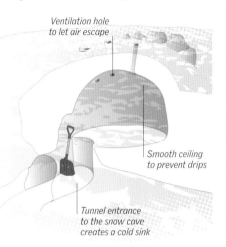

*Ventilation hole to let air escape*

*Smooth ceiling to prevent drips*

*Tunnel entrance to the snow cave creates a cold sink*

# SNOW LEDGE

You can build a snow ledge from a well-packed drift of snow out of the wind, or at least perpendicular to it.

### MAKING THE SNOW LEDGE

- Dig out blocks to form a doorway about 2 ft (70 cm) into the snow. Dig out blocks to form a horizontal rectangle above.
- Dig upward to create a sleeping platform and then form an arched ceiling.
- Place the cut blocks across the horizontal rectangle and seal any gaps with snow.
- Make a ventilation hole in the roof and one lower down to let fresh air circulate.

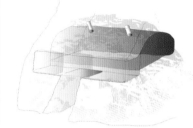

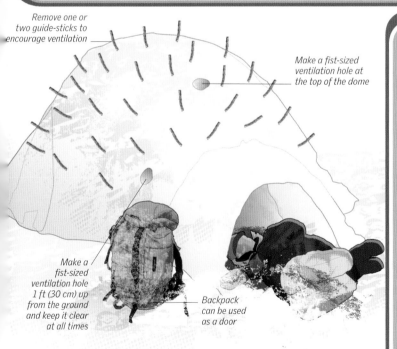

*Remove one or two guide-sticks to encourage ventilation*

*Make a fist-sized ventilation hole at the top of the dome*

*Make a fist-sized ventilation hole 1 ft (30 cm) up from the ground and keep it clear at all times*

*Backpack can be used as a door*

**5** When the snow has hardened, burrow into the mound, remove your backpack and tarpaulin, and excavate snow from the core.

- Use the guide-sticks to keep the walls at least 10 in (25 cm) thick.
- Don't use your hands to dig as they will get cold and wet.
- Smooth out the snow on the inside to prevent drips from forming.
- Build a raised sleeping platform. This creates a cold sink (an area into which the coldest air falls), taking cold air away from your sleeping area.

# CARBON MONOXIDE

Carbon monoxide is an odorless gas that's produced when there's not enough oxygen to create carbon dioxide from burning fuel. Carbon monoxide poisoning can be fatal in a well-insulated, non-ventilated environment.

### PREVENTION IS BETTER THAN CURE

Create one or more holes, 3–4 in (7.5–10 cm) in diameter, at the base and top of your shelter. Make sure the air flows out unobstructed.

### SIGNS OF POISONING

Carbon monoxide poisoning is cumulative and can build up over a few days. Mild effects are fatigue, faintness, and flu-like symptoms. As it progresses, the effects are severe headaches, nausea, and decreased mental coordination.

### TAKE ACTION

Get into the fresh air at once. You need to breathe fresh air for at least four hours to reduce the amount of carbon monoxide in your system by half.

### DETECTORS

Carbon monoxide detectors are widely available, but tend to be made for the home or RV. Some models are battery-operated, but they're too bulky for camping. You can wear a patch that changes color when carbon monoxide is in the air, giving an early visual warning.

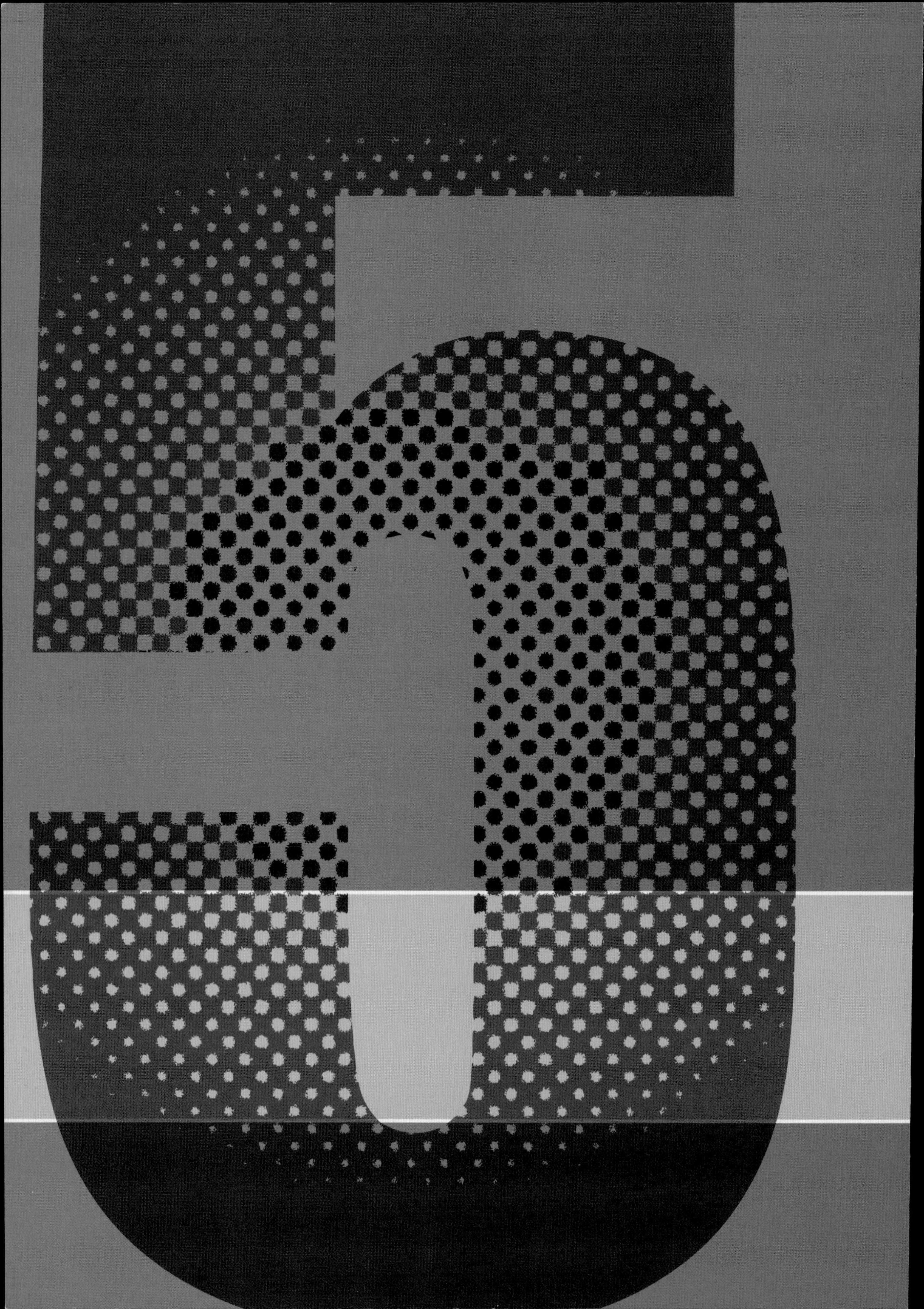
5

# WATER AND FOOD

# FIND AND TREAT WATER

**The importance of water**, even in a short-term survival situation, should never be underestimated. Water is essential to life, and a regular intake of 2–3 liters (4$\frac{1}{5}$–6$\frac{1}{3}$ pints) a day is needed just to maintain your water balance and prevent dehydration. The amount required can increase dramatically depending on factors such as the temperature of the environment, your age and physical condition, your workload, and whether you have been injured. It's not unusual for UK Royal Marines operating in desert or jungle environments to require 14 liters (3$\frac{3}{4}$ gallons) per day. We tend to take water for granted, not appreciating just how important it is until we don't have any—at which point it becomes the most important thing in the world.

You should always plan your treks around your need for water and your ability to replace it as required. There are many hydration systems available and many small and efficient methods of filtering and purifying water on the trail. In a survival situation, you should always strive to filter and purify any

## In this section YOU WILL DISCOVER...

- that **birds** can **show you** the **way** to **water**...

- when to **suck** on a **small pebble**...

- how to **make** a **gypsy well** and a **solar still**...

- why a **Finnish marshmallow** could **save your life**...

- how to **absorb water** without **drinking it**...

- how to **improvise** a **basic bladder**...

- the **importance** of **surgical tubing**...

**If a source of water** is undrinkable, such as salt or stagnant water, or even urine, you can still produce drinking water if you have the means to start and maintain a fire.

**THERE ARE MANY WAYS** to purify water, but if you have a fire you will always be able to distill it—and therefore make it drinkable. Build your fire close to the water source (if the water can be poured into a container or a hole dug in the ground where it will not seep away quickly, this will make the process more efficient). When the fire is established, place rocks in it (don't use slate or other layered rocks as they might shatter). Once the rocks are heated, use a forked stick or similar to transfer them into the salt or foul water. Then, suspend a piece of absorbent material, such as a T-shirt or moss, over the hot rocks to collect the steam. The steam will condense on the material and the resulting water, which you can wring out, will be fit to drink. If you have a cooking pot or survival tin, you can simply fill it with water, boil it over a fire, and collect the steam in the same way.

**If you have absolutely no means** of treating or boiling water, you should try to:
- Find the clearest flowing water and collect it from the surface.
- Filter debris out, even if only through a sock.
- Remember, it's better to drink foul water than not to drink at all.

water before drinking it. Bringing water to the boil will kill all water-borne diseases. In the short-term, stomach bugs from contaminated water may not kill you but they can seriously affect your ability to carry out other survival tasks. However, if you have no choice, it's better to drink contaminated water than not to drink at all. That way, a doctor will at least be able to treat you, whereas dehydration will kill you—and death can't be treated! Never drink urine or salt water, as these will only dehydrate you more.

We tend to take **water for granted** until we don't have any—at which point it becomes the most **important thing in the world**

# THE IMPORTANCE OF WATER

**YOU REQUIRE A STEADY** supply of water to sustain yourself in a survival situation and without it you will dehydrate. Left unchecked, dehydration will end in death. To survive, a balance between water intake and loss must exist.

## WHY YOU NEED WATER

Water is essential to life. It is needed, directly or indirectly, for every physical and chemical process that takes place in your body. Here are just a few of the functions that water performs:

- **Delivery service:** water carries oxygen, nutrients, and other essentials around the body.
- **Waste remover:** the kidneys use water to flush out toxins via urine.
- **Coolant:** water regulates the body's temperature.
- **Breathing aid:** the lungs use water to moisten inhaled air so that it doesn't irritate the sensitive pulmonary linings.
- **Sensory aid:** water helps conduct nervous impulses around the body.
- **Shock absorber:** water protects the vital organs and provides lubrication around the joints.

## HOW MUCH WATER DO YOU NEED?

How much water you need to survive a particular situation is dictated by a number of factors, such as your physical state, the environment you are in, and your exertion levels. Even when resting in the shade, the average person will lose more than 1 liter (1¾ pints) of water each day just through breathing and urination, a figure that increases dramatically once loss of water through sweat is taken into account. A minimum of 3 liters (5¼ pints) per day is required to remain healthy in a survival situation, with this amount increasing for higher temperatures and heavier workloads.

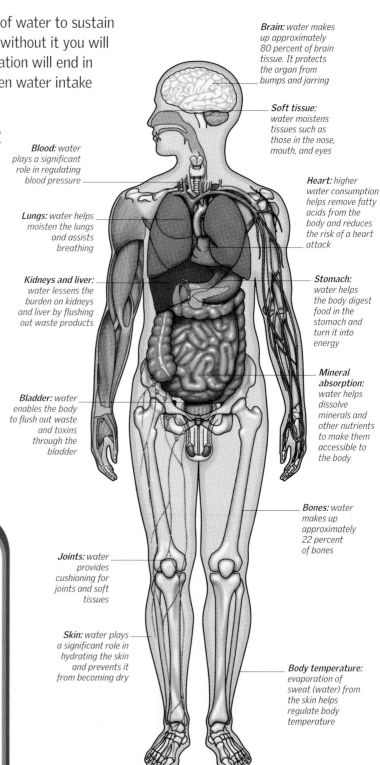

*Brain:* water makes up approximately 80 percent of brain tissue. It protects the organ from bumps and jarring

*Soft tissue:* water moistens tissues such as those in the nose, mouth, and eyes

*Blood:* water plays a significant role in regulating blood pressure

*Heart:* higher water consumption helps remove fatty acids from the body and reduces the risk of a heart attack

*Lungs:* water helps moisten the lungs and assists breathing

*Kidneys and liver:* water lessens the burden on kidneys and liver by flushing out waste products

*Stomach:* water helps the body digest food in the stomach and turn it into energy

*Mineral absorption:* water helps dissolve minerals and other nutrients to make them accessible to the body

*Bladder:* water enables the body to flush out waste and toxins through the bladder

*Bones:* water makes up approximately 22 percent of bones

*Joints:* water provides cushioning for joints and soft tissues

*Skin:* water plays a significant role in hydrating the skin and prevents it from becoming dry

*Body temperature:* evaporation of sweat (water) from the skin helps regulate body temperature

## WHAT IS DEHYDRATION?

Dehydration occurs when you fail to replace the water your body loses. It's vital to recognize the symptoms early. Factors that can lead to dehydration include high and low temperatures, humidity, work-rate, clothing, body size, fitness levels, and injury.

| THE EFFECTS OF WATER LOSS | | |
|---|---|---|
| **1-5% LOST** | **6-10% LOST** | **11-12% LOST** |
| • Thirst<br>• Discomfort<br>• Urine becomes darker<br>• Loss of appetite<br>• Impatience<br>• Drowsiness<br>• Lethargy<br>• Nausea<br>• Headache | • Dizziness<br>• Dry mouth<br>• Blueness of extremities<br>• Slurred speech<br>• Swollen tongue<br>• Blurred vision<br>• Tingling in limbs<br>• Inability to walk<br>• Difficulty in breathing | • Stiffness of joints<br>• Deafness<br>• Defective vision<br>• Shriveled skin<br>• Lack of feeling in skin<br>• Inability to swallow<br>• Delirium<br>• Unconsciousness<br>• Death |

## WATER-BORNE DISEASES

Water-borne diseases are caused by ingesting water contaminated by the faeces or urine of humans or animals that contains protozoa, viruses, bacteria, or intestinal parasites. Globally, they cause 10 million deaths a year.

| | DISEASE | SYMPTOMS |
|---|---|---|
| **PROTOZOA** | Cryptosporidium | Loss of appetite, nausea, and abdominal pain, usually followed by profuse, foul-smelling, watery diarrhea, and vomiting. |
| | Giardiasis | Loss of appetite, lethargy, fever, vomiting, diarrhea, blood in the urine, and abdominal cramps. |
| **VIRUS** | Infectious hepatitis (Hepatitis A) | Nausea, loss of appetite, mild fever, aching muscles, dark-colored urine, jaundice, and abdominal pain. |
| **BACTERIUM** | Amoebic dysentery | Feeling of fatigue and listlessness. Feces may be solid, but will smell foul and contain blood and mucus. |
| | Bacillary dysentery (Shigellosis) | Fever, abdominal pain, muscle cramps, high temperature, and blood, pus, and mucus in stools. |
| | Cholera | Vomiting, poor circulation, cold and clammy skin, muscle cramps, rapid dehydration, and increased heart-rate. |
| | E. coliform | Diarrhea and vomiting. Can cause death in vulnerable groups such as the very young or the elderly. |
| | Leptospirosis | Jaundiced appearance, lethargy, high temperature, aching muscles, and vomiting. Can be fatal if not diagnosed early. |
| | Salmonella | Nausea, diarrhea, headaches, stomach cramps, fever, possible blood in the feces, and vomiting. |
| **PARASITES** | Bilharzia | Irritation to the urinary tract and blood in urine, rash or itchy skin, abdominal pain, cough, diarrhea, fever, and fatigue. |
| | Hookworms | Anaemia and lethargy. Larvae travel to lungs and are coughed up and swallowed into the stomach, where they grow into worms. |

## TOO MUCH WATER?

Hyponatraemia is a condition caused when excess water accumulates in the body at a higher rate than it can be excreted. It results in a diminished sodium concentration in the body's plasma and the swelling of the body's cells. It can lead to a swollen brain and other neurological problems and, in extreme cases, coma and death. The way to prevent hyponatraemia is to control the amount of water that you drink, and to regulate your body's salt intake. If you don't have salt or sodium tablets in your survival tin, you can filter saltwater through fabric to sift out the salt content.

## RATIONING YOUR WATER

If your water supplies are limited, you'll have to use what rations you have efficiently until you're rescued. If your water rations will not last that long, you'll have to procure water yourself. There is much debate about the advantages and disadvantages of drinking no water for the first 24 hours of a survival situation, but at this early stage it's best to make sure you're adequately hydrated. Your particular circumstances will dictate what's best to do, but always consider the following:

• The incident that put you in the survival situation may have been both dramatic and stressful; this will make you thirsty.

• In the first 24 hours of a survival situation, you'll be addressing the principles of survival: protection (shelter) and location (see p. 27). This is hard, thirsty work.

• Physical factors—such as seasickness, injury, or the environment you're in, such as a desert—may dictate that water-rationing is not a viable option.

• If you only have a limited water supply, but drink nothing for the first 24 hours, you may end up being so dehydrated that what little water you have in your possession will have no positive effect on your dehydrated state.

# FINDING WATER: TEMPERATE CLIMATES

**THE ABILITY TO LOCATE** drinking water can challenge even the most experienced survivor and the challenges can vary dramatically according to the environment and the local conditions. It is, therefore, extremely important that you're aware of all the potential sources of water for the environment you're in.

## COLLECTING WATER

You can find water in a range of sources, which vary in terms of quality and accessibility. Your priority is to locate the best and most accessible source of water in your immediate environment.

### CATCHING RAINWATER

Collecting rain as it falls is the safest way to procure drinking water. It will need no treatment prior to drinking, as long as the catchment device itself has not been contaminated. Any number of non-porous materials—such as tarpaulins, ponchos, flysheets, survival blankets, or even large leaves—can be used as a rain-catchment device. Bear in mind that the larger the surface area of the material, the more rainwater you'll be able to catch.

**MATERIALS AND TOOLS**
- Tarpaulin
- Four sticks
- String
- Heavy stone
- Container

**1** Select a place as close to your camp as possible where your catchment device will be exposed to the most possible rain.

**2** Firmly secure the tarpaulin to four stakes (sticks of equal length could be used) using string. Make sure that one end is higher than the other to provide a natural run-off for the water.

**3** Place a heavy stone in the middle of the tarpaulin, roughly two-thirds of the way toward the lower end, to create a channel into which the rain will run down from the tarpaulin's sides.

**4** Place a container, such as a pan or can, beneath the end of the channel to collect the water as it starts to flow off the tarpaulin.

**WARNING!**
In a survival situation, even if you think your chances of rescue are high and that help is imminent, you should start to look for water sources as soon as you have addressed the immediate problems of protection and shelter (see pp. 154–81). Remember that you can survive for up to three weeks without food; without water, you won't be able to survive for more than a few days.

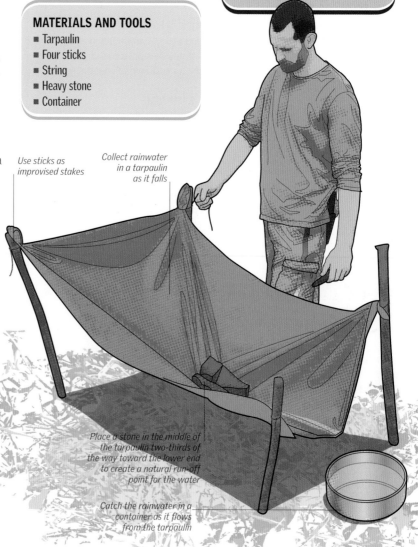

*Use sticks as improvised stakes*

*Collect rainwater in a tarpaulin as it falls*

*Place a stone in the middle of the tarpaulin two-thirds of the way toward the lower end to create a natural run-off point for the water*

*Catch the rainwater in a container as it flows from the tarpaulin*

# LOCATING OTHER NATURAL WATER SOURCES

If rainwater is not available, there may be other natural sources of water, from easily visible streams and rivers, to bores and holes, which can be hidden. Whatever your source, you should always treat the water before drinking.

| SOURCE | CHARACTERISTICS |
|---|---|
| SPRINGS | These occur when the water is forced to the surface as a result of subterranean pressures or from gravitational flow from higher sources. Found in low-lying areas, springs normally provide a permanent water source. Contrasting green vegetation is an indicator of their presence. |
| STREAMS AND RIVERS | Rivers and streams are an invaluable source of water, but there are still a few things you need to bear in mind when collecting water from them. The closer to the mountaintop the river or stream is, the clearer the fast-running water will be. The further downstream the water travels, the more likely it is to pick up minerals, debris, and pollutants that might be harmful to you. If possible, either check upstream for dead animals that may have contaminated the water, or follow the water downstream. Always try to collect the fast-flowing water near to the surface. In arid areas, rivers and streams tend only to flow during floods and will contain more pollutants and debris. |
| ROCK HOLES | Usually found in high ground, rock holes are natural collectors of rainwater. If the water appears to be trapped deep down, you can use your surgical tubing to retrieve it. Make sure you filter and purify the water before you drink it. |
| WELLS AND BORES | In some areas, you may find wells or old bore holes. Wells, which may be featured on local maps, can be deep and covered, making water procurement more difficult. In remote areas, wells are covered and marked in certain ways by the locals—find out what the markers are for your area. |
| LAKES AND PONDS | Rivers, streams, and water run-offs all flow into lakes or ponds. If you're collecting water from these sources, always try to collect it as it runs into the body of water, as lakes and ponds are more static than flowing water and can, therefore, become increasingly stagnant. Try to find the cleanest-looking area and avoid areas where debris has collected or where algae has formed. Note that the presence of fish indicates that the water is still oxygenated. |
| SEEPAGE | Usually located at the base of cliffs, high ground, or rocky outcrops, seepage is caused by slow-running channels that drain off these features. |
| SOAKS | Soaks are found close to rivers and creeks in low-lying areas, and are normally lower than the existing water table. The presence of soaks is often indicated by vegetation and they may be subject to pollution as a result of their use by animals. Make sure you filter and purify the water before you drink it. |

## AVOIDING POTENTIAL DANGERS

Most water sources are likely to be used by animals for drinking, bathing, urinating, and defecating, so always filter and purify any water collected before use (see pp. 200–01); the only exception to this rule is if you have collected rainwater. When collecting water, you should also be aware of the following dangers.
- It is possible that you'll encounter dangerous animals either using the water source, or on the way to or from the water source.
- Almost all major water sources will have a ranking system to determine which animals can use it. If all of the small gazelles suddenly disappear, ask yourself why.
- If you're collecting water from rivers, be aware of the potential dangers of river wildlife, such as crocodiles and snakes.
- If using dry riverbeds during the rainy season, be aware that flash floods can move quicker than you can run.

# LOCATING HIDDEN WATER SOURCES

The presence of water is usually indicated by signs of life, such as green vegetation, animal tracks, or human habitation. Even if the terrain you're in appears lifeless, there may be plenty of indicators of a possible water source.

## USE THE TERRAIN

- Observe the landscape for patches of green. Be aware that vegetation may not need obvious surface water for survival and may get its water from deep roots that tap into moisture below the surface.
- Water is subject to gravity and is more likely to be found downhill or in low-lying areas, such as valleys, dry riverbeds, narrow canyons, gullies, and at the base of cliffs or rock formations. Green vegetation forms next to a river and decreases as the ground rises away from the water source.
- Water will often seep inland on coastlines, leaving behind wetlands that contain water with tolerable levels of salt or that can be distilled in a solar still (see p. 189) to procure fresh water.

## WATCH THE ANIMALS

- The Bedouin listen to the twittering of birds at dawn and dusk and follow their flight path to discover where they drink.
- Flocks of birds circling over one spot are usually flying over a water source. This does not apply to meat-eating birds, such as vultures, eagles, or hawks, who get their fluid requirements from the meat they eat.
- All finches and grain-eaters need a regular supply of water. Observe their flight patterns to locate a water source.
- Bees need water, so beehives are never far from a water source.
- Animal tracks, especially those of herd animals, will often lead to a water source. Look for converging sets of tracks.
- Flies stay close to water and the presence of mosquitoes almost certainly means that water is nearby.
- Look out for herd animals, such as buffalo, hippos, elephants, impala, and wildebeest, as they depend on water.

# PROCURING WATER

Even if you find yourself in an environment without any obvious water sources, it doesn't necessarily mean that water will not be available to you. There are a number of water-procurement techniques that may mean the difference between you making it through a survival situation or not.

## SOURCING WATER FROM DEW

Dew is water in the form of droplets that form on exposed surfaces in the early morning or late evening and can provide an invaluable supply of fresh water. It occurs when the temperature of a surface is low enough to allow the moisture in the warmer air above it to condense. Dew can easily be collected from any non-porous surface—such as a car roof or a tarpaulin —with a piece of cloth that can then be wrung out into a container. You can also harvest or trap dew.

### HARVESTING DEW

You can harvest dew by walking through a field of long grass before sunrise or late in the evening with a piece of absorbent material—such as rags or a T-shirt—tied around your ankles.

**1** Tie the material tightly around each ankle and walk through the dew-covered grass. It will absorb the dew as you move.

**2** Wring the rags to extract the water. Repeat the process until you have an ample supply of water or the dew has evaporated.

### DELAYING DEHYDRATION

When water is scarce, the following points will help you delay the onset of dehydration:

- Conserve what water you have and use it as efficiently as possible.
- Work only in the coolest part of the day and avoid sweating.
- If the sun is shining, seek shade and keep covered.
- Suck a small, smooth button or pebble to help stimulate saliva and remove the sensation of thirst.
- Avoid eating protein-rich food as it requires more water to digest than those in other food groups.

### MAKING A DEW TRAP

Dig a hole about 18 in (45 cm) deep, line with a plastic sheet, and fill with smooth, clean stones. Water will condense on the stones overnight. Harvest as early as possible the next morning to ensure it does not evaporate.

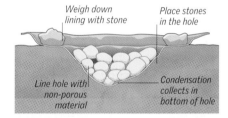

Weigh down lining with stone

Place stones in the hole

Line hole with non-porous material

Condensation collects in bottom of hole

## SOURCING WATER FROM PLANTS

Transpiration is the evaporation of water from a plant, primarily from its leaves. You can collect this vapor to boost your fresh water supply. All you need is a clear plastic bag.

### MAKING A TRANSPIRATION BAG

Place a smooth rock in the lower corner of the plastic bag, and place the bag over the leaves of a tree branch, tying the end. As water evaporates from the leaves, it will condense on the inside of the plastic bag and collect at its lowest point.

Water will collect in the bottom of the bag

### MAKING A VEGETATION BAG

Cut green vegetation and place it in a plastic bag. Place a smooth rock in the lower corner of the bag and tie off the open end. Secure the bag in direct sunlight. The sun causes water in the leaves to evaporate, condensation forms on the plastic bag and drips to the lower corner of the bag.

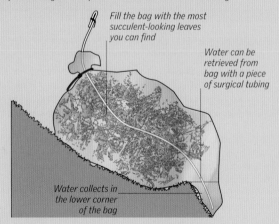

Fill the bag with the most succulent-looking leaves you can find

Water can be retrieved from bag with a piece of surgical tubing

Water collects in the lower corner of the bag

# MAKING A SOLAR STILL

A solar still works using the same principle as a vegetation bag (see opposite). It collects potable water from the vapor that is produced by vegetation, water that is unfit to drink, or moisture from the ground.

**1** Ideally find, or dig, a hole in the ground at least 2 ft (0.6 m) wide and 2 ft (0.6 m) deep. Place an empty container in the center of the hole. Fill the hole with vegetation, a receptacle containing undrinkable water, such as saltwater or urine, or fabric soaked in undrinkable water.

**2** Cover the hole with a plastic sheet, and secure it in place with stones. Place a stone in the center of the sheet to create a run-off point for the water. The sun's heat will evaporate water from the vegetation, or distill the undrinkable water, producing pure water vapor. The water vapor, which is now free of contaminants, will condense on the underside of the plastic sheet, and drip into the container where it can be collected.

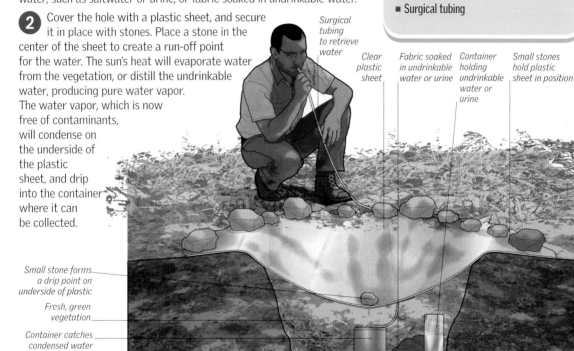

Surgical tubing to retrieve water

Clear plastic sheet

Fabric soaked in undrinkable water or urine

Container holding undrinkable water or urine

Small stones hold plastic sheet in position

Small stone forms a drip point on underside of plastic

Fresh, green vegetation

Container catches condensed water droplets

# MAKING A GYPSY WELL

A good method of using the ground to create cleaner water from stagnant water sources, a gypsy well can also be used to collect water from saturated ground. The water collected through this method will still need to be treated before it is safe to drink (see p. 201).

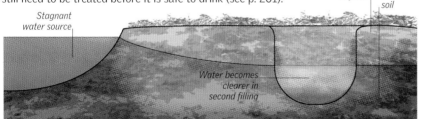

Stagnant water source

Dry soil

Saturated soil

Water becomes clearer in second filling

**1** Dig a hole a few feet away from a stagnant water source. It should be wide enough for you to be able to dip into it with a container and at least 12 in (30 cm) below the first layer of saturated soil. The hole will quickly fill with water.

**2** Bail out the muddy water and allow the hole to refill—you may have to repeat this process several times. Once the water is clear, it can be collected, treated, and used. Cover the well when not in use to prevent debris or small animals falling in.

**SURGICAL TUBING**
Always pack a length of surgical tubing in your survival kit. It doesn't take up much space and is an extremely versatile piece of equipment:
- It can be used as an improvised straw to reach water trapped in rocks, hollows, and trees.
- It allows you to access water procured from a solar still without taking the still apart.
- It can be built into transpiration and vegetation bags so that you can remove water without having to open the bag.

# FINDING WATER: HOT CLIMATES

**YOUR NEED FOR WATER** increases in hot climates as your body starts to use more of its water supply to regulate its temperature through perspiration. If you fail to drink more than you perspire, you will start to dehydrate and even approaching the first stages of dehydration can affect your chances of survival. Hot climates can be divided into two groups: hot-humid and hot-dry.

**WARNING!**
Water sources are plentiful in jungle and rain forest environments and, under normal circumstances, you should have no problem getting hold of enough water to satisfy your needs. However, rivers and streams may not be available during certain seasons, or if you have climbed too high, so knowledge of other water procurement methods could be crucial to your survival.

## HOT-HUMID CLIMATES

The hot-humid conditions found in jungles and rain forests mean that procuring water is rarely an issue. However, the body's need for water in these conditions should not be underestimated; it is not unusual to have to drink up to 3.7 gallons (14 liters) a day to avoid dehydration.

### SOURCING WATER FROM VEGETATION

Many plants, such as pitcher plants, have hollow parts that collect rainfall or dew. Some trees store and catch rainwater in natural receptacles, such as cracks or hollows. In an emergency, life-saving liquid can be garnered from a tree's roots or sap. You can find water trapped in the sections of green bamboo by carefully cutting into the bamboo with your machete or knife; or collect small, unripe coconuts and quench your thirst with the fluid they contain; or make a spigot and tap into the water contained inside the water tree. Life-saving fluid is everywhere in the jungle, and you don't have to look far to find it.

*After making a second cut in the water vine, the fluid it contains will start to flow*

### WATER VINES
Found throughout the jungles and rain forests of tropical regions, water vines are easily identifiable by their size and shape and can provide an excellent sort of fresh water. However, bear in mind that not all water vines are water-bearing; not all contain drinkable water and some even contain poisonous sap.

**1** Most water-bearing vines are about 2 inches (5 cm) in diameter. If you think you have found one, make a small cut in the vine with a machete and check the color of the sap. If the fluid is milky, don't drink it; if it's clear, then the water in the vine will be safe to drink, so cut through the vine as high as you can with a knife or machete.

**2** Cut off the vine at a point lower than the first cut. The liquid, which has a neutral, fruity taste, will start to flow. Don't let the vine touch your mouth as the bark may contain irritants.

**3** The pores in the upper end of the vine may re-close, stopping the flow of water. To rectify this, simply cut the top of the vine again with your machete.

## CATCHING RAINWATER

Catching rainwater is the best way to procure water: it is passive and requires no energy to collect once you place your containers. There are many forms of catchment device, but make sure you filter and purify the water (see pp. 200–01) before drinking it.

### BAMBOO ROOF
Construct a sloped bamboo roof with a bamboo gutter. This could be the roof of your shelter (see p. 169), but if water procurement is a problem, you will have to construct additional bamboo roofs.

### WIDE-LEAF ROOF
If you're in an area where there are wide-leafed plants, it's easy to construct a roof from them. Overlay the leaves as you would with roof tiles, working from the bottom to the top (see p. 170). Placed in this way, they will allow the water to run to the bottom. A length of bamboo cut in half lengthways can be placed as a collection gutter at the bottom.

### BAMBOO DRAINPIPE
Observe rainwater's route down a tree trunk and tie a length of bamboo that has been cut in half lengthwise in its path. Place the other end of the bamboo into a suitable container.

### DRIP RAGS
Wrapping any absorbent material around a leaning tree, such as a rag or a T-shirt, will result in the water running down the tree and soaking the material. Shape the rag to form a low point from which water will drip and place a suitable container underneath to catch the water.

# HOT-DRY CLIMATES

Anyone venturing into this environment should have sufficient water for their needs, plus an emergency supply just in case, otherwise they have no right to enter the desert. Green vegetation usually signifies water or moisture in some form, and many techniques of procuring water in temperate climates (see pp. 188–91) may work in some desert conditions.

## SOURCES OF EMERGENCY FLUID

If there is no surface water to be found, and you have no other means of procuring water, a water-yielding plant may be your only option. In some plants, the clear sap, fruit, or trapped rainwater, may quench your immediate thirst, but do not rely on these sources to keep you alive for long.

*The barrel-shaped cactus is characterized by numerous ribs and hundreds of sharp spines*

*Agaves have large clusters of thick, fleshy leaves surrounding a large central stalk*

### BARREL-SHAPED CACTUS

Barrel-shaped cacti contain a milky fluid that's safe to drink. Carefully remove the top of the cactus with a machete, mash up the flesh inside with a stick to make a pulp, and extract the juice from the pulp by sucking through a hollow grass stem. Alternatively, use a cloth to soak up as much of the fluid as possible and then wring the material to extract the fluid. The rewards from both techniques are minimal.

### AGAVES

Native to Mexico and the southern and western United States, agaves have a rosette of thick, fleshy leaves containing fluid that is safe to drink. Cut the huge flower stalk with a knife or machete and collect the juice.

*The prickly outer layer of the fruit has to be removed before consumption*

### PRICKLY PEARS

Found in low-spreading clumps measuring 3 ft (0.9 m) in height, and native to dry, sandy soils throughout the world, the prickly pear cactus has an edible fruit that can provide a life-saving amount of fluid.

### FINDING UNDERGROUND WATER

Water is life in the desert; wherever there is life there'll be water. Unusual clusters of green plants may indicate a minor presence of water; an abundance of greenery may indicate a more substantial water source. Water is rarely found above a depth of 6 ft (1.8 m) below the surface, so you will have to dig for it. If you do, make sure you only do so during the coolest part of the day. Bear in mind that, despite what you may have seen in movies, or read in other books, your chances of procuring water from the inside bend of a dry wadi in a real survival situation are slim to non-existent. In fact, you're more likely to waste what water you do have looking for the dry wadi and die in the process!

## THINK LATERALLY

The chances are that if you're having to procure water in the desert you'll already be in a desperate situation. Bear in mind that, in addition to the methods mentioned above, if you have knowledge of the techniques outlined in the temperate environment section (see pp.190–91)—such as solar stills, dew traps, and vegetation and transpiration bags—it could be enough to keep you alive in the desert.

## CHECKLIST FOR HOT-DRY CLIMATES

Even the best-laid plans can hit unforeseen problems, but many problems encountered in a desert environment can be avoided with some prior preparation.

- Always start hydrated.
- Carry enough water for your needs plus emergency water; your emergency supply should be enough to get you out of danger.
- Monitor your progress against the water you use. If you're using more than you thought, re-evaluate what you want to accomplish. It's better to turn back and learn from the mistake than to push on and create a survival situation that need not exist.
- Cache water ahead if necessary.
- Check your map for probable water sources. Confirm the reliability of these sources with locals and ask if there are any sources, such as wells, that are not shown on the map.
- Mark your map, or waypoint your GPS, with any water sources you sight as you progress. It's better to go back to a known source than to move on with nothing more than hope.
- To keep the water cool, always keep the bottles in the shade or in a windy location.

# FINDING WATER: COLD CLIMATES

**ADOPT THE SAME METHODS** of trying to find drinking water in cold climates as you would in temperate ones (see pp. 186–91), although the ability to procure water becomes a major problem in freezing temperatures. The cold-weather survivor faces a dilemma: he or she is surrounded by water, but could die of thirst because most of that water is frozen.

### WARNING!
Never try to melt ice or snow in your mouth, as it can cause freezing injuries to your mouth and lips. What's more, your body will expend heat as it melts the ice, and this could cause you to cross that very fine survival line between being cold or being hypothermic.

## CHECKLIST FOR COLD CLIMATES

You should prioritize water usage in cold-weather conditions in the same manner as you would in desert conditions (see p. 193).

■ One of your first thoughts should be about procuring water. You will have to find a water source that's close to everything you need to build and maintain a fire.

■ Always look for an alternative water source before trying to melt snow or ice. It's easier, less time-consuming, and more fuel-efficient to fill your water containers with natural meltwater than it is to melt snow or ice by the heat of a fire.

■ Your ability to procure water in freezing conditions will be directly related to your ability to start and maintain a fire.

■ Be aware that it takes time and patience to melt snow and ice. You'll also need enough fuel to maintain a fire for a considerable period of time.

■ Regulate your body heat to minimize overheating and sweating.

■ Keep drinking water close to your body to prevent it from freezing, but avoid having water containers directly next to your skin. Instead, keep them between layers of clothing and use the warmer air trapped between the layers to help raise the water's temperature.

■ Do not use recently frozen sea water, as it contains high levels of salt.

## MELTING ICE AND SNOW

If you have the choice between melting ice and snow, favor ice, as it melts more quickly than snow and is up to 17 times denser. However, if you can't find ice, use dense, compact snow. Always look for the whitest, purest-looking ice or snow.

### MELTING ICE

If you have some water to begin with, pour some into a container and heat it over a fire. Break the ice into small pieces—rather than adding it in one lump—and keep adding pieces to the container to melt them. Keep the water hot, but not boiling, so that you avoid losing water through evaporation.

### USING A HOT PLATFORM

If you don't already have water for the method above, you can melt ice slowly on a gently sloping platform fashioned from any flat piece of stone or wood positioned above a fire.

**1** Build a fire. Search for a large stone with a flat surface and two logs, or smaller stones, that are strong enough to support it. Place the small logs or stones on either side of the fire as a support for the flat-surfaced stone. Make sure that the platform is at an angle. This will create a natural run-off for the ice as it melts. Place a block of ice in the center of the platform.

**2** As the fire starts to heat up the platform, the ice will begin to melt. The meltwater will flow off the platform, where it can be collected in a container, such as a mess tin.

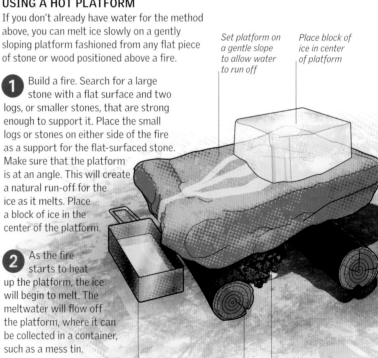

*Set platform on a gentle slope to allow water to run off*

*Place block of ice in center of platform*

*Collect the meltwater in a pan as it flows off the platform*

*Support the platform on two logs*

*Light a small fire to heat the platform and melt the ice*

# MELTING SNOW

If you already have water, follow the techniques for melting ice (see opposite), heating a little water and adding the snow little by little. Don't pack the snow too tightly; if an air pocket forms, the heat from the fire will be absorbed by the metal container rather than by the snow and could result in the fire burning a hole through the metal container before it melts the snow.

### MAKING A FINNISH MARSHMALLOW

Cut a solid piece of dense snow—often referred to as a "marshmallow" or a "snowman's head"—and skewer it with a stick. Secure the stick in the ground close enough to a fire that it receives heat, and position a suitable container underneath it to capture the water as it melts.

## STORING WATER

Snow is a great insulator: even if the temperature dips to -40°F (-40°C), water in a bottle will remain largely unfrozen if placed under at least 1 ft (0.3 m) of snow. Make sure you store the bottles upside down. That way, if some of the water does freeze, it will freeze at the bottom of the bottle and not at the top.

### USING A MELTING SACK

Using a similar principle to the Finnish marshmallow (see left), this technique involves using an improvised sack—made from any porous material, such as a T-shirt or a sock—suspended near to a fire. The heat from the fire will start to melt the snow, which can then be collected in a well-positioned container.

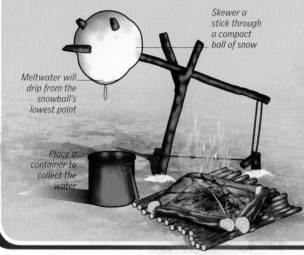

Skewer a stick through a compact ball of snow

Meltwater will drip from the snowball's lowest point

Place a container to collect the water

Make the sack from any porous material

Suspend the sack close enough to a fire for it to benefit from the heat

# IN A WORST-CASE SCENARIO

If you're caught out on barren snow or ice, you're unlikely to have access to natural fuel to burn in order to melt snow or ice into water. As long as you have your second-line survival equipment (see p. 42), you'll have all you need to procure life-saving water.

### USING YOUR FIRE TIN

Set up your fire tin on the ground and shelter it from any wind using either your body or your pack. Using your survival tin as a container, place small quantities of ice or snow into the tin. Light your fire tin and place your survival tin over the flame. Add more ice or snow as it starts to melt.

### USING YOUR MATCHLESS FIRESET

Place the lid of the matchless fireset tin on the ground. Light a hexi fuel block using the cotton wool and flint/striker. Using the fireset container or your survival tin, melt small quantities of ice or snow over the flame. Once the ice or snow has melted, let the container cool so you don't burn yourself. The water is then safe to drink.

Snow or ice placed in a metal container melts over the flame

Fire tin or matchless fireset + ice/snow = life saving water

## USING BODY HEAT

When Inuit hunters capture a caribou, they empty out the contents of its stomach, turn the stomach inside out, fill it with snow, and tie it shut with a length of intestine. They then put the stomach back in the cavity while they skin the caribou. By the time they have finished, the heat given off by the animal's body has melted the snow. The Inuit then open the bag carefully and suck out the water through a block of snow to filter it.

# FINDING WATER: AT SEA

**OF ALL ENVIRONMENTS**, the sea is possibly the most difficult in a survival situation. It offers no natural resources for protection against the extremes of temperatures, wind, rain, and sea state, and provides little to aid location. Being surrounded by water that you can't drink only adds to the difficulty. Some devices are capable of making seawater safe do drink, but if you don't have one, you'll have to find a way of procuring enough fresh water to keep you alive.

> **WARNING!**
> Never drink salt water. Its salt concentration is three times higher than that of blood and ingesting it will dehydrate you. Continued use over a prolonged period will lead to kidney failure and, ultimately, death.

## CONSERVING YOUR WATER RATIONS AT SEA

Rationing fresh water supplies when you're adrift at sea is a sensible precaution, as you have no idea how long it will be before you're rescued or before you reach land. Here are a few tips to help you conserve what water you have while you're at sea:

- Fix your daily water ration after taking stock of the amount of water you have, the output of solar stills and desalting kits, and the number and physical condition of your party.
- Prevent fresh water supplies from becoming contaminated by saltwater.
- Keep water supplies well shaded, both from the overhead sun and from the glare off the sea's surface.
- In hot conditions, dampening your clothes with saltwater can help to lower your body temperature—but don't overdo it. This is a trade-off between cooling yourself down and the saltwater boils and rashes that will result from continued exposure.
- Don't exert yourself. Relax and sleep whenever possible.
- Use every container you have—even a simple trash bag—to collect rainwater, and keep them well sealed and attached to the raft.
- If you don't have water, don't eat. Protein consumption will hasten the onset of dehydration.

## COLLECTING FRESH WATER

If you find yourself adrift with no hope of immediate rescue, obtaining drinking water will be a major priority. If you don't have a solar still or a reverse-osmosis pump, you must find another means of procuring fresh water. Fortunately, there are several ways of doing so.

### GATHERING RAINWATER

Most modern liferafts incorporate a built-in rainwater catchment system that channels rainwater and dew from the outer surface of the liferaft into collection pockets inside the liferaft. However, even if you're not in a liferaft, you can construct a similar system using a tarpaulin or any other waterproof material. Watch the clouds, be ready for the possibility of any showers (see pp. 80–81) and spread your tarpaulin in a bowl shape to catch the largest amount of rainwater possible. Always place a tarpaulin before nightfall, so that you don't miss out on any overnight rainfall.

### HARVESTING DEW

At night, secure the tarpaulin like a sunshade and turn up its edges to capture dew. It's also possible to harvest any dew that may have collected on the sides of the raft using a sponge or cloth that you then wring out.

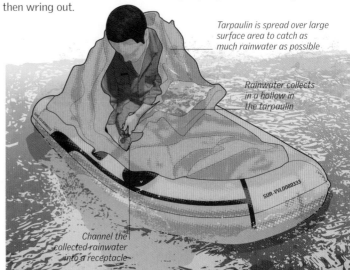

*Tarpaulin is spread over large surface area to catch as much rainwater as possible*

*Rainwater collects in a hollow in the tarpaulin*

*Channel the collected rainwater into a receptacle*

# TREATING SALTWATER

If you have no means of collecting rainwater or dew, there are several products capable of turning undrinkable saltwater into fresh water. Although these products are standard issue on most liferafts, you should always try to have at least one of them with you if you are venturing into a marine environment.

## SOLAR STILL

Solar stills are a simple way of distilling water using the power of the sun. Saltwater is placed at the bottom of the container, where it is evaporated by the sun through clear plastic. Pure water condenses on the top of the plastic and drips down to the side, where it can be collected, often via a tube. Most solar stills on modern liferafts are inflatable.

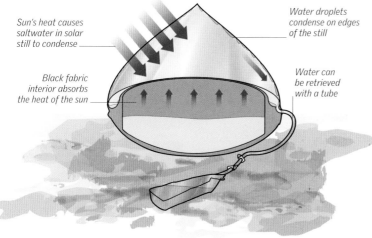

Sun's heat causes saltwater in solar still to condense

Water droplets condense on edges of the still

Black fabric interior absorbs the heat of the sun

Water can be retrieved with a tube

## MAKE YOUR OWN SOLAR STILL

If you have a chance to gather together the right materials, it's easy to make a small solar still. All you need are two containers (one larger than the other), a sheet of plastic, some string, and a weight to form a natural run-off point for the water as it condenses under the heat of the sun. If you have some surgical tubing, you can use it to retrieve the fresh water without taking the still apart.

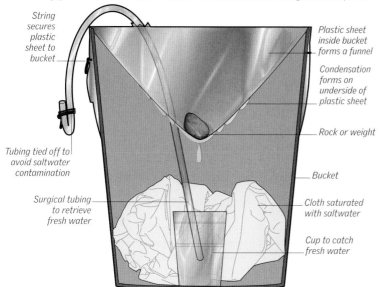

String secures plastic sheet to bucket

Plastic sheet inside bucket forms a funnel

Condensation forms on underside of plastic sheet

Rock or weight

Tubing tied off to avoid saltwater contamination

Surgical tubing to retrieve fresh water

Bucket

Cloth saturated with saltwater

Cup to catch fresh water

## REVERSE-OSMOSIS PUMP

These hand-powered devices pump seawater at a very high pressure through a membrane that filters out the salt. Depending on the model, they can produce around 23 liters (49 pints) of fresh water per day.

## DESALTING KIT

These kits turn seawater into freshwater through a process called "ion exchange." Because they only produce small amounts of fresh water over several hours, use desalting kits only during long periods of overcast weather when you can't use a solar still.

## THE LAST RESORT

In absolute emergencies, potentially life-saving forms of liquid can be obtained from the ocean.

### SEA ICE

In Arctic seas, you can obtain drinking water from old sea ice. This ice is bluish in color, has rounded corners, splinters easily and, more importantly, is nearly free of salt. New ice is gray, milky, hard, and salty. Water from icebergs is fresh, but icebergs are dangerous to approach, so you should only use them in an emergency.

### FISH

Drink the aqueous fluid found along the spine and in the eyes of large fish. Carefully cut the fish in half to get to the fluid along the spine and suck the eye. If you are so short of water that you need to do this, do not drink any of the other fluids: they are rich in protein and fat and your body will use up more of its water digesting them than it obtains from them.

### SEA TURTLE

Sea turtle blood has a salt concentration similar to that of humans. The blood can be collected by slitting the turtle's throat. Note that, although this may help prolong survival, sea turtles are an endangered species, so you should only kill one as a last resort.

### REHYDRATION ENEMA

If you have some water that is not salty or poisonous, but is too foul to take orally, you can absorb as much as a pint a day—enough to keep you alive—through the large intestine using an improvised tubing device.

# CARRYING AND STORING WATER

**YOU WILL NEED TO** make many decisions in any survival situation, some of which could mean the difference between life and death. One of these decisions will be whether to stay and wait for rescue or to attempt self-rescue. A major factor in this decision will be the availability of water and your ability to carry and store it.

*If your container has a lid, it can be used to scoop water from a stream before you pour it into a larger water bottle*

## WATER CONTAINERS

There are many different kinds of container for carrying both hot and cold liquids. They range from solid plastic or steel flasks or bottles, to collapsible waterproof bags that can be folded up when they're empty.

*Fitted with a push-pull nozzle for ease of use while on the move*

*Metal container can be used to boil water*

*A metal exterior and a glass interior makes a thermos a heavy alternative*

*Metal lid doubles up as a cup*

*Store purification tablets in pouch*

### PLASTIC WATER BOTTLE
Strong and lightweight, with screw-off tops or push-pull nozzles.

### METAL WATER BOTTLE
Slightly heavier, but stronger, than plastic water bottles.

### THERMOS FLASK
Although very heavy, thermos flasks allow you to store either hot or cold water.

### MILITARY WATER BOTTLE
A standard issue bottle used by most of the world's military forces.

### COLLAPSIBLE WATER CANTEEN
Heavy-duty plastic water canteen that can be hung round the neck.

## HYDRATION SYSTEMS

Hydration systems usually consist of a water-storage container (called a "reservoir"), an on-demand, one-way drinking tube, and a harness. However, a common problem with these systems is that, because you can't see the water, you can suddenly discover you have used all of it without realizing.

*Water container is filled and then carried in a backpack*

*Water is accessed via a one-way drinking tube*

*Use to store water once you're in camp*

*Stow water bags flat in your pack when not in use*

### COLLAPSIBLE WATER BOWL
Easy to pack, light, and can also be used to seperate items in your backpack.

### WATER BAGS
Useful for carrying water from its source back to your camp. Can also be used to keep your equipment dry.

# IMPROVISING WATER CONTAINERS

In an emergency, there's a strong chance that you won't have the luxury of having water bottles or storage systems at your disposal. However, with luck—and a little ingenuity—you should be able to find something that allows you to store and carry enough water to satisfy your needs.

## SEA SURVIVAL SUIT

Because they are designed to keep water out, they can also be used to keep water in. Most survival suits are packed with a layer of chalk to prevent the material from sticking together, so wash it out before use.

## DISCARDED MATERIALS

Always be on the lookout for anything that can hold water, from empty plastic bags and bottles, to large industrial-type containers. Clean and sterilize found items before use.

*Heavy-duty plastic bags can be used to carry water*

## EMERGENCY WATER

Sachets of emergency water can be bought and stored for emergency use. They usually come in a packet that contains five $1^7/_{10}$fl oz (50 ml) sachets of water, each being little more than a mouthful. These should always only be used as a last resort. Always try to procure water by other means before turning to your emergency water supply.

## WATERPROOF CLOTHING

Many types of waterproof clothing can be adapted to hold water. Jacket sleeves and trouser legs can be knotted to form a basic bladder; Gore-Tex® socks will hold water; and some waterproof backpacks can be used for water storage.

## GOURDS

The shell of a hollowed-out and dried fruit—a gourd—can hold water. Gourds made from large fruits, such as squashes, pumpkins, and melons, can hold a considerable amount of water.

*Look for a gourd with a shell thickness of $1/_4$in (60 mm)*

## BAMBOO

A bamboo cane will provide a natural cup if you cut 1 in ($2^1/_2$cm) below one joint and then 1 in ($2^1/_2$cm) below the next joint. Take care to smooth the edges after cutting.

*Bamboo can be cut into a ready-made cup*

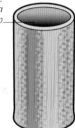

# MAKING A MINI-RESERVOIR

Your ability to store sufficient water for your needs in a survival situation may be limited and it may be impractical —because of injury or distance—to travel back and forth for water every time you need it. If you have some basic materials, making a mini-reservoir to catch rainwater (see also p. 188) solves this problem.

**1** To reduce the amount of effort required, choose a site that offers the least resistance (such as a natural hollow). Dig a shallow pit using whatever materials you have to hand, such as a stick.

**2** Smooth the edges of the pit and line it with waterproof material, such as a survival blanket. Weight the edges with rocks, soil, or logs, making sure that dirt can't run into the pond when it rains.

*Choose a site that will require the least amount of effort for you to dig a hole*

*Secure the survival blanket in place using rocks*

*Leave the pond uncovered when it rains, but cover it at other times to reduce evaporation*

## WATER HYGIENE

Water stored in a mini-reservoir for any period of time will need to be filtered and purified before it's safe to drink (see pp. 200–01).

# TREATING WATER

**WITH THE EXCEPTION OF** rainwater, all other water procured in a survival situation should be treated before it is safe to drink to remove or destroy harmful pathogens and microorganisms that could lead to gastrointestinal illness.

## FILTERING WATER

If you don't have a device that filters and disinfects the water, you will have to accomplish the same task in two stages. Before purifying the water, you will have to filter it to remove any debris. You could use the popular Millbank bag (see opposite), but it may be necessary for you to construct your own improvised filter.

> **MILLBANK BAG**
> Used extensively by military forces around the world, the Millbank bag is an effective water filter that packs down small and can be used many times to produce large quantities of filtered water. Set up the bag as soon as you arrive in camp, because the process is quite slow: the Millbank bag will filter 1 liter (2.1 pints) of water in five minutes. Note that water filtered in this way will still need to be purified.

### BUILDING A TRIPOD FILTER

If you're not carrying a filtration system with you such as a Millbank bag, you could make an improvised filter. All you need are three sticks to form a tripod, and some materials to create three separate layers.

**1** Use three sticks or a bent sapling to form a tripod. Using any materials you have, form layers, starting at the top with the coarsest material and working your way down using finer materials—such as parachute silk or nylon—as you go.

**2** Pour water into the top layer. It will become filtered as it passes through the increasingly fine materials.

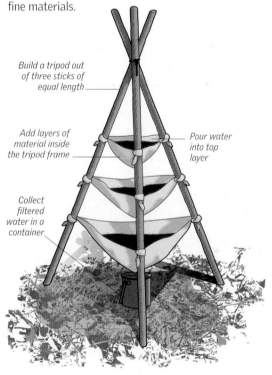

*Build a tripod out of three sticks of equal length*

*Add layers of material inside the tripod frame*

*Pour water into top layer*

*Collect filtered water in a container*

### MAKING A BOTTLE FILTER

To make an improvised bottle filter, take a container, such as a plastic bottle, and cut off the bottom (or make a hole). Note that a sock used in the same manner is still effective.

**1** Hang the bottle upside down from a branch. Fill the bottle with layers of different materials working from coarse to fine as you work your way down the container.

**2** Pour the water into the top end of the bottle and allow it to work its way down through the layers.

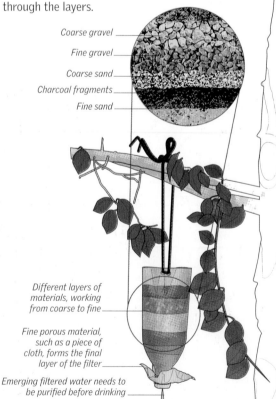

*Coarse gravel*

*Fine gravel*

*Coarse sand*

*Charcoal fragments*

*Fine sand*

*Different layers of materials, working from coarse to fine*

*Fine porous material, such as a piece of cloth, forms the final layer of the filter*

*Emerging filtered water needs to be purified before drinking*

# DISINFECTING WATER

If you drink untreated water, you run the risk of becoming infected with a water-borne disease (see p. 187), so it's vital that you treat any water first. If you have the ability to start a fire, the most effective way of making water safe to drink is by boiling it. However, if you are unable to make a fire, there are several devices available that are capable of filtering and purifying water to make it safe for drinking.

## MINI PORTABLE WATER PURIFIERS

These are specially designed units that filter the water and then purify it, by pumping the contaminated water through either microfilters, chemicals, or a combination of both. Sizes vary from small emergency pumps capable of purifying up to 13 gallons (50 liters) of water, to larger units that can filter huge quantities of water.

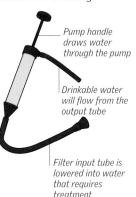

*Pump handle draws water through the pump*

*Drinkable water will flow from the output tube*

*Filter input tube is lowered into water that requires treatment*

## GRAVITY/PRESSURE FILTERS

These devices are incorporated within drinking bottles. The water is either allowed to flow naturally through the system via gravity, or is squeezed through by the operator. All bottles of this type usually employ: a filter to remove sediment and organic contaminants; a micron filter to remove protozoa; and a chemical that kills water-borne bacteria and viruses.

*The filter system is housed inside a water bottle*

*Water passes through a filter which removes debris and water-borne diseases*

## SURVIVAL STRAWS

Compact emergency water purifiers, survival straws contain a filter system and employ either carbon or iodine resin systems to eliminate water-borne diseases and harmful chemicals. You need to get the water to a point where you can reach it with your straw. If you want to draw a supply of water to carry with you, you'll have to draw the water into your mouth and decant it into a container—a laborious process.

*The filter end of the straw can be placed into any accessible non-saline water source*

*Water is sucked through the straw*

# OTHER METHODS

If you can't boil water, or if you don't have a water-purification device, you'll have to rely on non-mechanical techniques. The concentration and contact time required for some of these methods is dictated by the quality and temperature of the water being treated.

> **"BIG BUBBLES, NO TROUBLES"**
> Microorganisms and virtually all intestinal pathogens are killed at temperatures well below boiling point. The process of bringing water to the boil is sufficient to disinfect it—continuing to boil it just wastes fuel, time, and water.

| METHOD | DESCRIPTION |
|---|---|
| Iodine (Liquid and Tablets) | Iodine—which destroys bacteria, viruses, and cysts—can be used to disinfect water effectively and conveniently. Its action is dependent on its concentration, the water temperature, and duration of contact—a concentration of 8 mgs per liter at 68°F (20°C) will destroy all pathogens if left for ten minutes. |
| Chlorine tablets | Chlorine-based tablets will destroy most bacteria, but are less effective for viruses and cysts. They are more effective when used in combination with phosphoric acid and will destroy both Giardiasis and Cryptosporidium. |
| Potassium Permanganate | Potassium permanganate can be bought at most pharmacies. Mix a few granules with your water until it turns light pink. Leave for at least 30 minutes before drinking. |
| Bleach | Adding unscented household bleach is the cheapest way of adding chlorine to water (it contains 5 percent sodium hypochlorite). Be careful to add just one drop of bleach per liter of water—two if the water is cloudy—and leave for at least 30 minutes before drinking. This method is not always effective against Giardiasis and Cryptosporidium. |
| Ultraviolet (UV) Light | When many harmful microorganisms are exposed to UV light, the process of light absorption disrupts the cell's DNA, rendering the organism harmless. The quality of the water will affect the amount of exposure to UV light required: the cloudier the water the harder it will be for UV to penetrate. |
| UV Passive | Fill plastic bottles with water, replace the lids, and place them in direct sunlight, preferably on a dark surface. The sun's rays will kill the bacteria that cause common water-borne diseases. |
| UV Active (Steripen) | A small UV purifier that is placed in pre-filtered water and activated for a short time. Some models can purify up to 1 liter (2.1 pints) of water in as little as 48 seconds. |

# FIND AND PREPARE FOOD

**Your body converts food into fuel,** which provides you with heat and energy, and helps you to recover from hard work, injury, or sickness. If you are healthy, your body can survive for weeks without food by using the reserves stored in its tissues—although you will use approximately 70 calories per hour just breathing and up to 5,500 calories a day if laboring hard.

In a short-term survival situation, food should not be your major priority. You would probably have eaten recently and, if you'd prepared properly, you should have some basic emergency food in your pack. While you may go through food withdrawal symptoms—when your stomach complains because the food it's expecting doesn't arrive—you're not going to die of starvation within a few days. However, the body will react to its fuel not being replaced: hunger, a lack of energy, and a deterioration in coordination can be expected after a few days. If the opportunity to procure food arises, it should always be taken. Eat little and often but always make sure you have sufficient water to digest it.

## In this section YOU WILL DISCOVER...

- how to **cook** with **hot rocks**...
- how to **make** a **fishing reel** from a **beverage can**...
- why a **snare** must have a **perfect end**...
- how to **lasso a lizard** and **snare a squirrel**...
- that there's **more than one way** to **skin a rabbit**...
- which **grubs taste** like **scrambled eggs**...
- how to **catch** a **bird** in a **bush**...

**When gathering** food in the wild, always ensure that the energy gained from the food is more than the energy you expended in procuring it, otherwise it's a wasteful exercise.

**FOOD THAT'S EASY TO FIND** and gather should always be your first priority:

- **Plants** are easy to collect and, as long as they're readily available in the environment you're in, should be your first choice for food. However, make sure that you are absolutely sure that they are edible—mistakenly eating the wrong leaf or berry could cause vomiting and diarrhea, making your situation worse.
- **Fishing** requires little effort once the lines or traps have been set, and they will work for you around the clock. Fish is high in protein and relatively simple to prepare and cook.
- **Insects, reptiles, and amphibians** may also be available, but be careful that you don't expend more energy in catching them than you gain in nutrients from eating them. Remember also that many insects, snakes, and amphibians are poisonous, but they can still be used as bait for fish and mammals.
- **Birds and mammals** have their own survival mechanisms and are wary of humans, especially in remote areas where contact with humans is limited. Even if caught, the bird or mammal will need to be killed, plucked or skinned, and cooked.

In a long-term survival situation, your survival priorities will change and the need for food in order to simply survive will become more important. There is a thin line between food not being your priority and then subsequently finding that you're in no physical condition to do anything about it when it does become a priority—you should regularly reassess your situation and alter your plans accordingly. It takes effort, skill, and a certain amount of luck to obtain food in the wild, especially if you're not in your natural environment.

> Always ensure that the **energy gained** from the **food** is **more than** the **energy you expended** in **procuring it**, otherwise it's a **wasteful exercise**

# WILD COOKING

**IN A SURVIVAL SITUATION,** you must cook every item of food that you're not sure about in order to kill any parasites or harmful bacteria. While cooking reduces the nutritional value of food, it does help to improve the taste of many wild foods and to make them more digestible than if eaten raw.

## COOKING OVER AN OPEN FIRE

Use the fierce flames of a fire to boil water then, when the flames have died down, use the steady heat of the embers to cook on (see p. 121). The most basic method of cooking is roasting, using a spit made from green wood to suspend the food over a fire. Make sure the meat is thoroughly cooked.

## BOILING OR STEWING

When you boil food, fat and natural juices are retained in the water. It is important to drink the water to obtain the maximum nutrition from the meal, unless you have been boiling toxic substances out of the food.

> **FOUND MEAT**
> If you find a dead animal, you can eat the meat if you cut it into small pieces and boil it for 30 minutes. Don't touch it if you have cuts on your hands—you don't know how it died.

*Lash three sticks together to form the tripod*

*Forked stick allows you to adjust the pot height above the fire*

*A tripod is a very stable and therefore safe way to suspend a cooking pot over a fire*

*Wait until flames die down a little before you begin cooking*

## DAMPER BREAD

This simple method for making yeast-free bread was developed by stockmen working out in the Australian bush.

**1** Mix flour and water (and a pinch of salt, if you have it) into a pliable dough, then roll it into a long, thick sausage shape.

*Roll dough between your hands*

**2** Wind the dough around a stick, then hold it over the embers of a fire, turning regularly until it browns. It will slide easily off the stick when cooked.

*Use a green stick, which is less likely to burn*

## STEAMING FOOD

Steaming leaches fewer nutrients away than boiling and is a particularly good way of cooking fish and green vegetables—fresh leaves will be ready to eat in just a few minutes. To steam food, it must be suspended above boiling water in some way.

### BAMBOO STEAMER

Bamboo stems are tough, hollow, and divided into sections. Use a sharp stick to make small holes in the walls dividing a three-section piece of cane, leaving the wall at the base intact. Pour water into the stem until it's just below the bottom section ring. Add food to the top section and cover with grass and a loose-fitting bamboo lid. Lean the stem over a fire, propping it against a forked stick.

*Place grass on top of food to retain heat and cover with a lid*

*Steam rises up stem through holes in dividing walls*

*Food to be steamed is placed in top section*

*Water boils in bottom section*

## CLAY BAKING

Baking food in clay requires no cooking utensils. Animals must be cleaned and gutted first, but can otherwise just be covered in soft clay. When the meat is cooked, skin, spines, or feathers will remain embedded in the clay. Cooking root vegetables or fish in this way removes their skins, losing valuable nutrients, so it's best to wrap them in leaves first.

**2** Cover the food parcel with an even layer of clay, making sure it's well sealed.

*Layer of clay is 1 in (2.5 cm) thick*

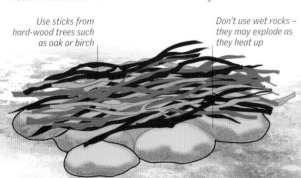

*Protect nutritious skin of fish by wrapping in fresh leaves*

*Select long, wide green leaves*

*Build a fire on top of clay to increase the heat and decrease the cooking time*

*Heat from embers radiates through clay to the food*

**1** Wrap the food in a bundle of fresh green leaves and tie them in place with some long strands of grass to make a secure parcel. Use only leaves from plants that you have identified as non-toxic.

**3** Place the parcel of clay in a bed of hot embers and build a fire up on top of it. Cooking time will be between 30 and 60 minutes, depending on the size of the food item. Break open the clay and remove the food.

## COOKING WITH HOT ROCKS

Rocks take a while to heat up but they stay hot for a long time, allowing food to bake steadily on them. To reduce cooking time, cover the food with some birch bark or a flat piece of wood. When cooking on rocks, don't use slate or other layered rocks as they are likely to shatter when heated. Another method of cooking with hot rocks is to place them in a pit. The food is covered with leaves and placed on the rocks, then the pit is filled in to retain the heat. The food is left buried until it is ready to eat.

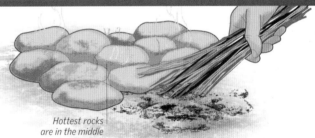

*Hottest rocks are in the middle*

**2** Brush the embers and ash off the rocks, taking care not to touch the rocks with your hands as they will now be extremely hot.

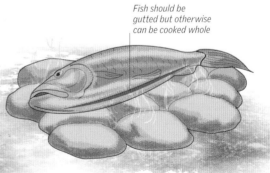

*Use sticks from hard-wood trees such as oak or birch*

*Don't use wet rocks – they may explode as they heat up*

*Fish should be gutted but otherwise can be cooked whole*

**1** Place some large, reasonably flat rocks close together. Light a fire on top of the rocks using some tinder and dry sticks, then leave the fire to burn down to hot ashes while you prepare your food.

**3** Place food on top of the rocks to bake. The hottest rocks will be in the center, so items that must be cooked more slowly should be put near the edges. Keep adding more food to cook until the rocks have cooled.

# EDIBLE PLANTS

**IN A SHORT-TERM** survival situation, food is not a priority—identifying edible plants uses energy, requires knowledge and skill, and the risks of getting it wrong far outweigh the benefits. In a long-term survival situation, however, your priorities would change, so being able to identify edible plants is advantageous.

## GATHERING PLANTS

When foraging for plants, take a bag or can with you and be careful not to crush what you collect. Gather only a few species to lessen the chances of mixing in something inedible or poisonous. Don't assume that because birds or mammals have eaten a plant it's safe for you to eat too. Unless you are absolutely certain, you will need to carry out the following test to find out whether a plant is edible.

**WARNING!**
The Universal Edibility Test (see below) does not apply to mushrooms. For this reason alone, you should never eat any mushrooms that you have gathered (especially in a survival situation) unless you are 100 percent positive that you can identify each specific mushroom as being edible. In 2008, a British woman died after eating a poisonous mushroom that had been foraged by mistake with edible mushrooms.

## DIGGING FOR ROOTS

Roots and tubers are a good source of carbohydrate and their skins contain vitamins. Take care when gathering in spring as some plants will only have small shoots and will be hard to identify.

**1** Cut a stick from a hard-wood tree, such as oak, sharpen one end to a chisel-shape then harden it in a fire.

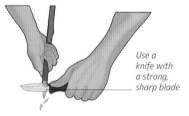

*Use a knife with a strong, sharp blade*

**2** Choose a larger plant, then dig down at its side, loosening the earth around the root until it can be pulled out in one piece.

*Take care not to damage the root*

## UNIVERSAL EDIBILITY TEST

This test enables you to check whether a plant is safe to eat. If you're in a group, only one of you should test the plant. Make sure that you have plenty of drinking water and firewood with you (see box, right), and eat nothing for eight hours beforehand. Test only one type of plant at a time, use only one part of that plant—roots, leaves, stalk, buds, fruit—at a time, and test it in the same state in which it will be eaten: either raw or cooked. Make sure that the plant you are testing is in plentiful supply (there's no point testing it otherwise) and avoid plants with milky or soapy sap, or bright colors—they are usually Nature's warning signal.

**1** First, inspect the plant—it should look fresh and in good condition. Avoid anything slimy. Next, sniff the plant. Discard it if it smells bad. If it smells of peaches or bitter almonds, it may contain cyanide.

**2** Take a small portion of the plant part you're testing and gently rub it on the sensitive skin inside your elbow or wrist. Wait for 15 minutes. If no irritation, stinging sensation, rash, or swelling develops, proceed to Step 3.

*If your skin reacts to the plant, wash it clean immediately*

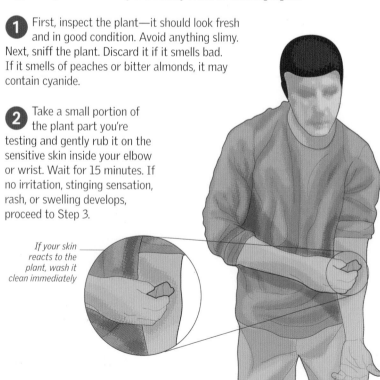

## NEEDLE TEA

The needles of evergreen trees such as pine and spruce are rich in vitamins A and C and can be used to make a refreshing—and potentially life-saving—tea.

**1** For each cup of tea, collect two teaspoons of fresh green needles and bruise them with a stone.

**2** Drop the needles into boiling water, then let them infuse for 10 minutes. Keep the pot warm and stir occasionally.

**3** Strain the tea through a cloth tied over a container. Sweeten with sugar or honey, if you have any.

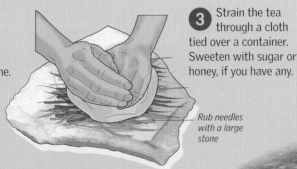

*Rub needles with a large stone*

*Needles are collected in cloth then discarded*

**3** Touch the corner of your mouth with the plant and wait 15 minutes. If no adverse reaction occurs, touch your lip and tongue with it. Wait another 15 minutes. If you suffer no ill effect, proceed to Step 4.

*If your lips or tongue start to tingle or become numb, reject the plant*

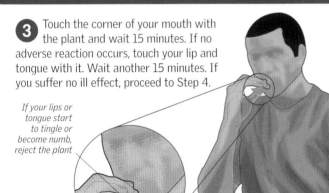

**4** Place the piece of plant on your tongue, wait 15 minutes, then chew it and hold it in your mouth for 15 minutes more. If there are no ill effects, swallow the piece and wait eight hours. Eat nothing else but continue to drink water.

*Place plant on tongue but do not chew or swallow it for 15 minutes*

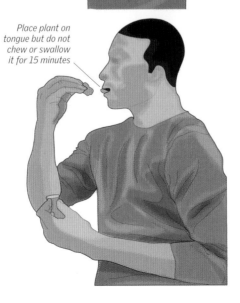

**5** If no ill effect occurs, eat a quarter of a cup of the same part of the plant, prepared in the same way, then wait another eight hours. If there is no reaction, it is safe to eat. Eat little and often rather than gorging.

### WHAT TO DO IF YOU HAVE AN ADVERSE REACTION

If at any stage you experience any type of adverse reaction to a plant during the edibility test, you should:

- Stop the test immediately.
- Avoid eating anything else until the symptoms cease.
- Wash the affected area thoroughly (if the reaction is external).
- Attempt to induce vomiting (if the reaction comes after eating the plant) by drinking salt water or by pushing a finger into the back of your throat.
- Drink lots of warm water (this is why you must ensure that you have a plentiful supply of purified water and firewood before you begin the test).
- Crush a teaspoonful of charcoal taken from a partially burned log and mix it into a paste with warm water, then swallow the mixture. It will either induce vomiting or, if you can keep it down, it may absorb the toxins.
- Try swallowing a paste made from white wood ash and water to reduce stomach pain.

**If the tester is unconscious:**
Do not induce vomiting if the tester is unconscious—get medical help and monitor the casualty.

# CATCHING FISH

**FISH CAN BE HOOKED**, netted, trapped, speared, or even caught by hand if you're lucky. Observe their behavior—where and when they feed, and what they eat—to determine which method to try. It must be noted that some fishing techniques are illegal in some parts of the world and should only be used in a genuine survival situation.

## FISHING TACKLE

Fishing equipment can be made from all kinds of material. Your survival kit should have some fishing line and a few hooks, but if you don't have a kit you can improvise. You can use a stick as a makeshift rod, for example.

## IMPROVISED HOOKS

Fishhooks can be fashioned from any piece of metal, such as a nail, pin, safety pin, needle, or some wire. You can also make them from natural materials, such as thorns, hard wood, coconut shells, bone, spines, or seashells. If you don't have any fishing line you can use parachute cord (see p. 136) or make cordage from plant fibers (see p. 138).

## BAIT AND LURES

Fish have a keen sense of smell to help them find their preferred food, so if one type of bait doesn't work, try another. Predatory fish are attracted to live bait by its movement—a worm wriggling on a hook, for example. You can make artificial bait out of shiny metal, cloth, or feathers. Try to imitate the fish's natural prey, such as an insect skimming across the water, to lure the fish into biting.

## MAKING A FISHING REEL

You can make a reel with an empty beverage can. Tie one end of a line to the tab, then wrap it around the can until you have about 2 ft (60 cm) left. Attach a hook, float, and some sinkers. Hold the top of the can in one hand and the float in the other. Point the bottom of the can toward where you want the hook to land and throw the float. The rest of the line will unwind and follow. If a fish bites, give the line a jerk then wind it in around the can.

Line sits inside a notch

Tie line tightly to the stems

Make a barb by tucking a splinter beneath the line tied to the twig

Attach the nail securely using line

Bend back of pin at an angle to form a barb

**SINGLE THORN**
Cut a 1 in (2.5 cm) length of bramble stem with a large, strong thorn. Tie a line to a notch at the other end.

**MANY THORNS**
Tie three strong thorns together securely with some fishing line. Cut a notch in the stems and attach the line.

**WOOD OR BONE**
Carve a splinter of bone into an arrow point or take a sliver of hard wood, like oak, and tie to a twig.

**NAIL**
Cut a notch at one end of a small piece of hard wood. Place the head of a nail in the notch and tie it in place.

**SAFETY PIN**
Remove the safety clasp. Bend the sharp point of the pin round to form a hook. Attach line to the wire loop.

## REMOVING A FISHHOOK

You should never try to remove a fishhook that is deeply embedded in flesh. Cut the fishing line as close to the hook as possible, then put a pad around the exposed part of the hook and secure with a bandage. Seek medical help as soon as possible and monitor for signs of infection. However, in a survival situation, you can try to remove the hook by doing the following:

Cut off the barbed end of the hook

**1** If the barb is visible, cut it off with a pair of pliers. If you can't see the barb, firmly and quickly push the hook in further until the barb emerges.

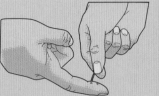

**2** Carefully ease the hook out by its eye. Clean the wound then cover it with a bandage.

## TYPES OF BAIT

Live bait includes creatures such as:
- Worms and slugs
- Grasshoppers, crickets, and beetles
- Maggots and caterpillars
- Frogs (including large tadpoles)
- Small fish—to catch larger fish

Examples of inanimate bait include:
- Meat, guts, and reproductive organs recovered from animals
- Nuts and small fruits
- Bread, cheese, and pasta

## FEATHER LURE

Make a hook, then attach it to a line. Tie a brightly colored feather just above the hook. Slowly move the lure across the water's surface to attract the fish.

*Hook hidden by feather*

## FLOATS AND SINKERS

A float keeps a baited hook at the best depth to attract the species of fish you're trying to catch. A sinker (weight) placed below the hook also helps to hold it in position. Your survival kit should include a few split-shot weights but, if it doesn't, you can tie small stones to the line instead. If the float bobs below the water's surface, you may have hooked a fish.

### MAKING A FLOAT

You can use any natural material that floats, such as a piece of bark or a rose hip (see below). If you find a bird's flight feather, you can make a float by trimming the feather until you are left with just the hollow quill, then folding it in half and tying the two ends together.

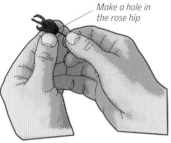

*Make a hole in the rose hip*

*Thread line through center*

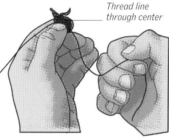

**1** Using a sharp pin, a piece of wire, or a long thorn, pierce through the center of a rose hip.

**2** Thread fishing line through the hole. If you don't have line, use a length of fine cordage.

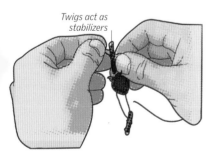

*Twigs act as stabilizers*

*Attach hook below float*

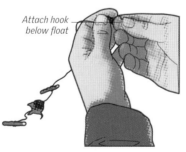

**3** Tie small twigs above and below the rose hip. These will act as stabilizers and will also prevent the float from slipping up or down the line.

**4** Attach the hook (in this example, a modified safety pin) to the line at the required depth below the float. If you have one, tie a sinker below the hook.

## LINE FISHING

The more hooks you can get in the water, the greater your chances of catching a fish. All the methods shown below are passive—you simply set them and leave them to work for you.

### SELF-STRIKING LINE

If a fish bites at the bait, the trigger will be jerked out of the catch and the bent rod will fly up. The line will be pulled tight, embedding the hook in the fish's mouth.

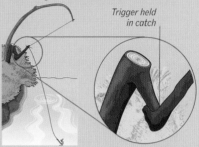

*Trigger held in catch*

### ICE FISHING

First check that the ice is at least 2 in (5 cm) thick and can bear your weight, then cut a fishing hole about 1 ft (30 cm) in diameter over the deepest part of the lake.

**1** Tie a hooked and baited line to a stick with a flag at the other end and a central crosspiece.

**2** If a fish takes the bait, the crosspiece will be jerked over the hole and the flagpole pulled upright.

*Ensure the ice doesn't freeze over*

### NIGHT LINES

To increase your chances of making a catch, you need to attract fish that live at all depths. Tie a rock to one end of a line and attach hooks with live bait at intervals along it. Tie the other end to a post at the edge of the bank and throw the line in the water, leaving it there overnight.

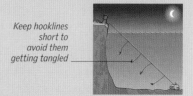

*Keep hooklines short to avoid them getting tangled*

# NETS, TRAPS, AND HARPOONS

You can leave a hooked line in the water, but unless you regularly check it any fish you catch may be eaten by bigger fish. In a survival situation, nets and traps are more convenient methods of fishing because once set you can leave them and they work for you all the time.

**WARNING!**
Gill nets and traps are illegal fishing methods in many parts of the world, so use them only in an emergency.

## MAKING A DIPPING NET

Fish that are too small to hook or harpoon may still be large enough to catch with a dipping net. Such fish are usually found at the edges of streams and lakes, and around rocks in pools. You can make a simple dipping net if you can split a branch or find a forked sapling and have a mosquito net—or a spare item of clothing, such as a sleeveless vest, T-shirt, or stockings.

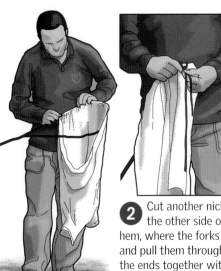

**1** Make two small nicks in the hem of the mosquito net, vest, or stockings, then thread the forks of the sapling through them.

**2** Cut another nick in the other side of the hem, where the forks meet, and pull them through. Tie the ends together with cordage, then push them back inside the hem.

**3** Tie off the net (or the vest above the armholes and neck), then either cut off the excess material or invert the net. This will prevent extra drag when you use the net.

## MAKING A GILL NET

Once it has been set in a river, a gill net is a highly effective way of catching fish, whether they are swimming up- or downstream. However, a gill net should only be set for short periods of time as fish of all sizes can be entangled or injured. Make the lines out of paracord or natural cordage (see pp. 136–39).

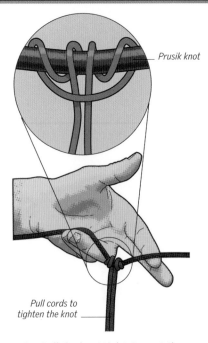

*Prusik knot*

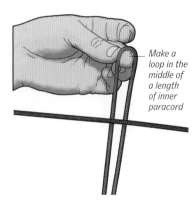

*Make a loop in the middle of a length of inner paracord*

**1** Take a section of the outer sheath of some paracord and suspend it between two trees. Loop the inner paracord behind this line.

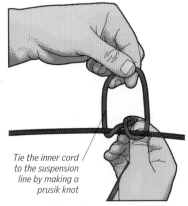

*Tie the inner cord to the suspension line by making a prusik knot*

**2** Holding the two ends of the inner cord in your other hand, pass them around the suspended line and through the loop.

*Pull cords to tighten the knot*

**3** Pull the knot tight. Repeat the process every 1½ in (4 cm) along the suspended line for the required width of the net.

# MAKING A HARPOON

Using a harpoon to spear fish takes time, patience, and a certain level of skill. Keep the point of your harpoon in the water to avoid splashing and scaring off the fish. Strike quickly when you see a potential catch, aiming just ahead of it. A spiked harpoon is the simplest to make.

*Wrap cordage around the sticks several times*

*Insert the thorny sticks into the notches*

**1** Gather a few short, thorny sticks to form the barbs of the harpoon. Cut a long, thick, straight branch and make notches around one end.

*These barbs will spear the fish*

**2** Bind the thorny sticks tightly to the shaft with cordage. They will need to be able to support some of the weight of the fish so wrap them securely.

**3** When using the harpoon, take care not to damage the barbs by driving them against rocks or onto the riverbed. Use a dipping net, if you have one, to land the fish.

**4** Make the mesh by tying a cord from one pair of cords to a cord from an adjacent pair, using a simple overhand knot (see p. 143).
■ Continue alternating along and down the line. Tie stones to the ends of the net to hold it down once it is in the water.

**5** To set the gill net, hang the suspension line between trees or poles on either side of the river, submerging the net in the water to a depth of about 6 in (15 cm).
■ The net can also be used to catch birds (see p. 226).

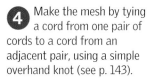

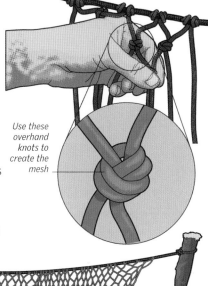

*Use these overhand knots to create the mesh*

# TRAPS

Fish traps can be made from a variety of materials. You can use rocks to build a wall or you can make a basket from sticks and cordage. You can even use man-made materials, such as bottles. If you only succeed in catching very small fish you can still use them as bait.

## BOTTLE TRAP

Also known as a "minnow trap," this method uses a large plastic bottle to catch small fish. Cut the bottle in two just below the shoulder. Invert the neck and insert it into the cut end, then tie the two pieces together. Make holes in the plastic with a hot pin so the trap will sink. Bait the trap, then place it in a stream. Check it regularly to remove any fish caught and replace the bait.

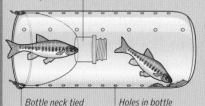

*Fish smells bait and swims into bottle but can't find its way back out*

*Bottle neck tied to bottle base*

*Holes in bottle let water in*

## SINGLE-WALL TRAP

If your camp is near a tidal creek, you can build a curved wall of large rocks out from the bank. Pick the location at high tide and build a low wall at low tide. Fish may be trapped in the pool created between the wall and the bank as the tide recedes.

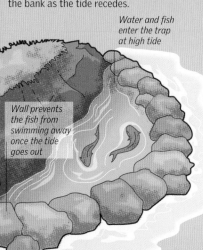

*Water and fish enter the trap at high tide*

*Wall prevents the fish from swimming away once the tide goes out*

# PREPARING FISH

**ALL FRESHWATER FISH** are edible but they must be cooked before eating as they are often infested with parasites and harbor bacteria. Saltwater fish are safer to eat raw, if necessary, but will taste better cooked. Never eat a fish that has pale gills, sunken eyes, flabby skin or flesh, or that smells bad.

## FISH HYGIENE

As soon as you have landed a fish, it should be killed and gutted, then cooked and eaten as quickly as possible, particularly in a warm climate. It doesn't take long for fish to go bad because their slimy skin provides a breeding site for flies and bacteria. In a cold climate, you can delay filleting for up to 12 hours, which will make the job easier.

## FILLETING A FISH

Filleting removes the parts of a fish that might quickly go bad, while leaving as much flesh as possible. With some species, you may find it easier to remove the bones after the fish has been cooked. Boil the bones and the head to make a nutritious stock. This must be done immediately and the stock should be kept in a cool place and drunk within a few hours.

**WARNING!**
When handling fish be careful not to accidentally touch your eyes. The slime may contain bacteria that can cause a painful inflammation of the eye covering (conjunctivitis). Make sure you wash your hands clean of all slime. If you have any cuts on your hands, cover them before touching the fish.

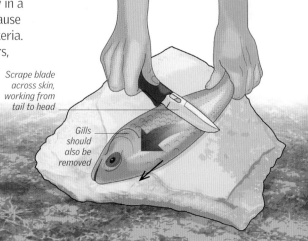

*Scrape blade across skin, working from tail to head*

*Gills should also be removed*

**1** Once you have killed the fish, cut its throat to bleed it and cut out the gills. Wipe the slime off its skin to make it less slippery.
■ Most fish don't need to be skinned—in fact, the skin is nutritious—but eels and catfish do (see panel, opposite).

**2** Fish can be cooked with their scales on but, if you have time, it is best to remove them, particularly if they are large, as they can be a choking hazard.
■ Hold the fish by the tail and scrape off the scales, holding the blade away from you and moving toward the head.

*Keep offal to use as bait*

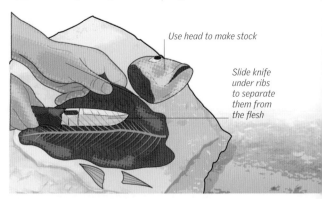

*Use head to make stock*

*Slide knife under ribs to separate them from the flesh*

**4** Pull out the internal organs then spread the fish open to check that you have removed everything. Keep the roe to eat (it lies down the side of the fish).
■ Wash the fish thoroughly, inside and out.

**5** Cut off the head, tail, and fins. Open out the body and slide the knife under the ribs to separate them from the body, working toward the head. Fish oils can make the knife slippery, so you can use your thumbs instead.
■ Repeat for the ribs on the other side of the backbone.

## SMALL FISH

Any fish that is less than 6 in (15 cm) long doesn't need to be filleted. After gutting, they can be fried, grilled, or roasted whole. Keeping the heads and tails on helps to prevent the fish from falling to pieces.

### SKEWERING FISH

Small fish, such as perch, can be grilled over an ember fire on a skewer to make a simple, yet tasty and nutritious meal. Impale the fishes on a green stick and hold them close to the embers. They won't take long to cook.

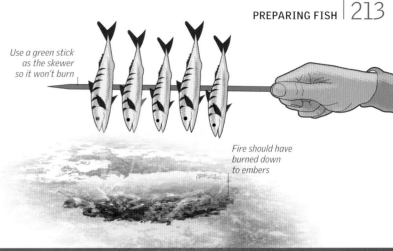

*Use a green stick as the skewer so it won't burn*

*Fire should have burned down to embers*

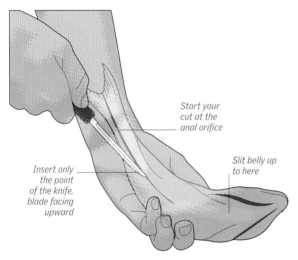

*Start your cut at the anal orifice*

*Insert only the point of the knife, blade facing upward*

*Slit belly up to here*

**3** Holding the fish with its tail toward you, insert the point of a sharp knife, blade up, into the anal orifice and slit the fish open along its belly to its throat. This prevents you from puncturing the internal organs.

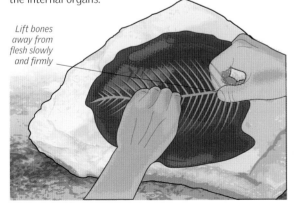

*Lift bones away from flesh slowly and firmly*

**6** Separate the top and bottom of the backbone from the flesh with the tip of your knife. Carefully pull the backbone and ribs away from the flesh in one piece.
- If you have any tweezers or needle-nose pliers, use them to remove any small bones that remain.

## SKINNING FISH

Eels and catfish are tasty but have to be skinned and gutted before cooking. To gut the fish, either use the filleting method shown opposite or Step 3 below. Catfish have a cartilage skeleton and can simply be cut crosswise into steaks.

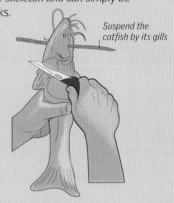

**1** Pass a stake through the gills of the fish and support on two strong uprights.
- Cut around the skin below the head with a sharp knife.
- Cut around the fins.

*Suspend the catfish by its gills*

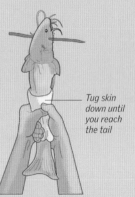

**2** Separate the top of the skin from the flesh then peel the skin downward.
- You will need to use both hands to get a good grip, and a firm, steady action. If the fish is very large, you may need to slit the skin.

*Tug skin down until you reach the tail*

**3** Remove the fish from the stake and break its backbone. When you pull the head off, the guts will come away with it.
- Remove tail and fins.

# EXTREME SURVIVAL— ADRIFT AT SEA

## USEFUL EQUIPMENT

- Liferaft, lifejacket, survival suit
- Water catchment devices
- Solar still/reverse-osmosis pump
- Emergency Locator Beacon
- Marine VHF radio
- First-aid kit, sunscreen, sunglasses
- Flashlight and batteries
- Map, compass, GPS
- Survival tin, bushcraft knife
- Cell/satellite phone
- Poncho/bivy sack

**IN 1972, A FAMILY OF FIVE SURVIVED** for 38 days adrift in the Pacific Ocean. The Robertson family were 18 months into a round-the-world sailing trip when their 43 ft (13 m) wooden schooner *Lucette* sank. They survived thanks to a combination of good seamanship, improvisation, and good fortune.

The family set off from Falmouth, England, on January 27, 1971—father Dougal at the helm, wife Lynn, and children Anne (who disembarked in the Bahamas), Douglas, and twins Neil and Sandy as crew—and safely navigated the Atlantic and Caribbean. On June 15, 1972, however, about 200 miles (320 km) west of the Galapagos, disaster struck—a pod of killer whales charged the boat, splintering the hull and holing her irreparably.

With *Lucette* sinking rapidly and no time to radio a distress call, the crew launched their inflatable liferaft and roped it to the boat's 10 ft (3 m) solid-hull dinghy, the *Ednamair*, which they used as a towboat after improvising a sail. Their supplies amounted to 2 gallons (10 liters) of water, a bag of onions, oranges and lemons, vitamin-fortified bread, glucose, four fishing hooks, a fishing line, a first-aid kit, a kitchen knife, and eight signal flares. They sailed north toward the Doldrums to find rain, which they collected with the use of a tarpaulin, and caught fish, eating some of the meat raw and drying the rest in the sun to be stored as rations.

**"A POD OF KILLER WHALES CHARGED THE BOAT...HOLING HER IRREPARABLY"**

After 16 days, the liferaft had deteriorated to such an extent that the family was forced to transfer to the dinghy, using the remnants of the raft as a canopy to provide shelter and aid in the collection of rainwater. They used the wind and currents to sail northeast toward Central America, and built up sufficient rations over the next three weeks to provide energy for the extra exertion of rowing toward the coast. Luckily for them, there was no need—their ordeal came to an end on July 23, when a Japanese fishing boat spotted a signal flare and picked them up.

# WHAT TO DO

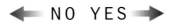
### ARE YOU IN DANGER? +
← NO   YES →

- If you are in a group, try to help any others who are in danger
- Prepare for the possibility of abandoning ship, and try to steer closer to either land or known shipping lanes
- Delegate responsibilities
- Ensure lifejackets and liferafts are ready for deployment

Get yourself out of it:
**Sinking vessel**—You need water, location aids, and protection from drowning and the elements
**Animals**—Try not to splash in the water as this will attract sharks
**Injury**—Stabilize condition and apply first aid

### ASSESS YOUR SITUATION
*See pages 234–35*

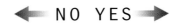
### DOES ANYONE KNOW YOU WILL BE MISSING OR WHERE YOU ARE?
← NO   YES →

If no one knows you are missing or where you are, you will need to notify people of your plight by any means at your disposal

If you are missed, a rescue party will almost certainly be dispatched to find you

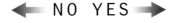
### DO YOU HAVE ANY MEANS OF COMMUNICATION?
← NO   YES →

You are faced with surviving for an indefinite period—until you are located or you find help

If you have a cell or satellite phone, let someone know your predicament. If your situation is serious enough to be worthy of emergency rescue, and you have a Personal Locator Beacon (PLB), you should consider this option

### CAN YOU SURVIVE WHERE YOU ARE? *
← NO   YES →

Abandon ship in a controlled manner and deploy all the liferafts. Always try to enter the liferaft dry. Use the rescue line to reach people in distress. Follow the "immediate actions" instructions printed inside the liferaft

Address the Principles of Survival: Protection, Location, Water, Food

**YOU WILL HAVE TO MOVE ****

**YOU SHOULD STAY ****

## DO

- Deploy the drogue—this will lessen drifting
- Inventory all food, water, and equipment and start rationing
- Prepare water procurement devices, such as solar stills and reverse osmosis pumps
- Protect yourself from the elements—sun, wind, and salt spray
- If you have no liferaft, then huddle together in a group with children in the center. If alone, adopt the H.E.L.P. position
- Improvise flotation aids from anything that can float or hold trapped air. Good examples are plastic bags, plastic bottles, and knotted clothing

## DON'T

- Cut the painter to the vessel until you know it will sink, as the vessel is what people will be looking for
- Drink seawater under any circumstances—this will only increase your rate of dehydration
- Eat unless you have sufficient water to digest the food—fish is high in protein and requires plenty of water to digest

## DON'T

- Neglect to take anti-seasickness tablets. Vomiting will dehydrate you and the effects are very demotivating
- Forget to wear your survival equipment and ensure everyone knows how to operate it
- Try to second-guess the rescuers when they arrive. Do exactly as they say, they know what they are doing

## DO

- Ensure that the rescue services are kept aware of your situation and updated with relevant information as the situation dictates
- Prepare to abandon ship: pack lifejackets and suitable clothing
- Ensure you know how to operate your survival equipment and that you have basic aids to location such as a whistle, flashlight, or plastic water bottle on your person
- Clear the deck of loose objects and be prepared to drop sail should rescue by helicopter be attempted
- Make an inventory and ration supplies

+ Never abandon a vessel unless you have to—searchers will be trying to locate it. Use the vessel's equipment while you can, and before you leave collect essential items to aid your survival.
* If cannot survive where you are, but you also cannot move owing to injury or other factors, you must do everything you can to attract rescue.
** If your situation changes (for instance, you are "moving" to find help, and you find a suitable location in which you can stay and survive) consult the alternative "Do" and "Don'ts."

# TRAPPING ANIMALS

**ALTHOUGH YOU SHOULD** be prepared to take down sitting prey if you get the opportunity, trapping small animals is easier than hunting them—it requires less skill and energy and leaves you free to carry on with other tasks. One of the simplest traps is a snare.

## MAKING A SNARE

Stainless steel snares of various strengths can be bought ready-made, with a running loop, or eye, at one end and a securing loop at the other. However, most survival kits contain a length of single-strand brass wire that can be used to make a snare.

**1** Decide on the strength of snare you want (see panel, below) and double or quadruple the wire accordingly.
- Pass the strands around a stick, place it on the ground, then loop the loose ends around a second stick.
- Rotate the second stick until the strands have entwined, forming a single, thick wire. Remove the sticks.

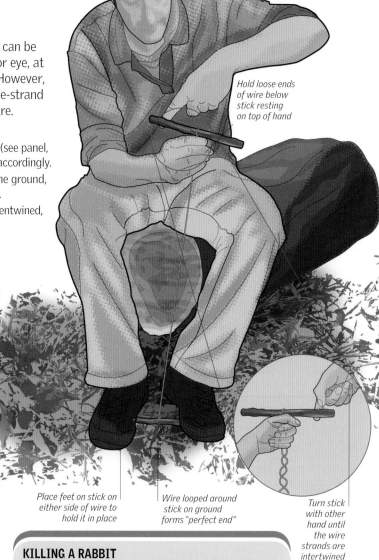

> **ALTERNATIVE MATERIALS**
> Guitar strings make great snares as they already have a "perfect end." Natural cordage can also be used.

*Hold loose ends of wire below stick resting on top of hand*

*Place feet on stick on either side of wire to hold it in place*

*Wire looped around stick on ground forms "perfect end"*

*Turn stick with other hand until the wire strands are intertwined*

### STRENGTHS OF SNARE

The single-strand wire found in most survival kits isn't strong enough to hold most animals you would want to catch. You'll need to double or quadruple the strands by winding them together to increase their strength.

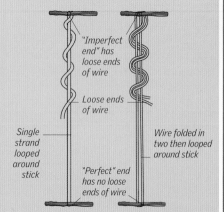

*"Imperfect end" has loose ends of wire*

*Loose ends of wire*

*Single strand looped around stick*

*Wire folded in two then looped around stick*

*"Perfect" end has no loose ends of wire*

#### TWO STRANDS
A two-strand snare will be sufficient to bear the weight of a squirrel-sized animal.

#### FOUR STRANDS
A four-strand snare will be strong enough to hold onto an animal the size of a rabbit.

> **KILLING A RABBIT**
> Unless you're an expert, breaking a rabbit's neck by holding its head and pulling on its legs can be difficult and could result in you dislocating its hips, causing it more pain. The best method is to strike the rabbit on the back of the neck with a solid stick, thus avoiding having to pick it up and risk being bitten or scratched. The eyes will glass over immediately when the animal is dead.

## LOOK AND LISTEN

To be successful at hunting and trapping, you need to decide which types of animal you are going to try to catch. To do that, you need to find out what animals are in the vicinity and where exactly they are to be found. Prey animals will use their keen senses to avoid being caught—so you will have to use your senses to find them. Look for any signs of animals, both on the ground and in the trees. And use your ears—you may be able to hear an animal even when you can't see it.

**SIGNS TO LOOK OUT FOR:**
- Runs, trails, and tracks
- Droppings
- Chewed or rubbed vegetation
- Feeding and watering areas
- Lairs, dens, and resting sites

## SQUIRREL POLE

Make several two-strand snares with nooses 3 in (8 cm) in diameter and stake-out cords 8 in (30 cm) in length. Place them around a long pole, with the lowest 2 ft (60 cm) off the ground. If you snare a squirrel, leave it, as others will come to investigate.

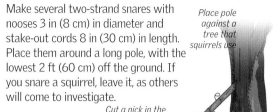
*Place pole against a tree that squirrels use*

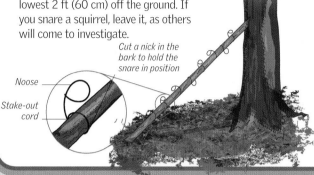

*Cut a nick in the bark to hold the snare in position*

*Noose*

*Stake-out cord*

---

**2** To make the noose, pass the imperfect end, or securing loop, through the perfect end, or running loop. The running loop has no loose ends of wire so it won't snag in an animal's fur and prevent the noose from tightening as it struggles.
- Use a single prusik knot (see p. 210) to tie a length of cord to the securing loop.

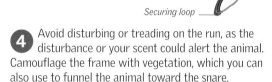

*Running loop, or "perfect end"*

*Using wire for the snare means the noose keep its shape*

*Securing loop*

**3** Before setting the snare, either bury it in the ground for a few hours or pass it over a flame for a few seconds to remove any human scent and dull its surface.
- Don't waste snares; always set them on runs you know the animals are using and set as many as you can.
- Use sticks to make a support from which to suspend the snare, or bend saplings into an arch.

**4** Avoid disturbing or treading on the run, as the disturbance or your scent could alert the animal. Camouflage the frame with vegetation, which you can also use to funnel the animal toward the snare.
- Use natural vegetation, such as holly or other prickly shrubs, to form a funnel on either side of the snare.
- The funnel helps to ensure that the animal has no option but to pass through the snare.

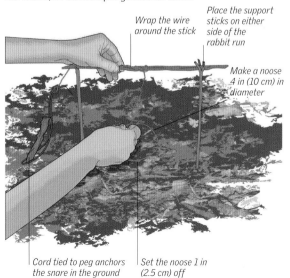

*Wrap the wire around the stick*

*Place the support sticks on either side of the rabbit run*

*Make a noose 4 in (10 cm) in diameter*

*Cord tied to peg anchors the snare in the ground*

*Set the noose 1 in (2.5 cm) off the ground*

*Branches in ground extend outwards from snare*

*Animal is funneled toward the snare*

# WEAPONS AND TECHNIQUES

A spear is the simplest weapon to make and use, but if you have the time and materials you can make more complicated weapons, although they require more skill to use. Learning other basic techniques, such as catching insects, is also invaluable when hunting.

*Hold at one end to throw*

*Weight is sufficient to kill or injure a rabbit-sized animal*

## THROWING STAR

With a throwing star you're four times more likely to hit prey than with a spear, and, if you don't succeed in wounding the animal with one of the sharp ends, the weight of the weapon will at least stun it. Keep it close at hand and ready to use, should the opportunity arise.

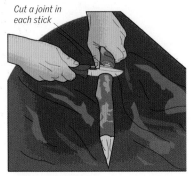

*Cut a joint in each stick*

**1** Find two sticks 2 in (5 cm) thick and 18 in (45 cm) long. Make a square-cut joint in the center of each, then sharpen each end.

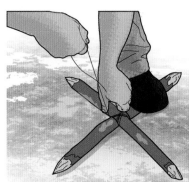

**2** Join the sticks together by overlapping the two square-cut joints and lashing them to each other with paracord or natural cordage.

**3** You can exert more force if you're throwing from a standing position. Aim for the animal's legs.

## RODENT SKEWER

A forked spear can be used to catch small mammals in their burrows. Thrust the pointed end into the hole. When you can feel the animal, twist the stick until you have snagged its fur, then carefully pull it out.

*Use a long sapling to make the skewer*

*Split one end into two then separate the fork with a piece of wood*

*The sharp point is used to snag the animal's fur*

## SLINGSHOT

A slingshot can be used to kill small animals. Cut a strong forked branch and make a notch in each fork. Take the rubber tubing from your survival kit (see pp. 60–61) and thread it through a piece of leather or plastic. Tie the ends of the tubing to the notches. Place a pebble in the pouch, stretch back the sling, and take aim.

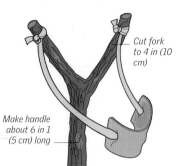

*Cut fork to 4 in (10 cm)*

*Make handle about 6 in 1 (5 cm) long*

## NOOSE STICK

You can use a noose stick to lasso lizards, slow-moving mammals, or roosting birds, jerking the pole to tighten the noose around the animal's neck. Use a wire or cordage snare (see pp. 216–17). When stalking prey, move slowly and very quietly.

*Select a stick strong enough to partly support the animal's weight*

*Make the loop large enough to fit over the animal's head*

# EASY PICKINGS

Ants are social insects, and most species are aggressive in defense of their nest. They have a stinging bite and some species will also squirt formic acid at their attacker. However, they make a nutritious meal if gathered with care. In summer months in northern temperate regions, you can eat the larvae of wood ants. And, if you use the technique shown below, you can get the ants to do all the work of collecting the larvae together for you. You'll have to vandalize the nest, but don't remove all of it.

## ANT CUISINE

Ant larvae are best fried—they taste like shrimp. Adult ants also make a tasty snack—in Bogotá, Colombia, movie theaters sell roasted leaf-cutter ant abdomens instead of popcorn.

*Ants carry the larvae into the protection of the shade*

*Wear gloves if you have them to protect your hands*

**1** Place a tarpaulin in a sunny patch next to the nest. Scoop the nest material, ants, and larvae into the middle of the tarpaulin.

**2** Lay some sticks on the tarpaulin, close to the edge, then fold over the sides to create shade. The ants will carry the larvae into the shade.

**3** After a while, throw back the folded sides of the tarpaulin and scoop up the larvae, which look like fat grains of white rice.

# CATCHING INSECTS

Many flying insects can be eaten, but catching them takes a bit of ingenuity. Crawling insects, such as ants (see above) and termites, can provide a good meal if you can collect them in sufficient quantities.

## TERMITE FISHING

Termites are found in the tropics and subtropics. Some species live in vast numbers inside mounds, which they build out of mud and saliva. If a foreign object breaches the walls, the termites will attack it with their powerful jaws.

## NIGHT FLIERS

Nocturnal flying insects, such as moths, are attracted to light. Stretch a white sheet between two branches and peg the bottom taut above a bowl of water. Hang a flashlight behind the sheet. Insects will fly into the sheet and fall into the water.

*Poke stick through wall into living chamber*

**1** Cut a long, thin, straight stick then peel it until smooth. Push it slowly into the termite hill.

*Termites cling to the stick with their jaws*

**2** Remove the stick and scrape off the attached termites into a container ready for frying or roasting.

*Ties at corners keep sheet taut*

*Stunned insects fall into water and drown*

# PREPARING SMALL MAMMALS

**PARASITES SUCH AS FLEAS** and lice will leave the body once a warm-blooded animal is dead so, if your circumstances permit, leave the carcass to cool before preparing it for cooking. In a hot climate, place the body in the shade. However, don't let it get too cold, as skin is more easily removed when a body is warm.

## RABBIT-SIZED MAMMALS

The method shown here applies to all furred mammals approximately the same size as a rabbit. Before gutting the animal, remove any urine by holding the body by the forelegs and progressively squeezing down from the chest toward the bowels, making sure that you direct the spray away from your own body. You'll need to remove any scent glands, which are usually inside the forelegs or around the anus, in case the musk taints the meat (take particular care when handling a skunk).

> **WARNING!**
> Rabbits, hares, and rodents may be infected with a bacteria called tularemia, which can be fatal to humans. Do not touch these animals with your bare hands if you have a scratch on your skin. If you have no gloves, cover your hands in soap lather before handling the animal, and wash your hands when you have finished. The germ is destroyed by heat, so cook the meat well. Myxamatosis, a viral disease that affects rabbits' mucous glands, is not harmful to humans.

## GUTTING

No part of a mammal carcass should be wasted. If your camp is near water, keep the guts as bait for fishing. The offal should be removed carefully and eaten if healthy – discard any organ that's pale or spotty. Liver is rich in essential vitamins and minerals and needs little cooking. It should be eaten as fresh as possible (removing the gall bladder from the middle first). Kidneys, which in most mammals are surrounded by fat, are also a valuable source of nutrition.

**1** Place the animal on its back on clean ground, such as a bed of pine boughs, with its head pointing toward you. Cut a small hole in its belly with the point of your knife, taking care not to pierce the guts.

> **WARNING!**
> Rabbits make an easy meal, but their flesh lacks fat and vitamins so, if your diet consists entirely of rabbit, your body will use its own vitamins and minerals to digest the meat. These are then lost from your body in your feces and, if not replaced, you'll get diarrhea and so become hungry and weak. Eating more rabbit makes the condition worse and you will eventually die of starvation. You must supplement your diet with some vegetation and fatty food.

**2** Pull the skin apart at the cut and insert a finger from each hand into the opening.

**3** Prise open the belly to expose the guts; remove them along with the heart, liver, and kidneys. Wash your hands before moving on to skinning.

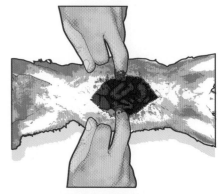

*Pinch up the skin before knicking it with your knife*

## SKINNING

If you wish to keep the skin for use later (to make a pair of mittens, for example), you should remove it as carefully as possible. You'll also need to cure it; stretch the skin as tight as possible and leave it in the sun or hang it close to the heat of a fire to dry. Rubbing wood ash into the skin will help to speed up the process.

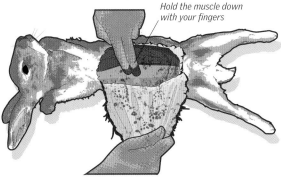

*Hold the muscle down with your fingers*

**1** Beginning at the belly, separate the skin from the muscle surrounding the gut cavity. You'll find that it pulls away quite easily. When you have reached the back on one side, repeat the process on the other.

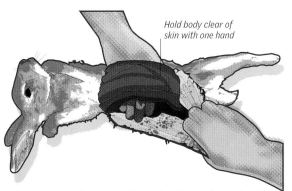

*Hold body clear of skin with one hand*

**2** Hold the flesh away from the skin with one hand and pull the skin over the rear legs, one by one. The hindquarters are now free of skin and fur, except for the tail, which should be cut off and the scent glands removed.

## GLOVE SKINNING

The preferred survival method of skinning and gutting a rabbit-sized mammal is to suspend it by its rear legs from a strong branch as this keeps the animal off the dirty ground.

- If you have no knife to hand, snap off the lower part of a foreleg and use the sharp edge of the broken bone to cut the skin.
- Gut the animal, then cut the skin around all four paws and between the rear legs.
- Tug the skin down toward the head.
- If you wish, pull the skin over the head. Otherwise just cut the head off.

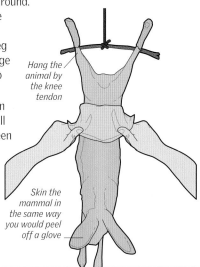

*Hang the animal by the knee tendon*

*Skin the mammal in the same way you would peel off a glove*

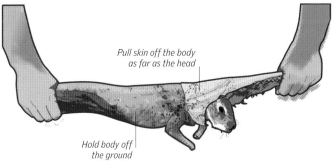

*Pull skin off the body as far as the head*

*Hold body off the ground*

**3** Hold the animal by the rear legs and pull the skin forward, easing out both forelegs. Pull the skin over the neck and then cut off the head. Wash the body to remove any traces of fur.

## HOW TO SKIN A SQUIRREL

Squirrel flesh is tender and tasty. Once you have skinned the squirrel, you can simply skewer it on a spit and roast it whole over a fire. Alternatively, you can cut the meat into pieces and make a stew. A large squirrel will feed two people.

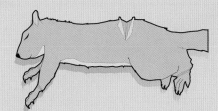

**1** Gut the squirrel following the method shown opposite. Cut the skin around the paws, then cut through the skin across the middle of its back.

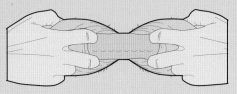

**2** Insert two fingers under the skin on either side of the cut and pull the two pieces apart and off the body. Wash off any traces of fur.

# PREPARING LARGE MAMMALS

**ALL LARGE MAMMALS** are edible, but you must not eat the livers of polar bears or bearded seals as they contain toxic levels of vitamin A. Wild game is sometimes infected with roundworm larvae and, if you eat the meat raw or undercooked, it will infect you with parasites, so always cook all wild game thoroughly.

## PREPARING THE KILL

Lifting large animals, such as deer, uses energy so, if you're alone, prepare the carcass on the ground. However, if you're in a group and circumstances permit, it's best to suspend the animal by its hocks (the tarsal joints of its hind legs) from a branch, as it will bleed better and will be easier to skin and gut. If you can't find a suitable tree from which to hang it, build a frame.

### WARNING!
Approach all game with caution, as the animal may still be alive and most wounded animals are extremely dangerous. To check, touch its eye with the tip of a long stick (or the muzzle of a gun). Even if the animal is unconscious, it will blink if it's alive. Always skin, gut, and butcher game at the site of the kill. You don't want the smell of fresh blood to attract predators or scavengers to your camp.

### BLEEDING

Bleeding is essential to preserve the meat and stops it from tasting too gamy. It also helps to cool the carcass. Slit the animal's throat from ear to ear and let the blood drain out. Blood is rich in vitamins and minerals, including salt, so, if you're able to, collect it in a container to use later in a stew. Cover the container to protect the blood from flies and to keep it cool.

### SKINNING

If you wish to preserve the hide, it's better to take the skin off before gutting. Cut the belly skin from throat to tail, cutting around the genitals. Cut along each leg from above the foot to the belly. Pull the hide off the carcass, severing connective tissue as necessary. If you're skinning on the ground and you don't want to keep the hide, you can use it to protect the meat—remove it fully only after jointing is complete.

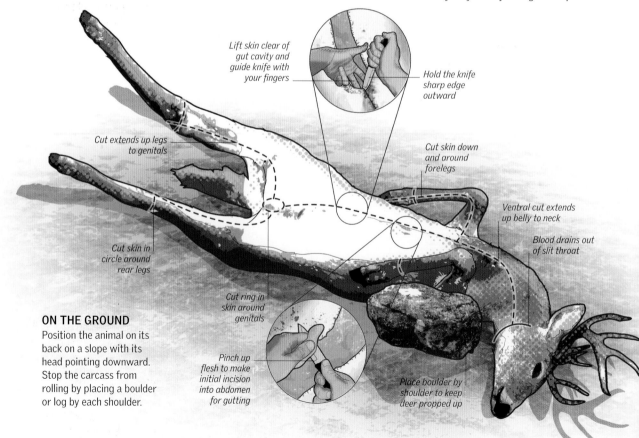

Lift skin clear of gut cavity and guide knife with your fingers

Hold the knife sharp edge outward

Cut extends up legs to genitals

Cut skin down and around forelegs

Ventral cut extends up belly to neck

Blood drains out of slit throat

Cut skin in circle around rear legs

Cut ring in skin around genitals

**ON THE GROUND**
Position the animal on its back on a slope with its head pointing downward. Stop the carcass from rolling by placing a boulder or log by each shoulder.

Pinch up flesh to make initial incision into abdomen for gutting

Place boulder by shoulder to keep deer propped up

# GUTTING

The method shown here is for gutting a carcass on its back. When finished, inspect the heart, liver, and kidneys for signs of worms or other parasites and, if the organs are healthy, keep them to eat. If the liver is spotted, a sign of disease, discard all internal organs and boil the meat.

**1** To avoid piercing the internal organs, pinch up the abdomen near the breastbone and make an incision big enough to insert two fingers.

■ Use your fingers to guide the knife, cutting toward, then around, the anus with the sharp blade-edge upward.

*Slice through the muscle covering the breastbone*

**2** Using a saw, if you have one, cut through the outer muscle and the breastbone to open up the chest cavity,

**3** Using the knife, slice through the diaphragm muscle, which separates the chest cavity from the gut cavity, getting as close to the spine as you can.

■ Remove the liver, taking care not to cut the gall bladder in the center.

*Ribs*

*Healthy liver is dark red-purple*

**4** Reach up through the chest cavity and cut the windpipe and esophagus. Hold them with one hand and pull out all the internal organs as one unit.

■ Check that the anus is clear of feces, pushing a hand through if you can't see daylight.

*Use the knife to cut organs where they adhere to body wall*

*Hold the top end of lungs to remove innards*

## KEEP THE GUTS

If you're able to carry them, take the guts, reproductive organs, and glands back to your camp in a sealed container. You can use them as bait in traplines or for fishing. Keep the fat that surrounds the intestines for cooking.

# JOINTING

Large game should be cut into manageable pieces that can be carried back to camp. Boning the meat helps to reduce the weight. Bag or wrap the meat as you remove it to keep it clean and free of flies, and keep it in the shade in hot climates. How a carcass is divided partly depends on the species, but the hindquarters contain the steaks and the best cuts.

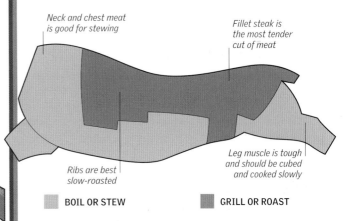

*Neck and chest meat is good for stewing*

*Fillet steak is the most tender cut of meat*

*Ribs are best slow-roasted*

*Leg muscle is tough and should be cubed and cooked slowly*

▮ BOIL OR STEW    ▮ GRILL OR ROAST

# USES FOR HIDES

Keep the skin if you can. When dried, it's light and can be used as a blanket, or it can be made into an item of clothing. Hide is one of the best materials for lashes. Sinew also makes good cordage (see p. 140).

## TANNING THE HIDE

The best way to clean a skin is to stretch it on a frame and then carefully scrape off the fat and any remaining scraps of flesh, using a flint or a piece of bone. Every mammal, with the exception of buffalo, has enough brain matter for use in tanning its own hide. Mash the brains well in warm water, then apply the mixture to the hairless side of the skin and leave it to dry for 24 hours.

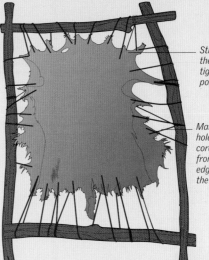

*Stretch the skin as tightly as possible*

*Make the holes for the cords away from the edges of the skin*

# PREPARING OTHER ANIMALS

**ALL TYPES OF ANIMAL** should be considered when searching for your next meal. Invertebrates are far more plentiful and widespread than other animals, and take less energy to gather and prepare. Reptiles and amphibians can also provide a vital source of nutrition.

## EATING FOR SURVIVAL

The thought of eating grubs or grasshoppers might not appeal, but experimentation is vital in a survival situation—don't forget that in some cultures such creatures are highly prized, if prepared properly. However, some animals are less palatable than others, in which case you should chop them finely and add to a stew.

### SLUGS, SNAILS, AND WORMS

Slugs should be avoided as they often feed on poisonous fungi. To prepare snails, either starve them or feed them safe food such as wild garlic for 24 hours to purge their guts before cooking. Either boil them in water or bake them in their shells in hot embers until the juices bubble over. Avoid all marine snails and any terrestrial snail with a brightly colored shell as they may be toxic. All earthworms are edible. Place them in salty water until they are purged, then boil, though they can be eaten raw if necessary.

## EDIBLE INSECTS

Insects are mostly protein and make good emergency food. Avoid any hairy or brightly colored insects or those that emit a foul smell (including larvae). As a general rule, avoid adults that sting or bite, but ants and honey bees can be eaten if collected carefully. Most insects, except those with a hard carapace, like beetles, can be eaten raw.

### HOPPING INSECTS

Grasshoppers and crickets have large leg muscles, and most are quite tasty when cooked (avoid brightly colored ones). Remove the antennas, wings, and leg spurs, and roast to kill any parasites.

### WITCHETTY GRUBS

Witchetty grubs are a highly nutritious Australian bush delicacy. They can be eaten raw but, if roasted quickly in hot ashes, they taste of scrambled eggs. Treat palm grubs in the same way.

*Large, white grubs high in protein and calcium*

## AMPHIBIANS AND REPTILES

All frogs in the *Rana* genus (see pp. 292–93) are edible. Skin and then boil or roast them. The best, most meaty part is the hind legs. Don't handle or eat toads or brightly colored tropical frogs as many have highly toxic skin secretions. Lizards and snakes are a good source of protein. They must be skinned and gutted, then either roasted on a stick if small, or cut into small pieces and boiled. All snake flesh is edible—and tastes like chicken—apart from the head, which must be removed.

**1** Hold the dead snake firmly behind the head and cut it off about 6 in (15 cm) down the body.

*Bury the head if the snake is venomous*

**2** Slit the belly with a sharp knife and remove the entrails and other organs. Either throw them away or keep as bait.

*Slice about 12 in (30 cm) along belly*

**3** Peel the skin back, then grasp the body in one hand and the skin in the other and pull it off.

*If the snake isn't too big, the skin will come off in one piece*

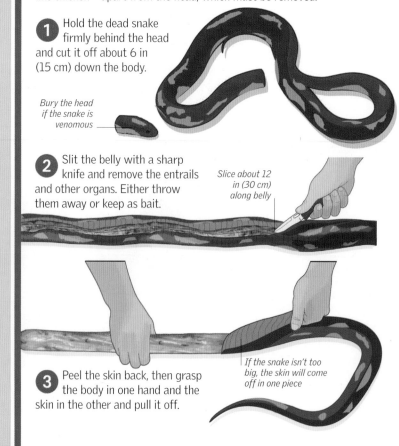

# PREPARING A CRAB

Avoid their strong claws (tie them up if you can). To kill a crab, plunge it in boiling water or stab it through the eye socket or the orifice under the shell flap on the body. Cook the crab for about 15 minutes.

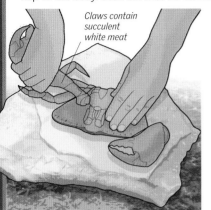

*Claws contain succulent white meat*

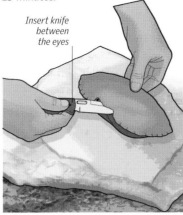

*Insert knife between the eyes*

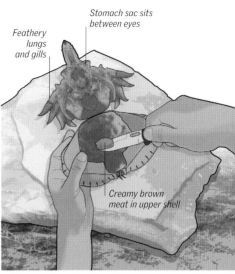

*Stomach sac sits between eyes*

*Feathery lungs and gills*

*Creamy brown meat in upper shell*

**1** Place the cooked crab on its back, then twist off its legs and the claws. They all contain edible meat, so crack them open with a rock.

**2** Open the shell by inserting the point of your knife between the two halves and twisting it. Lift back the lower shell.

**3** Remove and discard any green matter and the lungs, gills, and stomach as they're all poisonous. Scoop the meat out of the shell.

# SHELLFISH

Shellfish can be found in streams and on lake and sea shores. Don't collect marine shellfish that are not covered at high tide or are near any source of pollution. Shellfish must be alive when you collect them—bivalves, such as mussels, will close their shell if you tap them, and univalves, such as limpets, will cling tightly to their rock—and you must cook and eat them immediately.

## WARNING!

Tropical species of mussel should be avoided in the summer as they may be poisonous. The black mussel, which is found on Arctic and sub-Arctic coasts, may be poisonous at any time of the year. The symptoms of mussel poisoning are acute nausea, vomiting, diarrhea, abdominal pain, and fever.

## HOW TO SHUCK AN OYSTER

Oysters are rich in vitamins and minerals. To eat an oyster raw, first open its shell by inserting a blunt knife into the hinge at the thicker, more pointed end of the oyster and twisting. However, in a survival situation, play safe and boil oysters in their shells for five minutes after their shells open. Do not eat any whose shells do not open during cooking.

## SHRIMPS, CRABS, AND LOBSTERS

Small crustaceans, such as shrimps and crawfish, should be cooked in boiling water for five minutes. Larger crustaceans, such as some crabs and lobsters, should be boiled for up to 20 minutes. A tasty alternative to boiling shrimps or prawns is to roast them on skewers made of green wood, placed in the embers of a fire.

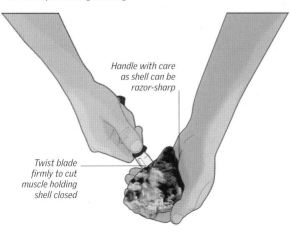

*Handle with care as shell can be razor-sharp*

*Twist blade firmly to cut muscle holding shell closed*

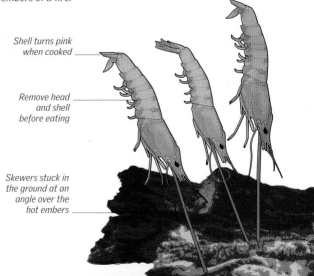

*Shell turns pink when cooked*

*Remove head and shell before eating*

*Skewers stuck in the ground at an angle over the hot embers*

# CATCHING BIRDS

**BIRDS CAN BE TRAPPED** in a variety of ways—in snares, nets, tunnels, or cages—and they can be hunted with noose sticks or any projectile weapon. The trick is to observe their behavior and to match your technique—and bait—to the bird. You need to discover their regular roosts, feeding spots, and flight paths.

**WARNING!**
Eggs are easy to collect, particularly from ground-nesters, although gulls, for example, will attack you if you try. However, taking eggs from nests is illegal in many countries and should only be done if absolutely necessary.

## FIGURE-4 CAGE TRAP

This trap enables you to catch ground-feeding birds (or rabbit-sized mammals) without killing or wounding them, so you can choose when you want to kill them and eat the meat fresh. The "Figure 4" is the trigger that's used to drop the cage over the animal.

### MAKING THE TRIGGER

To construct the Figure 4 trigger you need to make three notched sticks (bait stick, upright stick, and release stick) and then link them together as shown below.

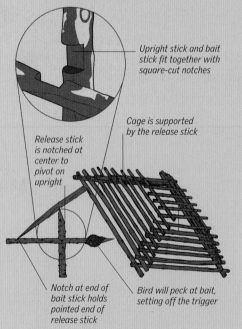

Upright stick and bait stick fit together with square-cut notches

Cage is supported by the release stick

Release stick is notched at center to pivot on upright

Notch at end of bait stick holds pointed end of release stick

Bird will peck at bait, setting off the trigger

### MAKING THE CAGE

Create a pyramid of sticks by placing progressively shorter sticks across longer sticks and lashing them together at the ends. Balance the cage over the bait.

## ON THE GROUND

Gamebirds, such as quail, and inquisitive scavengers, such as crows, can be lured into traps if you use the right bait. Migratory waterfowl, such as ducks and geese, molt in the late summer, which means they are easier to catch as they can't fly away.

### WALK-IN TUNNEL TRAP

A tunnel trap can be used to catch gamebirds, which have stiff feathers that lie in one direction and bend only with difficulty. As a bird tries to retreat from the trap, its feathers will become wedged in the tunnel walls.
- Dig a near-horizontal, funnel-shaped tunnel close to the ground.
- Lay a trail of bait (seed or berries) leading to the rear of the tunnel.
- As it eats the bait, the bird will move deeper into the tunnel and will be unable to back out.

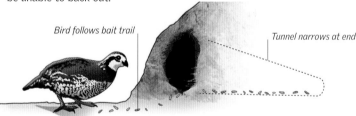

Bird follows bait trail

Tunnel narrows at end

## ON THE WING

A fine net stretched between two trees across a flight path is an effective method of catching birds in flight. Throwing a bola requires more skill, and works by entangling the bird in the spinning ropes.

### MAKING A BOLA

To make a bola, use an overhand knot (see p. 143) to tie three 3-ft (1-m) lengths of cord together about 3 in (8 cm) from one end. Find three rocks weighing about 7 oz (200 g), wrap each one in a piece of cloth, and tie it up with the free end of a cord.

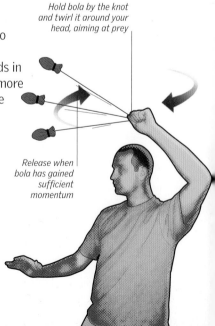

Hold bola by the knot and twirl it around your head, aiming at prey

Release when bola has gained sufficient momentum

# ON THE NEST

Birds are creatures of habit and will usually roost in the same place every night, such as in the branches of a tree as protection against ground predators. They rarely move once it's dark. Many birds are more accessible when breeding as, once you've located the nest, you'll always know where to find them. However, you should only take nesting birds in a genuine survival situation.

## MAKING A SNARE STICK

A snare stick is used to trap birds roosting in trees. Remove a bird once it has been snared, as its squawking and fluttering will alert other birds to the danger and scare them off.
- Make several single-strand snares (see pp. 216–27) with a loop diameter of about 1–2 in (2.5–5 cm), depending on the size of the bird.
- Place them close together along a stick, making notches in the stick to hold them in position with the loops uppermost.
- Tie the stick on top of a branch where you have seen birds roosting.

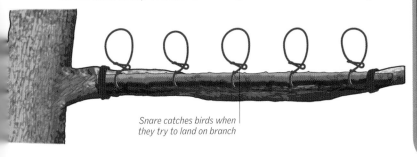

*Snare catches birds when they try to land on branch*

## BOUGH FENCE TRAP

This method is used to trap ducks, which often go ashore during the day to sun themselves, or at night to roost. They tend to favor small islands as protection against predators.
- Cut several saplings and make double-stranded snares (see p. 216).
- Place the boughs a few feet from the water's edge, and bend them into a series of overlapping hoops to form a fence around the island.
- If you only have a few snares, place them over the ducks' inward and outward tracks. Placing logs between the snares will then force the birds to pass through the hoops in order to get onto the island.
- Suspend a snare from the center of each bough arch.

# PHEASANT POLE

Pheasants roost in trees at night, usually returning to the same branch, and they won't leave once it's dark. To snare a sleeping pheasant, raise the pole up in front of it. The bird will wake and peck at the foil. As its head goes through the loop, pull the cordage and the snare will close around the bird's neck.

*Silver foil or shiny paper*

*Lash the snare loop to the fork with something that will break easily*

*Lash foil stick to long forked pole*

*Attach cordage to snare wire*

## TO MAKE THE POLE

Cut a long forked pole. Tie a stick in the V of the fork and attach a piece of silver foil to it. Weakly lash the loop of a snare to the fork, then run a length of cordage down the pole from the snare wire.

*Boughs overlap*

*Loop diameter is approximately 2 in (5 cm)*

*Loop of snare touches the ground*

# PREPARING BIRDS

**GAMEBIRDS AND WATERFOWL** are the most commonly eaten wild birds, but all birds are edible if prepared correctly. Skinning a bird is the quickest way to get at the meat, but this removes the nutritional value of the skin, so always pluck a bird if you have the time to do so.

> **WARNING!**
> Handle scavengers and carrion eaters, such as crows, buzzards, and vultures, as little as possible, because they are more likely to be infested with lice and ticks, and are prone to infection.
> ■ The meat of such birds must be boiled for at least 30 minutes to kill any infectious organisms. This will also tenderize the meat.
> ■ Always wash your hands after handling any bird.

## GETTING STARTED

If the bird hasn't already been killed by the method of capture you'll need to dispatch it—for example, by stretching its neck and cutting its throat (for the best way to kill gamebirds, see below). Whichever method you use to kill the bird, you must bleed it before plucking, but make sure you pluck it while the body is still warm.

## KILLING GAMEBIRDS

To quickly and humanely dispatch a gamebird, such as a pheasant, fold its wings into the body and hold it under your arm. Cover its head with your jacket to calm it down (this also reduces the chances of you being injured by its claws or beak). Still holding the bird firmly, take a 2 ft (60 cm) long, thick stick and place it on the ground. Put the bird's head underneath the stick, place your feet on the stick either side of the head, and pull the bird up sharply by the legs—the bird's head will come off.

### POACHER'S METHOD
The poacher's way to quickly get the meat from a dead pheasant that hasn't been decapitated is to place it face down on the ground with its head toward you, put a foot on each wing, take hold of the legs, and pull up sharply. This motion will tear the legs and breast meat away from the rest of the bird. Give it a sharp flick to detach the guts. In a survival situation, this is a good way to get meat off the bird if you don't have a knife or razor.

## PLUCKING A BIRD

It's not essential, but scalding a bird in a bucket of hot (not boiling) water for a couple of minutes usually helps to loosen the feathers; the exceptions are waterfowl and seabirds—their feathers will tighten instead. Be careful not to overscald the bird or the skin will start to cook.

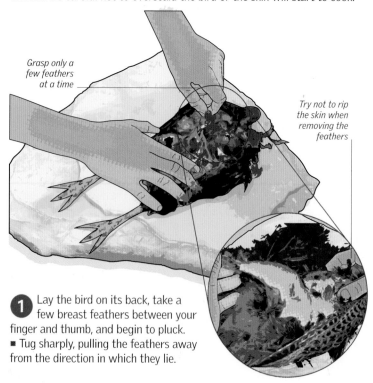

*Grasp only a few feathers at a time*

*Try not to rip the skin when removing the feathers*

**1** Lay the bird on its back, take a few breast feathers between your finger and thumb, and begin to pluck.
■ Tug sharply, pulling the feathers away from the direction in which they lie.

**2** Don't try to pluck too many feathers at once or you'll tear the skin. Work your way steadily around the front and back until you've plucked the whole body.
■ Keep the feathers (unless the bird is a scavenger, see box, above) to use for tinder, insulation, or fishing lures.

## OPTIONAL EXTRAS

Keep the crop (esophagus) contents of a gamebird—you can use the seeds and berries as bait to catch other birds. If the bird is female and has eggs in the oviduct, keep them and eat them. You should also eat the heart and the liver if they are in good condition; discard them if they look old or spotty, or show signs of parasites.

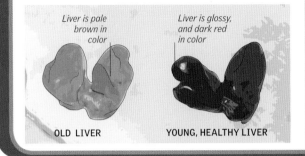

Liver is pale brown in color

Liver is glossy, and dark red in color

OLD LIVER

YOUNG, HEALTHY LIVER

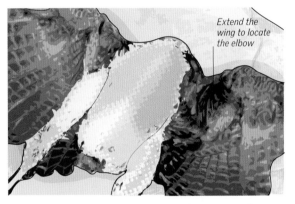

Extend the wing to locate the elbow

**3** Pluck the legs in the same way, then turn to the wings. Locate the elbows and cut off the lower wings at this joint. Pluck the upper wings.
- If the bird's head is still attached, cut it off as close as possible to the body.

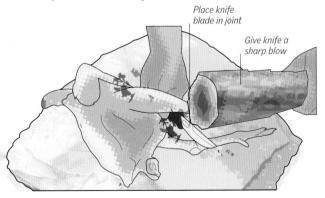

Place knife blade in joint

Give knife a sharp blow

**4** To remove the feet, find the ankle, insert the blade of a sharp knife into the joint, and press down hard.
- If you're dealing with a large bird, such as a turkey, hit the back of the knife with a thick stick for extra force.

## DRAWING METHODS

The usual way to remove the offal from a bird (known as "drawing") is to take the crop (esophagus) out of the neck end and the rest of the offal out of the rear end. The survival method is to make a cut from the throat to the tail with a sharp knife, reach in, and pull out all the offal (see below). Should you find yourself without a knife, you can still butcher a bird by pulling the skin apart with your fingers and working your way up the breast to the neck. The offal can be removed by ripping open the skin over the belly.

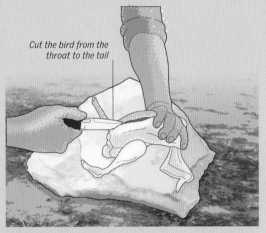

Cut the bird from the throat to the tail

**1** Hold the bird in one hand, breast upward and with its rear end toward you. Insert the point of a sharp knife into the throat.
- Make a single incision down toward the tail, being careful to not pierce the guts.

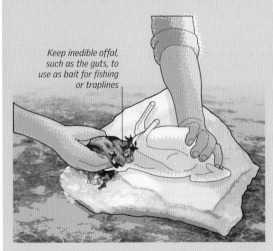

Keep inedible offal, such as the guts, to use as bait for fishing or traplines

**2** Reach into the gut cavity and pull out the offal, taking care not to break any eggs. Keep the liver and heart if healthy (see above left).
- Wash the bird clean with cold water and wash your hands thoroughly before further handling.

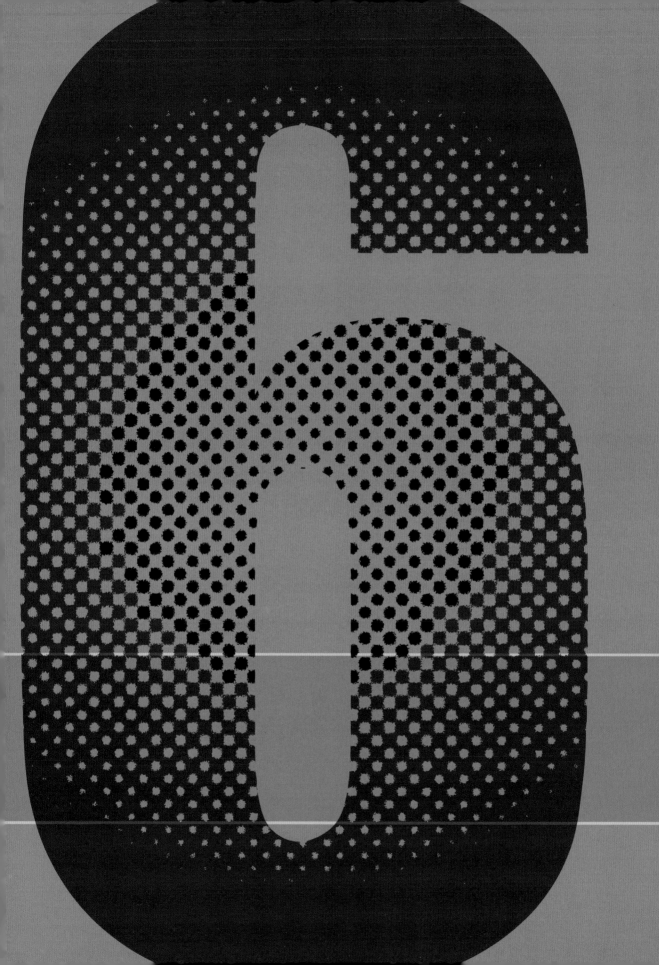

# IN AN EMERGENCY

# IN AN EMERGENCY

**You're only a survivor** when you have been rescued. This means that you must be able to either get yourself out of the predicament you are in (self-rescue) or be rescued from that situation by others. Sometimes you will be able to choose whether to undertake self-rescue; at other times the decision will be out of your hands. There may be several reasons why you cannot achieve self-rescue: you could be utterly lost; local conditions such as flooding or bad weather could trap you; or injury to yourself or a group member could make movement impossible. In this situation, the onus is on you to attract attention. You must be able to make contact with rescuers, using location aids you have with you or those you can improvise. Never delay any form of rescue because of the embarrassment factor—the only important factor is the outcome, and I would always rather be embarrassed and alive than eventually found dead!

Preparation is key—informing people of your intentions and timeframes will at least have someone wondering why you are not back yet. Equally, taking the best

## In this chapter YOU WILL DISCOVER...

- how to **recognize** the **enemies** of **survival**...
- why **LEOs** are so **important**...
- when to **set fire** to a **log cabin**...
- that **tinsel** isn't just for **Christmas**...
- what to **do** if a **hippo yawns**...
- that you **should go** with the **flow** in an **avalanche**...
- how to **inflate** your **pants**...

location aids for your environment and knowing how best to use them will increase the chances of you being found.

In many survival situations, a major decision will be whether you remain where you are or move to a location that offers a better chance of survival, rescue, or both. There are numerous factors that will dictate your best option but, in general, it's always best to stay where you are. It's all too easy to make a rash decision and attempt to walk out of a situation only to put yourself in even greater danger.

## A location aid can make the difference between life and death. A comparatively recent invention is the multi-tasking Skystreme device.

**SKYSTREME** is a silver, inflatable foil kite, which weighs just $1\frac{1}{2}$ oz (43 g) and packs down to a small and convenient size. It can perform four tasks in a survival situation:

**Location aid** The kite is orally inflated and its wedge shape means it can lift off from the ground unaided in 4 mph (6 kph) winds.

- The 165 ft (50 m) of line attached to the kite (this much cordage is invaluable in itself) allows it to rise above tree levels and reflect sunlight. It can be seen by the naked eye at a distance of 2 miles (3 km).
- At night, you can hang a small flashlight or lightstick underneath the kite to aid visibility.
- The metallic surface reflects radar and can be detected by aircraft at a distance of 10 miles (17 km). A UK Royal Marine on a polar crossing flew his Skystreme behind his sled so that support aircraft could find and track him.

**Emergency first aid splint** The kite can be inflated around a broken or sprained limb.

**Thermal vest** The kite can be inflated and put inside clothing to act as a body warmer.

**Water storage** Instead of being inflated with air, the kite can be used to carry and store water.

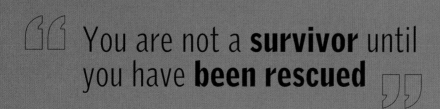
You are not a **survivor** until you have **been rescued**

# ASSESSING YOUR SITUATION

**ONCE YOU'RE OUT** of immediate danger, assess your situation and plan accordingly. At this initial stage, it's crucial to think clearly—the decisions you make now could mean the difference between life and death. In most cases, remaining where you are is the preferred option, but no two situations are ever the same: the circumstances, environment, conditions, and you—the individual—all have a major impact on what can and cannot be achieved.

## THE STRATEGY FOR STAYING ALIVE

In an emergency situation, think of the four priorities of survival: protection, location, water, and food. Your situation will determine which is the most important. In most cases, as long as you're in no further danger from injury or the elements, you should focus your efforts on establishing a safe location and getting yourself rescued. The strategy for staying alive, known by the acronym SURVIVAL (see below), gives you a framework to use and helps you remember what you need to do to remain alive and get rescued.

### THE RULE OF THREES

A common understanding among those concerned with survival is that various key time limits have a numerical value linked to the number three. Remembering the "rule of threes" can help you focus your decision-making, particularly if you are injured, at risk of further injury, or in immediate danger from the elements. In most cases:

- **Three seconds** is the psychological reaction time for making a decision.
- **Three minutes** is the length of time your brain can do without oxygen before it suffers irreparable damage.
- **Three hours** is the critical time you can survive unprotected in extreme climates.
- **Three days** is the approximate length of time you can live without water.
- **Three weeks** is the approximate length of time you can live without food.

| SIZE UP YOUR SITUATION | USE ALL YOUR SENSES | REMEMBER WHERE YOU ARE | VANQUISH FEAR |
|---|---|---|---|
| - First, assess the particulars of your surroundings, physical condition, and equipment.<br>- If you're in a group, you can share tasks and responsibilities, but remember that everyone will be affected by the consequences of your decisions. | - Most people react to a true survival situation through either training (they automatically do what they've been trained to do in a particular situation) or by instinct (they automatically do what their mind and body tell them to do). | - In any survival situation, it always helps to know where you are so that you can make the best decisions about what to do and where to go next. | - Fear and panic can be formidable enemies, so it's imperative that you have the knowledge and training to counteract them and prevent them from making your situation worse. |
| - Your surroundings: every environment has its own idiosyncrasies—hot and dry, hot and wet, cold, exposed, or enclosed. Determine what you need to do in order to adapt to that environment.<br>- Your equipment: assess your equipment and consider how it can best be used in your particular situation.<br>- Your physical condition: remove yourself and others from danger. Check for injuries and administer first aid as necessary. Remember that the trauma and stress of a survival situation may cause you to overlook, or subconsciously ignore, injuries that you yourself may have received. | - Whatever has happened, approach your predicament in a calm and rational manner. The situation requires careful thought and planning.<br>- If you act in haste, you may overlook important factors, lose vital equipment, or simply make matters worse. The saying "Undue haste makes waste" is especially true in a survival situation.<br>- Listen to your subconscious survival senses and gut feelings, and learn to act on them when they send you warning signals. | - Knowing your precise location can clarify whether rescuers are likely to find you or if you'll have to rescue yourself. You'll get a good idea of the obstacles you may face, whether you should remain where you are, and where best to position your aids to location.<br>- If you have made an Emergency Plan of Action (see pp. 24–25), someone will know your approximate location, and when you're due back.<br>- Channel your efforts into making sure that when rescuers are looking for you, your aids to location are in place. | - If uncontrolled, fear and panic can destroy your ability to make intelligent and rational decisions. They can cause you to react to your feelings and imagination rather than to your actual situation and your abilities. Moreover, they can incapacitate you and drain your energy, thus triggering other negative emotions.<br>- If you're in a group, your responses can have a direct effect on others—positive responses are productive and can motivate, while negative responses can undermine confidence and morale. |

# THE ENEMIES OF SURVIVAL

In a survival situation, there are seven factors, known as "the enemies of survival," that can work against you. In many cases, you can deal with them by knowing what they are and understanding their effects. One way to memorize these is by using a mnemonic such as: "Be Prepared To Face These Hostile Factors".

## BOREDOM AND LONELINESS

When boredom sets in, you become inactive and lose the ability to deal with your situation effectively, so you need to keep busy. Loneliness makes you overwhelmed by what you need to achieve, leading to a feeling of helplessness.

## PAIN

If you're injured, don't ignore the pain. Attend to a minor injury, as it could grow into a major problem that could impair your ability to survive. A positive mental attitude coupled with keeping busy helps to distract the mind from pain.

## THIRST

Thirst is not a good indicator of the body's need for water. Your body can be dehydrated before you feel thirsty. Stay ahead of dehydration, rather than have to deal with it. Prioritize your need for water in a way that's relevant to your environment.

## FATIGUE

Tiredness leads to mistakes that, at best, cause frustration and, at worst, may result in injury or death. In a survival situation, it's unlikely that you'll replace the energy you use effectively, so everything becomes harder to achieve. Never underestimate the importance of quality rest to your physical and mental wellbeing.

## TEMPERATURE

Temperature is a major factor in any survival situation and it will be affected by wind, rain, and humidity. You should dress to suit the environment you're in and be aware of the signs and symptoms of temperature-related injuries, such as dehydration, hypothermia, heat stress, and heat stroke (see pp. 272–73).

## HUNGER

In a short-term survival situation (one to five days), procuring food is not a high priority. You can offset your reduced energy and stamina levels by drinking water and pacing yourself so you work within your limits. However, take every opportunity to procure food without expending energy.

## FEAR

Fear is one of our body's greatest survival tools, as it can stimulate you, so that you're ready to act—however, it can also debilitate. Fear is good as long as you have control over it, and the key to controlling fear in a survival situation is knowledge.

| IMPROVISE | VALUE LIVING AND LIFE | ACT LIKE THE LOCALS | LEARN BASIC SKILLS |
|---|---|---|---|
| ▪ The true skill of a survivor is to understand what's required and improvise solutions to particular problems. Do you have the skills and knowledge to keep yourself alive and in a condition to be proactive in your own rescue? | ▪ Some people without training and equipment have survived the most horrendous situations. In many cases, this was simply because they had the will to live and refused to give up! | ▪ Whatever environment you're trying to survive in, you can be sure that the local or indigenous people and the local wildlife have developed ways of adapting to it in order to survive. | ▪ Learning basic skills increases your chances of survival. Without training your prospects of survival are down to luck, which is never the best place to start. There is a saying: "Luck favors those who are best prepared." |
| ▪ You may start out with all the right equipment, but it may get lost or broken, or simply wear out. Your ability to improvise may mean the difference between your continued struggle to survive in relative comfort, or absolute misery.<br>▪ Think laterally, like the climber who was stranded on the side of a mountain with no aids to location. He used the flash on his camera to signal his location to a rescue helicopter. Improvise and overcome! | ▪ The stories of prisoners of war often reveal what kept them alive: religious beliefs, thoughts of family and friends, or a determination not to let the enemy win. While these alone may not always be enough, they're certainly a key factor in any survival situation.<br>▪ It helps to bear in mind that hardship means different things to different people and in different cultures.<br>▪ Survival is about dealing with hardships and having the will to live. If the will to live is not there, then just having the knowledge and equipment may not be enough. | ▪ Look at how the local people dress and act: in hot countries they leave manual work until the coolest parts of the day and work in a slow and deliberate manner to reduce sweating and therefore conserve water.<br>▪ If you're in a desert, for example, watch where animals go to find shade: they're mostly nocturnal and spend the day underground. Learn their tricks to find water, like the darkling beetle in the Namib Desert that drinks water from the fog that condenses on its carapace.<br>▪ If you're in a jungle, pay attention when the animals go quiet or quickly leave an area—danger is usually around the corner. | ▪ Prior preparation is the key to survival: discover what you need to know about the environment you're going to; familiarize yourself with all your equipment; and practice your basic skills until they become second nature. This thorough preparation will help you to combat the fear of the unknown and give you the self-confidence to meet the challenges of any survival situation you may be in. |

# ATTRACTING RESCUERS

**TO BE A SURVIVOR** you need to rescue yourself or be rescued by others. If you can't rescue yourself—perhaps you're injured, completely lost, or trapped by bad weather—you must attract attention with location aids that you've either brought with you or have improvised.

## AIDS TO LOCATION

Location aids can save your life, so make sure you know how to use them effectively. A helicopter on a search pattern may make only one pass over an area before moving on, so you'll only have a few minutes to act decisively.

## COMMUNICATING WITH SATELLITES

When activated, a Personal Locator Beacon (PLB) transmits a radio distress signal to two complementary satellite systems called LEOSAR and GEOSAR. Together, these form the "COSPAS-SARSAT" system. The signal is then relayed to a rescue coordination center closest to the beacon's location. PLBs mainly use 406Mhz; the military also use 243.5Mhz and 282.8Mhz.

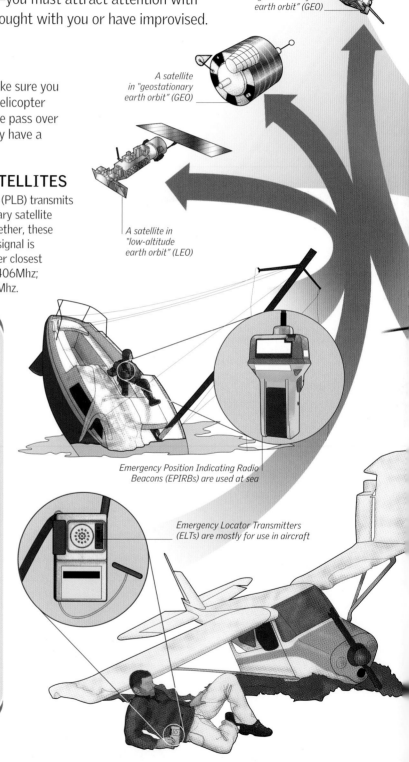

*A satellite in "geostationary earth orbit" (GEO)*

*A satellite in "geostationary earth orbit" (GEO)*

*A satellite in "low-altitude earth orbit" (LEO)*

*Emergency Position Indicating Radio Beacons (EPIRBs) are used at sea*

*Emergency Locator Transmitters (ELTs) are mostly for use in aircraft*

### ATTRACTING ATTENTION

When you're in a survival situation, you need to employ your location aids in the best way possible. There are three main principles for attracting attention:

■ **Attract:** pick a place that maximizes your chances of attracting attention using your location aids, such as open or high ground. Place your aids carefully so they can be detected from as wide an area as possible. The more obvious the signal the better.

■ **Hold:** you need to hold the attention of rescuers by maintaining the signal until they indicate they've seen you. Try to send some critical information (the type of assistance you require or the number of survivors and their condition, for example) via a May Day, or Help message (see pp. 237–41).

■ **Direct:** regardless of which location aids you use, once rescuers have been alerted, do all you can to direct them to your present location. If you have voice communication, direct them to your position. If you leave notes before moving on from places, make sure they contain dates and precise details of your intentions.

## SHOULD I STAY OR SHOULD I GO?

You need to decide whether to stay where you are or to move to a location where you have a better chance of rescue or self-rescue. If you move on, remember the following:

■ Keep your aids to location at hand. It's no good having your signal mirror at the bottom of your backpack when you may have only seconds to attract a passing vehicle or plane.

■ Deploy your aids to location at the end of each day, even though it takes effort and you'll be moving in the morning.

■ To show where you've been and where you're heading, leave markers, such as a note left in a visible position and visual clues on the ground or vegetation, to indicate your direction of travel.

## MOBILE TELEPHONES AND RADIOS

Always take a cell or satellite phone with you when traveling—they are essential in an emergency. On a sea trip, take a marine VHF radio to contact would-be rescuers.

### CELL AND SATELLITE PHONES

Wherever you are in the world, you can rent or buy a cell phone linked to local networks. Choose one with a GPS unit for fixing and racking your position and a camera so you can send pictures of your location and any injuries you've sustained. Alternatively, rent or buy a satellite phone that's connected to the Iridium Satellite Phone System, in which 66 low-earth orbiting (LEO) satellites provide complete coverage of Earth (including oceans, airways, and polar regions).

### MARINE VHF RADIOS

All large ships and most motorized small craft are equipped with marine VHF radios. These hand-held units transmit and receive on frequencies between 156 to 174MHz—usually on Channel 16, the international calling and distress channel. Channel 9 can also be used in some places. Transmission power ranges between 1 and 25 watts, giving a maximum range of up to about 60 miles (110 km) between aerials mounted on tall ships and hills, and 5 miles (9 km) between aerials mounted on small boats at sea level. Your VHF radio should be waterproof, able to float, and kept on charge. Follow the instructions whenever transmitting and receiving on VHF.

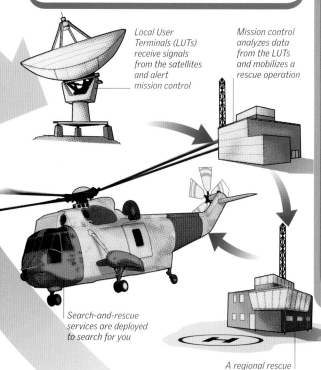

*Local User Terminals (LUTs) receive signals from the satellites and alert mission control*

*Mission control analyzes data from the LUTs and mobilizes a rescue operation*

*Search-and-rescue services are deployed to search for you*

*A regional rescue coordination center alerts the search-and-rescue teams*

*Personal Locator Beacons (PLBs) are for personal use and kept on the body*

*A PLB is activated manually and sends a signal to one of the search-and-rescue satellites*

## WARNING!

PLBs are for emergency use only and should always be used responsibly.

# BUILDING SIGNAL FIRES

A signal fire is a very effective way of attracting the attention of rescuers, but you do need the right materials and building one requires some effort. A well-constructed signal fire located in a good position will generate a large amount of smoke that can be seen from a long way away. Two variations—the dome and the log cabin—are shown here.

## TOOLS AND MATERIALS
- Knife and saw
- Poles and long saplings
- Green vegetation
- Tinder, kindling, and fuel
- Lighter or matches

## SIGNAL FIRE ESSENTIALS

Whichever signal fire you make, there are several important principles to follow in order to make it as effective as possible.

### FIRE FORMATION

If you can, prepare three signal fires in a recognized formation, such as a triangle or in a straight line. If the fires are random, they could be misread as a bush fire or a group of native fires. The distance between each fire should be at least 65 ft (20 m) but needs to be dictated by how quickly you can effectively light each one in turn.

### FIRE COMPONENTS

Essentially, each signal fire is composed of a ready-to-light firebase made of dry tinder, kindling, and fuel. When you add the merest spark or flame to the tinder, the firebase immediately turns into a sustainable fire.
- Site the firebase off the ground to prevent damp from reaching it, and to allow enough airflow to help it ignite more effectively.
- Cover the top of the firebase with large amounts of green vegetation and anything else that produces smoke, such as tires. The covering keeps the firebase dry.
- Place a second stack of green vegetation near the firebase and add this as the original vegetation burns out.

### AT THE READY

Once you have prepared the signal fire, you need to keep the following nearby, ready for use at a moment's notice:
- Dry tinder in a waterproof container underneath the firebase.
- Hexamine fuel tablets, stove fuel, gas, paper, or birch bark to guarantee the fire gets going again if it starts to dwindle.
- Something to create a spark or flame.
- A witch's broom, made of a cleft stick stuffed with kindling or bark, next to your camp fire, so you can quickly light the broom and transfer it to the signal fire.

## MAKING A DOME SIGNAL FIRE

Prepare a large fire on a raised platform under a dome-shaped structure made from bent saplings. Fueled by air from below, the fire creates plumes of smoke from the green vegetation. If you have no saplings, use poles to a make a teepee shape.

*Bend two long saplings to form the dome*

*Lash poles to each side of the dome to steady it*

*Peg the long poles to the ground*

*Four stakes steady the platform*

*Green wood poles act as a firebase*

*Large log or rock*

*Stick the ends of the saplings firmly into the ground.*

**1** Lay two long poles parallel to each other. Prop them up over a log or rock at one end, and tie them to four stakes at the other. Lay lengths of green wood side by side on the long poles under the dome, to act as a firebase.
- Bend two long saplings at 90 degrees to each other to form a dome.

**4** Layer green vegetation on top of the dome to form a roof over the fire platform.
- Keep additional green vegetation nearby to add to the fire when it's alight.

*Leave an access point for lighting the fire, but keep it closed so the tinder, kindling, and fuel stays dry*

# MAKING A LOG CABIN SIGNAL FIRE

This signal fire is known as the "log cabin" because of the way the fuel wood is stacked.

■ The framework for the fire is a stack of green wood, made up of pairs of poles arranged in alternating layers set at 90 degrees to each other.

■ Place an additional supply of green vegetation nearby to be used as required, but not so close that it catches fire by accident.

*Green wood poles produce more smoke than dead wood*

*Pile on as much green vegetation as you can find*

**1** Lay a platform of green wood on the ground and build a firebase of dry tinder, kindling, and fuel on top.
■ Build a "log cabin" over the firebase using green wood.

**2** Heap green vegetation over the platform to generate thick plumes of smoke when the fire is lit.
■ Leave an access point at the front to allow you to light the firebase.

*Tinder, kindling, fuel, and vegetation*

**2** Prepare a fire (see pp. 124–25) on the platform and load it with green vegetation.
■ Lay the vegetation close enough to the fuel below to catch easily when the fire is lit—but don't smother it.

*Stab a thin branch or vine into the bundle, wrap it around a few times and tuck it in under itself*

**3** Prepare some kindling bundles which will help turn the initial flame into a fire.
■ Make the bundles by breaking small, dead branches (as thick as a small finger) from the lower trunks of trees.
■ Fold them into a small bundle held together with a thin branch or vine.

*Make a witch's broom out of kindling or bark*

**5** Light a witch's broom (see panel, left) from your camp fire, take it to the dome, and light the fire.
■ Use kindling bundles (see Step 3) to fuel the fire.

*Orange smoke from the flare mingles with the fire smoke, increasing its visibility*

**6** When smoke billows upward, light a preprepared signal flare (see p. 241), if you have one, taped or tied to a long pole.
■ Use the pole to position the flare as high into the smoke as you can.

# OTHER RESCUE SIGNALS

As well as signal fires, there are other visual devices for attracting potential rescuers. Some are unusual and others, such as a whistle, quite obvious. Whatever device you use, you have to try to hold the rescuers' attention by persisting with your signal.

## LIGHT WINDMILL

You can create a highly visible, illuminated "windmill" effect by whirling a chemical lightstick (cyalume) in front of you attached to the end of a cord 3 ft (1 m) long. Depending on local conditions it can be seen up to 2 miles (3 km) away—or further by an aircraft. Blow your whistle at the same time, using the International Distress Signal of six blasts over one minute, then one minute's silence. The reply is three short blasts.

Activate the lightstick and whirl it in front of you

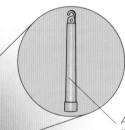

A lightstick is filled with a luminous substance known as cyalume

### CREATING A STROBE EFFECT
LED strobe lights are compact, robust, waterproof, and are sometimes incorporated within standard flashlights. They are very powerful and can be seen from a long way away. Many strobes can be set to produce a variety of sequenced flashes, including flashing SOS in Morse Code. Even if you don't have a dedicated strobe light, you can still switch your regular flashlight on and off repeatedly to attract attention.

## TINSEL TREE

The signaling device known as a "tinsel tree" is best used when you're remaining in one place for a while. It's effective only during daylight hours, so you'll need to find a suitable and easily visible tree or bush in a sunny position.

■ Cut a silver survival blanket, a roll of aluminum foil, or any reflective material into strips.

■ Attach the strips to the tree so that they move in the breeze, catching the sunlight and glinting like small mirrors.

## WHISTLE

Take a whistle with you when you venture out into the wilderness because sound, especially in remote areas where there's little or no noise pollution, travels incredible distances. A whistle is an item of first-line gear (see pp. 42–43), and should be kept on a cord around your neck.

# SIGNALING DISTRESS

Two of the most recognized signs of distress are a little red star shooting up into the sky or a billowing cloud of orange smoke. There are many different types of signal flares and rockets, ranging from simple, handheld devices that fire flares into the sky to specialized kits designed to penetrate thick jungle canopy. Usually found in the emergency survival packs of aircraft and liferafts, flares are also available from specialized shops.

## SIGNAL FLARES

One end of a signal flare has an orange-colored smoke signal for daytime use. The other end has a flare for night-time use (but it can be operated during the day, too). Remember the following:

- Follow the instructions on the outside of the device.
- Wear gloves to protect your hands.
- The heat from a flare can damage a liferaft, so keep your flare well clear when you light it.
- Don't discard flares unless you have used both ends.

Hold the signal flare as high as you can to make it more visible

# GROUND-TO-AIR MARKERS

You can improvise internationally recognized emergency signals on the ground that rescuers in the air can see.

## GETTING NOTICED

To make a ground-to-air marker, use anything that contrasts with the ground, such as orange lifejackets, seaweed, clothing, rocks, branches of trees, or soil.

- Whatever you use, make sure the message is big and visible from all directions.
- Check on your markers regularly.
- When appropriate, use one of the emergency codes shown below. SOS or HELP written in big letters will attract attention too.

| V | ■ Require assistance |
|---|---|
| X | ■ Require medical assistance |
| N | ■ No/Negative |
| Y | ■ Yes/Affirmative |
| ↑ | ■ Proceed this way (arrow points) |

# SIGNAL MIRROR

A signal mirror, or "heliograph," has a shiny surface that reflects the sun and sends flashes over distances exceeding 30 miles (50 km), depending on the strength of the sun, the size of the mirror, and the clarity of the air. You can even use the light from the moon when it's full. By interrupting the flashes you can send messages in Morse Code.

## IMPROVISING A SIGNAL MIRROR

If you don't have a heliograph or any other mirror, try using anything with a shiny, reflective surface, such as a foil food packet, a CD, or the bottom of a beverage can.

### WARNING!

Don't dazzle your would-be rescuers by continuing to flash directly at them. Using your signal mirror intermittently is more effective for attracting attention.

**1** Polish the base of a can to a shine with a slightly abrasive paste. You can use charcoal and water, toothpaste, or even chocolate.

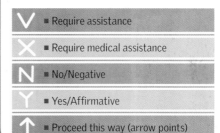

Polish the concave base—it will only take a couple of minutes

**2** Hold the can in front of your face with the polished base facing the sun.

- Direct the flash of reflected sunlight on to the palm of your other hand to practice controlling the light.
- Aim the can toward a rescuer and send a signal, either by moving your palm up and down to interrupt the flash or by directing the flash between a "V" made with your thumb and fingers.

The V-shape helps you direct the light

Hold the can up to your eye to help direct the light

# WILD ANIMALS

**WALKING IN THE WILDS** of Alaska and coming across a fresh deposit of bear feces is a sobering experience. It quickly dawns on you that you're potentially a part of the natural food chain. What do you have to do to protect yourself, and will it be effective or just provoke the animal? Fortunately, the survival instincts of wild animals are such that, with only a few exceptions, most animals, regardless of their size, will avoid confronting you. However, they will defend themselves by attacking you if provoked, cornered, or surprised, particularly when they have young.

## FERAL ANIMALS

Wherever you go in the world there are animals that have escaped into the wild from zoos, wildlife parks, and domestic situations. These feral animals include pigs, cats, dogs, mink, and muntjacs. In many cases, they have become particularly aggressive and seem to have lost any fear of confrontation with humans. Try to find out which feral animals are common in the region you're traveling in and avoid them if at all possible.

| | BEARS | BIG CATS | HIPPOS | ELEPHANTS | CROCODILIANS |
|---|---|---|---|---|---|
| **ANIMAL FACTS** | • Brown bears stand taller then black bears and weigh more. Polar bears are the largest land predator. All bears are powerful, with claws on their strong paws. Brown bears can run faster than humans.<br>• Bears are found in the Northern Hemisphere and parts of South America. | • Tigers are the largest cat, with lions a close second. All big cats have sharp teeth and claws.<br>• Other dangerous cats include cougars (also called pumas, mountain lions, and panthers), leopards, and jaguars.<br>• Big cats are found on all continents, except for Australasia. | • The hippopotamus is the third-largest animal in Africa after the elephant and white rhino.<br>• Hippos can weigh more than 3 tonnes. They have long, razor-sharp incisors and tusklike canines. | • African elephants have larger ears than Indian elephants and are more aggressive.<br>• Elephants stand up to 13 ft (4 m) tall and weigh up to 6 tons.<br>• They can reach speeds of 25–30 mph (40–48 kph). | • Crocodilians include alligators, gharials, and crocodiles.<br>• They can stay submerged for more than an hour at a time, can swim up to 20 mph (32 kph), and run as fast as 11 mph (17 kph) over short distances.<br>• Crocodilians live in many subtropical and tropical parts of the world. |
| **PRECAUTIONS** | • Look for signs of bears and check with locals about bear activity.<br>• Stow and cook food away from the campsite. Keep unused food and garbage out of reach.<br>• Avoid thickets and streams where bears rest and feed.<br>• Carry a stick, knife, or spray (see opposite). | • Avoid coming into contact with big cats. They are most unlikely to attack unless you provoke them or threaten their cubs.<br>• An exception is the cougar, which is responsible for an increasing number of unprovoked attacks in urban areas of North America. | • Avoid provoking a hippo. Many encounters are the result of hitting a partially submerged hippo with a canoe or boat. Almost all hippo attacks are fatal.<br>• Stay vigilant on or beside rivers that hippos are known to frequent.<br>• Don't get between a hippo and water. | • Keep away from places that elephants frequent, such as watering holes.<br>• If you do come across them, don't get too close, especially if there's a baby elephant nearby.<br>• Look for a safe place to retreat to, such as a vehicle, rocky outcrop, or a tree, before you need it. | • Stay away from waters and river banks where crocodilians live. Be vigilant at all times.<br>• If you need to go near the water, watch the area for at least 30 minutes first.<br>• Don't go to the same spot twice, as crocodiles may lie in wait the next time.<br>• Keep a defensive weapon, such as a knife, close by. |
| **WHAT TO DO IF...** | • Make a noise to let a bear know you're there.<br>• If you see a bear, stay calm. Make yourself look as big as possible by raising your arms.<br>• Walk slowly backward. Don't run. If the bear follows, stop and hold your ground.<br>• If the bear attacks, play dead, or fight back. | • If a big cat approaches, stare at its eyes, shout, and make a noise to confuse it. Use a spray if you need to (see opposite).<br>• Don't turn your back or run away.<br>• If a big cat sees you, do not crouch or bend down. An upright human makes less attractive prey than a four-legged animal. | • If you encounter a hippo, go back on your tracks and find another route.<br>• If a hippo yawns at you, he's not feeling sleepy—this is a threat. He's showing you his teeth, tusks, and jaws that can snap a canoe in half! Make every effort to escape. | • If an elephant squares up to you with flared ears, trumpeting, and kicking the dirt in front of it, then back away.<br>• If an elephant charges, run to your safe place (see above).<br>• As a last resort, play dead and hope the elephant loses interest. | • If you meet a crocodilian on land, run away.<br>• If a crocodilian does grab you, it may let go—if it does, run.<br>• If it drags you into the water, fight back. Stab under its throat with a knife, hit or poke its eyes, strike its nostrils hard, or bang the large valve at the back of its throat. |

# ARMING YOURSELF

If you're traveling in areas where encounters with wild animals are possible, be ready with a weapon such as a knife, large stick, or deterrent spray. Remember, avoidance is always better than confrontation.

## PEPPER SPRAY

One type of deterrent spray contains the pepper ingredients capsaicin and capsaicinoids. It shoots a cloud or stream that irritates an animal's eyes. The animal usually withdraws, but take care until the danger has passed.

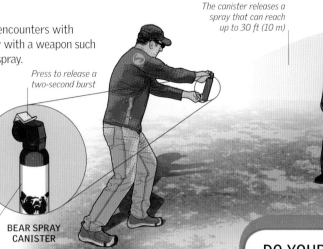

*Press to release a two-second burst*

**BEAR SPRAY CANISTER**

*The pepper spray is under pressure in a canister*

*The canister releases a spray that can reach up to 30 ft (10 m)*

| | SHARKS | SNAKES | AMPHIBIANS | |
|---|---|---|---|---|
| **ANIMAL FACTS** | • There are more than 450 species of shark, but only a few of them pose any danger to humans. These include great white, bull, and tiger sharks.<br>• Most attacks occur in coastal waters in the tropics and subtropics, especially where the water is murky or stirred up by the surf of breaking waves. | • Less than 15 percent of the 3000+ types of poisonous snake are regarded as being dangerous to humans.<br>• Depending on the snake, venom either affects the blood, the nervous system, or the heart.<br>• Snakes live in every part of the world except for very cold environments. | • Many frogs, toads, and salamanders secrete poison through their skin. The most poisonous frog known is the golden poison-dart frog from South America.<br>• Amphibians live where the climate is sufficiently warm and wet for them to breed. | |
| **PRECAUTIONS** | • Avoid shark-infested waters or waters where sharks are known to feed or frequent. Ask the locals about recent sightings of shark activity.<br>• Carry something, such as a pole or spear, that you can use as a weapon. | • Wear long pants and boots, and cover your neck.<br>• As you walk, tap the ground in front of you with a stick to alert snakes to avoid you.<br>• Step onto logs rather than over them.<br>• At night, place your boots upside down on sticks.<br>• Don't put your hands into holes or cracks where snakes might be hiding. | • You can touch a poisonous frog or toad with no ill effect. The poison only takes effect if it enters your system via an open wound or your mouth or eyes. If this happens, get emergency help without delay. | |
| **WHAT TO DO IF...** | • If you see a shark, stay calm and move to safety.<br>• If it makes a move toward you, swim away smoothly but keep watching it.<br>• If it rushes at you, hit it on the nose with whatever you have at hand.<br>• If it grabs you, aggressively strike its eyes or gills. | • If you come across a snake, try to remain completely still. Most snakes will instinctively move away and are more likely to attack a moving target.<br>• Don't panic. If you have a stick, slowly bring it to a position ready for use.<br>• If a snake attacks, hit it hard on the head. | • If contact with a poisonous amphibian is unavoidable, immediately wash the affected area. Keep the water you use away from open cuts or abrasions.<br>• Thoroughly wash your hands and don't put your fingers in your mouth or rub your eyes. | |

# DO YOUR RESEARCH

Spend some time researching the area you'll be traveling in and find out which animals present the greatest dangers. Discover as much as you can about their habits and how best to avoid coming into contact with them.

## SPOT THE SIGNS

Understand the habits of these dangerous creatures: when do they forage, sleep, and drink? What are their habits?

■ Learn to recognize the natural signs that indicate their presence: tracks or prints; feces/droppings; territory markings, such as flattened vegetation where the animal rubs its scent on the ground; telltale signs, such as where bears have clawed the bark from trees.

■ Be aware of other animals disappearing quickly from a watering hole, or a noisy jungle suddenly going quiet.

■ Ask local people if there have been any reports of animals attacking people.

■ Find out the best ways to ward off an attack or defend yourself should you have no option (see left). Adopting a certain stance or submissive posture, or avoiding or maintaining eye contact, could make the difference between safety or danger, life or death.

# EXTREME SURVIVAL— IN COLD CONDITIONS

## USEFUL EQUIPMENT

- Waterproof, layered clothing
- Trekking pole or ice ax
- Collapsible snow shovel
- Light, whistle, avalanche beacon
- Tarpaulin
- Goretex® gloves and gaitors
- Map, compass, GPS
- Survival tin, bushcraft knife
- Cell/satellite phone
- Poncho/bivy sack

**34-YEAR-OLD ICE HOCKEY PLAYER ERIC LEMARQUE** became lost in the snowy wilderness of the Sierra Nevada mountains in California after snowboarding at Mammoth Mountain ski resort. Despite being under-equipped and ill-prepared, his improvisation helped him to survive for seven days.

LeMarque was snowboarding alone late on Friday, February 6, 2004, setting off down an unmarked run of virgin powder snow just as the lifts were shutting for the day. Coming to a stop on a flat section, and with visibility reduced to just 10 ft (3 m), he realized he had lost the trail. Wearing uninsulated ski trousers and jacket, and with just an MP3 player, a cell phone with a dead battery, and wet matches, he was ill-prepared for survival, so he began to search for the trail.

LeMarque chose the wrong direction and walked away from the ski resort. Realizing he faced a night in the open, he used his snowboard to dig a crude trench, lining it with bark scraped from a pine tree for insulation from the snow. He tried to light a fire with pine needles and lint from his clothing, but his matches were too wet. He also ate pine needles and bark.

**"WITH VISIBILITY REDUCED TO JUST 10 FT (3 M), HE REALISED HE HAD LOST THE TRAIL"**

Over the next five days, LeMarque walked further into the wilderness, leaving scraps of clothing for rescuers and attempting to signal to passing planes with the blue LCD screen of his MP3 player. Fortunately for LeMarque, rescuers spotted his snowboard tracks and followed it for 24 hours, finding him on February 13. He was barely conscious, dehydrated, hypothermic, and malnourished—having lost 35 lb (16 kg) in body weight—and was suffering from severely frostbitten feet, which later required both legs to be amputated below the knees. But he was alive.

# WHAT TO DO

**ARE YOU IN DANGER?**

NO    YES

If you are in a group, try to help any others who are in danger

Get yourself out of it:
**Cold/wind/wet**—These can quickly lead to hypothermia, so get yourself out of the elements quickly
**Animals**—Avoid confrontation and move away from danger
**Injury**—Stabilize condition and apply first aid

**ASSESS YOUR SITUATION**
*See pages 234–35*

**DOES ANYONE KNOW YOU WILL BE MISSING OR WHERE YOU ARE?**

NO    YES

If no one knows you are missing or where you are, you will need to notify people of your plight by any means at your disposal

If you are missed, a rescue party will almost certainly be dispatched to find you

**DO YOU HAVE ANY MEANS OF COMMUNICATION?**

NO    YES

You are faced with surviving for an indefinite period—until you are located or you find help

If you have a cell or satellite phone, let someone know your predicament. If your situation is serious enough to be worthy of emergency rescue, and you have a Personal Locator Beacon (PLB), you should consider this option

**CAN YOU SURVIVE WHERE YOU ARE? ***

NO    YES

If you cannot survive where you are and there are no physical reasons why you should remain, you will have to move to a location that offers either a better chance of survival, rescue, or both

Address the Principles of Survival: Protection, Location, Water, Food

**YOU WILL HAVE TO MOVE ****     **YOU SHOULD STAY ****

## DO

- Make an informed decision on the best location to move to
- Keep hydrated by wrapping snow in a wet item of clothing and suck it as it melts—but only if you are walking or working and generating heat
- Improvise a walking staff that can be used to check depth and quality of snow, and unseen drop-offs
- Check regularly for signs of frostnip or frostbite and hypothermia
- Have aids to location accessible while moving and deployed while static
- Protect all extremities from the elements—tie gloves to cord threaded through your jacket so they don't get lost

## DON'T

- Underestimate the need for water just because it is cold—you are just as likely to get dehydrated in a cold environment as in a hot one
- Post-hole through virgin snow—it is exhausting. Instead, improvise a pair of snow shoes
- Sleep directly on the ground. Ventilate your shelter and first check for natural dangers (avalanche)

## DON'T

- Use your body heat to melt snow as it lowers your body temperature and can induce hypothermia
- Breathe air onto cold hands—breath contains moisture which will then cool and conduct heat away from your hands
- Sit or lay directly on the cold ground. Use whatever is available to improvise a sitting or sleeping platform

## DO

- Select a suitable shelter site away from dangers. Build it big enough for you and your equipment. Incorporate a cold sink and a sleeping platform higher than the sink
- Keep cutting and digging tools in the shelter in case a very heavy snow fall or an avalanche requires you to dig your way out
- Mark the entrance to the shelter so you can find it easily
- Keep a fire going: once established, you can use it to melt snow and benefit from warmth
- Prepare all of your aids to location for immediate use

* If you cannot survive where you are, but you also cannot move owing to injury or other factors, you must do everything you can to attract rescue.
** If your situation changes (for instance, you are "moving" to find help, and you find a suitable location in which you can stay and survive) consult the alternative "Do" and "Don'ts."

# ENVIRONMENTAL HAZARDS

**SOME PARTS OF THE WORLD** have a reputation for sudden or extreme weather conditions, and unpredictable environmental hazards that cause havoc for everyone, not just travelers. Before you set off, make sure that you're aware of any such potential hazards in the areas you're visiting, and be ready for them, just in case.

## BEING PREPARED

Many environmental hazards—from avalanches and volcanoes to forest fires, tornadoes, and hurricanes—can suddenly propel you into an emergency situation. While you can never be sure of escaping the worst excesses that Nature can throw at you, you can prepare yourself. A combination of the right equipment, local knowledge, and an awareness of evasive techniques will mean that you shouldn't have to find yourself in a survival situation thinking "if only".

### COMMONSENSE ADVICE
No fail-safe guidelines will protect you from every environmental danger and hazard, but there is some commonsense advice that you will do well to heed before you venture into the wilderness:
■ Check the prevailing weather conditions of your destination at the time of your journey. Log onto the internet or tune into local radio stations.
■ Find out if you're heading into a particularly risky season of weather—for example, monsoons in India or hurricanes in the Caribbean.
■ Take an emergency survival kit (see pp. 58–59).
■ Learn the relevant survival techniques either before you go or as soon as you arrive at your destination—you may not get a second chance.
■ Don't challenge Nature—it rarely loses.

### EQUIPPING YOURSELF FOR AN AVALANCHE REGION
Before heading for the mountains, find out whether the prevailing conditions make avalanches more likely (see right).
■ Take a collapsible shovel for moving snow and a probe for checking the depth of the snow.
■ Keep some survival aids in your pockets in case you lose your backpack.
■ Carry an avalanche transceiver—when activated, its signal can be detected by rescue services.

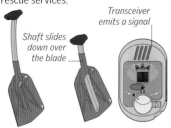

*Shaft slides down over the blade*

*Transceiver emits a signal*

**COLLAPSIBLE SHOVEL**

**AVALANCHE TRANSCEIVER**

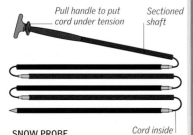

*Pull handle to put cord under tension*

*Sectioned shaft*

**SNOW PROBE**

*Cord inside hollow shaft*

## SURVIVING AN AVALANCHE

There's always the danger of an avalanche on slopes that face away from the sun in the middle of winter, when a fresh layer of heavy snow sits on top of a weak layer of snow. An avalanche may be triggered when snow is disturbed by loud noises, an earth tremor, or the movement of skiers or snowboarders. Learn the warning signs, take the right equipment, and practice the emergency steps in case you get caught.

### SPOTTING THE WARNING SIGNS
As you cross the snowbound mountains, hills, and valleys, look out for signs that warn of a possible avalanche:
■ Convex slopes at an angle between 30 and 45 degrees.
■ Slopes without trees or rocks.
■ Loose, dry snow that doesn't settle.
■ Soft, newly fallen snow that's more than 1 ft (30 cm) deep.
■ Snow that sounds hollow.
■ Snow that falls as crystals or pellets.
■ Snow that falls at more than 1 in (2.5 cm) an hour.

### TAKING EVASIVE ACTION
If you see or hear an avalanche, and you think it might be coming your way, take evasive action at once:
■ Activate your avalanche transceiver in case you get caught in the snow.
■ Try to take cover—for example, under a solid rock overhang if you can see one nearby (see below).
■ If you can't find or reach suitable cover, try to sidestep the avalanche by skiing out of the way—at right angles to its potential path.

*Shelter under a rock overhang*

*Cover mouth and nose with hands*

# HAZARDOUS GROUND

All kinds of local conditions can prove treacherous if you don't keep your wits about you. Walking through wetlands can be risky, as the ground can suddenly give way under foot and you can find yourself in a swamp or, worse still, a patch of quicksand.

### SURVIVING A SWAMP

Freshwater swamps are found in low-lying inland areas and contain masses of thorny undergrowth, reeds, and grasses, and there may be dangerous animals, such as crocodilians and snakes. The water may be foul and mosquitoes, which can cause malaria, are often present. Moving through a swamp is difficult: you can be on solid ground one moment, and chest-deep in water the next. Where possible, try to build a raft or some kind of flotation aid to help you escape. Use the waterways to navigate your way to open water, where you have the best chance of either being seen by rescuers or finding your way back to civilization.

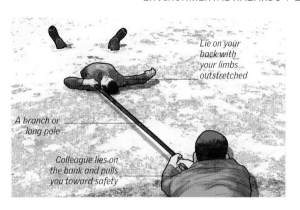

*Lie on your back with your limbs outstretched*

*A branch or long pole*

*Colleague lies on the bank and pulls you toward safety*

### ESCAPING FROM QUICKSAND

If you step into quicksand, try to fall onto your back with your limbs outstretched to spread your weight. Try to get to the bank by paddling with your hands. Don't struggle as you will sink faster. If you're with someone, he or she needs to lie on firm ground and pull you to safety, reaching you with the help of a long pole, rope, or branch.

*Keep your head clear of the snow*

*"Swim" in the snow by flailing your arms and legs to create as big a space as possible*

### ESCAPING FROM AN AVALANCHE

If you can't take evasive action and find yourself below an advancing avalanche with no prospect of escape, try to keep calm and remember the following advice:
- Remove the bindings from your skis and and the loops from your ski poles. Put your rucksack on one shoulder, but ditch it rather than risk dislocating your shoulder.
- If you're overtaken by snow, "swim" with the flow (see above) to make a big space around you before the snow compacts and "sets". Use your hands or a collapsible shovel to clear the snow around your head and to create a space for you to breathe, as often people suffocate before they freeze.
- If you don't know which way is up, dribble saliva to find out which way is down—then dig in the opposite direction.
- Get out quickly, as time is of the essence, and shout when you hear potential rescuers to attract their attention.

### ESCAPING A VOLCANIC ERUPTION

Find out if there's an active volcano in the region you're visiting. If there is, and its eruption is imminent, leave the area as soon as you can. It will pump enormous quantities of lava from the mantle below the crust and produce huge amounts of ash, toxic gases, debris, and mud. However, if you do get caught in an eruption:
- Be careful when driving to safety, as the ash and mud make roads slippery.
- Take cover to avoid the flying fiery debris, hot gases, and suffocating clouds of ash. Sulfur dioxide in the ash chokes your lungs and, when mixed with rain to form sulfuric acid, burns your skin.
- If you're caught in an ash cloud, cover your face with a wet cloth (or use a mask if you have one). Wash your skin afterward.

### SURVIVING AN EARTHQUAKE

Find out if an earthquake is likely to happen in the region you're visiting. If you feel an earthquake coming:
- Get into the open, away from structures or trees that can fall on you. Then lie down.
- Stay in open ground until aftershocks and tremors have stopped altogether.
- If you're in a building, go to the lowest floor, and stay beside a wall or under a sturdy table. Turn off the gas if you have time.
- If you're in a vehicle, stop, but stay inside.

## SURVIVING A FOREST FIRE

When vegetation on the ground is tinder dry, the slightest spark can start a fire that gets out of control and sweeps through a forest. A forest fire may be caused by lightning, a piece of glass focusing the sun's rays, a discarded cigarette, or a spark from a camp fire. Forest fires produce intense heat, thick smoke, and toxic gases—and they use up all the available oxygen in the air, making it impossible to breathe.

### PREPARATION AND SPOTTING THE WARNING SIGNS

If you're going to a place where forest fires are a hazard, find out from local radio reports whether conditions are making them more likely. If you venture into a forest, make sure you carry a cell phone or some electronic means of signaling, and let others know your route and destination. The following warning signs may help you gain time before a fire is upon you:
- You'll probably smell a fire first, and you'll hear it crackling as it burns before you see it. If you smell a fire and you notice animals growing agitated, a forest fire may be close by.
- The smoke will help you establish how close the fire is. The direction of the smoke tells you which way the wind is blowing.

Road or natural break in the trees

Trees on fire

Run towards the wind

Wind direction

### TAKING EVASIVE ACTION

If the wind is blowing toward the fire then move into it quickly. However, if the wind is behind the fire you could be in serious danger because the fire will be moving very fast.
- Try to find a river, lake, road, or natural break in the forest. Stay there until you're rescued or the fire has passed you by.
- Don't go up to high ground as fire is drawn faster uphill.
- Many forest fires spread on a wide front, so avoiding the fire by going around it may be impossible.
- If the fire is upon you, and the wall of flame is fragmented, the best course of action may be to run through the flames: take off man-made clothes (as they will melt onto you), cover as much of your skin as you can, and douse yourself in water if you have any. Take a deep breath, press a damp cloth to your mouth and nose, pick a spot where the wall of flames is thinnest, and run without stopping until you're through.
- If you're in a vehicle, stay inside. Park it as far away from the trees as possible, turn off the engine, close the windows, lie down on the floor, and cover yourself if you can.
- If escape is impossible, try to dig and bury yourself under soil. Dampen all clothing and get as low as possible.

# EXTREME WEATHER

High winds and torrential rain are common seasonal occurrences across the world. From tornadoes and whirlwinds to tropical storms such as hurricanes and typhoons, these extreme weather patterns cause enormous damage and threaten many lives.

## AVOIDING HURRICANES AND TORNADOES

Weather forecasts can predict approximate directions and paths of impending hurricanes and local emergency services will give advice on the predicted severity. If you're planning a trek in an area known for hurricanes and tornados, check long-range weather forecasts and be prepared to cancel or alter your plans if necessary—if you're caught in the open your chances of survival are extremely limited. If you're going to be in the wilderness during a "storm season" then take a battery- or solar-powered radio, check for weather updates, and be prepared to head back to civilization. If your home is in a tornado or hurricane area, follow the advice of local services, but most importantly be prepared with a plan that will ensure you don't get caught out.

The advancing path of the tornado's vortex

If you cannot evade a tornado, you may have to wedge yourself into a ditch or between rocks

## PREPARING TO EVACUATE

The arrival of a hurricane or tornado is a time when you can find yourself in a survival situation on your own home turf. The following advice can help you prepare to evacuate.

■ Secure anything outside that could be picked up by winds and cause damage, such as rubbish bins and garden furniture.

■ Prepare an evacuation plan (including pets if you have them). Find out where you will evacuate to and make several route plans to the location in case roads are unusable. Fuel your vehicle as soon as a hurricane warning is forecast.

■ Put together a hurricane survival pack that contains what you need for a 72-hour period. Include drinking water, a change of clothing, non-perishable food, sleeping bags, radio, flashlights, and contact numbers for family and emergency services.

■ Protect your house by securely boarding up all windows and doors. Turn off the water, gas, and electricity.

## STAYING PUT

If you decide to stay put, you should still follow the guidelines above. As the storm approaches, move everyone and your supplies to an underground shelter or a room without windows.

■ Monitor the radio reports and comply with the advice of the emergency services.

■ Don't go outside until the "all-clear" has been given.

## TAKING COVER OUTDOORS

If it appears that you are, or could be, in the path of a tornado or hurricane, do everything you can to move out of its way—choose a direction at a right angle to its path.

■ If you're driving but can't get out of the way, try to park in an underpass. Leave the vehicle and wedge yourself into a secure position as high as you can under the underpass. If you're in the open, shelter upwind of your abandoned vehicle, so that it does not become a hazard to you.

■ If you're out in the open, head for the lowest ground and find a ditch or depression (see below), in which you can shelter, or wedge yourself between rocks.

Lie face down with your hands over the back of your head

## SURVIVING AN ELECTRICAL STORM

An electrical storm may develop when warm air rises and meets colder air. Electricity sparks between water droplets in the clouds, forming lightning that takes the shortest route to the ground. The following advice will help you avoid being struck by lightning, or minimize its effects if you are:

■ Avoid getting caught in open ground—seek shelter but not under a lone tree: when lightning strikes a single tree a tremendous voltage fans out from its base.

■ Remain in your vehicle if there is no other cover: it acts as a Faraday Cage (a metallic enclosure that prevents the entry or escape of an electromagnetic field).

■ If caught in the open: make yourself as small as possible and limit the amount of area you cover. Do not lay down or stand up, crouch down low with feet together and hands off the ground.

Keep your elbows by your side

Bend your head forward

Clasp your knees

Raise your heels from the ground

## SURVIVING A FLASH FLOOD

A sudden deluge of rain doesn't always drain away quickly, instead flowing rampantly over the surface of the land in torrents, and causing flash floods. Soil, animals, vegetation, and even buildings can be quickly washed away. There may be landslides, too, and rivers may break their banks. The following advice can help in the event of a flash flood:

■ If you're inside a building, move to the upper floors, taking with you essentials such as bedding, food, and matches. Unless the building is threatened, stay there until the waters have receded or you have been rescued.

■ If you're outside, head for higher ground.

■ Never walk or drive through a flood.

■ Filter and boil water for drinking, as the sources of water around you may have been contaminated. Alternatively, collect rainwater to drink.

## ESCAPING A SANDSTORM

If you can see a sandstorm coming, mark your direction of travel before it strikes and find somewhere safe to shelter—for example, behind some rocks. Face away from the direction of the wind and cover yourself as completely as you can, particularly your head, face, and neck.

# SURVIVING AT SEA

**THE SEA IS ARGUABLY THE HARSHEST** environment of all and you could be thrown into a sea-survival situation for any number of reasons: bad weather, fire, mechanical failure, or collision. However, there's plenty of good advice to follow and equipment designed to protect you.

> ### BE PREPARED
> If you're venturing onto the open seas, you should plan for the worst and be prepared with knowledge, skills, and equipment.

## KNOW YOUR VESSEL

Regardless of the size of your vessel, find out everything you can about what to do in the event of a major problem that requires you to abandon ship and take to the water. The points below are generic and may not apply to all situations or types of vessel.

### LARGE PASSENGER VESSELS

If you're a passenger on a large vessel, such as a ferry, liner, or cruise ship, make sure you learn the safety procedures.
- Attend the "Abandon Ship" drills.
- Find out which emergency alarms indicate fire, collision, and abandon ship.
- Find out where the lifejackets are stowed, and how to put them on and operate them.
- Learn the escape routes.
- Locate the Emergency Lifeboat Stations and find out what your responsibilities are.
- If you have children or people with special needs with you, make sure you have a system for getting them on deck and providing them with suitable survival equipment.

### SMALL VESSELS

These craft include yachts, small boats, canoes, and kayaks, so crew members need to agree on an emergency plan of action and delegate responsibilities relevant to the situation and the skills of each person.
- Know where the emergency equipment is stowed and how it's operated.
- If your vessel has an EPIRB (see p. 236), make sure everyone knows where it is and how it's operated. Those activated automatically are released hydrostatically from a bracket at a water depth of 3–10 ft (1–3 m). The buoyant EPIRB then floats to the surface and begins transmitting.
- Make sure your EPIRB has been registered so that, once the signal is detected, the rescue services know who it belongs to.
- Keep a grab bag to hand (see box, right).

## SURVIVAL SUIT AND LIFEJACKET

A survival suit is designed to keep you warm and dry in extreme conditions and rough seas, and a lifejacket will keep you afloat with your head out of the water, even if you're unconscious.

### PROTECTION

Survival suits and lifejackets are equipped with various protection features to help you survive in the sea.

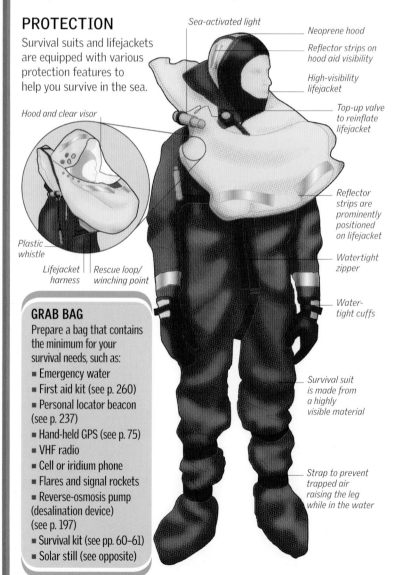

Sea-activated light

Neoprene hood

Reflector strips on hood aid visibility

High-visibility lifejacket

Top-up valve to reinflate lifejacket

Reflector strips are prominently positioned on lifejacket

Watertight zipper

Water-tight cuffs

Survival suit is made from a highly visible material

Strap to prevent trapped air raising the leg while in the water

Hood and clear visor

Plastic whistle

Lifejacket harness

Rescue loop/ winching point

> ### GRAB BAG
> Prepare a bag that contains the minimum for your survival needs, such as:
> - Emergency water
> - First aid kit (see p. 260)
> - Personal locator beacon (see p. 237)
> - Hand-held GPS (see p. 75)
> - VHF radio
> - Cell or iridium phone
> - Flares and signal rockets
> - Reverse-osmosis pump (desalination device) (see p. 197)
> - Survival kit (see pp. 60–61)
> - Solar still (see opposite)

# TYPES OF LIFERAFT

Single-seater and multi-seater liferafts contain similar design features and survival aids. As well as being able to accommodate more people, multi-seaters carry larger quantities of fresh water and more anti-sea sickness tablets, for example.

## SINGLE-SEAT LIFERAFT

Only one person can fit into a single-seat liferaft. You can inflate it with carbon dioxide, by pumping air in manually, or by oral inflation.

## MULTI-SEATER LIFERAFT

Many vessels carry multi-seater liferafts in a valise or a hard container. Multi-seaters can accommodate between four and 25 people and may be open-topped or covered. Many larger multi-seaters may also include locator beacons (see p. 236), paddles, and a solar still (see below).

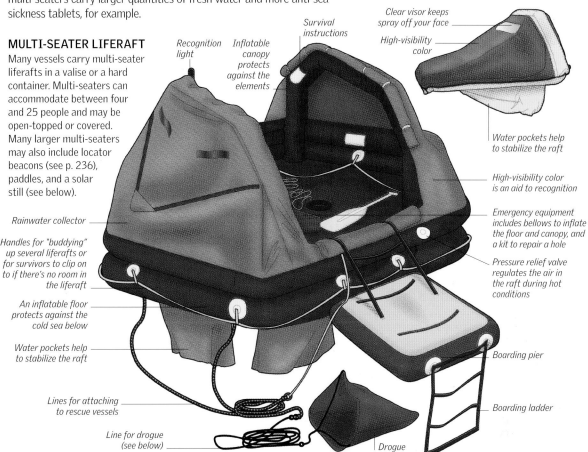

*Recognition light*

*Inflatable canopy protects against the elements*

*Survival instructions*

*Clear visor keeps spray off your face*

*High-visibility color*

*Water pockets help to stabilize the raft*

*High-visibility color is an aid to recognition*

*Emergency equipment includes bellows to inflate the floor and canopy, and a kit to repair a hole*

*Pressure relief valve regulates the air in the raft during hot conditions*

*Rainwater collector*

*Handles for "buddying" up several liferafts or for survivors to clip on to if there's no room in the liferaft*

*An inflatable floor protects against the cold sea below*

*Water pockets help to stabilize the raft*

*Lines for attaching to rescue vessels*

*Line for drogue (see below)*

*Boarding pier*

*Boarding ladder*

*Drogue*

## SOLAR STILL

A solar still is a light, compact, and easy-to-use device for producing drinking water from sea water. Heat from the sun evaporates the salty water inside the still. Condensation on the walls collects in a channel around the rim and is directed to a store. Depending on the prevailing conditions and the availablilty of sunshine, a solar still can produce as much as 2 liters (3½ pints) of fresh drinking water a day.

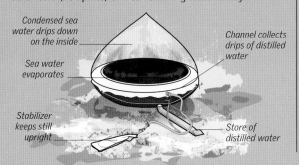

*Condensed sea water drips down on the inside*

*Sea water evaporates*

*Channel collects drips of distilled water*

*Stabilizer keeps still upright*

*Store of distilled water*

## DROGUE

A sea anchor, known as a "drogue," is a critical piece of equipment because it helps to reduce drift and keeps the liferaft stable and seaworthy, particularly in heavy seas.

### STEADYING A RAFT

A drogue stops a liferaft from overturning by creating drag that "anchors" the trailing side of the raft to the water.
- A drogue can position a liferaft either downwind or 90 degrees to the wind.
- It helps to keep the raft near the ditching location, thereby improving the chance of rescue. Even in a 2-knot current a liferaft can drift 50 miles (80 km) a day.

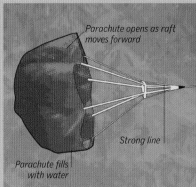

*Parachute opens as raft moves forward*

*Strong line*

*Parachute fills with water*

# ABANDONING SHIP

Unless your vessel is an immediate danger to you, don't abandon it until you really need to. Even a badly damaged vessel can provide you with protection from the elements, equipment such as radios and flares, and provisions such as water and food. In addition, it is a big target for rescuers to spot. Make every effort to keep the vessel afloat.

## THE DANGERS THAT AWAIT

When you do decide to abandon ship, you will be faced with the following dangers. If you have prepared yourself properly before heading out to sea, you will—in many cases, at least—be able to deal with them.

- Hypothermia brought on by inadequate clothing and exposure to wet, windy, and rainy conditions.
- Drowning because you have no lifejacket.
- Dehydration caused by a lack of water or an injury.
- Malnutrition due to a lack of food.
- Cold shock (see p. 254) due to sudden immersion in cold water.

## BEFORE ABANDONING SHIP

Where time and circumstances permit, don't abandon your ship until absolutely necessary. Send a May Day signal with your name, position, group size, physical condition, and circumstances. Then carry out the following measures:

- Activate the 406 EPIRB (see p. 236).
- Ensure everyone on the vessel wears layers of clothing, and has a survival suit and lifejacket (see p. 250).
- Check the liferafts are ready for launch.
- Get the grab bag (see p. 250).
- Prepare to take the jerry-cans of water on board the liferafts.
- Fill spare containers with water.
- Gather up as much food as you can.

## TAKING TO THE LIFERAFT

If you have to abandon ship, make every effort to launch all available liferafts. Even the craft that are not used will make it easier for search and rescue teams to detect the "footprint" of the survivors. They also contain additional supplies of water, flares, and other useful items.

- Many liferafts have a painter. This is a line that attaches the liferaft to the vessel to ensure it does not blow away when thrown overboard and inflated.
- Should the vessel sink, the painter has a weak link that breaks under pressure, or you can cut it.

*Painter line attached to vessel*

*Multi-seat liferaft (see p. 251)*

## PREVENTING HYPOTHERMIA

Getting wet greatly reduces your survival chances. At 41°F (5°C), a normally dressed person has only a 50 percent chance of surviving for one hour. You are six times more likely to survive in protective clothing.

- Climb into the liferaft carefully so that you don't get wet.
- Wear several layers of clothing to trap air. Even wet layers retain some heat around the body. Don't forget your head, hands, and feet.
- Wear a survival suit (see p. 250) to increase your survival time.

**1** Move slowly and deliberately into the liferaft, keeping out of the water, and trying to stay as dry as possible. If you have to enter the water, climb down or lower yourself into it, rather than jumping.

- Look for the Day-Glo instruction patch inside the liferaft. Follow the recommended advice under "Immediate Actions" (see panel, opposite).

# IN THE LIFERAFT

Once you have successfully negotiated the tricky procedure of abandoning ship and climbing into the liferaft, there are a number of actions you need to take. These are prioritized into immediate, secondary, and subsequent.

## IMMEDIATE ACTIONS

■ Inflate the floor of the liferaft with the bellows, while carrying out a roll call of your group to check for missing members.
■ If the vessel is still afloat, keep the raft attached via the painter. Someone should be ready to cut the painter close to the vessel in case it starts to sink.
■ Once clear of the vessel, set up the drogue (see p. 251).
■ In difficult weather conditions, close the entrances of the raft in order to keep in heat, and keep out wind, rain, seawater, or spray.
■ Bale out water, check for leaks, use the sponge to dry the liferaft, and use the leak stopper and clamps if necessary.

## SECONDARY ACTIONS

■ Treat the injured.
■ Take anti-seasickness tablets.
■ Post lookouts.
■ Bring liferafts together.
■ Warm up as best you can.

> ### WARNING!
> Never drink seawater, because the salt it contains will increase your rate of dehydration. If you're in hot conditions without any water, dehydration can set in within one hour.

## SUBSEQUENT ACTIONS

■ Delegate a leader based on experience.
■ Find out who has useful skills, such as first aid and sea survival training.
■ Ask everyone to look for sharp objects that could puncture the liferaft. At the same time, ask them if they have anything that could have a survival use.
■ Find out what survival aids you have. Prepare aids to location (see p. 236) and show everyone how to operate them.
■ Establish a routine and detail a watch system for inside and outside the liferaft.
■ Delegate one member of the group to make repairs, another to keep the rations, and another to administer first aid.
■ Establish how much water and food you have and start to ration in accordance with your particular situation.
■ Procure water as soon as possible—don't wait until you need it. Deploy solar stills (see p. 251) and use the reverse-osmosis pump (see p. 197).

*If you are helping people on board, for stability, you should straddle the entrance of the liferaft, with one leg inside and the other outside*

*If you are waiting to board you can hold on to the handles, or clip yourself on*

*Wear a lifebelt at all times*

*Kneel to the side of the raft and steady yourself before throwing*

*Throw the quoit and line at the person in the water*

*The person in the water aims to catch the quoit*

*Ring*
*Rescue line*

**2** If your group does end up in the water, the first two people on board the liferaft should help others on, one at a time, lifting them under the arms.
■ Don't overload the raft. Those least vulnerable can hang on to the raft's handles, or tie their lifejacket lifeline to one.

**3** Look for anyone who is struggling to make their way upward you. Use the rescue line and ring to pull them to safety in the liferaft.
■ Avoid entering the sea unless you have to rescue an unconscious person from the water.

# TAKING TO THE WATER

About two-thirds of people who drown in open water were within 10 ft (3 m) of a safe refuge and 60 percent of them were "good" swimmers. Here are some useful tips to prevent drowning.

## JUMPING INTO THE WATER

Abandoning ship can be a dangerous procedure. If you have to enter the water, climb down using ropes or nets. If you have no option but to jump into the sea, these straightforward steps should improve your chances of survival. Jumping into the water is a last resort, as you will be prone to cold shock (see box, right) and at immediate risk of hypothermia and drowning. If you have to do it, first ensure your lifejacket is fitted correctly and check the surface of the water to find a safe entry point. Watch out for people, debris, and burning fuel. If you can't avoid the fuel, swim under it and, before coming up for air, poke your hand through the surface to ensure you're clear of it. As you come up, keep your face down to protect your nose, eyes, and mouth.

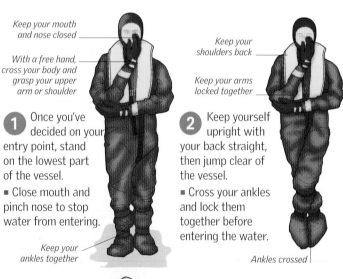

Keep your mouth and nose closed

With a free hand, cross your body and grasp your upper arm or shoulder

**1** Once you've decided on your entry point, stand on the lowest part of the vessel.

- Close mouth and pinch nose to stop water from entering.

Keep your ankles together

Keep your shoulders back

Keep your arms locked together

**2** Keep yourself upright with your back straight, then jump clear of the vessel.

- Cross your ankles and lock them together before entering the water.

Ankles crossed

Pull the hood or visor of your lifejacket down over your head

Inflated lifejacket

Move upright and force your legs down

**3** Once you're in the water, inflate your lifejacket.

- If you're in a survival suit, raise your arms and gently pull one seal away from your wrist to let the excess air escape.

Don't kick with your legs or feet, just float to the surface

Raise your hips to the surface of the water

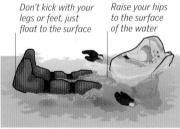

**4** Lie on your back and swim as calmly as you can away from hazards, such as burning fuel.

- Push your head back onto the neck of the lifejacket to help raise your hips.
- Keep your feet and knees together, and use a backward butterfly stroke to swim upward the liferaft.

## COLD SHOCK

Cold shock response is the body's reaction to immersion in very cold water—for example, if abandoning a ship in winter in the North Atlantic Ocean. It is a common cause of death in such circumstances. Symptoms include gasping for breath and hyperventilation, which can lead to the inhalation of water, disorientation, panic, and the possible onset of hypothermia. A sudden increase in blood pressure and heart rate can cause cardiac problems in some people. Prolonged immersion in water will make it hard to perform physical movements, making swimming, climbing aboard a liferaft, or firing a flare extremely difficult.

- Body type or mental conditioning can help some people survive swimming in icy water.
- Dressing in layers and/or wearing a survival suit improves your chances of survival.
- Avoid entering the water if you possibly can.

## IF YOU HAVE NO LIFERAFT

Even without a liferaft, you stand a better chance of surviving at sea if you're in a group. More survivors create a larger target for rescuers to see, and being with others can be good for morale.

- Collect any floating debris before it disappears with the current, as this can increase your "footprint" so that rescuers can see you more easily.
- Determine what location aids and other equipment are available and prepare these for use.
- If there are children or injured among your group, place them in the center of the group and huddle close together.
- If you are alone, get into a position known as H.E.L.P. (see below), which stands for "Heat Escape Lessening Position." This will help to keep heat within the core of your body.

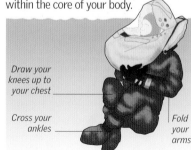

Draw your knees up to your chest

Cross your ankles

Fold your arms

# FLOATING FACE DOWN

Don't panic if you have to enter the water without a lifejacket. Your body's natural buoyancy will keep at least the top of your head above water. To keep your face above water, too, make small windmill motions with your arms extended. However, if the water's rough, your only option may be to float face down.

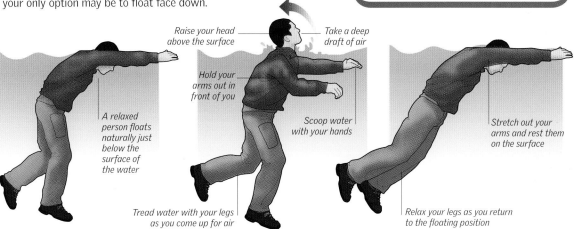

Raise your head above the surface

Take a deep draft of air

Hold your arms out in front of you

Scoop water with your hands

A relaxed person floats naturally just below the surface of the water

Tread water with your legs as you come up for air

Stretch out your arms and rest them on the surface

Relax your legs as you return to the floating position

**1** It's important to relax, even though this seems hard when your life is in danger.
- Let your face lie in the water, and put your arms out in front of you.

**2** Begin to exhale into the water as you raise your head up.
- Lift your head as it breaks through the surface and empty your lungs completely before inhaling more air.

**3** With fresh air in your lungs, duck your face back into the water, keeping your mouth closed.
- Let your body float again, before you repeat the sequence.

# IMPROVISING A BUOYANCY AID

If you're in the water and wearing pants, you can improvise a buoyancy aid that will help you to keep your head above water. Initially, it may be awkward to organize, but the benefit outweighs the effort involved.

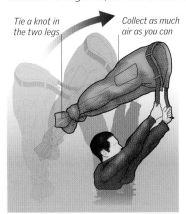

Tie a knot in the two legs

Collect as much air as you can

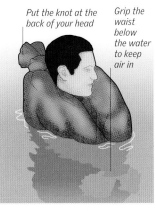

Put the knot at the back of your head

Grip the waist below the water to keep air in

**1** Take off your pants and tie the legs together near the bottom. Tighten the knot as much as you can with your teeth.
- Flick the pants over your head from behind until they fill with air. Tread water as you do this.

**2** Quickly catch the waist with your hands and grip it tight to hold air in.
- Put your head between the trouser legs and float.
- You will need to repeat the process regularly.

# FIRST AID

# FIRST AID

**Regardless of the events** that put you in a survival situation, a major factor that will dictate your options and actions will be whether anyone has been injured. Someone's survival may depend on the treatment they receive at the time of the incident, and during the ongoing survival ordeal, so it's essential that everyone should be proficient and confident in basic first aid techniques. In a true survival situation, the term "seek medical help" really means "deal with it yourself." While it would be impossible to be able to treat all injuries—a task even a paramedic would find daunting without the right equipment—the vast majority can be either dealt with or stabilized using a combination of basic first-aid techniques and common sense.

The "Protection" element of the survival principles (see p. 27) applies to your situation at all times—you should continually look at the consequences of every action in relation to protection against injury. Prevention is always a better option than cure. In hot climates, being able to recognize the first stages

## In this chapter YOU WILL DISCOVER...

- that **maggots** have their **uses**...
- how to **improvise goggles** to prevent **snow blindness**...
- when to **stop**, **drop**, and **roll**...
- how to treat **snake bites** and **jellyfish stings**...
- when to **eat charcoal** or drink **bark tea**...
- how to prevent **frostnip** from becoming **frostbite**...
- when to **perform** a **firefighter's lift**...

of heat stress will allow you to take action with them before they develop into life-threatening dehydration and heatstroke. In cold climates, being able to recognize the first stages of frostnip will allow you to stop it from becoming frostbite. In many cases, further injury can be avoided by adopting the basic principles detailed throughout this book, such as being able to assess the best course of action in a given situation, plan a route and move safely over terrain, and protect yourself against the elements.

**The will to survive** is often the only factor that determines whether you live or die—regardless of your equipment, training, knowledge, and skills.

**WHEN FACED WITH** everything that man and nature can throw at you, when there appears to be no hope, you'll be faced with two choices: will you accept your situation and wait and see what hand fate deals you, or will you endure the pain and discomfort and fight for you own survival?

**This determination** was clearly shown by Aron Ralston during a hike in Blue John Canyon, Utah. After accidentally dislodging a 800 lb (363 kg) boulder, which pinned his right arm, he was faced with a bleak outlook. After five days, aware that no one knew he was missing and having run out of water, Ralston decided to amputate his own arm with his knife, applied a tourniquet, and hiked off to safety.

**In another famous example**, Simon Yates took the agonizing decision to cut the rope that held his injured climbing partner, Joe Simpson (who Yates thought had died), over a crevasse in the Peruvian Andes. Incredibly, Simpson survived the fall and chose to endure. He spent three days without food and only splashes of water from melting ice as he crawled and hopped the 5 miles (8 km) back over frozen mountainous terrain to reach their camp.

The **vast majority** of **injuries** can be either **dealt with** or **stabilized** using a **combination** of **basic first aid techniques** and **common sense**

# FIRST AID ESSENTIALS

**SAFETY IS KEY** on any expedition. Before you set off, make sure that you and everyone in your party has the necessary medical equipment—especially medications. If someone is injured, he or she should be treated immediately. If you can't contact the emergency services (and if there are enough of you), one person should stay with the casualty while two others go for help.

> ### WARNING!
> Protect yourself from danger at all times. You can't help anyone if you become a casualty as well. If the area is unsafe, don't approach the casualty—get emergency help and monitor the casualty's condition from a safe distance.

## BASIC FIRST AID KIT

Keep your first aid kit (see panel, opposite) dry and readily accessible. Check the seals on sterile dressings; if they're not intact they're not sterile. Replace anything you use as soon as you can.

## PRIORITIES AFTER AN INCIDENT

Assess a situation quickly and methodically. Find out what happened. Check casualties for life-threatening conditions such as unconsciousness or severe bleeding (see p. 264) and treat those first.

- **Response** Is the casualty conscious or unconscious? If the casualty is responding to you, he or she is conscious. Shake the shoulders gently if you're not sure.

- **Airway** Is it open and clear? If the casualty can talk, it is. If he or she is unconscious, open and clear it (see p. 276).

- **Breathing** Is it normal? Treat any difficulty such as asthma (see p. 275). If he or she is unconscious and not breathing, call for emergency help and begin CPR (see p. 277).

- **Circulation** Are there any signs of severe bleeding? If so, treat immediately. Once life-threatening conditions are under control, you can make a more detailed assessment. Examine the casualty methodically from head to toe. Ask how the incident occurred, as it can indicate likely injuries.

*Large scissors are useful for cutting clothing*

*Safety pins for securing bandages*

*Lightweight carrier*

*Combined sterile dressings*

*Antibiotic eye ointment*

*Tablets such as antihistamine and paracetamol*

*Antiseptic cream*

*Disposable gloves*

*Take fabric, waterproof, and hypoallergenic plasters*

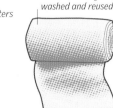

*Gauze roller bandage to secure dressings—can be washed and reused*

*Zinc-oxide tape can be used to secure dressings*

## IMPROVISED SLINGS

Hand, arm, or shoulder injuries need to be immobilized and supported in a raised position. If you don't have a triangular bandage with you, use a piece of strong cloth about 3 ft (1 m) square, folded in half to form a triangle (see p. 270). You can also use your jacket or even rucksack straps. The jacket corner "sling" is the only one that provides enough support for a hand, wrist, or forearm injury. Ask the casualty to support the arm with his or her other hand while you secure the sling.

### JACKET CORNER
To support an injured forearm or hand, fold the jacket up over the arm and pin it.

### BUTTON-UP JACKET
Undo one of the buttons and slide the injured arm into the opening for support.

### BELT SUPPORT
Support an upper arm injury in a raised position with a belt looped into a figure-eight.

### PINNED SLEEVE
Pin a sleeve to a jacket or the strap of a backpack for support.

### SHOULDER STRAP
Rest a sprain by tucking your hand in your backpack strap.

## PROTECTING AGAINST INFECTION

Disposable gloves prevent cross-infection between you and the casualty; they must be latex-free, since contact with latex can cause an allergic reaction. Antiseptic wipes are also invaluable when cleaning wounds.

*Use latex-free gloves*

*Use alcohol-free antiseptic wipes*

**LATEX-FREE DISPOSABLE GLOVES**

**ANTISEPTIC WIPES**

### COMBINED STERILE DRESSING

This is a sealed dressing consisting of a pad attached to a bandage. It's easy to apply, and can be used as a sling. It should be taped on to your backpack strap for easy access in an emergency.

*Sterile pad is sewn onto a bandage*

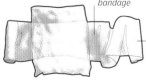

## CHECK LIST

Make sure that your first aid kit and medicines are suited to the environment you will be visiting.

### BASIC KIT
- Alcohol-free antiseptic wipes
- Latex-free disposable gloves
- Alcohol gel for handwashing
- Antiseptic cream
- Antibiotic eye ointment
- Adhesive dressings—fabric, waterproof, and hypoallergenic
- Gel blister bandages
- Combined sterile dressings, or sterile pads and bandages in assorted sizes
- Roller bandages—take self-adhesive for supporting joints and gauze for securing dressings
- Two triangular bandages
- Micropore or zinc oxide tape
- Scissors and tweezers
- Safety pins
- Disposable syringes

### PERSONAL MEDICATION
- Painkillers
- Anti-inflammatories
- Medical alert bracelet/pendant
- Prescription medicines such as asthma inhaler and/or adrenaline (epinephrine) autoinjector
- Antihistamines
- Anti-diarrhea medicine
- Packets of oral rehydration salts
- Hydrocortisone cream

### ENVIRONMENT-SPECIFIC EXTRAS
- Malaria tablets
- Mosquito repellent
- Anti-poison-ivy cream
- Sunblock
- Tick remover
- DEET powder for removing leeches

# FLESH WOUNDS

**ANY INJURY THAT BREAKS THE SKIN** carries a risk of infection as germs can enter the body. These can come from the cause of injury, air, dirt, or clothing embedded in the wound. In the wilderness, keeping the injured area clean can be a real challenge, but it is essential. Tetanus is a potentially lethal infection caused by bacteria that live in soil. It can be prevented by immunization, so ensure that your vaccinations are up to date.

> **MAGGOT THERAPY**
> If a wound is seriously infected and you have no antibiotics, expose it to flies for one day, then cover. Maggots will develop and eat any dead tissue. Check daily, and flush the maggots out of the wound with sterile water before they start to eat healthy tissue.

## BLISTERS AND BRUISING

A blister is a fluid-filled "bubble" of skin that occurs when skin is rubbed repeatedly against a surface (a friction burn). A bruise is bleeding into the skin and surrounding tissue from a blow that does not break the surface of the skin.

### HOW TO TREAT BLISTERS

The ideal treatment for a blister is to rest and wait until it has healed, but this may not be possible in a survival situation. Cover it with a gel blister dressing if you have one or, if the blister is large, you may have to pierce it to enable you to continue walking. However, never pierce a blister caused by a burn—you risk infection.

*Hold the foot steady with your free hand*

*Keep the foot flat*

*Use only a sterilized needle to pierce a blister*

**1** If you have to burst a blister, first sterilize a needle by holding it in a flame until it's red hot, then letting it cool.
■ Clean the area with water or wipes, pat dry, then pierce the edge of the blister.

> **BLISTER PREVENTION**
> Following these simple rules when out hiking should prevent blisters from developing in the first place:
> ■ Ensure boots or shoes fit properly and are well "broken in" before you set out.
> ■ Always wear clean, dry, comfortable socks next to your skin. Avoid wearing two pairs as they may bunch up, increasing friction.
> ■ Keep toenails cut short and straight.
> ■ Remove boots and air your feet during rest periods.
> ■ If you feel a "hot spot," treat it before it becomes a problem: stop immediately and apply moleskin, a gel pad, or zinc-oxide tape.

**2** Carefully apply pressure to the side of the blister opposite the hole made by the needle. Continue to apply pressure until all of the fluid has been squeezed out.

**3** Gently clean and dry the blister, then protect the wound from infection by applying a dressing.
■ Use a gel blister plaster or padded moleskin, if possible.
■ Alternatively, use a pad held in place with zinc-oxide tape.

### HOW TO TREAT BRUISING

To reduce the swelling and pain of a bruise, raise the injured area, and apply a cold compress. If you have access to cold running water, ice, or snow, soak a cloth and hold it against the bruised area for at least ten minutes. Severe bruising may indicate a more serious injury, such as a broken bone (see p. 271) or internal injury (see Shock, p. 274), which will require immediate treatment.

# WOUNDS AND BLEEDING

Severe bleeding can be distressing for both you and the casualty, but it can usually be controlled by a combination of direct pressure and elevation of the injury. Remain calm and reassure the casualty while treating the wound. Treat for shock (see p. 274).

## FOREIGN OBJECT IN A WOUND

Any loose foreign objects, such as pieces of dirt or gravel, should be removed from a wound, otherwise they may cause infection or delay healing. Either rinse them off with cold running water or carefully pick loose pieces off the wound with tweezers. However, if an object is embedded in a wound don't remove it, but treat as shown below.

## MINOR CUTS OR GRAZES

Any break in the skin, however minor, needs to be cleaned and protected from infection. Rinse the wound with clean cold water and pat it dry. Then cover the injury; the dressing pad must be larger than the wound. For small grazes, use a plaster; for larger ones, use a sterile pad and a bandage.

### NATURAL WOUND DRESSING

The birch polypore, or razorstrop fungus, which grows on the sides of old birch trees, can be used as a natural wound dressing. Cut a thin slice from the top of the fungus and secure it over the wound. If you are in any doubt about the identity of the fungus, do not use it.

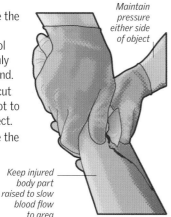

**1** Don't try to remove the object as it may be plugging bleeding. Control bleeding by pressing firmly on either side of the wound.
- Push the edges of the cut together but take care not to press directly on the object.
- Raise the wound above the level of the heart.

*Maintain pressure either side of object*

*Keep injured body part raised to slow blood flow to area*

**2** Place a piece of gauze over the object to protect it, then build up padding on either side (rolled bandages are ideal). Bandage over the pads and the object.
- Check the circulation beyond the bandage every ten minutes (see p. 264).

*Bandage over the object to prevent further injury*

# TYPES OF WOUND

Different types of object and force produce different kinds of wound. It's useful to identify the type of wound you or the casualty has incurred so that the correct method of treatment can be applied.

### BRUISE (CONTUSION)
A blunt blow will break blood vessels under the skin, causing blood to leak into the tissues. This results in a bruise: the skin is tender, swollen, and blue-black in color.

### GRAZE (ABRASION)
A friction burn from a rope, or a sliding fall, will scrape off the top layers of skin, leaving a raw, tender area. Grazes often contain embedded foreign matter.

### TEAR (LACERATION)
If the skin is torn open, the wound may not bleed as badly as an incised wound, but a larger area of tissue may be damaged and vulnerable to infection.

### PUNCTURE WOUND
Sharp objects such as nails or sea urchin spines can puncture the skin. The entry hole will be small but the wound will be deep, with a high risk of infection.

### INCISED WOUND
If a sharp-edged object cuts across the skin, blood vessels will be sliced open and bleeding will be severe. Nerves or tendons may also be damaged.

### STAB WOUND
A penetrating wound from a long, bladed instrument is a very serious injury. A stab wound to the torso can damage vital organs and cause internal bleeding.

# GUNSHOT WOUND

Check if the casualty has an exit wound. Treat entry and exit wounds separately.

### ENTRY WOUND
Bullets drive deep into, or through, the body. They leave a small, neat entrance wound and cause serious internal damage and contamination.

### EXIT WOUND
If a bullet passes through the body, the exit wound will be large and ragged. Don't remove the bullet if there is no exit wound.

## SEVERE EXTERNAL BLEEDING

Control the bleeding with direct pressure over a wound and, if possible, call for emergency help. Never use a tourniquet as this can cause severe tissue damage. Life-threatening shock is likely to develop if blood loss is severe (see p. 274).

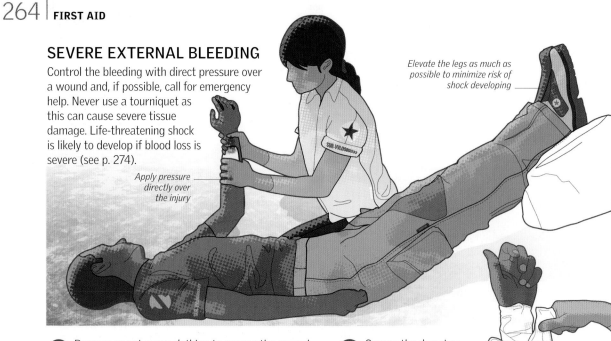

*Elevate the legs as much as possible to minimize risk of shock developing*

*Apply pressure directly over the injury*

**1** Remove or cut away clothing to expose the wound. Apply direct pressure to the wound, over a sterile dressing or pad if you have one. Raise the injured limb above the level of the casualty's heart to reduce blood flow to the area. Help him to lie down and raise his legs.

**2** Secure the dressing with a bandage. If blood soaks through, apply a second dressing on top of the first.

**3** Every ten minutes, check the bandage is not too tight. Gently press a fingernail beyond the dressing. If the skin color does not return quickly, rebandage more loosely.

## VARICOSE VEINS

When the one-way valves in veins fail, blood pools behind them, causing raised knobbly skin. The taut, thin-walled veins can easily be burst by a knock. Bleeding will be profuse.

**1** Help the casualty to lie down and raise and support the injured area as high as you can. This reduces bleeding straight away. Expose the wound and apply direct pressure over a sterile dressing or pad.

**2** Bandage the pad firmly to maintain pressure on the wound. Keep the area raised. Check the bandage is not too tight (see step 3, above). If necessary, loosen it but maintain pressure.

## SCALP WOUNDS

A scalp wound can bleed profusely, making it appear worse than it actually is. However, it may mask a more serious head injury. If a casualty becomes drowsy, has a headache, or double vision, get emergency help if possible.

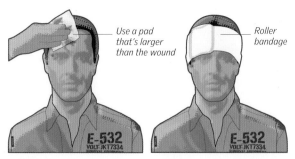

*Use a pad that's larger than the wound*

*Roller bandage*

**1** Sit the casualty on the floor. Carefully replace loose flaps of skin, cover the wound with a sterile pad, and apply pressure.

**2** Secure the dressing with a roller bandage. If the casualty doesn't quickly recover or if he deteriorates, get help.

# EYE INJURIES

The eye can be seriously injured by a blow or contact with sharp objects, such as a tree branch, risking scarring, infection, or even loss of vision. Always wear eye protection when hiking through dense vegetation.

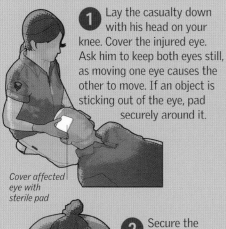

**1** Lay the casualty down with his head on your knee. Cover the injured eye. Ask him to keep both eyes still, as moving one eye causes the other to move. If an object is sticking out of the eye, pad securely around it.

*Cover affected eye with sterile pad*

**2** Secure the dressing with a bandage. If you're on your own, fix the dressing in place with plasters or tape and try not to move your eyes.

*Secure pad with bandage*

## FOREIGN OBJECT IN THE EYE

If you can see an object on the surface of the eye, try lifting it off with the corner of a handkerchief, or wash it out with sterile water, washing away from the good eye. Don't remove anything that is sticking to the eye.

## SNOW BLINDESS

Also known as "flash burn," this occurs if the surface of the eye is damaged through exposure to ultraviolet light, such as the glare from sun reflected off snow or water. Wearing sunglasses can prevent this. In an emergency, make your own goggles from cardboard or birch bark. If a person is affected by snow blindness, give him gauze pads to hold against his eyes. Bandage them in place if help is delayed.

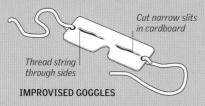

*Cut narrow slits in cardboard*

*Thread string through sides*

**IMPROVISED GOGGLES**

# BURNS AND SCALDS

There is a serious risk of infection with all burns. Burns may affect only the outermost layer of skin, the upper layers, or the full thickness. Severe burns will affect all three layers. If the burn is larger than the casualty's hand it needs hospital treatment.

## SMALL SUPERFICIAL BURNS

Cool the injury for ten minutes with cold running water or any cold, harmless liquid. Remove jewelry or watches from the affected area before it swells. Cover the burn to prevent infection.

## LARGE OR DEEP BURNS

If a burn is extensive or deep, then fluid will be lost from the body and life-threatening shock is likely to develop (see p. 274). If the injury occured in a fire, the casualty could also have burns to his air passages so may have breathing difficulties. Don't burst any blisters as you will increase the risk of infection.

**STOP, DROP, AND ROLL**
If clothing is on fire:
- Stop moving
- Drop to the ground
- Roll over on the ground until flames are extinguished

**1** Help the casualty lie down and protect him from the ground if possible. Cool the injury by dousing it with cold water for ten minutes; this also reduces swelling and relieves pain.

*Cool for at least ten minutes*

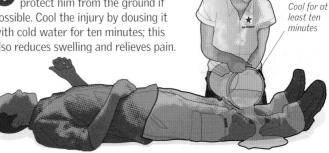

**2** While cooling the burn, remove or cut away clothing from around the burn. Don't touch or remove anything that's sticking to the burn.

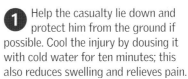

*Cut clothing to expose burned area*

**3** Cover the entire area with plastic kitchen wrap, a clean plastic bag, or a clean, lint-free dressing. Get emergency help as soon as possible.

*Protect the injury to reduce risk of infection*

# BITES AND STINGS

**MANY BITES OR INSECT STINGS** are painful, but most can be treated with simple first aid. However, there is a risk of an allergic reaction called anaphylactic shock. If a casualty develops a red blotchy rash, watery eyes or puffiness around the eyes, and/or breathing difficulties, get urgent medical help (see p. 274).

## TREATING BITES

An injury that breaks the skin carries a risk of infection. This is greatest with animal bites, since the mouth harbors so many germs. For a snake bite, you'll need to get emergency help, as the casualty needs to be transported on a stretcher in the treatment position to prevent the venom spreading through the body.

> ### PORCUPINE QUILLS
> If you are pierced by a porcupine's barbed quills, you must remove them or they will continue to work their way into the flesh and may pierce a vital organ.
> - Cut off the ends of the quills, which are hollow, to allow them to deflate slightly.
> - Pull the quills out, using pliers if you have them.
> - Clean the puncture wounds and apply an antiseptic ointment.

## SNAKE BITES

Relatively few snakes are venomous, but it's generally safer to assume that all of them are. Most snakes cause a painful bite that leaves small puncture marks in the skin; however, the bite of a poisonous snake may in fact be painless. Symptoms also include nausea and vomiting, disturbed vision, and breathing difficulties.

**1** Keep the casualty calm. Help her to lie down with her head, chest, and shoulders supported.
- Advise her to keep still.
- Make a note, if you can, of the time the bite occurred.

**2** Apply a bandage around the site of the injury. Do not wash the area, remove any footwear or clothing, or attempt to suck the venom.

**3** Tie another bandage around the affected limb that extends from the bite as far up the limb as possible.
- Check the circulation (see p. 264).
- Immobilize the affected limb.
- Move the casualty only with the use of a stretcher.

## MAMMAL BITES

Bites from mammals—animals or humans—carry a serious risk of infection because the sharp teeth cause puncture wounds that transport bacteria deep into the tissue (see p. 263). As always, wear gloves to protect yourself. The bite can also crush surrounding tissue, and bleeding may be severe (see p. 264).

### CLEAN WOUND
Raise the injury. Wash the wound with clean gauze and water. Pat dry, and cover it with a wound dressing.

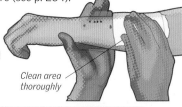

*Clean area thoroughly*

> ### SNAKE IDENTIFICATION
> Identify the snake if you can, since this will help medical teams find the correct antivenom. If you're not certain of the identity, make a note of its color or distinguishing features. If it's safe, put the snake in a secure container, but bear in mind that venom is active even if a snake is dead. Don't wash the venom off the bite; it can be used to identify the antivenin.

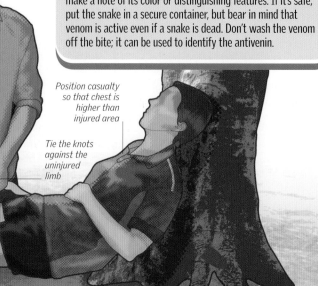

*Position casualty so that chest is higher than injured area*

*Tie the knots against the uninjured limb*

*Immobilize legs with folded triangular bandages*

*Bandage the limb from the bite site as far up the leg as possible*

## TICK BITES

Ticks are tiny, spider-like parasites that live in grass or woodland. They feed on blood, attaching themselves to the skin with spiked mouthparts, and swell to the size of a pea. They carry Lyme Disease, so must be removed.

### TRADITIONAL METHOD

Using tweezers, grasp the tick's head as close to the skin as you can. Pull the head upward using steady pressure (don't twist). Keep the tick in a container so it can be checked for Lyme Disease.

*Don't squeeze the body*

### SPECIALIZED REMOVAL HOOK

Tick extractor tools that "unscrew" the mouthparts of the tick from the skin are available from pet shops. Slide the hook along the skin to grab the tick. Raise the hook very slightly and rotate it to lift the tick clear.

*Slide the hook until it engages with the tick*

## HANDLING LEECHES

When in leech-infested territory, inspect your clothing and limbs every few minutes. Never pull a leech off if it's attached, as the jaws will remain in the skin and cause infection. To remove:

- Apply the juice of a raw lime, DEET, alcohol, or a dash of salt. If you're a smoker, put your cigarette butts in a piece of cloth, moisten the cloth, and squeeze nicotine onto the leech.
- Once the leech has dropped off, wash the area to remove the anticoagulant in and around the wound. Treat any bleeding (see p. 263) and cover the wound.

# TREATING STINGS

Many stings are painful, but they are rarely life-threatening. Scorpion stings can be very painful and cause severe illness, and treatment should be as for snake bite (see opposite). Multiple insect stings of any type can produce a more serious reaction (see anaphylactic shock, p. 274).

**WARNING!**
A sting in the mouth or throat can cause swelling that blocks the airway. To minimize this, give the casualty cold water to sip.

## INSECT STING

A bee, wasp, or hornet sting is often painful and followed by swelling and redness at the site. Some people have an allergy to stings, so monitor the casualty for signs of anaphylactic shock.

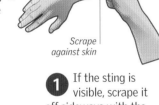

*Scrape against skin*

**1** If the sting is visible, scrape it off sideways with the edge of a credit card, knife, or a fingernail.
- Don't squeeze the sac as you may squeeze more venom into the area.

**2** Raise the affected part and place a cold pad against it for at least ten minutes to minimize swelling.
- Monitor the casualty for signs of allergy such as wheezing, or swelling around the face.

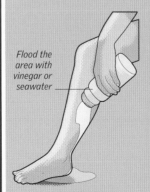

## SEA CREATURES

When touched, sea anemones, corals, jellyfish, and Portuguese men-of-war release venomous cells that stick to the skin. Treat jellyfish stings as below; apply a cold compress to other stings to minimize swelling and relieve pain. Creatures such as weever fish have sharp spines that, if trodden on, become embedded, and may become infected.

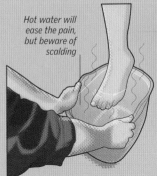

*Flood the area with vinegar or seawater*

*Hot water will ease the pain, but beware of scalding*

### JELLYFISH STING

Pour vinegar or seawater over the area to neutralize the sting. Help the casualty to sit down; treat as for snake bite (see opposite).

### SEA URCHIN SPINES

Immerse the injured part in water as hot as the casualty can tolerate for about 30 minutes. Get medical help, as the spines must be removed.

# POISONOUS PLANTS AND INTESTINAL PARASITES

**IT'S ESSENTIAL TO MAINTAIN** personal hygiene in camp, to purify all drinking water from natural sources (see pp. 198–201), and to observe the rules of food safety if you wish to remain healthy in the wilderness. You should also learn how to recognize and avoid the poisonous plants in the region you're traveling in.

## CONTACT POISONING

Poisonous plants don't always have to be ingested to cause damage. If they come into contact with the skin, the result can be pain, swelling, redness, a rash, and itching. Get medical help fast and, in the meantime, rinse the skin with cold water for 20 minutes. If the water splashes an eye, rinse for ten minutes. Although plants are the most common cause of contact poisoning, chemicals such as camp fuel can also be harmful.

## POISONOUS PLANTS

Poison ivy, poison oak, and poison sumac are the most well known of the plants that contain urushiol, an irritant oil. If you damage the plant and get the oil on your skin, you must wash it off immediately with soap and cold water. You should also remove and wash any contaminated clothing to prevent the oil spreading. Apply an anti-poison-ivy cream as soon as possible. Many people will develop an itchy rash and often painful blistering within 4 to 24 hours of contact with the plant (see warning panel, above).

### POISON SUMAC
Found in wet acid swamps in eastern North America, poison sumac can grow as tall as 18 ft (6 m).

*Oval leaflets grow in opposite pairs*

### POISON IVY
Native to wooded areas of North America, poison ivy is now found worldwide.

*Berries are white when ripe*

### STINGING NETTLES
Found in many countries, stinging nettles usually cause only a temporary stinging sensation where the plant's hairs touch the skin. Apply a soothing cold compress or rub the affected area with a dock leaf if you can find one. Watch for an itchy red rash that indicates an allergic reaction.

### POISON OAK
Like poison ivy, the leaflets of poison oak grow in threes. This plant is found in wooded parts of North America.

*Leaflets are shaped like oak leaves*

### WARNING!
If you think you've handled a poisonous plant, don't touch especially sensitive parts of your body such as the eyes, mouth, or genitals until you have washed your hands thoroughly.
■ If you develop blisters on your skin, don't scratch them—however much they itch. If you break the skin, you'll run the risk of getting an infection.
■ As well as painful blistering, some people may have an extreme reaction to the toxin. They should be monitored and treated for shock (see p. 274). Get medical help as soon as possible.

### NATURAL REMEDIES
Where nature causes a problem, she sometimes provides the solution. The following counter the effects of urushiol:
■ Jewelweed has a sticky juice that will dry out blisters in a few days. Cut a piece of stem, split it down the middle, and rub the pieces on the affected skin.

*Jewelweed has distinctive pale yellow or orange, spotted flowers*

■ To soothe itching, make a poultice of witch hazel leaves. Mash up the leaves, adding water if too dry, then apply to the affected area.
■ Try washing with a tannic acid solution. Tannic acid is found in tea, or you can make it from oak bark (see opposite).
■ Tea tree oil, from the leaves of the melaleuca tree, is also said to counter the effects of urushiol. Apply directly to the affected area.

# SWALLOWED POISON

Try to find out what the casualty ingested, how much, and when. If you suspect the casualty has swallowed a caustic chemical, such as camp fuel, do not induce vomiting as it will burn again on the way back up. Get medical help and monitor the casualty. If the lips are burnt, give frequent sips of cool milk or water. If you know the casualty has swallowed a poisonous plant or fungus and he or she is conscious, induce vomiting by tickling the back of the throat. Dilute the poison by getting him or her to drink large quantities of water or milk, or tea mixed with charcoal.

## DIARRHEA AND VOMITING

In the wilderness, diarrhea and vomiting can kill, because they lead to dehydration (see p. 272) or even shock (see p. 274). The most likely causes are food poisoning or drinking contaminated water, although infectious diseases are a possibility, so get medical help if symptoms persist. You should rest, keep warm, and replace lost fluids. If you're hungry, you can eat small amounts of bland foods such as pasta for 24 hours.

### NATURAL REMEDIES

In a survival situation, there are various natural remedies you can try to stop diarrhea or alleviate symptoms such as stomach pain, although some are more palatable than others:

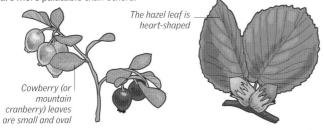

The hazel leaf is heart-shaped

Cowberry (or mountain cranberry) leaves are small and oval

- **Tea:** Drink tea made from hazel, cowberry, or cranberry leaves.
- **Bark:** Pull some bark off a tree (preferably oak), remove the inner bark and boil it for at least 12 hours, adding more water as necessary. The resulting black brew smells and tastes vile, but it contains tannic acid and will cure diarrhea. Drink one cup every two hours.
- **Charcoal:** Take a partially burned piece of wood, scrape off the char, then swallow about a handful with water.
- **Bones:** Burn to ashes then grind, or grind bones into a powder between two rocks. Make a paste with water, then swallow about a tablespoonful.
- **Chalk:** Grind into a powder, mix with water to a paste, then swallow about a tablespoonful.
- **Ash:** Make a paste of wood ash and water, then swallow. This will alleviate stomach pain.

### REST AND REHYDRATE

Drink water to maintain your fluid levels. To help replace lost salts, dissolve a packet of rehydration salts in the water, or one teaspoon of salt in a liter of water, before drinking.

## INTESTINAL PARASITES

There are two main types of intestinal parasite: helminths (tapeworms, pinworms, and roundworms) and protozoa (giardia, for example). The usual causes of infection are ingesting contaminated water or food, or poor personal hygiene. Symptoms include nausea or vomiting, diarrhea (see left), dysentry, bloating, stomach pain, weight loss, or a rash or itching around the rectum. Seek medical advice as soon as possible.

### WILDERNESS CURE FOR WORMS

If you have passed a worm in your stool, swallow a couple of tablespoons of kerosene. While this method may make you sick, it will make the worms sicker. Gasoline will also work but is not as effective.

### HOW TO AVOID BEING INFECTED

Prevention is far better than cure and to avoid being infected by parasites present in water or spread in feces you should always do the following in the wilderness:
- Boil all water, or use other reliable methods of purification (see pp. 198–201).
- Don't clean your teeth or rinse your mouth with water that isn't pure.
- Don't swim or stand in rivers or lakes in places where you could be at risk unless absolutely necessary.
- Cover any cuts or wounds on your skin.
- Maintain strict personal hygiene in camp (see pp. 116–17) and when handling food.
- Boil any meat you think might be infected for at least 20 minutes, or ideally until it falls off the bone, before eating it.

# BONES, JOINTS, AND MUSCLES

## CRAMP

This painful muscle spasm can be caused by dehydration and a reduction of body salts through perspiration—so make sure you have enough to drink when exercising. Sit down, rest, and stretch the affected muscles.

### FOOT

Help the person stand on his good foot and stretch the muscles to reverse the spasm. Once the cramp has eased, massage the affected area of the foot.

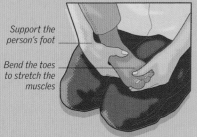

*Support the person's foot*

*Bend the toes to stretch the muscles*

### CALF

Sit the person down and support the affected leg. Help him to straighten his leg, and flex his toes to reverse the spasm. Then massage the painful muscle.

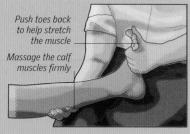

*Push toes back to help stretch the muscle*

*Massage the calf muscles firmly*

### THIGH

If the cramp is in the back of the thigh, straighten the leg to stretch the muscle; if it's in the front of the thigh, bend the leg. Once the pain eases, massage the affected area.

*Support the leg on your shoulder*

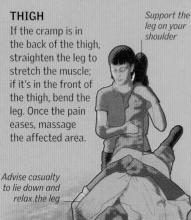

*Advise casualty to lie down and relax the leg*

---

**IT CAN BE DIFFICULT TO TELL** whether an injury is a sprain, a broken bone, or a dislocation. The ends of broken bones can move, damaging blood vessels or nerves nearby, so treat the casualty in the position found and immobilize the injured area before letting him or her move. Anyone with a spine injury or broken leg must be carried by stretcher.

## SPRAINS AND STRAINS

A strain is a pulled muscle. A sprain occurs when ligaments that hold a joint together are damaged. The ideal treatment is to raise the injury, cool, and rest it. If you provide comfortable support, gentle movement can help the injury. If in any doubt, treat the injury as a broken bone (see opposite).

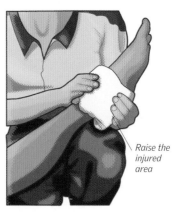

*Raise the injured area*

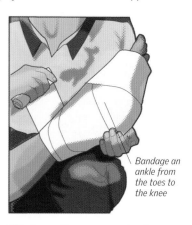

*Bandage an ankle from the toes to the knee*

**1** Rest and support the injury. Wrap a cold compress around it for at least 10 minutes to reduce swelling and bruising.

**2** Leave the compress in place, or wrap padding around the injury. Apply a crêpe bandage from below the injury to the next joint.

## ARM INJURY

Falling onto an outstretched hand can cause a broken wrist, forearm, upper arm, or collar bone. Support the affected arm in a sling. If a casualty can't bend his arm, he may have injured his elbow, in which case don't use a sling. Instead wrap padding around the joint and secure the arm to the body with triangular bandages. To make sure that the bandage isn't too tight, check the wrist pulse.

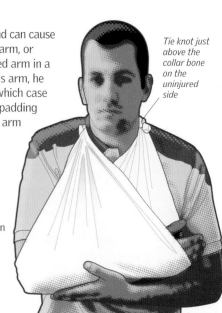

*Tie knot just above the collar bone on the uninjured side*

### USING A SLING

Slide a triangular bandage between the arm and the chest. Bring the front up over the arm and tie a reef knot on the uninjured side.

# LEG INJURY

Injuries to the legs can be serious, as any fracture is likely to be unstable, which means that the ends of the bones can move easily, and could pierce one of the large blood vessels in the leg, resulting in severe bleeding. Don't move the casualty unless you have to, and, even then, only when the legs have been immobilized. If you see any signs of shock (see p. 274) ensure the head is low, but do not raise the legs.

# HAND INJURY

Injuries to hands are often complicated by bruising or bleeding. Raise the injured hand and treat bleeding with direct pressure (see p. 264). Remove jewelry before the area starts to swell. Wrap the hand in padding and support it in a raised position with a sling.

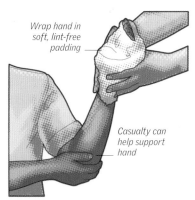

*Wrap hand in soft, lint-free padding*

*Casualty can help support hand*

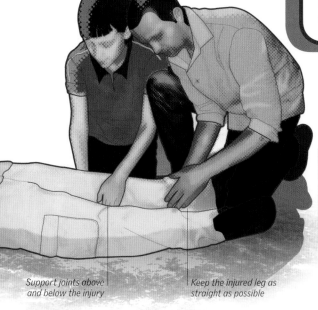

*Support joints above and below the injury*

*Keep the injured leg as straight as possible*

*Put first bandage around the knees*

*Secure third and fourth bandages above and below injury*

*Tie second bandage in a figure of eight around the ankles and feet*

*Secure bandages with reef knots on the injured side*

**1** Lay the casualty down and support the injury to minimize further damage. Call for emergency help. If this is nearby just maintain this support. You can put rolled-up coats or blankets on either side for extra support.

**2** If help is delayed or you need to transport the casualty, put bandages around the knees and ankles (and pelvis, if the thigh is injured), and above and below the injury. Place padding between the legs, then tie the bandages.

# SPINAL INJURY

If a person falls and lands on his back, or falls from a height, it is best to assume that he has a spinal and, probably, a head injury. Don't move him—support his head and neck in line with the rest of his back. Moving him could damage the spinal cord, which may result in permanent loss of movement below the injured area. Call for emergency help, or send someone to get help while you stay with the casualty. If you have to move him because he is in danger, use the log-roll technique (see p. 279).

*Make sure you are comfortable because you may have to wait for help to arrive*

### SUPPORT THE HEAD AND NECK

Kneel or lie behind the casualty's head. Keep your arms steady by resting your elbows on your thighs and place your hands on either side of his head to keep it in line with his body. Wait for help.

*Don't cover the casualty's ears as he must be able to hear you*

# TREATING EXPOSURE

**EXTREMES OF HEAT AND COLD** can prevent the body's temperature-regulation mechanisms from functioning properly. Both extremes can cause life-threatening injures, so it's vital to act quickly. Don't leave a casualty—call for help or, if possible, send someone to seek help while you treat him or her.

> **WARNING!**
> If a casualty becomes unconscious, be prepared to give cardiopulmonary resuscitation (see p. 277).

## HEAT INJURIES

In hot weather, wear a hat, reapply sunscreen frequently, and stay in the shade when you can to avoid heat injuries such as sunburn. You'll quickly become dehydrated if you don't drink enough water to replace fluids lost through sweating.

## DEHYDRATION

Help the casualty to sit down and give him fluids to drink; water is usually sufficient, but rehydration salts mixed with water is best. If the casualty complains of cramp, help him stretch the affected muscles, then massage them firmly (see p. 270).

## HEAT EXHAUSTION

If a casualty feels dizzy and starts to sweat profusely, but has cold, clammy skin, get him into the shade and give him fluids to drink. Help him to lie down then raise his legs—support his feet on a backpack—to help improve blood flow to the brain. Monitor him while he recovers.

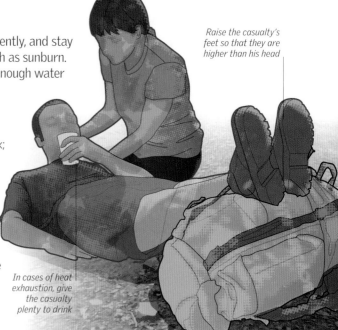

*Raise the casualty's feet so that they are higher than his head*

*In cases of heat exhaustion, give the casualty plenty to drink*

## HEATSTROKE

This life-threatening condition may follow heat exhaustion or develop with no warning. Heatstroke causes the body's temperature-control mechanism to fail. If a person complains of headache, feels dizzy, has hot, dry skin, and begins losing consciousness, he or she may have heatstroke and will need urgent medical help.

**1** Move the casualty to as cool a place as possible—out of the sun. Help him to sit or lie down with his head raised and remove all of his outer clothing.

**2** Do anything possible to quickly reduce the body temperature. Ideally, wrap him in a cold, wet sheet. Keep the sheet cool by continually pouring water over it.

**3** When the body temperature drops below 104°F (40°C), replace the wet sheet with a dry one.

**4** Monitor the level of response, pulse, and breathing. If his temperature starts to rise again, repeat the treatment.

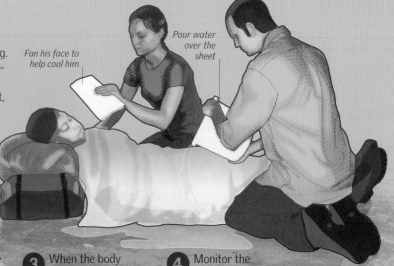

*Fan his face to help cool him*

*Pour water over the sheet*

# COLD INJURIES

Exposure to cold can result in parts of the body freezing (frostnip and frostbite) or the body's core temperature becoming dangerously low (hypothermia).

## FROSTNIP AND FROSTBITE

Frostnip is the freezing of the top layer of skin, usually on the face and extremities. The skin turns numb, white, and hard. Untreated, it can lead to frostbite, which is much more serious—the deeper tissues, and even the bone, freeze. The skin turns white or blue and feels solidly frozen.

### WARM GRADUALLY

Frostnip and frostbite can both be treated by warming the affected area, though frostbite requires more intensive treatment. Warm the affected area with body heat—place the casualty's hands in his own armpits, or place his feet in your armpits. Remove any rings and raise the injured part to reduce swelling. Ideally, place the affected area in warm water. Dress the injury in sterile dressings.

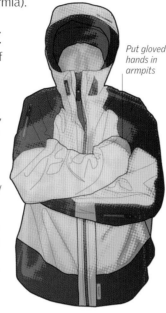

*Put gloved hands in armpits*

## HYPOTHERMIA

This life-threatening condition develops if the body's core temperature falls below 95°F (35°C). Treatment aims to prevent further heat loss. It's vital that a casualty is warmed up gradually. If he or she is warmed up too quickly, blood is diverted away from vital organs, such as the heart and brain, to the skin, which can actually speed up cooling of the body. A casualty with hypothermia must be moved on a stretcher.

## DROWNING

If a person has been immersed in cold water, there is a high risk of hypothermia. In addition, the cold can cause the heart to stop, or throat spasms can block the airway. Water can also enter the lungs and cause secondary drowning (see p. 255) hours after the person appeared to have recovered.

### RESCUING A CASUALTY

If you have rescued a person from water, help him or her to lie down with the head low. Replace wet clothes with dry ones. Treat for hypothermia (see left). If the person is unconscious and not breathing, give five rescue breaths before beginning chest compressions (see p. 277).

### ALTITUDE SICKNESS

Symptoms of altitude sickness include nausea, loss of appetite, shortness of breath, and a headache that's not relieved by medication. The casualty may also have difficulty sleeping and will feel unwell. The only solution is to start the descent immediately and remain at a lower altitude for a few days. Severe cases will need to be carried.

**1** Help the casualty to a sheltered place where he should rest to prevent his body temperature falling further. Send someone else to get help.

**2** If possible, and if there is no risk of further cold, remove any wet clothing and replace with warm, dry clothes—but don't give up your own clothes.

**3** Put a thick layer of dry leaves underneath him to insulate him from the ground. Help him to lie down in a sleeping bag and, if you have one, cover him with a survival blanket.

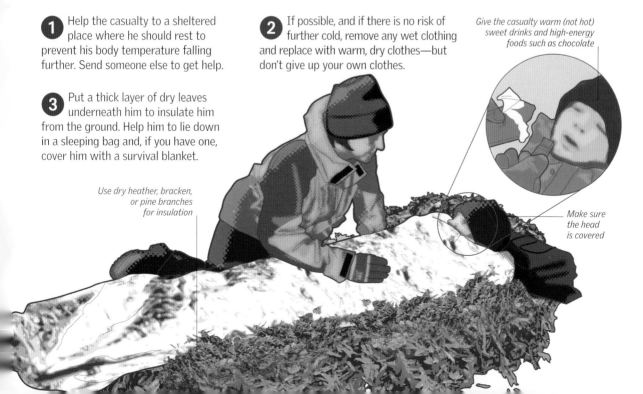

*Give the casualty warm (not hot) sweet drinks and high-energy foods such as chocolate*

*Use dry heather, bracken, or pine branches for insulation*

*Make sure the head is covered*

# TREATING SHOCK

**SHOCK IS A LIFE-THREATENING CONDITION** that occurs if the circulatory system fails. The most common cause is severe bleeding, but it can also be a consequence of burns. Initially, there will be a rapid pulse and pale clammy skin. As the condition progresses, breathing becomes rapid and shallow, pulse weakens, and skin becomes pale gray-blue. If untreated, unconsciousness results.

> ### ANAPHYLACTIC SHOCK
> Anaphylactic shock is a rare but severe allergic reaction affecting the whole body. People who know they are susceptible to this carry a special adrenaline (epinephrine) autoinjector for use in an emergency. If the casualty has one, but is too weak to use it, take off the safety cap and, holding it in your fist, press it against the casualty's thigh (through clothing if necessary).

## DEALING WITH SHOCK

Do not give the casualty anything to eat or drink as an anaesthetic may be needed; moisten his lips with water if he's thirsty. Call for help; the casualty must be transported in the treatment position.

**1** Treat the cause of shock, for example bleeding or burns (see p. 265). Suspect shock, too, if you notice any symptoms, yet can't see any obvious injury—it could be caused by internal bleeding.

**2** Help the casualty to lie down; insulate him from the ground with blankets or bracken. Raise and support his legs as high as you can above the level of his heart.

**3** Loosen tight clothing, for example at the neck, chest, and waist. Keep his head low; this may prevent him from losing consciousness. Keep the casualty warm; cover him with a blanket or sleeping bag if you have one.

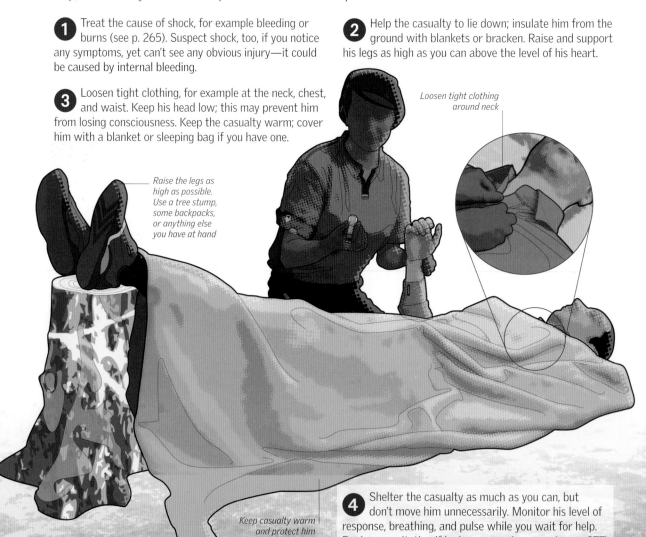

*Loosen tight clothing around neck*

*Raise the legs as high as possible. Use a tree stump, some backpacks, or anything else you have at hand*

*Keep casualty warm and protect him from the ground*

**4** Shelter the casualty as much as you can, but don't move him unnecessarily. Monitor his level of response, breathing, and pulse while you wait for help. Begin resuscitation if he loses consciousness (see p. 277).

# BREATHING DIFFICULTIES

**RESPIRATORY PROBLEMS** need prompt treatment because they can prevent sufficient oxygen reaching the body tissues. The cause may be temporary, for example choking, suffocation, or smoke inhalation, or it can be a long-term condition such as asthma that requires medication. You may need to get emergency help.

> **WARNING!**
> If at any stage the casualty loses consciousness, open the airway (see p. 276) and check breathing; the throat muscles may relax enough to allow breathing. If he or she is not breathing, begin resuscitation as this may dislodge the blockage (see p. 277).

## CHOKING

When an object becomes stuck in the throat it can cause a muscular spasm that blocks the airway. Always ask the casualty if she is choking, to make sure. If she can speak, cough, or breathe, the obstruction is mild and she will probably be able to clear it herself.

**1** If the casualty is breathing, tell her to continue coughing. If she can't speak or cough, help her to bend forward. Support her upper body and give up to five back blows in between her shoulder blades with the heel of your hand.

**2** If back blows fail, stand behind her. Put your arms around her abdomen, clench one fist and grasp it with the other hand. Pull sharply inwards and upward up to five times. Check the mouth and remove any obvious blockage.

**3** If the obstruction has still not cleared, repeat the five back slaps and five abdominal thrusts three times, then call for help if it's not already on the way. Continue until help arrives or the casualty becomes unconscious (see pp. 276–77).

*Pull against the abdomen— not the chest*

## ASTHMA

This is a condition in which breathing becomes difficult because the muscles in the air passages go into spasm. Most people who suffer from asthma carry inhalers with them. Many have two inhalers—a brown or white "preventer" inhaler and a blue "reliever" inhaler to use in an attack. If the person does not have any medication, sit him or her down and call for emergency help.

**1** Sit the casualty down and advise her to take a puff from her reliever inhaler. Tell her to take slow, deep breaths and to sit as upright as she can. The attack should start to ease in a few minutes.

**2** If the attack does not ease, tell her to take another dose from her inhaler and rest while she recovers. If the attack still does not ease, or is becoming worse, emergency help is needed as she could lose consciousness.

### WHAT TO DO IN A SURVIVAL SITUATION

The best advice is prevention—know what triggers the asthma and avoid those things if at all possible. However, should someone have an asthma attack and not have an inhaler, try the following:

- Tell her to exhale as completely as she can. This expels the "stale" air, with little or no oxygen in it. It may be difficult—and will seem strange—to blow air out when the basic instinct is to gulp air in, but this does work.
- Then, tell her to inhale, slowly and steadily, and to close her eyes to help calm herself while doing so.

*Take slow, deep breaths*

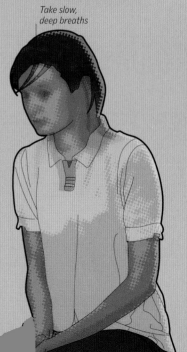

# UNCONSCIOUSNESS

**IF SOMEONE FALLS UNCONSCIOUS,** your priority is to make sure their airway is open so that they can breathe. Call for emergency help immediately (ideally ask someone to do this while you treat the casualty). Don't move the casualty and don't leave him or her alone unless you have to go and get help.

Talk to the casualty and ask him to open his eyes

Shake an adult casualty's shoulder

## CHECK FOR RESPONSE

Gently shake the casualty's shoulders (if it's a child, tap the shoulders). Talk to him and watch for a response. If he's alert, he's conscious. If, for example, he reacts weakly, he may not be fully conscious—monitor him for any change (deterioration or improvement). If there's no response, he's unconscious.

## OPEN THE AIRWAY

If an unconscious casualty is on his back, he's at risk of swallowing his tongue—thereby blocking his air passages. Tilting the head and lifting the chin will "lift" the tongue, clearing the air passage.

## CHECK THE BREATHING

Tilt a casualty's head back with one hand and lift the chin with two fingers of your other hand; don't press on the soft tissues under the chin. Keep the airway open, and look, listen, and feel for normal breathing. If the casualty is breathing normally, place him in the recovery position (see below). If he's not breathing, begin chest compressions right away (see opposite).

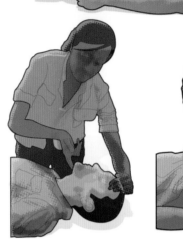

**1** Place a hand on the forehead to tilt the head; lift the chin.

**2** Look along the casualty's chest; listen, and feel, for breath against your cheek for no more than ten seconds.

## RECOVERY POSITION

If an unconscious casualty is breathing, place him in the recovery position to keep his airway open and clear. Remove anything bulky from his pockets. Kneel beside him. Bend the arm nearest you at a right angle to his body then bring the other arm across his chest until his hand rests against his near cheek, and hold it there. Bend the far leg at the knee, and, still holding the knee, pull the casualty toward you until he is on his side.

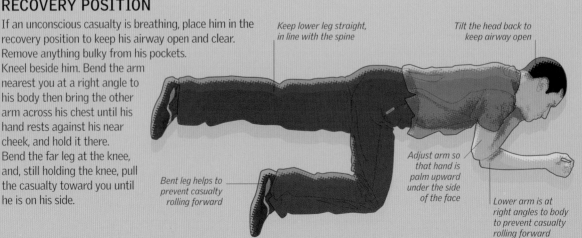

Keep lower leg straight, in line with the spine

Tilt the head back to keep airway open

Bent leg helps to prevent casualty rolling forward

Adjust arm so that hand is palm upward under the side of the face

Lower arm is at right angles to body to prevent casualty rolling forward

# CARDIOPULMONARY RESUSCITATION (CPR)

If a casualty is not breathing, you must try to keep the body supplied with oxygen by using chest compressions and rescue breaths until emergency help arrives. This is known as cardiopulmonary resuscitation, or CPR. If an adult collapses, the cause is most likely to be a heart problem so treat as below. If you have rescued an unconscious casualty from water, start with rescue breaths as for a child (see right). If you are unable to achieve rescue breaths, you can give chest compressions alone.

## HOW TO GIVE CPR

Kneel beside the casualty, level with his chest so that you don't have to change position. If you have someone else with you, take it in turns to give CPR so you don't become too exhausted. Change over at the end of each two-minute cycle.

> ### CPR ON A CHILD
> - Start by giving the child five rescue breaths.
> - Give 30 compressions using the heel of one hand only and slightly less pressure than you would for an adult. Depress the chest by approximately one third of its depth.
> - Continue with 30 compressions followed by two rescue breaths until the child recovers, help arrives, or you become exhausted.
> - If you are on your own, give CPR for one minute before you try to call for help.

**1** Put one hand on the center of the casualty's chest—make sure you don't press on the lower abdomen, the tip of the breastbone, or the ribs.

**2** Place the heel of your other hand on top of the first and link your fingers together. Keep your fingers off the casualty's chest.

**3** Begin chest compressions. Lean over and, keeping your arms straight, press straight down on the casualty's chest, depressing it by $1^1/_2$–2 in (4–5 cm). Release the pressure and let the chest come back up, but don't move your hands. Repeat 30 times.

**4** Tilt the casualty's head to open the airway and pinch his nose to close the nostrils. Let his mouth fall open slightly. Lift his chin with the fingers of your other hand.

**5** To begin rescue breaths, take a normal breath and seal your lips over those of the casualty. Blow into his mouth until you see his chest rise, then lift your mouth away and watch his chest fall. If his chest doesn't rise, adjust his head and try again. Repeat to give a second breath, but don't make more than two attempts at giving rescue breaths before compressing again.

**6** Continue the cycle of 30 compressions followed by two rescue breaths until the casualty recovers, help arrives, or you are too exhausted to keep going.
- If at any stage the casualty starts breathing normally, place him in the recovery position (see opposite) and monitor his condition until help arrives.

*Place heel of hand on center of chest*

*Keep fingers clear of the ribs*

# MOVING A CASUALTY

**IDEALLY, AN INJURED PERSON** should be treated in the position in which he or she was found. Make the casualty as comfortable as possible and wait for help. In a survival situation, if you have to move someone, it's essential to immobilize an injury first to avoid aggravating it.

## PREPARING FOR A MOVE

Plan your move before you start. Choose a method appropriate to the injury. Don't attempt to move anyone by yourself if you have help. Encourage the casualty to do as much as possible himself.

## FIREFIGHTER'S LIFT

This is a technique that can be used to move a conscious casualty if you're on your own and need to carry an injured person a short distance. It gets its name from the firefighters who originally used it. Don't use it if a casualty has head or facial injuries or a broken arm or leg. To prevent injuring your back, use your legs to power the move.

**1** Support the casualty's injury with padding and bandages. Help him to stand up.
- Stand at right angles to the casualty, then squat down in front of him, staying as close to him as possible.
- Your shoulder should be level with the top of the casualty's legs.

*Put your arm between his legs so that your shoulder is against the top of his leg*

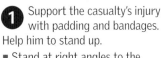

*Hold his wrist to help support him*

**2** Pass your nearest arm between the casualty's legs, wrap it around his thigh, and grasp his leg. Grasp the casualty's wrist firmly with the other arm.

*Tell the casualty to keep his weight off the injured foot*

**3** With your feet shoulder-width apart to ensure you're well balanced, encourage the casualty to lean across your shoulders.
- Keeping your back straight, hold his wrist firmly, and use the strength of your legs to stand up.

## IMPROVISING A STRETCHER

If you need to move a casualty who is unconscious, has a broken leg, or a spine injury, he must be carried by stretcher. Ideally, call the emergency services, and wait for them to arrive. If you can't contact them and you need to get the casualty to medical assistance, you may need to make a stretcher. Use a hurdle or gate, or make the stretcher from poles and coats.

**WARNING!**
Rescuers should not use their own clothing to make a stretcher if this might put them at risk of exposure.

*Push sleeves inside jacket for added strength*

*Place cross-piece at each end of the stretcher*

*Place the side of the stretcher against the casualty's back*

**1** Zip or button up two or three jackets. Cut two support poles, strong enough to bear the casualty's weight and 3 ft (1 m) longer than the casualty. Lash a short forked branch across each end (see pp. 166–67) to keep the support poles apart.

**2** Immobilize any injury (see p. 271), and roll the casualty onto his uninjured side. One person should support his head while others help to keep his body straight, ideally one for the upper body and one for the legs. Slide the stretcher in place then roll him gently back on to it.

## TWO-PERSON SEAT

If there are two of you, this method can be used to carry a conscious casualty who can't walk, but who can support himself with his arms. Nominate one person to be in charge of the move and give the instructions. Keep your backs straight at all times.

**1** Stand facing each other behind the casualty. Grasp your left wrist with your right hand, then grasp each other's free wrist to make a seat.

**2** Ask the casualty to put her arms around your shoulders. Let her sit back on to your hands. Rise and take her weight. Set off together, leading with your outside feet.

## SUPPORTING THE UPPER BODY

If a casualty has an injured arm, the seat carry (see left) can be adapted to support the upper body. As before, one of you should direct the move and always move together. Keep your backs straight as you walk, and stop if it causes you or the casualty any discomfort.

**1** Stand facing each other, on either side of the casualty. Put your arms around her back and grasp her clothing on the side farthest from you.

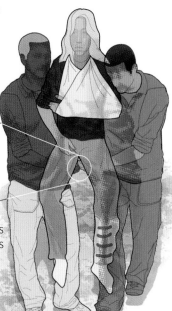

**2** Pass your free hands behind the casualty's thighs. Link your fingers together or grasp each other's wrists. Help the casualty back on to the "seat," and lift her.

# WILD FOOD

**MANY POISONOUS PLANTS** in temperate regions resemble edible ones, so you should only eat plants that you can positively identify. If you're in any doubt at all, carry out the Universal Edibility Test (UET) first (see pp. 206–07). Don't forget that some plants are edible only at certain stages of their growth. Never eat wild plants if you have any known

| NAME | WHERE | IDENTIFICATION | EDIBLE PART | |
|---|---|---|---|---|
| **BISTORT/KNOTWEED** *Polygonum* spp. | ▪ Damp, grassy habitats, such as meadows, in North America and Eurasia. | ▪ Perennial plant, 16–40 in (40–100 cm) tall. Green, triangular leaves. Small pink or white flowers form dense, cylindrical flowerheads at end of long, unbranched stem. | ▪ Young shoots and leaves ▪ Roots | |
| **BRAMBLE/BLACKBERRY** *Rubus fruticosus* | ▪ In most temperate habitats worldwide, but particularly scrubland, hedges, and woodland. | ▪ Scrambling deciduous shrub with thorny stems forming thickets. Green, toothed leaves. White or deep pink five-petaled flowers. Fruit ripens to blue-black in late summer. | ▪ Fruit ▪ Young shoots ▪ Leaves | |
| **BUCKWHEAT** *Fagopyrum esculentum* | ▪ Open grassland worldwide. | ▪ Red-stemmed plant up to 2 ft (60 cm) tall. Green, triangular leaves. Small pink, five-petaled flowers grow in clusters. Triangular seeds. | ▪ Seeds | |
| **DANDELION** *Taraxacum* spp. | ▪ Widely distributed in temperate areas of Eurasia; introduced to the Americas, Australia, and New Zealand. | ▪ Rosette of green, jagged-edged leaves grows close to the ground from a central taproot. Large, bright yellow flower head matures into a spherical "clock" of several seeds. | ▪ Leaves ▪ Roots | |
| **DOG ROSE** *Rosa canina* | ▪ In hedgerows, woodland margins, and scrubland in Europe, northwest Africa, and western Asia; introduced to other regions. | ▪ Scrambling deciduous shrub with spiny stems. Dark green, toothed leaves. Scentless, white, pink or deep pink five-petaled flowers. Fruit, or "hip," is orange-red and oval. | ▪ Hips ▪ Buds and flowers ▪ Young leaves | |
| **STINGING/ COMMON NETTLE** *Urtica dioica* | ▪ By hedgerows and woodland margins in North America, Eurasia, and North Africa. | ▪ Perennial herbaceous plant, 20–60 in (50–150 cm) tall. Green, oval, strongly toothed leaves covered in stiff stinging hairs. Small green flowers sometimes have a red tinge. | ▪ Young shoots and leaves | |
| **SUGAR MAPLE** *Acer saccharum* | ▪ Woods and forests in northeastern North America. | ▪ Deciduous tree, usually 82–115 ft (25–35 m) tall. Gray-brown bark smooth on young trees, furrowed and flaky on old trees. Green, five-lobed leaves turn bright red in fall. | ▪ Sap ▪ Inner bark | |
| **WALNUT** *Juglans* spp. | ▪ Temperate areas in Eurasia and North America. Common in the Himalayas. | ▪ Large deciduous tree up to 82 ft (25 m) tall with distinctive gnarled bark. Green leaves have narrow leaflets. Nut has a thick, green husk, which rots away once it falls to the ground. | ▪ Nuts | |
| **WATER CHESTNUT AND WATER CALTROP** *Trapa natans* and *T. bicornis* | ▪ In slow-moving water in warm temperate areas of Eurasia and Africa; introduced to North America and Australia. | ▪ Green, triangular, saw-toothed leaves float on surface. White four-petaled flowers. Fruit is borne underwater and has four sharp spines and one hard gray seed. | ▪ Seeds | |
| **WILD GRAPE** *Vitis* spp. | ▪ In most habitats in North America and Eurasia. | ▪ Sprawling, high-climbing vine with large, lobed leaves. Fruit grows as hanging bunches of berries, which are amber or dark purple when ripe. | ▪ Fruit ▪ Young leaves | |

# TEMPERATE PLANTS

allergies, a pre-existing medical condition, or are pregnant. The UET doesn't apply to mushrooms, so never eat any mushrooms unless you can positively identify every single one as being edible. As part of your preparation for your trip, you should familiarize yourself with the edible plants in the region you're visiting, and their seasonal availability.

| PREPARATION | SIMILAR PLANTS | BEWARE OF | EXTRA INFORMATION |
|---|---|---|---|
| ■ Young leaves and shoots can be eaten raw or boiled.<br>■ Soak roots, then boil or roast. | ■ Alpine bistort (*P. viviparum*) is common on rocky soils in northern alpine regions and the Arctic. | | ■ Roots are twice twisted and are said to resemble two snakes. They contain starch and can be used to make flour. |
| ■ Fruit and peeled young shoots are edible raw.<br>■ Infuse the leaves to make tea. | ■ Wild raspberry (*R. idaeus*) fruit ripens to a bright red. Tea made from the leaves can be used to treat diarrhea. | ■ Catching yourself on thorns. | ■ Blackberries and raspberries are high in vitamin C and sugars. Blackberry leaf tea can be used to treat colds and coughs. |
| ■ Hull and grind the seeds to make buckwheat flour.<br>■ Roast seeds and cook with water to make porridge. | | ■ Buckwheat leaves are edible but can cause photosensitivity of the skin if eaten in large quantities. | |
| ■ Young leaves can be eaten raw; boil old leaves to remove the bitter taste (change the water once).<br>■ Boil the roots. | | | ■ Roots can be roasted and ground to make a substitute for coffee. The leaves are high in vitamins A and C, iron, and calcium. |
| ■ Buds and flowers are edible raw.<br>■ Chew the pulp of raw hips, or dry and eat later.<br>■ Boil leaves in water to make tea. | | ■ The hips of all wild roses (*Rosa* spp.) are edible, but do not eat the seeds if they are prickly as they will irritate the throat and stomach. | ■ Rose hips remain on the shrub all year. They are rich in vitamin C. Boil crushed hips in water then strain to make a nutritious syrup. |
| ■ Boil the plants for 10 minutes to destroy the formic acid and histamine in the stinging hairs. | ■ Dead nettles (*Lamium* spp.) are also edible if cooked. They have heart-shaped leaves and white or purple flowers. No stinging hairs. | ■ Gather and handle the plants carefully, wearing gloves if you have them, to avoid being stung by the hairs. | ■ Fresh nettles are rich in protein and vitamin K. The fibers in mature stems can be woven into cordage (see pp. 138–41). |
| ■ Boil sap into a high-energy syrup.<br>■ Eat inner bark raw or boil into a gelatinous mass, then roast and grind into a flour. | ■ Red maple (*A. rubrum*) also produces sweet sap.<br>■ White birch (*Betula* spp.) has edible inner bark. | | ■ To collect the sap, cut a V-shape into the trunk, make a hole below the cut, and insert a leaf to guide the drips into a container below. |
| ■ Crack the shell and eat the ripe nut raw. | | | ■ Rich in fat, protein, and vitamins.<br>■ Crushed green husks of black walnut (*J. nigra*) are toxic to fish. Use to poison and catch them. |
| ■ Seeds can be eaten raw or roasted. | | | ■ Water chestnuts are a source of carbohydrate. |
| ■ Ripe fruit is best eaten raw.<br>■ Boil young leaves. | | ■ Moonseed vines (*Menispermum* spp.) have grapelike fruits, which are poisonous. Unlike edible grapes, they only have one seed. | ■ Ripe grapes are rich in vitamin C and sugar. Water can be obtained from the vine stem (see p. 192). |

# WILD FOOD

**SOME OF THE PLANTS** listed below are good sources of water/liquid. In a survival situation in the desert, don't eat food if you don't have any water, as your body will use up its own water to digest it. Only eat plants that you can positively identify and, if you are in any doubt at all, carry out the Universal Edibility Test (UET) first (see pp. 206–07).

| NAME | WHERE | IDENTIFICATION | |
|---|---|---|---|
| **ACACIA/WATTLE** *Acacia* spp. | ▪ Africa, southern Asia, Australia, and the Americas. | ▪ Thorny, medium-sized trees with gray-white bark. Green leaves divided into many small, oval leaflets. Small, ball-shaped yellow, white or pink flowers. | |
| **AGAVE** *Agave* spp. | ▪ Southern USA and Mexico, Central America, the Caribbean, and northeastern South America. | ▪ Rosette of fleshy leaves with sharp tip and spiny margin. Central, tall flower stalk. | |
| **AMARANTH** *Amaranthus* spp. | ▪ The Americas, Africa, and Asia. | ▪ Tall herb with alternating leaves and erect fleshy stems. Tiny brown/black seeds (one plant produces 40,000–60,000 seeds). | |
| **BAOBAB** *Adansonia* spp. | ▪ Africa and northern Australia. | ▪ Large trees with swollen trunks, up to 30 ft (9 m) in diameter. Green leaves have 5–7 digit-like leaflets. Oblong fruit up to 8 in (20 cm) long. | |
| **CAROB TREE** *Ceratonia siliqua* | ▪ Mediterranean, northern Africa, Middle East, and India. | ▪ Evergreen tree up to 50 ft (15 m) tall. Shiny green leaves up to 8 in (20 cm) long. Small red flowers. Flat leathery seed pods; dark-green/black when ripe. Hard brown seeds. | |
| **CARRION FLOWER** *Hoodia* spp. | ▪ Southwest Africa. | ▪ Numerous thorny, succulent stems up to 6 ft (2 m) tall. Star-shaped or shallowly bell-shaped flowers give off the smell of rotting meat. | |
| **DATE PALM** *Phoenix dactylifera* | ▪ West and North Africa, Middle East, and India; introduced to Mexico and USA. | ▪ Tall slender palms with a large crown of green leaves, divided into many narrow leaflets. Fruit reddish-brown when ripe. | |
| **PRICKLY PEAR CACTUS** *Opuntia* spp. | ▪ The Americas; introduced to the Caribbean, the Mediterranean, Africa, and Australia. | ▪ Thick, jointed, flat, pad-like, green stems covered in spines. Red or yellow flowers. Fruit red when ripe. | |
| **WILD GOURDS** *Cucurbitaceae* | ▪ Kalahari Desert (Namibia), the Sahara, islands in the Mediterranean, the Middle East, and southeastern India. | ▪ Ground-trailing green vine. Bright yellow flowers. Orange-sized green or yellow fruit. | |

# DESERT PLANTS

Don't forget that some plants are edible only at certain stages of their growth. Don't eat wild plants if you have any known allergies, a preexisting medical condition, or are pregnant. When planning your trip, it's advisable to familiarize yourself with the edible plants in the region you are visiting and their seasonal availability.

| EDIBLE PART | PREPARATION | BEWARE OF | EXTRA INFORMATION |
|---|---|---|---|
| • Seeds (from dark brown pods)<br>• Young leaves and shoots | • Roast seeds.<br>• Boil leaves and shoots. | • Catching yourself on thorns. | • Roots may be tapped for water. |
| • Stalk, before in flower<br>• Buds and flowers | • Roast the stalk.<br>• Boil buds and flowers. | • Juice from many species can cause acute contact dermatitis, with reddening and blistering lasting 1–2 weeks. Leaves have needle-like ends. | • Roasted stalk tastes sweet, like molasses. |
| • Young shoots and leaves<br>• Seeds | • Eat shoots and leaves raw or boiled or stir-fried.<br>• Remove chaff from seeds, then cook like popcorn or grind into flour to make bread. | • Amaranth leaves are high in oxalic acid, which can irritate the gut and cause kidney stones, so eat in moderation. | • Amaranth leaves are a common leaf vegetable in the tropics and warm temperate regions. |
| • Shoots and young leaves<br>• Fruit<br>• Seeds | • Eat the fruit pulp raw.<br>• Boil shoots and leaves.<br>• Roast seeds. | | • Tap the trunk for water. Kalahari bushmen suck water through holes in the trunk using the hollow stems of grasses. |
| • Pods<br>• Seeds | • Eat the sweet, nutritious pulp of the pods raw.<br>• Grind the seeds into flour and make into porridge. | | |
| • Stems | • Tap the stems for their water. | | • The stems contain an appetite suppressant. Kalahari bushmen chew the stems of several *Hoodia* species before and during their long, arduous hunts. |
| • Fruit<br>• Growing tip of the palm (heart)<br>• Young leaves<br>• Sap | • Eat the fruit (dates) raw or sun-dried.<br>• Boil the leaves and heart.<br>• Boil the sap down to a syrup. | | • Date palms always grow near water. The leaves can be used to thatch a shelter. |
| • Fruit<br>• Seeds<br>• Pads | • Peel fruit and eat raw.<br>• Roast and grind seeds to a flour.<br>• Boil or grill young pads, first removing thorns by peeling or scorching over a fire. | • Spines. Avoid any similar-looking plant that has milky sap as it may be poisonous. | • The non-milky sap from the pads is a good source of water. |
| • Fruit (Tsamma melon only)<br>• Flowers<br>• Seeds<br>• Young leaves and shoots | • Pound fruit to a pulp and eat raw.<br>• Eat the flowers raw.<br>• Roast or boil seeds.<br>• Chew leaves and shoots for water. | • The fruit of the wild desert gourd or colocynth (*Citrullus colocynthis*) is very bitter and is a strong laxative. | • The Tsamma melon (*C. lanatus*) is also known as the wild watermelon. The fruit pulp is a good source of water. |

# WILD FOOD

**A GREAT NUMBER OF PLANTS** flourish in the tropics, growing all year round in the warm and humid conditions—those listed below are just a few of the most common varieties. When you plan your trip, you should familiarize yourself with the edible plants in the region you are visiting. In tropical forests, most fruits are borne high in the canopy—out of reach,

| NAME | WHERE | IDENTIFICATION | EDIBLE PART |
|---|---|---|---|
| **BAMBOO** <br> *Bambuseae* | ▪ Tropical and subtropical forests. | ▪ Tree-like grasses with woody, segmented, hollow stems ranging from black to green to gold in color. Green blade-like leaves. Species range in height from $1^2/_3$–$11^1/_2$ ft (0.5–3.5 m). | ▪ Young shoots <br> ▪ Seeds |
| **BANANA AND PLANTAIN** <br> *Musa* spp. | ▪ Native to Australia and Southeast Asia; introduced to other tropical regions. | ▪ Tree-like herbaceous plants up to 33 ft (10 m) tall. Large, green, strap-like, split leaves. Flowers and fruit grow in dense hanging clusters. | ▪ Fruit <br> ▪ Buds and flowers <br> ▪ Shoots and young stems <br> ▪ Roots |
| **BRAZIL NUT** <br> *Bertholletia excelsa* | ▪ Along river banks in rain forests in South America. | ▪ Large dry-season deciduous tree up to 150 ft (45 m) tall. Green, oblong, crinkly leaves. Yellow flowers. Fruit is the size of a coconut with a hard, woody shell and contains 8–24 seeds. | ▪ Seeds or "nuts" |
| **CEYLON/VINE SPINACH** <br> *Basella alba* | ▪ Widespread in tropical forests. | ▪ Trailing, vine-like plant reaching 100 ft (30 m) in length. Beet-red stems. Fleshy, oval or heart-shaped, green or red-purple leaves. | ▪ Young leaves and stems |
| **FIG** <br> *Ficus* spp. | ▪ Variety of habitats in tropical and subtropical regions. | ▪ Evergreen tree with long aerial roots growing from the trunk and branches. Leathery green leaves. Pear-shaped fruit grow directly from the trunk or branches. | ▪ Ripe fruit |
| **PAPAYA/PAWPAW** <br> *Carica papaya* | ▪ Native to tropical rain forests in the Americas; introduced to other tropical and some temperate regions. | ▪ Small tree up to 20 ft (6 m) high, with a soft hollow trunk. Large green leaves have seven lobes. Large melon-like fruit turn yellow or orange when ripe. | ▪ Fruit <br> ▪ Young flowers, leaves, and stems |
| **PEANUT** <br> *Arachis hypogaea* | ▪ Native to tropical rain forests in the Americas; introduced to other tropical and some temperate regions. | ▪ Small, bushy plant up to $1^2/_3$ ft (50 cm) tall. Paired, oval green leaves grow four to a stem. Yellow flowers. Underground legume (pod) contains 1–4 nuts. | ▪ Seeds or "nuts" |
| **SAGO PALM** <br> *Metroxylon sagu* | ▪ Damp lowlands of tropical rain forests in Southeast Asia; introduced elsewhere. | ▪ Spiny-trunked palm up to 33 ft (10 m) tall. Crown of pinnate (feather-like) green leaves. | ▪ Pith <br> ▪ Young shoots <br> ▪ Young nuts |
| **WATER LILY** <br> *Nymphaea* | ▪ Lakes, ponds, and rivers in tropical and subtropical regions worldwide. Also found in temperate regions. | ▪ Flat, green, heart-shaped leaves float on surface of water. Large, white, yellow, pink, or blue fragrant flowers. | ▪ Tubers <br> ▪ Stems <br> ▪ Seeds |

# TROPICAL PLANTS

unless you can climb the tree. Only eat plants that you can positively identify. If you are in any doubt at all, carry out the Universal Edibility Test (UET) first (see pp. 206–07). Don't forget that some plants are edible only at certain stages of their growth. Don't eat wild plants if you have a known allergy, a preexisting medical condition, or are pregnant.

| PREPARATION | SIMILAR PLANTS | BEWARE OF | EXTRA INFORMATION |
|---|---|---|---|
| ▪ Split the tough outer sheath of the shoots, and boil or steam. ▪ Boil the seeds or grind, mix with water, make into cakes, and bake. | | ▪ Shoots of the giant bamboo or volohosy (*Cathariostachys madagascariensis*) contain prussic acid (cyanide). | ▪ Bamboo stems often hold water (see p. 190). The stems can be used for cooking (see p. 204) and building a shelter (see p. 169). |
| ▪ Fruit and flowers are edible raw or cooked. ▪ Cook shoots, stems, and roots. | | | ▪ Banana and plantain fruit is rich in potassium and vitamins A, B6, and C. Hard, unripe plantain fruit is only edible when cooked. |
| ▪ Break fruit capsule open, crack the nut's shell, and eat raw. | ▪ The sapucaia tree (*Lecythis* spp.) produces edible seeds in a similar fruit capsule. They are called paradise nuts. | | ▪ Ripe fruit capsules fall to the ground. Rodents and monkeys are attracted to the nuts, which are rich in fats and selenium. |
| ▪ Steam, boil, stew, or stir-fry the leaves and stems. | | ▪ Don't eat too much, as the plant can have a mild laxative effect. | ▪ Young leaves and stems are rich in vitamins. |
| ▪ Eat the fruit raw or cooked. | | ▪ Don't eat any hard, woody fruit, or those covered in hairs. | ▪ Edible figs are soft when ripe and green, red, or black in color. |
| ▪ Flesh of ripe fruit is edible raw. Unripe fruit is edible cooked. ▪ Flowers, leaves, and stems must be boiled, and the water must be changed at least once. | | ▪ Don't get the milky juice of green, unripe fruit in your eyes as it will cause temporary blindness. | ▪ Ripe fruit is rich in vitamin C. Unripe fruit will ripen quickly if placed in the sun. |
| ▪ Remove the shell and eat the nuts raw. | | ▪ Don't handle or eat if you are allergic to peanuts. | ▪ Peanuts are a good source of protein, B vitamins, and minerals. |
| ▪ Crush the pith, knead it in water, strain into a pot, and let the fine sago settle. Squeeze and let it dry. Mix to a paste with boiling water. | ▪ Many palms have edible parts. The sugar palm (*Arenga pinnata*) has an edible sap which can be boiled down to a thick syrup. | ▪ Don't eat a palm's fruit unless you have positively identified it as an edible variety as the fruit of some species contain harmful crystals. | ▪ A mature palm will yield 330-660 lb (150–300 kg) of sago starch—almost pure carbohydrate. |
| ▪ Peel and slice the tubers, which can be eaten raw. ▪ Stems are best cooked. ▪ Dry and grind the seeds into flour. | ▪ All parts of the lotus (*Nelumbo* spp.) are edible raw or cooked. | | ▪ The tubers are rich in starch. The seeds have a bitter taste but they are edible. |

# WILD FOOD

**WHEN PREPARING FOR YOUR TRIP,** you should familiarize yourself with the edible plants in the region you are visiting and their seasonal availability. Only eat plants that you can positively identify and, if you are in any doubt at all, carry out the Universal Edibility Test (UET) first (see pp. 206–07). Don't forget that some plants are edible only

| | NAME | WHERE | IDENTIFICATION | |
|---|---|---|---|---|
| **LICHENS** | **ICELAND MOSS** *Cetraria islandica* | ▪ Mountainous areas in Arctic, sub-Arctic, and cold temperate regions in North America and Europe; lava slopes and plains of Iceland. | ▪ Mat-forming lichen, up to 4 in (10 cm) high. Gray-green to pale chestnut branches, rolled into tubes terminating in flattened lobes with fringed edges. | |
| | **REINDEER MOSS** *Cladonia rangiferina* | ▪ Tundra, bogs, and open woodlands in Arctic, sub-Arctic, and northern temperate regions. | ▪ Mat-forming lichen, 2–4 in (5–10 cm) high. Gray, rounded branches resemble antlers. | |
| | **ROCK TRIPE** *Umbilicaria* spp. | ▪ On rocks in Arctic, sub-Arctic, and northern temperate regions. | ▪ Rounded lichens with curling edges, usually gray or brown. | |
| **PLANTS** | **ARCTIC WILLOW** *Salix arctica* | ▪ Tundra in North America, Europe, and Asia; mountainous areas in some northern temperate regions. | ▪ Mat-forming shrub, 1–2 ft (30–60 cm) high. Rounded, shiny green leaves. Flowers grow as yellow catkins. | |
| | **BEARBERRY** *Arctostaphylos uva-ursi* | ▪ Mountainous areas in Arctic and sub-Arctic regions. | ▪ Dwarf evergreen shrub. Thick, leathery, club-shaped green leaves. Pink or white flowers. Bright red berries grow in clusters. | |
| | **BOG LABRADOR TEA** *Rhododendron groenlandicum* | ▪ Bogs and alpine areas in Arctic, sub-Arctic, and temperate regions in North America and Europe. | ▪ Evergreen shrub, 1–3 ft (30–90 cm) high. Narrow, leathery, green leaves are hairy underneath and fragrant. Small, fragrant, white flowers grow in clusters and are sticky. | |
| | **CLOUDBERRY** *Rubus chamaemorus* | ▪ Bogs, marshes, and wet meadows in alpine and sub-Arctic regions of North America, Europe, and Asia. | ▪ Perennial shrub, 4–10 in (10–25 cm) high. Soft, green leaves have 5–7 lobes. White flowers have five petals. Rasberry-sized, amber berries grow at the top of the plant. | |
| | **CROWBERRY** *Empetrum nigrum* | ▪ Tundra, moorlands, bogs, and spruce forests in Arctic, sub-Arctic, and northern temperate regions. Also found in the Andes. | ▪ Dwarf, evergreen, mat-forming shrub. Short, pale green, needle-like leaves. Small, purple-red flowers. Black berries. | |
| | **KERGUELEN CABBAGE** *Pringlea antiscorbutica* | ▪ Rocky areas of sub-Antarctic islands in the Indian and Southern Oceans. | ▪ Cabbage-like plant. | |

# PLANTS IN COLD CLIMATES

at certain stages of their growth. Don't eat wild plants if you have any known allergies, a preexisting medical condition, or are pregnant. There are no poisonous types of lichen (although see rock tripe entry, below), but they must all be soaked in water overnight and boiled well before they can be eaten.

| EDIBLE PART | PREPARATION | BEWARE OF | EXTRA INFORMATION |
|---|---|---|---|
| • All | • Soak for several hours then boil well. | • All lichens contain an acid that will cause stomach irritation unless soaked and boiled before eating. | • Lichens are low in protein but high in carbohydrates (lichen-starch). |
| • All | • Soak for several hours then boil well. | • All lichens contain an acid that will cause stomach irritation unless soaked and boiled before eating. | • High in vitamins A and B. Important source of food for reindeer (caribou). Partially digested lichens from the reindeer's stomach are considered a delicacy by herders. |
| • All | • Soak for several hours then boil well. | • There have been some reports of rock tripe poisoning so apply the Universal Edibility Test first. | |
| • Young shoots<br>• Leaves<br>• Young roots | • Peel off outer bark and eat inner shoots raw.<br>• Eat the leaves raw.<br>• Peel roots and eat raw. | | • Arctic willow leaves have 7–10 times more vitamin C than an orange. |
| • Berries | • Cook before eating. | • Bears feeding on the berries. | • Forms mats in Arctic regions. |
| • Leaves | • Infuse to make tea. | | • Pick individual leaves rather than whole branches and harvest from several shrubs. Northern Labrador tea (*R. tomentosum*) leaves also make a fragrant tea. The plant grows in peaty soils and on tundra. |
| • Berries | • Edible raw. | • Bears feeding on the berries. | • Berries initially pink, ripening to amber in fall. High in vitamin C. |
| • Berries | • Eat raw or cooked. | • Bears feeding on the berries. | • Previous year's berries will last on plant until spring if not picked. Fresh berries can be dried for storage. Low in vitamins. |
| • Leaves | • Boil well. | | • Leaves have a bitter taste so must be well-boiled. High in potassium and vitamin C. Antarctic explorers and whalers used to eat Kerguelen cabbage to ward off scurvy, hence its scientific name. |

# WILD FOOD

**THERE ARE NO POISONOUS SEAWEEDS,** but some may cause gastrointestinal upset. The seaweeds listed below are common and safe to eat if gathered when still growing, but should only be eaten in small quantities at first. Don't eat seaweed if you are short of fresh water to drink. Only eat plants that you can positively identify and, if you are in

| | NAME | WHERE | IDENTIFICATION | |
|---|---|---|---|---|
| SEAWEEDS | **GUTWEED**<br>*Enteromorpha* spp. | ▪ Saltmarshes and rock pools in cold-temperate waters worldwide. | ▪ Pale or bright green, tubular, unbranched stems, 8–16 in (20–40 cm) long. | |
| | **KELP**<br>*Alaria* spp., *Laminaria* spp., and *Macrocystis* spp. | ▪ Rocky coasts of the Atlantic and Pacific oceans. | ▪ Very long, strap-like, olive-green to brown fronds. Giant kelp (*M. pyrifera*) is the largest seaweed on Earth, reaching lengths of 150 ft (45 m). | |
| | **LAVER**<br>*Poryphyra* spp. | ▪ Rocky coasts worldwide. | ▪ Very thin, irregularly shaped membranous frond, up to 20 in (50 cm) long. Color varies from olive-green to purple-brown or blackish. | |
| SEASHORE PLANTS | **COCONUT PALM**<br>*Cocos nucifera* | ▪ Sandy, rocky, and coral coasts in tropics and subtropics worldwide. | ▪ Woody perennial tree, up to 72 ft (22 m) tall, with a crown of pinnate (feather-like) leaves. Gray trunk is ringed with growth scars. | |
| | **GLASSWORT/ MARSH SAMPHIRE**<br>*Salicornia* spp. | ▪ Salt marshes and coastal mudflats of western and eastern North America, western Europe, and the Mediterranean. | ▪ Bright green, jointed, fleshy stems, 4–12 in (10–30 cm) high. Scale-like leaves and tiny flowers are sunk into the stems. | |
| | **ORACHE/SALTBUSH**<br>*Atriplex* spp. | ▪ Sandy and shingle beaches worldwide. | ▪ Sprawling plant with spikes of small, greenish flowers. Pale- or silvery-green leaves are either triangular or spear-shaped, sometimes lobed. | |
| | **SCREW PINE**<br>*Pandanus* spp. | ▪ Tropical coasts from Madagascar to southern Asia and islands in the southwestern Pacific. | ▪ Tree up to 30 ft (9 m) tall, supported by stilt-like aerial roots. Strap-like, saw-toothed leaves are grouped in spirals. Large, globular knobbly fruit ripens from green to orange or red. | |
| | **SCURVY-GRASS**<br>*Cochlearia* spp. | ▪ Salt marshes and rocky coasts of northern North America and northern Europe and Asia. | ▪ Creeping plant, 4–16 in (10–40 cm) high, with thick, fleshy, dark green, heart-shaped leaves. Small, white, four-petaled flowers. | |
| | **SEA BEET**<br>*Beta vulgaris maritima* | ▪ Salt marshes, shingle beaches, and cliffs in Europe. | ▪ Sprawling plant up to 40 in (1 m) high, with glossy green, stems and leaves often tinged red. Tiny green flowers grow in clusters on the stems. | |
| | **SEAROCKET**<br>*Cakile* spp. | ▪ Sandy shores in North America, Europe, Asia, and Australia. | ▪ Up to 16 in (40 cm) high with deeply lobed, fleshy, green leaves. Pale lavender, four-petaled flowers. | |

# COASTAL PLANTS

any doubt at all, carry out the Universal Edibility Test (UET) first (see pp. 206–07). Don't eat wild plants if you have any known allergies, a preexisting medical condition, or are pregnant. When planning your trip, it is advisable to familiarize yourself with the edible plants in the region you are visiting and their seasonal availability.

| EDIBLE PART | PREPARATION | BEWARE OF | EXTRA INFORMATION |
|---|---|---|---|
| ▪ All | ▪ Eat raw or dry in the sun and grind to a powder, for ease of storage. | | ▪ Gutweed is a good indicator of where fresh water runs across a seashore as it is particularly abundant in such sites. |
| ▪ Fronds | ▪ Best boiled, though young fronds can be eaten raw. | ▪ Large doses of iodine can be harmful. | ▪ Sugarwrack (*L. saccharina*) tastes sweet, as its name implies, and can be eaten fried or boiled. Kelp is high in iodine, small amounts of which are needed for good health. |
| ▪ All | ▪ Boil, then mash. | | ▪ The Welsh make a cake of out of laver and oatmeal, called laverbread. The Japanese produce thousands of tons of paper-thin sheets of dried, processed laver, called nori. |
| ▪ Seeds (coconuts) | ▪ Drink the milk fresh. ▪ Eat the flesh raw or sun-dried. | ▪ Mature coconut milk needs extra water to be digested. It's also a laxative, so don't drink too much. | ▪ Green, unripe coconuts are a good source of water (see p. 190). Coconut milk is rich in sugar and vitamins and contains protein. The oily flesh is also nutritious. |
| ▪ Stems | ▪ Steam or boil. | | ▪ Also known as Poor Man's Asparagus. Rock samphire (*Crithmum maritimum*), which is found on cliffs and rocky shores, is unrelated but has edible succulent leaves. |
| ▪ Leaves | ▪ Young leaves can be eaten raw, older leaves should be boiled. | | ▪ *Atriplex* species are restricted to saline soils. As well as coasts, they are also found inland on the shores of alkaline lakes and in deserts. Gray saltbush (*A. cinerea*) is a type of bushfood in Australia. |
| ▪ Fruit | ▪ Inner flesh of ripe fruit can be eaten raw. Partly ripe fruit can be eaten if baked for two hours. | ▪ The leaves have small, thorn-like spines at the edges, which can scrape and irritate the skin. | ▪ Unripe, green fruit is inedible. |
| ▪ Leaves | ▪ Eat the leaves raw or pulp and drink. | | ▪ Scurvy-grass leaves are rich in vitamin C—sailors used to eat (or drink) them to prevent scurvy. They are very bitter, so are best leached in water, but you should eat them in a survival situation. |
| ▪ Leaves | ▪ Eat raw or boiled. | | ▪ Sea beet is the wild ancestor of beets, sugar beets, and Swiss chard. |
| ▪ Leaves ▪ Young pods | ▪ Leaves and young pods can be eaten raw. | | ▪ Searocket leaves have a peppery taste. One species of *Cakile* grows in the deserts of the Arabian Peninsula. |

# WILD FOOD

**ALL MAMMALS ARE EDIBLE,** but some species or groups of mammals are in danger of extinction and are protected by law; the mammal groups listed below contain many species that are common in their areas of distribution, and are not usually dangerous if approached and handled correctly. However, when preparing for your trip, you must

| | NAME | WHERE | IDENTIFICATION | |
|---|---|---|---|---|
| AERIAL | **BATS** *Chiroptera* | ▪ Temperate and tropical regions worldwide. | ▪ The only mammals with true wings and the ability to fly. Wingspans vary from 6 in (15 cm) to over 5 ft (1.5 m) in the large fruit bats, or flying foxes (*Megachiroptera*). | |
| TREES / GROUND | **TREE SQUIRRELS** *Sciurus* | ▪ North and South America, Europe, and temperate parts of Asia. | ▪ Small or medium-sized rodents, with large, bushy tails. | |
| TREES / GROUND | **PORCUPINES** *Hystricomorpha* | ▪ North and South America, Africa, and tropical Asia. | ▪ Large, rounded rodents, with a coat of sharp quills. | |
| GROUND / BURROWS | **ANTELOPE AND DEER** *Bovidae* and *Cervidae* | ▪ North and South America, Africa, and Eurasia. | ▪ Hoofed mammals, with long legs and barrel-shaped bodies. Male antelope have permanent horns; male deer have antlers, which they shed and regrow each year. | |
| GROUND / BURROWS | **GUINEA PIGS** *Cavia* spp. | ▪ Northwestern, central, and southeastern South America. | ▪ Small rodent, with dark, coarse fur, short legs, and no tail. | |
| GROUND / BURROWS | **HEDGEHOGS** *Erinaceinae* | ▪ Europe, Africa, and Asia; introduced to New Zealand. | ▪ Small, short-legged insectivorous mammal, with spines on back and sides of body. | |
| GROUND / BURROWS | **KANGAROOS** *Macropus* spp. | ▪ Australia. | ▪ The largest of the marsupials (pouched mammals), with long, strong tails, large back legs, and short forelegs. | |
| GROUND / BURROWS | **RABBITS AND HARES** *Leporidae* | ▪ Most habitats worldwide, from arctic tundra to semi-desert. | ▪ Small or medium-sized herbivorous mammals, with large ears and small, round, furry tails. Fur is usually brown or dark gray; the Arctic hare (*Lepus arcticus*) has a winter coat: white with black ear tips. | |
| GROUND / AQUATIC | **BEAVER** *Castor* spp. | ▪ North America and northwestern Eurasia. | ▪ Large semi-aquatic rodents, with coarse, brown fur, webbed feet, and a flat, scaly tail. | |
| GROUND / AQUATIC | **CANE RATS** *Thryonomys* spp. | ▪ Sub-Saharan Africa. | ▪ Large rodents, with coarse, brown fur and a long, naked tail. The greater cane rat (*T. swinderianus*) is semi-aquatic. | |

# MAMMALS

familiarize yourself with those mammals that can be hunted in the region you are visiting and their seasonal movements. Some countries and/or states will require you to have a hunting license or permit. For trapping and preparation methods, see pp. 216–23, and for cooking suggestions, see pp. 204–05.

| HOW TO FIND | BEWARE OF | EXTRA INFORMATION |
|---|---|---|
| ■ Active at night. Roost in colonies in caves and trees during the day. Temperate species hibernate in the winter. | ■ Sharp teeth. Some bats carry rabies or other diseases (see pp. 300–01), so cook the meat thoroughly. Bats are protected in Europe and some parts of North America. | ■ Large, plump, fruit-eating bats, such as the Indian flying-fox (*Pteropus giganteus*), are considered a delicacy in many tropical areas. |
| ■ Mostly active by day, feeding in branches and on the ground on shoots, nuts, and birds' eggs. Nest in trees in a range of woodland habitats. | ■ Sharp teeth and claws. | ■ Flying squirrels (*Pteromyini*) are nocturnal, tree-living members of the squirrel (*Sciuridae*) family. They glide from tree to tree rather than fly. |
| ■ Some New World porcupines climb trees to feed, but all Old World porcupines spend all their time on the ground across a range of habitats. | ■ Barbed quills (see p. 266 for how to remove). | ■ Slow-moving, so can easily be run down and speared. Unlike most small game, the meat is fatty rather than lean. |
| ■ Antelope are mainly found in savanna, or marshland habitats, and deer mainly in woodland, forests, or tundra. | ■ Horns or antlers. | ■ Most active at dawn and dusk. Usually live in groups. |
| ■ Feed mostly at dawn and dusk, in shrubby grassland in mountainous regions. | ■ Sharp teeth. | ■ Have communal feeding runways. Traps can be baited with leafy vegetables. |
| ■ Habitats range from woodland, hedgerows, and grassland to desert. Feed at night on small animals, such as worms and insects. | ■ Sharp spines. Usually infested with parasites, so handle carefully and cook well. | ■ Traditionally prepared for eating by covering with clay and baking in embers of a fire (see p. 205). |
| ■ Live in open savanna woodland, feeding mainly at night on vegetation. Gather at waterholes in times of drought. | ■ Sharp claws and a powerful kick. | ■ Kangaroos are protected in some Australian states, but can be hunted (if you have a permit) in others. |
| ■ Rabbits live in burrows, often in large numbers, coming above ground to feed on vegetation, using well-worn runs. Hares live above ground. | ■ Rabbits and hares may be infected with germs, so handle them carefully and cook well. Their meat is very lean, and must be eaten with green vegetables (see p. 220). | ■ In most areas, these are the first animals to try to trap. The European rabbit (*Oryctolagus cuniculus*) is an invasive pest species in Australia. |
| ■ Look for the distinctive mud-and-stick lodges in the middle of a pond or lake. Beavers leave the lodge at night to feed on water plants and trees along the riverbank. | ■ Strong, chisel-like teeth. The Eurasian beaver (*Castor fiber*) is protected in many of the countries in which it is found. | ■ Use regular runs along streams. The tail can be eaten as well as the flesh. |
| ■ Feed at night on reeds and grasses in marshland and on riverbanks, or on grasses in moist savanna, and on rocky hillsides. | ■ Sharp teeth. | ■ Cane rats are a valuable source of bush meat in West and Central Africa. "True" rats (*Rattus* spp.) are edible but often carry diseases, so handle with care. |

# WILD FOOD

**ALL BIRDS ARE EDIBLE,** although a few taste horrible (birds-of-paradise, for example), and pitohuis have poisonous feathers and skin. Some species or groups of birds are in danger of extinction and are protected by law; the bird groups listed below contain many species that are common in their areas of distribution. When planning your trip,

| NAMES | WHERE | IDENTIFICATION | |
|---|---|---|---|
| **GAMEBIRDS** <br> *Galliformes* | ▪ Worldwide, except Antarctica. | ▪ Typically have plump bodies, small heads, and short, rounded wings. Range in size from quail , which can weigh as little as 2 oz (50 g), to the wild turkey (*Meleagris galloparvo*), which can be as heavy as 22 lb (10 kg). | |
| **OSTRICH** <br> *Struthio camelus* | ▪ From West to East Africa south of the Sahara, and southern Africa. | ▪ The world's tallest and heaviest bird, reaching 220 lb (100 kg), the ostrich is flightless. Long neck and long, strong legs, with two-toed feet. Males have black and white plumage, females brown. | |
| **OWLS** <br> *Strigiformes* | ▪ Every continent, except Antarctica. | ▪ Upright posture and a flattened face with large, forward-facing eyes. Strong, hooked bill and sharp talons (claws). | |
| **PIGEONS AND DOVES** <br> *Columbiformes* | ▪ Worldwide, except the polar regions. | ▪ Plump, full-breasted bodies, with a small head and bill. Thick, soft plumage, which can be brown or gray, or brightly colored in some tropical species. | |
| **STORKS AND HERONS** <br> *Ciconiiformes* | ▪ Worldwide, except the polar regions. | ▪ All have large bodies, with long legs, long necks, and bills. Range height from 10 in (25 cm) for the smallest bitterns to 5 ft (1.5 m) for the largest storks. | |
| **VULTURES** <br> *Accipitridae* and *Cathartidae* | ▪ All continents, except Antarctica and Australasia. | ▪ Large carrion-eating birds, with large wings, powerful feet with sharp talons, and a strongly hooked bill. Head and neck is often bald or sparsely feathered. | |
| **WADERS AND GULLS** <br> *Charadriiformes* | ▪ Worldwide. | ▪ Vary greatly in size and shape, but most have subdued brown, gray, black, or white plumage. Waders (or shorebirds) usually have lightweight bodies and long legs. Gulls have compact bodies. | |
| **WATERFOWL** <br> *Anseriformes* | ▪ Worldwide, except Antarctica. | ▪ Typically have plump bodies, powerful wings, and short legs with webbed feet. Most species have a broad, flattened bill. Ducks usually have short necks, while geese and swans have long necks. | |

# BIRDS

you must familiarize yourself with those birds that can be hunted in the region you are visiting and their seasonal availability. Some countries and/or states will require you to have a hunting license or permit. For trapping and preparation methods, see pp. 226–29; for cooking suggestions, see pp. 204–05.

| HOW TO FIND | BEWARE OF | EXTRA INFORMATION |
|---|---|---|
| • Wide range of terrestrial habitats, from high mountains, to tropical forests, to Arctic tundra. | • Short but sharp beak and claws. In some species (including pheasants), the males have sharp spurs on their ankles. | • Nearly all gamebirds feed and nest on the ground. At night, many gamebirds roost in trees. |
| • Open semi-arid plains (from desert to savanna) and open woodland. | • Can run fast and deliver a powerful kick. Very protective of eggs in the nest and the young birds. | • The eggs are the largest of any bird, weighing 3 lb (1.4 kg). The nests are communal and contain up to 40 eggs. |
| • In most habitats, from tundra to dense forest. | • Sharp bill and talons. | • Most species hunt at night and roost in trees during the day. Usually nest in holes in trees, under rocky overhangs, or, sometimes, in burrows. |
| • Variety of forest habitats, from open woodland to dense, tropical rain forest, and grassland and semi-arid areas. | | • Often feed in flocks on the ground or in trees, and usually roost communally in trees. Can be taken by hand from the roost if you approach slowly and quietly. |
| • Freshwater habitats, ranging from wetlands, rivers, lakes, marshes, swamps, mangroves, and lagoons to tidal mudflats. | • Sharp bill. | • Usually feed alone at the water's edge, but often nest communally in trees. |
| • Open areas, including mountains, plains, deserts, and savannas. | • Sharp bill and talons. Handle as little as possible, as prone to parasites and infection. Boil meat for at least 30 minutes. | • Carrion eaters and scavengers, such as crows (*Corvus* spp.) and gulls (see below), can be lured into traps baited with meat. |
| • Tundra and a variety of wetland and coastal habitats, including tidal mudflats, beaches, and cliffs. | • Sharp bill. Gulls and terns will aggressively defend their nest sites. | • Most birds in this group nest on the ground or on rock ledges, laying about four well-camouflaged eggs. Often nest in large colonies. |
| • Arctic tundra, wetlands, rivers, and lakes. Ducks and swans usually feed on the water, while geese graze on the land. | • Geese and swans can be very aggressive, particularly in the breeding season. Mute swans (*Cygnus olor*) can weigh up to 26 lb (12 kg). | • Many species migrate between their breeding grounds in the Arctic and their wintering grounds further south. They molt their feathers in the late summer, rendering them flightless for a couple of weeks and thus easier to catch. |

# WILD FOOD

**SOME AMPHIBIAN AND REPTILE SPECIES** are at risk of extinction and are protected by law; the animals listed below are common in their areas of distribution, and are non-venomous. As part of preparation for your trip, it is advisable to familiarize yourself with the reptiles and amphibians in the region you are visiting. Many countries and/or states

| | NAME | WHERE | IDENTIFICATION | |
|---|---|---|---|---|
| **FROGS** | **AFRICAN CLAWED FROG** *Xenopus* spp. | ▪ Sub-Saharan Africa; introduced to North America, South America, and Europe. | ▪ Flattened, brown body, 2¼–5 in (6–13 cm) long, with a line of white "stitch marks" along the sides. Clawed toes on the muscular legs. | |
| | **AMERICAN BULLFROG** *Rana catesbeiana* | ▪ North America; introduced to Europe and Asia. | ▪ Body is green with brown markings above and white below, 3½–8 in (9–20 cm) long. Large legs and large eardrums. | |
| | **SOUTH AMERICAN BULLFROG** *Leptodactylus pentadactylus* | ▪ Central and northern South America. | ▪ Smooth yellow or pale brown body with some dark markings, 3–9 in (8–22 cm) long. | |
| **TURTLES** | **AFRICAN HELMETED TURTLE** *Pelomedusa subrufa* | ▪ Sub-Saharan Africa. | ▪ Flattened, brown shell, 8–12½ in (20–32 cm) long. | |
| | **ASIAN LEAF TURTLE** *Cyclemus dentata* | ▪ Southeast Asia. | ▪ Oval, light to dark brown shell, 6–9½ in (15–24 cm) long, with serrated edge near tail. Reddish brown head and legs. | |
| | **PAINTED TURTLE** *Chrysemys picta* | ▪ Southern Canada, USA, and northern Mexico. | ▪ Flattened, smooth shell, 6–10 in (15–25 cm) long; brown above and yellow below, sometimes patterned. Yellow or red stripes on the neck. | |
| **SNAKES** | **CARPET PYTHON** *Morelia spilota* | ▪ Indonesia, New Guinea, and Australia. | ▪ Several subspecies, all of which have a bold pattern of irregular markings, which can be reddish brown, brown, black or gray. Average length is 6½ ft (2 m), but can reach 13 ft (4 m). | |
| | **COMMON BOA** *Boa constrictor* | ▪ Central America, South America, and some Caribbean islands. | ▪ Several subspecies but all have characteristic dark saddle markings along the back and a dark stripe behind each eye. Narrow head and pointed snout. | |
| | **COMMON EGG-EATING SNAKE** *Dasypeltis scabra* | ▪ Sub-saharan Africa | ▪ Reddish-brown or gray body with dark, angular markings. A slender snake, 28–39 in (70–100 cm) long. Rounded snout. | |
| | **COMMON RATSNAKE** *Elaphe obsoleta* | ▪ Southern Canada, and central and eastern USA | ▪ Subspecies coloration varies from bright yellow-orange to pale gray with darker blotches. Length range is 4–6 ft (1.2–1.8 m). Long head with rounded snout. | |
| **LIZARDS** | **COMMON/VIVIPAROUS LIZARD** *Zootoca vivipara* | ▪ Europe, extending to the Arctic Circle. and central to eastern Asia, including Japan. | ▪ Body is usually brown olive, sometimes black, with males having bright yellow or orange bellies and females creamy white ones. Length range is 4–7 in (10–18 cm) | |
| | **GREEN IGUANA** *Iguana iguana* | ▪ Central America and northern South America. | ▪ Green or grayish body, 3¼–6½ ft (1–2 m) long, including the long striped tail. Long, stout legs for climbing trees. Adults have a fleshy dewlap beneath the throat, which is large in males. | |
| | **RAINBOW LIZARD** *Agama agama* | ▪ West, Central, and East Africa. | ▪ Males turn brightly colored in the sun, with an orange-red head and a blue or turquoise body; females and juvenile males remain gray. Length range is 12–16 in (30–40 cm). | |
| | **WESTERN FENCE LIZARD** *Sceloporus occidentalis* | ▪ Southwestern USA and northwestern Mexico. | ▪ Brown body with raised, pointed scales. Blue patches on belly are most pronounced in males. Length range is 6–9 in (15–23 cm). | |

# AMPHIBIANS AND REPTILES

will require you to have a hunting license or permit. See p. 218 for some trapping methods and p. 224 for how to prepare the animal for cooking. Avoid brightly colored tropical frogs as they are often highly toxic. In addition, don't eat box turtles, as they sometimes eat poisonous fungi and their flesh may be toxic.

| HOW TO FIND | SIMILAR SPECIES | EXTRA INFORMATION |
|---|---|---|
| Wetlands and waterholes in savannas and tropical and subtropical forests. | | Also known as the African clawed toad. |
| Wetlands. | All frogs in the *Rana* genus are edible. The genus includes New World true frogs and the European common frog (*R. temporaria*). | American bullfrog legs can be the size of chicken drumsticks. All temperate species of frog hibernate in the winter. |
| Tropical forests and rain forests. | | Active at night. If picked up, the South American bullfrog emits a loud scream to startle the predator into dropping it. |
| Watering holes and rain pools in open country. | | In the rainy season, this turtle wanders from pool to pool to forage. In the dry season, it buries itself in mud. |
| Shallow streams in mountains or lowlands. | | Very active on land and in water. |
| Lakes, ponds, and slow-moving streams and rivers. | | Active by day. You will often find several painted turtles piled up together on a log in the water, basking in the sun. |
| Wide range of habitats. | | The carpet python is non-venomous, but it can inflict a nasty bite. It is one of Australia's most widespread snakes. |
| Wide range of habitats, from tropical forest to dry savanna. | There are several species in the boa family, which includes the world's largest snake, the green anaconda (*Eunectes murinus*). | Kills its prey by coiling around it and suffocating it. Don't tackle large common boas—they can be up to 13 ft (4 m) long. |
| Desert and open habitats. | | This nocturnal African snake feeds on eggs during the bird-breeding season then fasts for the rest of the year. It has no teeth. |
| Rocky hillsides with open woodland. | Ratsnakes (*Elaphe* spp.), which include the brightly colored corn snake (*E. guttata*), are found in both the New and Old Worlds. | Like the common boa (see above), all ratsnakes kill their prey by constriction. |
| Wide range of terrestrial habitats. | | There's no point trying to catch a common lizard by its tail as, like many lizards, it can shed the tail and regrow it. |
| Tropical forest and rain forest. | | Defends itelf by lashing out with its tail and claws. |
| Open habitats. | | Rainbow lizard can shed and regrow its tail. |
| On rocks and other prominent places in temperate and coniferous woodlands. | The eastern fence lizard (*S. undulatus*) is widely distributed across southeastern USA and northeastern Mexico. | Fence lizard can shed and regrow its tail. |

# WILD FOOD

**WHEN PLANNING YOUR TRIP,** it is advisable to familiarize yourself with the species of fish in the region you are visiting, their seasonal availability, and the best method of catching them (see pp. 208–09 for how to make tackle and techniques to use in a survival situation). Many countries and/or states will require you to have a fishing

| NAME | WHERE | IDENTIFICATION | |
|---|---|---|---|
| **BARRAMUNDI** <br> *Lates calcarifer* | ▪ Western and eastern Indian Ocean, and northwestern and western Pacific Ocean. | ▪ Up to 6½ ft (2 m) long, with a rounded tail fin. Dark greenish-gray upper body fading to silver below. | |
| **COMMON/BRONZE BREAM** <br> *Abramis brama* | ▪ Europe to Central Asia. | ▪ Up to 2¾ ft (82 cm) long, with a deep, narrow, bronze-colored body and a deeply forked tail. | |
| **COMMON/KING CARP** <br> *Cyprinus carpio* | ▪ Europe and Asia; introduced in North America and Australasia. | ▪ Up to 5 ft (1.5 m) long, with a dark gold upper body paling to silver below. | |
| **EUROPEAN TURBOT** <br> *Psetta maxima* | ▪ Northeast Atlantic Ocean up to the Arctic Circle and the Mediterranean. | ▪ Almost circular flatfish, up to 3¼ ft (1 m) in diameter. Sandy brown with brown or black speckles on top. | |
| **NILE PERCH** <br> *Lates niloticus* | ▪ Northern, central, and eastern Africa. | ▪ Up to 6¼ ft (1.9 m) long, with a rounded tail fin. Dark gray-blue upper body fading to silver below. | |
| **RUDD** <br> *Scardinius erythrophthalmus* | ▪ Europe and Asia. | ▪ Up to 17 in (45 cm) long, with a deeply forked tail. Dark greenish upper body paling to silver below. Red pelvic, pectoral, and anal fins. | |
| **ATLANTIC SALMON** <br> *Salmo salar* | ▪ North Atlantic and Arctic oceans, and Baltic Sea and adjacent rivers; introduced to Argentina and Australasia. | ▪ Up to 5 ft (1.5 m) long, with a powerful, streamlined, silver blue-green body. | |
| **TARPON** <br> *Megalops atlanticus* | ▪ Eastern and western Atlantic Ocean, the Gulf of Mexico, and the Caribbean. | ▪ Up to 8 ft (2.5 m) long, with a deeply forked tail. Bright silver body, with large, hard scales. | |
| **TENCH** <br> *Tinca tinca* | ▪ Europe and Asia; introduced in North America. | ▪ Olive green upper body, golden below, with a square tail fin. Small barbel at corners of mouth. Average length is 27 in (70 cm). | |
| **BROWN TROUT AND SEA TROUT** <br> *Salmo trutta* | ▪ Temperate waters worldwide. | ▪ Streamlined body with an average length of 3¼ ft (1 m). The brown trout has a brownish body flecked with distinctive black and red spots. The sea-going form, the sea trout, is silver-blue with black spots. | |

license or permit, and some species of fish can only be caught at certain times of the year. Before fishing, you should also check with the locals that fish in the area are safe to eat—in some regions the waters may be contaminated. See pp. 212–13 for how to prepare a fish for cooking.

| HOW TO FIND | SIMILAR FISH | EXTRA INFORMATION |
|---|---|---|
| ▪ Tropical, slow-moving creeks and estuaries, hiding in mangrove roots and rocky outcrops. | | ▪ Beware of the sharp dorsal fin. |
| ▪ Bottom of still and slow-moving waters, typically in lakes, rivers and ponds. Swim in large shoals. | ▪ Silver bream (*Blicca bjoerkna*) and white-eye bream (*Abramis sapa*). | |
| ▪ Still and slow-moving waters, often among vegetation near banks of lakes or ponds. | ▪ Wild carp, mirrored carp, and leather carp are all varieties of the common carp. | |
| ▪ Sandy, rocky, or mixed sea beds in shallow coastal and brackish water. | ▪ Other flatfish (*Pleuronectiformes*) found in shallow water, such as sole, plaice, and flounder. | |
| ▪ Lakes and large rivers. | ▪ Other perch (*Perciformes*). | ▪ Beware of the sharp dorsal fin and teeth (the Nile perch is a voracious predator). This species weighs up to 440 lb (200 kg). |
| ▪ Still and slow-moving waters, often near banks of ponds and marshlands. | ▪ Roach (*Rutilus rutilus*) | |
| ▪ Cold, fast-flowing rivers and coastal waters. | ▪ Pacific salmon (*Oncorhynchus* spp.) | ▪ The salmon run (when the fish migrate from the sea to their birth rivers) is in the autumn, with spawning between November and January. |
| ▪ Estuaries, lagoons, tidal flats and mangrove swamps. Feed in shoals. | ▪ Indo-Pacific tarpon (*M. cyprinoides*), which is smaller and rarer. | ▪ This species is hard to hook because of its bony mouth. It weighs up to 160kg (350lb). |
| ▪ Still and slow-moving waters, in ponds, lakes and rivers. The best time of day to catch tench is at dawn, at the edges of dense vegetation. | | |
| ▪ Streams, rivers, lakes, and coastal waters. | ▪ Rainbow trout and steelhead trout (*Oncorhynchus mykiss*) and the cutthroat trout (*O. clarki*). | ▪ Sea-going forms migrate from the sea to rivers to spawn in the autumn. Beware of small bones when eating. |

# WILD FOOD

**SOME SPECIES OF INVERTEBRATE** are in danger of extinction and are protected by law; the animals listed below are common in their areas of distribution. When preparing for your trip, it is advisable to familiarize yourself with the edible invertebrates in the region you are visiting and the best way to catch them (see p. 219 for some techniques to use in a survival

| | NAME | WHERE | IDENTIFICATION |
|---|---|---|---|
| **MOLLUSCS** | **COMMON/BLUE MUSSEL** *Mytilus edulis* | • Intertidal zones of estuaries and coasts of North and southeastern Atlantic and northeastern and southwestern Pacific. | • Dark-shelled bivalve, reaching 4–6 in (10-15 cm) in length. |
| | **GIANT AFRICAN LAND SNAILS** *Achatina* spp. | • Sub-tropical and tropical parts of Africa; introduced to the Asia-Pacific region. | • Large terrestrial snails, reaching up to 12 in (30 cm) in length when body is extended, and 4 in (10 cm) in diameter. Whorled, conical, brownish shell with darker bands. |
| **ARTHROPODS** | **GRASSHOPPERS** *Acrididae* | • Worldwide, on vegetation and the ground. | • Winged insects with powerful hindlegs, ²/₅–3¹/₄ in (1–8 cm) long, usually with camouflage coloring and patterning. |
| | **HONEYPOT/HONEY ANTS** *Myrmecocystus* spp. | • Semi-arid and arid regions of southwest USA, Mexico, Africa, and Australia. | • Segmented bodies with six legs and a pair of antennae, and a constricted waist. Range in colour and size, from ¹/₁₀–¹/₂ in (2–12mm). Special members of the colony, called repletes, have abdomens that can swell to the size of a grape. |
| | **WITCHETTY GRUB** *Endoxyla leucomochla* | • Underground, in the roots of the witchetty bush (*Acacia kempeana*), central Australia. | • The larva of this species of cossid moth reaches about 2³/₄ in (7 cm) in length. It is white with a brown head. |
| **CRUSTACEANS** | **CRAYFISH/CRAWFISH/ YABBIES/KOURAS** *Astaclidea* | • Worldwide, in freshwater streams. | • Segmented bodies, which can be sandy yellow, green, dark brown, or blue-gray in color. Ten legs, the front two of which are large claws. Average length is 4 in (8 cm), but some species grow much larger. |
| | **WOODLICE** *Oniscidea* and *Armadillidiidae* | • Worldwide, in damp terrestrial microhabitats, such as in rotting wood and leaf litter. | • Flattened, segmented bodies up to ³/₄ in (2 cm) in length. Gray or light brown or black in color. Pill millipedes will roll up into a ball when threatened. |
| **WORMS** | **COMMON EARTHWORM** *Lumbricus terrestris* | • Temperate regions of Europe; introduced to most parts of the world. | • Reddish worm, reaching 14 in (35 cm) in length when extended. |

# INVERTEBRATES

situation). Many countries and/or states will require you to have a hunting license or permit, and some species of shellfish can only be caught at certain times of the year. Also check with the locals that the shellfish are safe to eat—in some regions the waters may be contaminated. See pp. 224–25 for some preparation and cooking methods.

| SIMILAR INVERTEBRATES | BEWARE OF | EXTRA INFORMATION |
|---|---|---|
| • Most species of marine and freshwater bivalves and univalves are edible if alive and healthy when gathered. | • Don't collect marine shellfish that aren't covered at high tide. The black mussel (*Musculus niger*), found in Arctic waters, can be poisonous year-round. Mussels in tropical zones are poisonous during the summer. | • Healthy bivalves should close their shells when tapped and the shells should open when cooked. Healthy univalves, such as limpets, should be difficult to pry off the rocks on which they live. |
| • Many terrestrial and freshwater snails are edible. The winkle or common periwinkle (*Littorina littorea*) is an edible sea snail. | • Avoid any terrestrial snails with brightly colored shells and all sea snails unless you can positively identify them as an edible species, as they may be poisonous. | • Snails should be starved for 24 hours or fed a diet of edible green leaves to purge their guts before cooking. Boil for at least 10 minutes. |
| • Most species of cricket (*Gryllidae*) and katydid (*Tettigoniidae*) are edible. | • Avoid any brightly colored grasshoppers as they may be toxic. | • Remove the antennae, wings, and leg spurs, and roast to kill any parasites. |
| • Most species of ant are edible if gathered carefully. The larvae of wood ants (*Formica* spp.) in northern temperate regions make a nutritious meal in summer months. The abdomen of the green or weaver ant (*Oecophylla smaragdina*) found in southeast Asia and Australia tastes like citrus sherbert. Termites (*Isoptera*) are also edible. See p. 219 for catching methods. | • Most species of ant are aggressive in defense of their nest and have a stinging bite. Some will then squirt formic acid at the site of the bite. | • The swollen abdomens of the repletes contain a nutritious fluid.<br>• The repletes live deep underground in the ants' nest so you would have to dig them out. |
| • The term "witchetty grub" is also applied to the edible larvae of other cossid moths, ghost moths (*Hepialidae*), and longhorn beetles (*Cerambycidae*). Palm grubs are the edible larvae of the palm weevil (*Rhynchophorus* Spp.). They live in the trunks of sago palms (see pp. 284–285) in Southeast Asia. | • Do not eat any insect larvae that are already dead when you find them, or that look sick, smell bad, or that irritate the skin if handled. | • Should be eaten raw or roasted quickly in hot embers. |
| • Marine decapods such as crabs, lobsters, and prawns are also edible. | • May contain harmful parasites so cook well. | • Keep alive until ready to eat. See p. 225 for preparation and cooking methods. |
| | | • Boil or fry gently. Will turn slightly pink, like shrimp, when cooked. |
| • All earthworms are edible. | | • The common earthworm is unusual in that it feeds at the surface, making it easier to find and gather than other worms. |

# NATURAL DANGERS

**FOR INFORMATION ON LARGER** dangerous animals, such as bears, big cats, and sharks, and venomous animals, such as snakes, see pp. 242–43. When planning your trip, it is advisable to familiarize yourself with the potentially harmful wildlife in the region you are visiting, the nature of the threat, and how to avoid it if possible. In the case of suspected

| | NAME | WHERE | IDENTIFICATION | |
|---|---|---|---|---|
| **MAMMALS** | **VAMPIRE BATS** *Desmodontinae* | ▪ In rain forests, deserts, and grasslands, from Mexico to northern and central South America. | ▪ Small bats, with a body length of 2¾–3½ in (7–9 cm) and a wingspan of 14–16 in (35–40 cm). Dark brownish gray fur, paler on the belly. Razor-like upper incisors. | |
| | **RATS** *Rattus* spp. | ▪ Worldwide, except for the polar regions. | ▪ Medium-sized rodents, with a minimum body length of 5 in (12 cm), and long, naked tails. Coarse brown, gray-brown, or black fur, paler on belly. Pink feet. | |
| **SNAKES** | **SPITTING COBRAS AND RINKHALS** *Naja* spp. and *Hemachatus haemachatus* | ▪ Warm temperate, subtropical, and tropical regions of Asia and Africa. | ▪ Pale brown to black snakes up to 6 ft (2 m) long. When threatened, will rear up and spread their hoods, revealing striped patterns on their necks. | |
| **FISH** | **ELECTRIC EEL** *Electrophorus electricus* | ▪ Amazon and Orinoco river systems, South America, often in shallow water. | ▪ Not a true eel, but an eel-like fish up to 8¼ ft (2.5 m) long and can be as thick as a human thigh. Continuous fin along lower body. | |
| | **STONEFISH** *Synanceia verrucosa* | ▪ In tropical coastal waters of northern Indian Ocean and southwestern Pacific Ocean. | ▪ Up to 16 in (40 cm) long, this lumpy fish can match its color to the rock or sediment on which it lies while waiting for passing prey. Venomous spines in the dorsal fin. | |
| **OTHER ANIMALS** | **BOX JELLYFISH/ SEA WASPS** *Cubomedusae* | ▪ At the surface of tropical waters of southwest Pacific and eastern Indian Ocean. | ▪ Box-shaped, transparent jellyfish, up to 10 in (25 cm) in diameter. Up to 15 long tentacles, which bear stinging cells, at each corner. | |
| | **CENTIPEDES** *Chilopoda* | ▪ In soil, leaf litter, cracks, and crevices in temperate, subtropical, and tropical regions worldwide. | ▪ Elongated, flattened bodies divided into at least 16 segments, most of which have one pair of legs. Tropical species are typically brightly colored—yellow, red, orange, or green—with dark stripes. The world's largest centipede, *Scolpendra gigantea*, reaches 12 in (30 cm) in length. | |
| | **CONE SHELLS/ CONE SNAILS** *Conidae* | ▪ In inter-tidal zones and on coral reefs in warm temperate, subtropical, and tropical seas and oceans worldwide. | ▪ Brightly colored and patterned, cone-shaped shells, up to 9 in (23 cm) long. These predatory snails have venomous, harpoon-like mouthparts. | |

# WILD ANIMALS

poisoning, call the emergency services immediately. For further information regarding treatment for bites and stings, see pp. 266–67. If a casualty becomes unconscious, open the airway and check breathing (see p. 276). Be ready to begin CPR—chest compressions and rescue breaths (see p. 277), use a plastic face mask or face shield, if you have one.

| DANGER | TREATMENT | HOW TO AVOID |
|---|---|---|
| • Many mammal species are infected with rabies, but because vampire bats feed by biting their victims, then lapping blood from the wound, the virus can be transmitted via their saliva. Symptoms include fever, headache, fear (especially of water), and seizures. | • If bitten by a vampire bat, or other potentially rabid mammal, clean the wound thoroughly and seek immediate medical help. Symptoms usually appear 2–8 weeks after infection, by which time the disease is almost always fatal. | • Vampire bats roost in hollow trees and caves, emerging at night to feed. Don't shelter in bat caves (bat dung can cause a respiratory disease). Keep covered at night, and sleep under a mosquito net. Get vaccinated before traveling to a high-risk area. |
| • Can be infested with parasites and can also carry infectious diseases. Leptospirosis is a water-borne bacterial disease spread by infected rats' urine; the acute form in humans is called Weil's disease. | • If you've been in contact with potentially contaminated water and develop flu-like symptoms (fever, headache, muscle pain) you must get your blood tested as soon as possible. Antibiotics are effective in the early stages of the disease. | • If handling a rat, beware of its teeth and claws, and wash thoroughly afterward. Cook the meat thoroughly. In rat-infested areas avoid getting water into any cuts; if you do, wash with soap and boiled water. |
| • Will eject a fine spray of venom from their fangs upward the eyes of an aggressor. Causes intense pain, tearing, and discharge from the eyes, spasm and swelling of the eyelids. Ulceration of the cornea can lead to infection resulting in blindness. | • Call the emergency services. Rinse the eyes with cool water for 10 minutes. Apply an antibiotic eye ointment. | • If you come across a spitting cobra, try to remain completely still and allow the snake to move away, if possible (see p. 243). |
| • Can generate shocks of up to 600 volts, used to stun or kill prey when hunting, or in self-defense. Such a shock can be discharged up to 8 hours after its death, and is potentially lethal to humans. | • Call the emergency services. If the casualty becomes unconscious, open the airway and check breathing (see p. 276). Be ready to begin CPR (see p. 277). | • Keep your boots on if crossing a tributary and take care when washing. These waters are also home to piranhas (*Serrasalminae*), which have razor-sharp teeth. |
| • The world's most venomous fish. If trodden on, the spines inject poison into the puncture wound. This is extremely painful and can be fatal. The injured body part will swell and muscular paralysis may set in. | • Call the emergency services—anti-venin is available. Immerse the injured part in water as hot as the casualty can stand for at least 30 minutes (see p. 267). Don't immobilize the injured limb. Be ready to begin CPR if the casualty loses consciousness (see pp. 276–77). | • Wear something on your feet when walking in shallow water. Weaverfish (*Trachinidae*) and scorpionfish (*Scorpaenidae*) also have venomous stings; the treatment is the same. |
| • Sting is extremely painful—it will damage the skin and can cause permanent scarring. In severe cases, box jellyfish (*Chironex fleckeri*) stings can lead to cardiac arrest and death within minutes. | • Call the emergency services—anti-venin is available. Flood the stung area with vinegar or sea water for at least 30 seconds to neutralize the stinging cells (see p. 267). Be ready to begin CPR if the casualty loses consciousness (see pp. 276–77). | • Never touch jellyfish, even when dead. All jellyfish, sea anemones, corals, and the Portuguese man-of-war (*Physalia physalis*) release venomous cells when touched. Some are more toxic than others. |
| • Have a pair of large, venomous claws on their heads, which in some species can be dangerous to humans. The sting is painful and leads to swelling. May result in anaphylactic shock. | • Call the emergency services. Apply a cold compress for at least 10 minutes to reduce pain and swelling. Monitor the casualty for anaphylactic shock (see p. 274) and be ready to begin CPR (see p. 277). | • As a general rule, avoid all multiple-legged arthropods. If you discover one on your body, gently brush it off in the direction in which it is walking. |
| • Will fire its harpoon in self-defense if touched. Sting of most species is painful; that of the larger tropical species can be fatal. Symptoms include swelling and numbness, and may be followed by severe breathing difficulties. | • Call the emergency services and treat as for snake bite (see p. 266). Monitor the casualty for shock (see p. 274) and be ready to begin CPR (see p. 277). | • Don't pick up any cone shells in rock pools or when snorkeling or diving. (There is no anti-venin: treatment entails providing life support until the venom is metabolized by the casualty's body.) |

# NATURAL DANGERS

**IN THE CASE OF SUSPECTED POISONING** from a spider bite or a scorpion sting, you must call the emergency services immediately. For further information regarding treatment for bites and stings, see pp. 266–67. If a casualty becomes unsconscious, open the airway and check breathing (see p. 276). Be ready to begin CPR—chest compressions and rescue

| | NAME | WHERE | IDENTIFICATION | |
|---|---|---|---|---|
| **INSECTS** | **BEES, WASPS, AND HORNETS** *Hymenoptera* | ▪ In a variety of terrestrial habitats worldwide. | ▪ Narrow-waisted bodies, often striped black and yellow. Bees are hairy, while wasps and hornets have hairless bodies. Up to 1½ in (3.5 cm) long. Bees have barbed stingers, wasps and hornet stingers are smooth. | |
| | **MOSQUITOES** *Culicidae* | ▪ In a variety of terrestrial habitats near water worldwide, especially in warmer regions. | ▪ Narrow bodies and long, slender legs. Up to ¾ in (2 cm) long. Females have syringe-like mouthparts for piercing skin. | |
| **ARACHNIDS** | **BROWN RECLUSE/ FIDDLEBACK SPIDER** *Loxosceles reclusa* | ▪ Southern midwestern states of USA, south to the Gulf of Mexico. | ▪ Small brown spider, about ½ in (1.25 cm) long) with a distinctive dark, violin-shaped mark on the back of its cephalothorax (head). | |
| | **FUNNEL-WEB SPIDERS** *Atrax robustus* and *Hadronyche* spp. | ▪ Moist, cool, sheltered habitats in eastern and southern Australia. | ▪ Large spiders, up to 1½ in (4.5 cm) long, with glossy dark brown or black bodies and short legs. | |
| | **TARANTULAS** *Theraphosidae* | ▪ Deserts and forests in subtropical and tropical regions worldwide. | ▪ Very large spiders with bodies up to 5 in (12 cm) long and a legspan of up to 11 in (28 cm). Bodies and legs are covered in bristly hairs. Pale brown to black in color, with pink, red, brown, or black markings. | |
| | **WIDOW SPIDERS** *Latrodectus* spp. | ▪ Warm temperate, subtropical, and tropical regions worldwide. | ▪ Small spiders, with dark, glossy bodies and distinctive red, yellow, or white markings on the abdomen, which are shaped like an hourglass in some species. | |
| | **SCORPIONS** *Scorpiones* | ▪ Deserts, grasslands, woodland, and forests in warm temperate, subtropical, and tropical regions worldwide. | ▪ Segmented bodies, with large, claw-like pedipalps and sting-bearing tails. Yellow, brown, or black bodies, 3–8 in (8–20 cm) long, depending on the species. | |
| | **TICKS** *Ixodidae* | ▪ Grassland and woodland habitats worldwide. | ▪ Rounded bodies with no distinct divisions. Yellow to red– or black–brown in color. Up to ⅖ in (1 cm) long, but larger after feeding. They have spiked mouthparts, which they use to attach themselves to the skin of warm-blooded animals to feed on their blood. | |

# INSECTS AND ARACHNIDS

breaths (see p. 277). If you need to give rescue breaths and there is poison in the casualty's mouth, or on his or her face, use a plastic face mask or face shield, if you have one. Before your trip, it is advisable to familiarize yourself with the harmful insects and arachnids (spiders, scorpions, and ticks) in the region you are visiting, and the nature of the threat.

| DANGER | TREATMENT | HOW TO AVOID |
|---|---|---|
| ■ When a bee stings you, the stinger is ripped out of its body with the venom sac. Wasps and hornets can sting repeatedly. The stings are painful, followed by redness and swelling. A single sting may result in anaphylactic shock (see p. 274) | ■ Scrape the sting off sideways at the base of the sting if it is visible, using a fingernail or a credit card. Raise the affected part and place a cold compress against it for at least 10 minutes (see p. 267). Monitor for signs of allergic reaction. | ■ Watch out for flowers where bees may be feeding. Be careful when gathering fruit, or cleaning fish or game, as wasps or hornets will be attracted to the smell. Don't disturb their nests. |
| ■ Female mosquitoes feed on blood and their bites can irritate the skin. They are carriers of infectious diseases such as malaria, yellow fever, and dengue fever. | ■ Apply an antihistamine cream to the bites if they itch, and do not scratch them, as there is a risk of infection. If casualty develops a headache and fever, get medical help. Get casualty to rest, drink plenty of water, and take anti-malarials, if directed. | ■ Cover your arms and legs after sunset, use mosquito repellent, and sleep under a mosquito net. Take anti-malarial medication as directed. Get a yellow fever vaccination before traveling, where advised. |
| ■ Bite can cause fever, chills, vomiting, and, pain in the joints. In most cases the bite is minor, but in some cases the tissue around the wound will die, leaving a deep scar. Rarely fatal. | ■ Sit casualty down, treat as for snakebite (see p. 266), and call the emergency services. Apply a cold compress to the site of the sting. Monitor for signs of allergic reaction, such as wheezing, and anaphylactic shock (see p. 274). | ■ This spider likes to hide in dark places, so be careful where you put your hands and bare feet, and always check your bedding. |
| ■ Bite is very painful and cause profuse sweating, nausea, vomiting, tingling around the mouth and tongue, salivation, and weakness. Rarely fatal. | ■ Sit casualty down, treat as for snakebite (see p. 266), and call the emergency services— anti-venin is available. Monitor for signs of allergic reaction and anaphylactic shock (see p. 274). | ■ Take care when moving rocks and logs. |
| ■ Bite can be painful but is only mildly venomous. If provoked, tarantulas will flick irritating hairs from their abdomen which will cause itching and swelling of the skin and nasal passages, and watering of the eyes. | ■ Give pain relief and apply a cold compress to the site of the bite. Monitor for signs of allergic reaction, such as wheezing, and anaphylactic shock (see p. 274). Wash any hairs away with cool water. | ■ Tarantulas are nocturnal and hunt prey in trees and on the ground. Move away if you disturb one; don't touch it. |
| ■ Bite is painful and results in localized redness and swelling. More severe reactions include profuse sweating, abdominal and chest pains, nausea, and vomiting. Rarely fatal. | ■ Apply a cold compress (ice if available) and give pain relief. If symptoms worsen, call the emergency services – anti-venin is available. Monitor for signs of allergic reaction, such as wheezing, and anaphylactic shock (see p. 274). | ■ Widow spiders, which include Australia's redback spider (*L. hasselti*), build their webs in dry, sheltered spots, such as in shrubs or among rocks or logs, so take care when moving among them. |
| ■ Scorpion stings can be very painful and may cause severe illness. A few species have neurotoxins in their venom, resulting in temporary paralysis for 1–2 days. Rarely fatal and only in young children, the elderly, or the ill or infirm. | ■ If swelling occurs, sit casualty down, treat as for snake bite (see p. 266). Apply an ice pack or cold compress to the site of the sting. Call the emergency services, monitor for anaphylactic shock (see p. 274) and allergic reaction. Try to identify the scorpion. | ■ Scorpions are mostly nocturnal and take shelter during the day. Check your boots and clothing before putting them on and check your bedding at night. Take care when gathering firewood or turning over rocks. |
| ■ Ticks are carriers of infectious diseases such as Lyme disease and Rocky Mountain spotted fever. Sufferers of Lyme disease may develop a red, ringed "bull's-eye" skin lesion at the bite site. | ■ Carefully remove an attached tick with tweezers or a specialized tool (see p. 267). Clean and monitor the wound for symptoms. Get medical help if casualty develops a severe headache, stiff neck, or a fever. | ■ Wear light-shaded, tightly woven clothing and apply tick repellent. Check your skin and clothing for ticks at regular intervals. |

# NATURAL DANGERS

**IN THE CASE OF SUSPECTED PLANT POISONING,** you must call the emergency services immediately. If a casualty becomes unconscious, open the airway and check their breathing (see p. 276). Be ready to begin CPR—chest compressions and rescue breaths (see p. 277). If you need to give rescue breaths, use a plastic face mask or face shield, if you have one, to

| | NAME | WHERE | IDENTIFICATION | POISONOUS PART | |
|---|---|---|---|---|---|
| **CONTACT POISONING** | **COWHAGE/COWAGE/ COWITCH** *Mucana pruriens* | ▪ Scrub and light woodland in the the tropics and USA. | ▪ Vine-like plant with green, oval leaflets growing in threes. Spikes of hairy, dull purplish flowers. Hairy brown seedpods. | ▪ Flowers ▪ Pods | |
| | **POISON IVY** *Toxicodendron radicans* | ▪ Wooded areas in North America; widely introduced elsewhere. | ▪ See p. 268 for illustration. | ▪ All | |
| | **WHITE/GRAY MANGROVE** *Avicennia marina* | ▪ Mangrove swamps from tropical Africa to Indonesia and Australasia. | ▪ Slender tree with pale bark and long aerial roots. Green, oblong, leathery leaves. Yellow flowers and fleshy, pale orange seed capsules. | ▪ Sap | |
| **INGESTION POISONING** | **BANEBERRY** *Actaea* spp. | ▪ Temperate woodland in the northern hemisphere. | ▪ Low shrub with, toothed green leaves. Small white flowers. White, black, or red berries grow in clusters. | ▪ All, but the berries are the most poisonous. | |
| | **CASTOR OIL PLANT/ CASTOR BEAN** *Ricinus communis* | ▪ Throughout the tropics in scrub and wasteland; introduced to temperate regions. | ▪ Tall shrub with glossy dark green or dark purple, star-like leaves. Spikes of yellow flowers. Spiky red pods. | ▪ All, but the seeds contain particularly high levels of the poison ricin. | |
| | **DEATH CAMAS/ DEATH LILY** *Zigadenus* spp. | ▪ Grassy, wooded, and rocky areas in temperate regions of North America. | ▪ Long grass-like leaves arise from a bulb. Flowers have six white petals with a green heart at base. | ▪ All | |
| | **PANGI** *Pangium edule* | ▪ Tropical forests in Southeast Asia. | ▪ Tall tree with green, heart-shaped leaves. Green flower spikes. Large brownish pear-shaped fruits grow in clusters. | ▪ All, but especially the seeds, which contain prussic acid (cyanide). | |
| | **PHYSIC NUT** *Jatropha curcas* | ▪ Woodland throughout the tropics and southern USA. | ▪ Large shrub with large, green, ivy-like leaves. Small greenish-yellow flowers. Apple-sized yellow fruit has large seeds. | ▪ All, but particularly the seeds. | |
| | **POISON HEMLOCK** *Conium maculatum* | ▪ Wet or moist ground in temperate parts of Eurasia; introduced to North America and Australia. | ▪ Tall herb with branching purple-spotted stem; toothed leaves; small clusters of white flowers grown in flat umbrellas. | ▪ All, but the root has the highest level of toxins. | |
| | **STRYCHNINE TREE** *Strychnos nux-vomica* | ▪ Tropical and subtropical forests in India, Southeast Asia, and Australia. | ▪ Evergreen tree with paired oval leaves. Small clusters of greenish flowers grow at end of branches. Large orange-red berries. | ▪ All, but the seeds contain lethal levels of strychnine. | |

# POISONOUS PLANTS

protect yourself from any poison on the casualty's mouth. When planning your trip, it is advisable to familiarize yourself with the poisonous plants in the region you are visiting. For further information regarding plant contact poisoning and ingestion poisoning, and their treatment in a survival situation, see pp. 268–69.

| EFFECT | TREATMENT | ADDITIONAL INFO |
|---|---|---|
| • Skin irritation. Contact with the eyes can cause blindness. | • Call the emergency services. Rinse the skin with cold water for 20 minutes, the eye(s) for 10 minutes. Don't let the water collect under the casualty or you. | |
| • Reddening, itching, swelling, and blistering of skin within 4–24 hours of contact with the plant. Some people may suffer an allergic reaction called anaphylactic shock (see p. 274). | • Wash the affected area with soap and cold water. Apply anti-poison ivy cream. Monitor and treat for shock (see p. 274) if necessary. For natural remedies, see p. 268. | • Western poison oak (*T. diversilobum*), Atlantic poison oak (*T. pubescens*), and poison sumac (*T. vernix*) also cause contact poisoning (see p. 268). |
| • The sap blisters the skin and will cause temporary blindness if it gets in the eyes. | • Call the emergency services. Rinse the skin with cold water for 20 minutes, the eye(s) for 10 minutes. Monitor casualty and treat for shock (see p. 274). | • Blinding or milky mangrove (*Exoecaria agallocha*) also has poisonous sap. |
| • Can be fatal—ingestion of berries can lead to cardiac arrest and death. Other symptoms include dizziness, vomiting, and severe internal irritation. | • Call the emergency services. Induce vomiting if casualty is still conscious. Dilute the poison by getting him or her to drink large quantities of water or milk, or tea mixed with charcoal. | |
| • Can be fatal—ingestion of raw seeds causes severe diarrhea. | • Call the emergency services. Induce vomiting if casualty is still conscious. Dilute the poison by getting him or her to drink large quantities of water or milk, or tea mixed with charcoal. | • The seedpods explode when ripe, scattering the large, oval, glossy, brown-mottled seeds, which can be mistaken for beans. |
| • Deadly poisonous. Symptoms include profuse salivation, vomiting, diarrhea, confusion, slow, irregular heartbeat, low temperature, difficulty breathing, and unconsciousness, leading to death. | • Call the emergency services. Induce vomiting if casualty is still conscious. Dilute the poison by getting him or her to drink large quantities of water or milk, or tea mixed with charcoal. | • This plant looks similar to wild onions, which are edible, but the death camas does not have the onion smell. |
| • Deadly poisonous. Causes unconsciousness and severe breathing difficulties, which, if untreated, may lead to death. | • Call the emergency services (antidotes are available). Induce vomiting if casualty is still conscious. Dilute the poison (see Death Camas, above). Keep casualty warm and at rest. | • If the casualty is unconscious and stops breathing, give rescue breaths, using a face shield. Alternatively, use an oxygen bag and a mask, if possible. |
| • Severe diarrhea and vomiting. | • Call the emergency services. Induce vomiting if casualty is still conscious. Dilute the poison by getting him or her to drink large quantities of water or milk, or tea mixed with charcoal. | • The seeds look like betel nuts and taste sweet. Several species in the *Jatropha* genus are poisonous, for example, the aptly named bellyache bush (*J. gossypifolia*). |
| • Deadly poisonous. A small amount can result in death by respiratory failure from muscular paralysis. Early symptoms include nausea, vomiting, and rapid heartbeat. | • Call the emergency services. Induce vomiting if casualty is still conscious. Dilute the poison (see Physic Nut, above). If the casualty is unconscious and stops breathing, begin CPR, using a face shield. | • Water hemlock or spotted cowbane (*Cicuta* spp.), which looks similar, is also deadly poisonous. Don't mistake these plants for wild carrots or wild parsnips. |
| • Deadly poisonous. Muscle spasms occur 10–20 minutes after exposure, leading to seizures followed by death from severe breathing difficulties or exhaustion within 2–3 hours. | • Call the emergency services. Induce vomiting if casualty is still conscious. Dilute the poison by getting him or her to drink large quantities of water or milk, or tea mixed with charcoal. | • Warning: strychnine can also enter the system through contact with the eyes. |

# RESOURCES

## SCOUTS AND SCOUTING

### Boy Scouts of America

1325 West Walnut Hill Lane
P.O. Box 152079, Irving,
Texas 75015-2079

Phone: 972-580-2000

Fax: 972-580-2413

www.scouting.org

Boy Scouts of America prepares young people
to make ethical and moral choices over their
lifetimes by instilling in them the values of
the Scout Oath and Law.

### Girl Scouts of the USA

420 Fifth Avenue
New York, New York 10018-2798

Phone: 800-GSUSA-4-U [800-478-7248]
or 212-852-8000

www.girlscouts.org

Girl Scouts is one of the largest organizations
dedicated specifically to girls. It encourages
them to develop skills and values such as
leadership, social conscience, and self-worth that
will stand them in good stead in the wider world.

### National Scouting Museum

Boy Scouts of America, S505,
1329 West Walnut Hill Lane, Irving,
Texas 75038

Phone: 800-303-3047 and 972-580-2100

e-mail: nsmuseum@netbsa.org

www.bsamuseum.org

This museum is a tribute to the rich history
of the Boy Scouts of America and features
a Norman Rockwell art gallery, virtual reality
adventures, hands-on learning experiences,
and a collection that traces the Scouting
movement from its beginnings.

## WEATHER AND ENVIRONMENTAL HAZARDS

### National Oceanic and Atmospheric Administration (NOAA)

1401 Constitution Avenue, NW,
Room 6217, Washington, DC 20230

Phone: 202-482-6090

Fax: 202-482-3154

www.noaawatch.gov

The NOAA has several departments, such as
the National Severe Storms Laboratory (NSSL),
the Storm Prediction Center (SPC), which is part
of the National Weather Service (NWS), and the
National Centers for Environmental Prediction
(NCEP). The SPC provides regular, timely, and
accurate storm forecasts, and watches out for
severe thunderstorms, tornadoes, heavy rain,
heavy snow, and fire weather events over the
contiguous United States.

### National Weather Service

1325 East West Highway, Silver Spring,
Maryland 20910

www.weather.gov/om/severeweather/index

Provides weather, hydrologic, and climate forecasts
and observations for the whole country and the
waters and oceans around it. The service offers
a national information database for the use of
public, private, and global communities.

### NOAA Weather Radio All Hazards (NWR)

www.weather.gov/nwr

A nationwide network of radio stations broadcasts
continuous weather information directly from the
nearest National Weather Service office. NWR
broadcasts official Weather Service warnings,
watches, forecasts, and other hazard information
24 hours a day, seven days a week.

### National Interagency Coordination Center (NICC)

www.nifc.gov/nicc/index.htm

The NICC serves as a focal point for
coordinating the national mobilization of
resources, such as heavy airtankers, helicopters,
smokejumpers, area command teams, and
Remote Automated Weather Stations (RAWS),
for wildland fire and other incidents throughout
the United States.

### The Forest Fire Lookout Association (FFLA)

2590 W. Versailles Drive, Coeur d'Alene,
Idaho 83815

Phone: 208-765-1714 and 800-GRN-TREE

Email: weblookout@imbris.net

www.firelookout.org

The FFLA investigates former forest-fire lookout
sites, ground cabins, and early forest fire detection
methods to encourage public groups and others
in restoring forest-fire lookouts.

### U.S. Geological Service

Western Distribution Branch,
P.O. Box 25286, Denver, Colorado 80225

Phone: 303-236-7477

www.usgs.gov

This multi-disciplinary science organization
focuses on biology, geography, geology, geospatial
information, and water, and is dedicated to the
timely, relevant, and impartial study of the US
landscape, and natural resources and hazards.

### DesertUSA

www.desertusa.com

This website is a comprehensive resource
for North American deserts and Southwest
destinations. It includes information about desert
biomes, and the ways plants and animals adapt
to them, and about national and state parks.

## HEALTH AND MEDICAL

### Centers for Disease Control and Prevention

1600 Clifton Rd, Atlanta, Georgia 30333

Phone: 800-232-4636 and 888-232-6348

Email: cdcinfo@cdc.gov

www.cdc.gov

Provides the expertise, information, advice,
and tools that individuals and communities need
to protect their health, including the promotion
of healthy living and the prevention of disease,
injury, and disability.

### U.S. Department of Health and Human Services

200 Independence Avenue, S.W.,
Washington, D.C. 20201

Phone: 202-619-0257

Toll Free: 1-877-696-6775

www.hhs.gov/disasters/index.shtml

For information and advice on coping with
disasters and related medical emergencies.

### American Medical Association

515 N. State Street, Chicago, Illinois 60610

Phone: 800-621-8335

www.ama-assn.org/ama/pub/
category/6206.html

The AMA's Center for Public Health Preparedness
and Disaster Response is an important national
educational resource for enhancing the disaster
preparedness and response capabilities of both
civilian and military providers.

## American Red Cross

National Headquarters, 2025 E Street NW
Washington, DC 20006

Phone: 800-733-2767

www.redcross.org/services

The nation's premier response organization that provides relief for communities during natural and manmade emergencies. It belongs to a worldwide movement that offers neutral humanitarian care and assistance to victims of war and devastating natural disasters such as earthquakes.

## National Capital Poison Center

3201 New Mexico Ave, Suite 310,
Washington D.C. 20016

Emergency Phone: 800 222 1222

www.poison.org

Affiliated with The George Washington University Medical Center, the Poison Center is committed to prevent poisonings, save lives, and limit injury from poisoning.

# SEARCH AND RESCUE

## National Association for Search & Rescue (NASAR)

PO Box 232020, Centerville,
Virginia 20120-2020

Phone: 703-222-6277

Toll Free: 877-893-0702

Email: info@nasar.org

www.nasar.org/nasar

A not-for-profit association dedicated to the advancement of professional, literary, and scientific knowledge in fields related to search and rescue throughout the United States and around the world.

## National Institute for Urban Search & Rescue

PO Box 91648, Santa Barbara,
California 93190

Phone: 800-767-0093 and 805-569-5066

Cell: 805-798-0169

Email: niusr@cox.net

www.niusr.org

A non-profit organization dedicated to finding ways of saving lives by improving disaster readiness and response through public awareness, collaboration, research, and engineering.

## Mountain Rescue Association

www.mra.org

Represents highly skilled and active mountain rescue teams throughout the country, who work for local government authorities and who are dedicated to saving lives through rescue and mountain safety education.

## International Association of Dive Rescue Specialists

201 North Link Lane, Fort Collins,
Colorado 80524-2712

Phone (toll free): 800-IADRS-911

Phone (international): 1-970-482-1562

Fax (international): 970-482-0893

www.iadrs.org

An association of public safety divers and water rescue personnel who, over the years, have educated and assisted professionals in all 50 states and 15 foreign countries.

## Association of Air Medical Services

526 King Street, Suite 415,
Alexandria, Virgina 22314

Phone: 703-836-8732

Fax: 703-836-8920

www.aams.org

An international not-for-profit organization that represents providers of air and surface medical transport systems, and aims to ensure that everyone has access to quality air medical and critical care support.

# FEDERAL

## Environmental Protection Agency (EPA)

EPA Headquarters, Ariel Rios Building
1200 Pennsylvania Avenue, N.W.,
Washington, DC 20460

EPA Hotlines: Various phone numbers and websites for assistance.

www.epa.gov/ebtpages/
emeremergencypreparedness.html

The EPA develops, implements, and coordinates preparations for chemical and other emergencies in order to be able to respond quickly and effectively to environmental crises and to keep the public informed about hazards in their community.

## Federal Emergency Management Agency (FEMA)

500 C Street S.W., Washington, D.C. 20472

Phone: 800-621-FEMA-3362

TDD: TTY users can dial 1-800-462-7585 to use the Federal Relay Service.

www.fema.gov

FEMA aims to reduce the loss of life and property, and protect the country from all hazards, including natural disasters, acts of terrorism, and other manmade disasters.

## U.S. Dept of the Interior National Parks Pass

1849 C Street, NW, Washington, DC 20240

Phone: 202-208-3100

Email: webteam@ios.doi.gov

www.doi.gov/parkpass.html

You can buy an annual pass for entry into national parks from the US Geological Survey store and through the government's federal lands recreation web portal at www.recreation.gov.

# CANADA

## National Search and Rescue Secretariat (NSS)

400-275 Slater Street, Ottawa,
Ontario K1A 0K2

Phone: (toll-free) 1-800-727-9414

Email: inquiry@nss.gc.ca

www.nss.gc.ca

An independent government agency that coordinates the search-and-rescue requirements of the military, coastguard, police, transport, parks, and meteorological services.

## Search and Rescue Volunteer Association of Canada

8 Paradise Road, Paradise,
Newfoundland and Labrador A1L 3B4

Phone (toll free): 1-866-9SARVAC
(1-866-972-7822)

Phone (office): 709-368-5533

Fax: 709-368-1298

Email: info@sarvac.ca

www.sarvac.ca

A not-for-profit organization that provides a national search-and-rescue service, and is committed to fostering the exchange of information between other rescue services.

## Meteorological Service of Canada

www.msc-smc.ec.gc.ca

Provides information and conducts research on water, climate, weather, atmospheric science, and other environmental issues.

## Environment Canada

Inquiry Center, 351 St. Joseph Boulevard
Place Vincent Massey, 8th Floor
Gatineau, Quebec K1A 0H3

Phone: 1-800-668-6767
or 819-997-2800

Fax: 819-994-1412

TTY: 819-994-0736

Email: enviroinfo@ec.gc.ca

www.ec.gc.ca

Government department committed to preserving and enhancing the country's environment, and to providing weather forecasts.

# GLOSSARY

**A-frame** A type of shelter design in which the roof is suspended by a single support running from the front to the back.

**Air mass** A large body of air in a weather system with its own temperature and humidity.

**Altitude sickness** An illness brought on by low air pressure at high altitudes.

**Anabatic winds** Daytime, upslope winds.

**Anaphylactic shock** A dangerous allergic reaction brought on by a bite or sting.

**Attack point** See *Stand-off.*

**Avalanche transceiver** A personal beacon that can be activated to alert rescuers by someone caught in an avalanche.

**Base layer** The bottom layer of clothing that sits directly against the skin and is designed to "wick" sweat away from the body.

**Base rate** The heart rate, as measured at rest.

**Beaufort scale** A way of describing wind speed on land and at sea, using a scale from 0 (calm) to 12 (hurricane).

**Belaying** A rope technique used by climbing partners to safeguard each other.

**Bivy pup tent** A basic one-man tent that uses a bivi bag as a covering.

**Bivy sack** A large waterproof sack suitable for use as a basic shelter; smaller than a tent.

**Blazes** A general term for markers on a trail.

**Bola** A hunting device made of a rope with weights attached, designed to be spun and thrown.

**Boot skiing** A technique for descending slopes without skis.

**Bothy bag** A large waterproof bag that provides shelter from the wind, rain or sun.

**Bow-and-drill** set One of the oldest methods of creating a glowing ember (coal) for use in lighting a fire.

**Boxing an object** See *Detouring.*

**Breathable clothing** Clothing that allows sweat in the form of water vapor to escape but keeps liquids (rain or snow) out.

**Bungee** A type of elasticated cord, often with hooks at either end.

**Bushcraft knife** A versatile survival knife used primarily for carving, cutting, and splitting small logs.

**Button compass** A small, simple compass, ideal as a back-up compass.

**Button tie** A method of attaching cordage to fabric that has no hoops or grommets, without ripping a hole in it.

**Cairn** Trail marker consisting of a pile of rocks of varying sizes, designed to be visible in fog.

**Canoe** A open-deck paddle boat, for one or more people, and equipment.

**Carabina** A metal clip used for joining ropes.

**Carbon monoxide** A colourless, odourless, tasteless, but highly toxic gas.

**Cardiopulmonary resuscitation (CPR)** An emergency system of chest compressions and rescue breaths designed to restart a casualty's heart and lungs.

**Cerebral edema** Accumulation of excess water in the brain that causes reduced brain function and potentially fatal swelling.

**Char cloth** Cotton cloth that has been combusted in the absence of oxygen. Used for lighting fires.

**Chimneying** A climbing technique used for climbing up the inside of large rock clefts.

**Cirrus** A wispy cloud that forms high in the sky and is made from ice crystals.

**Cold shock** An involuntary gasp reflex followed by hyperventilation, caused by sudden immersion in very cold water.

**Commando saw** A small saw consisting of a serrated wire blade with a ring at each end.

**Compacted snow trench** A shelter dug into compacted snow. The excavated snow can then be cut into blocks and used to form a roof.

**Compass baseplate** A plate to which some compasses are fixed, containing additional markings useful for orientation and navigation.

**Compass scale** Scaled markings on a compass baseplate that measure distances on a map and help in working out grid references.

**Compass** An instrument used for orientation and navigation, using a freely rotating needle that indicates Magnetic North.

**Coniferous tree** A needle-leaved, cone-bearing, mostly evergreen tree, such as pine, spruce, or fir.

**Continental air mass** Air that has tracked over land and carries comparatively less moisture than maritime air mass.

**Contour lines** Lines on a map that show points of equal height above sea level, thus detailing the changing height of natural features.

**Contour navigation** Walking at a constant height around a high natural obstacle.

**Contouring** See *Contour navigation.*

**Contusion** A bruise.

**Cordage** A type of light rope—an essential piece of survival equipment.

**COSPAS–SARSAT system** A satellite system, made up of LEOSAR and GEOSAR satellites, that picks up signals from distress beacons.

**Cramp** Painful muscle spasm, often a result of dehydration.

**Crampons** Spiked metal plates that attach to boots to provide grip on icy surfaces.

**Cumulonimbus** A type of cloud that starts low in the sky and builds upward, producing short, heavy downpours or thunderstorms.

**Cumulus** A billowing, puffy cloud that is generally small and develops on bright, sunny days, indicating fine weather.

**Damper bread** Yeast-free bread, suitable for making on a campfire.

**Deadfall** A trap in which a weight falls onto prey. Also a mass of fallen dead timber.

**Defensive swimming** A type of swimming technique designed to keep the swimmer protected from obstacles in the water.

**Degree** A unit of latitude or longitude, equal to $1/360$ of a circle.

**Dehydration** A low level of water in the body. A very dangerous condition if not reversed.

**Deliberate off-set (aiming off)** Deliberately aiming left or right of a known feature.

**Desalting kit** An emergency kit for turning saltwater into freshwater.

**Detouring** Walking around an obstacle as a method of clearing it, using a point in the distance as a reference.

**Dew point** The temperature at which water vapor held in the air cools to become liquid.

**Dew trap** A method of collecting dew to form usable water.

**Digging stick** A sturdy piece of wood with a pointed end.

**Dipping net** A fishing net used for scooping up fish that are too small to catch on a line.

**Drill and flywheel** A friction-based method of starting a fire.

**Drip rag** A method of collecting rainwater dripping down a tree using cloth.

**Drogue** A sea anchor used to stabilize a vessel.

**Dysentery** A waterborn disease that causes severe diarrhea.

**Eastings** The vertical grid lines on a map. They increase in value the further east they are.

**Emergency plan of action (EPA)** A document left with relevant authorities that contains vital details about you and your intended route, should you need to be rescued.

**Emergency rendezvous (ERV)** A predetermined point at which all members of a group should meet in the event of separation.

**Equator** An imaginary circle running around the Earth's diameter that is equidistant from the North and South Poles at all points.

**Eskimo roll** A technique for righting a capsized kayak.

**Feather stick** A stick that has been feathered to use as kindling and fuel.

**Fighter trench** A type of snow trench dug into soft snow. Ideally uses a tarpaulin for the roof.

**Finnish marshmallow** A method of melting chunks of ice over a fire then collecting the water in a container.

**Fire can** A can filled with waxed cardboard, used for lighting a campfire in difficult conditions, or as a basic cooking device.

**Firebase** A stable, non-flammable base suitable for building a campfire on.

**Firefighter's lift** A method of moving a casualty by carrying them over your shoulder.

**Fire set** A set of components necessary to generate a glowing ember that can start a fire.

**Firesteel** A metal bar which, when hit with a striker, produces a spark for lighting campfires.

**Flash burn** See *Snow blindness*.

**Föhn effect** A dry downslope wind which occurs on the lee-side of a mountain or hill.

**Four-wheel drive (4WD)** A system on a vehicle where drive is provided by all four wheels, resulting in superior traction.

**Frostbite** A serious condition caused by excessive exposure to extreme cold, in which body tissues actually freeze, sometimes to the bone. Often starts with the extremities.

**Frostnip** The freezing of the top layer of skin, usually on the face and extremities, caused by exposure to extreme cold. Can develop into frostbite if left untreated.

**Gaiters** Protective fabric that wraps around the lower leg and ankle, designed to keep out water and guard against sharp objects.

**Gill net** A fishing net in the form of a mesh stretched across a stream.

**Global positioning system (GPS)** A hand-held unit that uses orbiting satellites to determine the user's position accurately.

**Gourd** The shell of hollowed-out, dried fruit.

**Grab bag** A pre-prepared bag of essential survival equipment suitable for quickly picking up in an emergency at sea.

**Gravity filter** An effective method of filtering and purifying water, incorporated into a bottle.

**Grid bearing** A horizontal direction expressed in degrees east or west of north or south.

**Grid magnetic angle (GMA)** The difference between magnetic north and grid north, expressed as an angle.

**Grid north** A northerly direction that runs parallel to vertical gridlines on a map. Different from true north because a map is flat.

**Grid reference** A method of pinpointing the location of a place or object anywhere on a map, using coordinates provided by a numbered grid system printed on the map.

**Grommet** A metal-ringed eyelet in clothing.

**Groundsheet** The waterproof floor of a tent.

**Gypsy well** A method of using a hole in the ground to filter non-potable water.

**Hand jam** A crack in a rockface suitable for wedging your whole hand into when climbing.

**Handrailing** A method of navigating using long linear features on the landscape that run in the general direction of your travel, such as rivers, roads, or paths.

**Hank** A small coil of cordage.

**Heat exhaustion (heat stress)** Dehydration resulting in dizziness and profuse sweating. Often a precursor to heatstroke.

**Heatstroke** A life-threatening condition brought on by severe overheating.

**HELP (Heat Escape Lessening Posture)** A posture that reduces heat-loss from the body when floating in water.

**Hexamine stove** A stove that uses hexamine solid fuel instead of gas or liquid fuel.

**Hot platform** A method of melting ice over a fire then collecting the liquid in a container.

**Hyperthermia** An abnormally high body temperature, potentially fatal.

**Hyponatremia** An accumulation of excess water in the body, leading to a dangerously low concentration of sodium.

**Hypothermia** A life-threatening condition caused by exposure to cold.

**Hypoxia** Inadequate levels of oxygen in the blood or body tissues. Potentially fatal.

**Igloo** A shelter made from cut blocks of snow.

**Iodine** A chemical used to purify water.

**Isobar contours** Lines on a weather chart that connect points at which the barometric pressure is the same.

**Katabatic winds** Cool, light downslope winds that form on clear nights.
**Kayak** A closed-deck paddle boat.
**Kindling** Small pieces of fuel for a fire, added to burning tinder.
**Kukri** A large-bladed knife from Nepal, mainly used for chopping.

**Land breeze** A night-time wind that blows from land to sea.
**Lanyard** A small cord or rope used for securing or suspending an item.
**Latitude** The angular distance north or south of the Equator, in degrees along a meridian.
**Layering** Wearing several light layers of clothes rather than just one or two thick ones. Layers can be added or taken off to maintain a consistent body temperature.
**Lean-to** A shelter with a sloping roof that leans against a horizontal ridgepole.
**Lee-side** The side of hill that is out of the wind.
**Lensatic compass** A type of compass used for precise navigational work.
**Longitude** The angular distance east or west across the Earth betweeen one meridian and the prime meridian at Greenwich, England.

**Machete** A large-bladed knife mainly used for chopping, about 18–20 in (45–50 cm) long.
**Magnetic north** The direction indicated by a magnetic compass.
**Magnetic variation** The difference between magnetic north and grid north.
**Mantelling** A technique used for climbing overhanging rock.
**Maritime air mass** Air that has tracked over the sea, typically carrying a lot of moisture.
**Mayday** The internationally recognized distress signal for a grave emergency.
**Matchless fire set** Small kit that includes everything you need to start a fire – tinder, fuel, and spark device.
**Melting sack** An improvised sack that can hold snow or ice and is positioned close to a fire to provide water.
**Meridian** An imaginary arc on the Earth's surface from the North to the South Pole, connecting all locations running along it.

**Mid-layer** An insulating layer of clothing that sits between the base layer and the outer layer.
**Motor impairment** A limitation or loss of muscle control or movement.

**Naismith's Rule** A method of calculating the time it will take to arrive at a destination, taking into account distance and topography.
**Natural hollow** A natural dip in the ground that can be used as an emergency shelter.
**New World** Non-Eurasian and non-African regions of the world – specifically the Americas and Australia.
**Noggin** A piece of wood used to help support a structure, reducing the amount of cordage required.
**Non-potable water** Water that is not suitable for drinking.
**Northings** The horizontal grid lines on a map that increase in value the further north they are.

**Occluded front** A point at which two air masses meet in a weather system.
**Old World** Europe, Asia, and Africa.
**Outer layer** Outer clothing that keeps out rain but lets sweat (as water vapor) escape.

**Pace counting** A method of determining distance, involving knowing how many paces you take to cover a set distance.
**Pack animal** An animal such as a mule or horse used for carrying heavy loads.
**Paracord** A useful type of cordage originally developed as rigging lines for parachutes. Usually comprises an outer sheath over an inner section of yarn.
**Parang** A large-bladed knife from Malaysia mainly used for chopping.
**Pathogen** A microorganism, especially bacteria or fungi, that causes disease.
**Permafrost** Permanently frozen soil.
**Personal Locator Beacon (PSB)** A personal beacon that can send a distress signal to an orbiting satellite to initiate a rescue.
**Poncho** A multi-purpose waterproof outer garment made from one sheet of fabric; also useful for building a basic tent.
**Post-holing** A technique for walking in deep snow without snow shoes.

**Potable water** Water suitable for drinking.
**Potassium permanganate** A chemical used for a variety of tasks, from lighting fires to purifying water.
**Precipitation** Moisture in a cloud that may fall as rain, snow, or hail.
**Prismatic compass** See *Lensatic compass*.
**Protractor** A semicircular device for measuring angles.
**Psychogenic shock** A very high level of psychological and emotional stress brought on by a sudden disaster situation.
**Pulk** A simple plastic sled used for carrying equipment over snow.
**Pulmonary edema** Swelling and fluid accumulation in the lungs that causes potentially fatal breathing problems.
**Pygmy hut** A domed hut made from a circle of bent saplings or limber poles and thatched with natural materials.
**Pygmy roll** A method of rolling fibers together to make cordage.

**Quicksand** A bed of loose, wet sand that yields easily to pressure and can engulf anything on its surface.
**Quinzhee** A basic dome-shaped, snow-covered overnight shelter.

**Ranger flint and steel** A rod of flint which, when hit with a striker, produces a spark for lighting campfires.
**Recovery position** The position an unconscious person should be placed in to minimize further injury and help recovery.
**Reflector** A device for directing heat from a campfire toward shelter.
**Reverse-osmosis pump** A survival pump system that turns saltwater into freshwater.
**Ridgepole** A long horizontal pole that forms the apex of a roof.
**Romer measure** See *Compass scale*.

**Salting** A salt marsh.
**Scrambling** Climbing without ropes.
**Scrape** A type of basic shelter built in a natural hollow or depression in the ground.
**Sea breeze** A daytime wind that blows from sea to land.
**Secondary drowning** Potentially fatal biological changes that can take place in the lungs after a person nearly drowns,

caused by the body's response to inhaling water.

**Shock** A life-threatening condition that occurs if the circulatory system fails, often triggered by severe bleeding, burns, or sudden cold.

**Show-stopper** A failure in planning that could cause delays to, or stop a trip or expedition.

**Sighting mirror** An advanced component on a high-end compass used for helping in orientation and navigation.

**Signal fire** A fire specifically designed to produce lots of smoke to attract attention.

**Signal flare** A hand-held distress flare that gives off orange smoke in daylight and a bright light at night.

**Signal mirror** A simple signaling device that works by reflecting sunlight.

**Silva compass** A type of basic compass useful for hiking.

**Sip well** A method of extracting water trapped under rocks by sandy ground.

**Skidoo** A motorized vehicle used for traveling over snow and ice.

**Slingshot** A hunting weapon that fires small stones and is made from a Y-shaped stick with an elastic strip stretched between the prongs.

**Snare** A wire noose used for trapping animals.

**Snow blindness** Eye damage caused by ultraviolet light reflected from snow or water.

**Snow cave** An effective cave-like shelter dug into compacted snow on the lee-side of a hill.

**Snowshoes** Wide-soled strap-on shoes designed to stop the wearer sinking into the snow.

**Soak** A water source found close to rivers and creeks in low-lying areas that are normally lower than the existing water table.

**Solar still** A method of extracting drinking water from any source of moisture by a process of evaporation and condensation.

**Space blanket** A plastic blanket covered in aluminum foil that can be used as a shelter or a reflective signalling device; to carry, store, and heat water; or to cook in.

**Stand-off** A technique for navigating to a specific point that may be difficult to

locate by orientating from a nearby prominent feature.

**Standing dead wood** Wood from a tree that has died but is still standing.

**Straddling** A climbing technique used for ascending wide chimneys.

**Stratus** Dense, grey cloud that forms a sheet. Deep clouds mean rain can fall for l ong periods.

**Strobe lights** An effective signaling device in the form of a rapidly flashing LED light.

**Survival blanket** See *Space blanket*.

**Survival kit** Essential items for survival carried on your person.

**Survival straw** A compact emergency water purifier.

**Survival suit** A waterproof, buoyant suit designed for survival in open water.

**Survival tin** An essential, compact container carried at all times; addresses basic survival needs: protection, location, water, and food.

**Taiga** A subpolar region characterized by coniferous forest.

**Tarp** Shortened form of "tarpaulin," a type of sturdy waterproof sheet.

**Temperate climate** A climate without extremes of temperature or rainfall.

**Tetanus** A potentially lethal infection caused by bacteria that live in soil.

**Throwing star** An improvised four-pointed hunting weapon used for throwing at prey.

**Tinder** A dry, light, combustible material that is the first fuel used when lighting a fire.

**Tinder bundle** A firelighter made of dead twigs folded into small, tied bundles.

**Topographic map** A map that shows the main features on a landscape, and elevation via use of contour lines.

**Transpiration bag** A method of evaporating, condensing, and siphoning off water from foliage using a plastic bag and sunlight.

**Triangulation** A method of determining your location by taking bearings with a compass from recognizable landscape features.

**True north** The direction of a meridian of longitude that converges on the North Pole.

**Tundra** A polar region characterized by permafrost and stunted vegetation.

**Universal Edibility Test (UET)** A test that checks whether a plant is safe to eat via a methodical process of testing small amounts on the skin, in the mouth, and in the stomach.

**UV active purification** Purifying water using a battery-operated ultraviolet (UV) purifier.

**UV passive purification** Purifying water by leaving filled bottles in strong direct sunlight. The UV rays eventually kill most pathogens.

**Vegetation bag** See *Transpiration bag*.

**Water balance** The difference between water lost from the body through sweat and the water taken in through drinking.

**Water purifier** A device that filters and purifies water by pumping it through micro filters, chemicals, or a combination of both.

**Weather chart** A map of major weather systems and their predicted direction of travel.

**Wicking material** A material that moves moisture away from your body to evaporate.

**Wickiup** A small hut made from straight poles lashed together at the top, with an interwoven framework covered with animal hides or grass.

**Witch's broom** A cleft stick stuffed with thin, dry bark suitable for lighting a fire.

**Withies** The strong, flexible stems of plants, such as willow, birch, ash, and hazel.

**Zig-zag route** Method of climbing a steep slope using a zig-zag path to reduce the effort required to achieve the climb. Also effective when walking down steep slopes.

# INDEX

# ABOUT THE AUTHOR

After joining the Royal Navy in 1977, Colin Towell qualified as a Combat Survival Instructor with 22 Regiment SAS (the British army's elite Special Air Service), and has spent over 30 years teaching land, sea, desert, jungle, and cold-weather survival skills—as well as survival and conduct in captivity—to UK Army, Navy, Royal Marines, and Air Force personnel. He was the Royal Navy's Chief Survival Instructor and also served three years as Chief Instructor at the US Navy SERE (Survival, Evasion, Resistance, and Extraction) school. Colin saw service in the Falklands, Bosnia, Germany, USA, and Northern Ireland, and still serves as a Reserve Chief Instructor with the UK Defence SERE Training Organisation, training both instructors and students. He provided the survival training, equipment and rescue coordination for Sir Richard Branson's balloon global circumnavigation attempts, and also trials, evaluates, and instructs in the use of specialized survival equipment, both in the UK and abroad.

www.colintowell-survival.com

# ACKNOWLEDGEMENTS

## FROM THE AUTHOR

I have undertaken as a student every survival course I have ever subsequently taught as an instructor, mainly because I have had to, but also as a reminder of what my students experience, both physically and mentally, when they undergo survival training. In writing this book, it is safe to say that I have again been the student, and the instructors have been the team at Dorling Kindersley, and I would like to take this opportunity to thank them for their dedication, professionalism, vision, and sense of humor. Thank you to Stephanie, Lee, Nicky, Richard, and Michael for heading up the team; and to Phil and Pip, Clare and Katie, Gill and Sarah, Chris and Tracy, Jill, Bob, Brian, Sharon, Chris, Gareth, and Conor, for learning how to translate my Cumbrian into English and for creating the wonderful design for this book; thanks also to the team of illustrators who possess an unnerving ability to decipher my drawings and turn them into works of art!

My warm thanks also go to the following people for generously sharing their expertise: Flt Lt John Hudson, Royal Air Force, Defence SERE Training Centre; Lt Carlton Oliver, Royal Navy, Defence SERE Training Centre; Chief Petty Officer (SE) Keith Spiller; Petty Officer (METOC) Kirk Davidson; Petty Officer (SE) Stephen Paris-Hunter; Tony Borkowski (Royal School Military Survey); Mike Dymond M.R.I.N N.DipM (RYA); Robert (Baldy Bob) Whale; Charlie Tyrrell; Colin Knox (Pre-Mac); Murray Bryars; and Paul Baker (Bushman.UK Knifes).

Finally, I would like to thank the Defence SERE Organisation and the Survival Equipment Branch of the Royal Navy for giving me an amazing career that, if the truth is known, I would have done for free, and for allowing me the opportunity to learn from the very best, both at home and around the world.

## FROM THE PUBLISHER

In addition to those mentioned above, Dorling Kindersley would like to thank the following people for their help in making this book happen. At the Royal Navy: Cdr. Alan George RN, Lt. Cdr. Adrian Mundin RN, Lt. Cdr. Paula Rowe RN, and Lt. Cdr. Phil Rosindale RN. At IMG: Olivia Smales and Simon Gresswell.

Thanks also to: Gareth Jones, Chris Stone, and Conor Kilgallon for editorial assistance; Jillian Burr and Tracy Smith for design assistance; and Sue Bosanko for compiling the index.

**VENTURING® · BSA**

Thank you for your purchase of *The Survival Handbook: Essential Skills for Outdoor Adventure*, an officially licensed product of the Boy Scouts of America. For more than ten years, the Boy Scouts of America Venturing program has been at the forefront of educating and preparing young men and women ages 14 through 20 to enjoy the outdoors in a responsible and safe manner.

In fact, every Venturer subscribes to a standard philosophy regarding the outdoors, the Outdoor Code.

## OUTDOOR CODE

**As an American, I will do my best to . . .**

■ **Be clean in my outdoor manners.** I will treat the outdoors as a heritage. I will take care of it for myself and others. I will keep my trash and garbage out of lakes, streams, fields, woods, and roadways.

■ **Be careful with fire.** I will build my fires only where they are appropriate. When I have finished using a fire, I will make sure it is cold out. I will leave a clean fire ring, or remove all evidence of my fire.

■ **Be considerate in the outdoors.** I will treat public and private property with respect. I will use low-impact methods of hiking and camping.

■ **Be conservation-minded.** I will learn how to practice good conservation of soil, water, forests, minerals, grassland, wildlife, and energy. I will urge others to do the same.

This code and those who follow it represent the highest ideals regarding the outdoors and the conduct necessary to not only survive, but to enjoy its full splendor.

For more information on Venturing and the exciting leadership-building programs offered, please see
**www.scouting.org/venturing**